AESTHETICS IN A MULTICULTURAL AGE

Aesthetics in a Multicultural Age

Edited by
Emory Elliott
Louis Freitas Caton
Jeffrey Rhyne

OXFORD
UNIVERSITY PRESS

2002

OXFORD

UNIVERSITY PRESS

Oxford   New York

Athens   Auckland   Bangkok   Bogotá   Buenos Aires   Cape Town
Chennai   Dar es Salaam   Delhi   Florence   Hong Kong   Istanbul   Karachi
Kolkata   Kuala Lumpur   Madrid   Melbourne   Mexico City   Mumbai   Nairobi
Paris   São Paulo   Shanghai   Singapore   Taipei   Tokyo   Toronto   Warsaw

with associated companies in
Berlin   Ibadan

Copyright © 2002 by Oxford University Press

Published by Oxford University Press, Inc.
198 Madison Avenue, New York, New York 10016

Oxford is a registered trademark of Oxford University Press

Library of Congress Cataloging-in-Publication Data
Aesthetics in a multicultural age / edited by Emory Elliott,
Louis Freitas Caton, and Jeffrey Rhyne.
p. cm.
Includes bibliographical references and index.
ISBN 0-19-514632-8; ISBN 0-19-514633-6 (pbk.)
1. Aesthetics, American—Congresses.   2. Aesthetics, Modern—20th century
—Congresses.   3. Pluralism (Social sciences)—United States—Congresses.
I. Elliott, Emory, 1942–   II. Caton, Louis Freitas.   III. Rhyne, Jeffrey.
BH221.U53 A33   2001
11'.85—dc21   2001021316

3 5 7 9 8 6 4 2

Printed in the United States of America
on acid-free paper

Preface

On October 22–24, 1998, the Center for Ideas and Society at the University of California, Riverside, conducted a major conference entitled "Aesthetics and Difference: Cultural Diversity, Literature, and the Arts." This conference had 140 participants and drew more than 600 people to its various presentations. It received substantial coverage in the *Los Angeles Times* both for the intellectual innovations of its theme and contents and for its accompanying photographic exhibits held at the University of California, Riverside/California Museum of Photography and the University's Marilyn and Jack Sweeney Art Gallery. The conference also was the subject of a cover story in the December 6, 1998, *Chronicle of Higher Education*, with a web site forum on the critical issues that lasted for several weeks. Although substantially expanded and revised, the essays in this volume began as papers at this conference.

The intentions of the conference organizers were to emphasize both the multidisciplinary and multicultural nature of the subject of aesthetics, especially as it has developed in the United States in recent decades. The conference sessions included artists and creative writers as well as scholars and critics who together explored a wide range of theoretical and methodological issues in the fields of literature, art, music, film, photography, and drama. Central to many of the debates and topics was the relation of the arts and criticism to contemporary social, political, and cultural issues in the United States having to do with ethnicity, race, class, and gender. The major purpose of the conference was to advance the research and teaching of the arts and humanities by examining some of the issues of the so-called "cultural wars" and by bridging the gap that has existed for two decades between those scholars and critics who generally hold opposing views of the purposes of art and criticism. Most of the participants agreed that the objectives of the conference were attained.

In a final session designed to offer a critique of the conference, the remarks of four panelists, Professors Martha Banta, Masao Miyoshi, Nellie McKay, and Amalia Mesa-Bains, suggested that the main objective of the conference had been achieved: the beginning of a serious assessment of the role of aesthetic theories and practices within the arts and literature as these are being redefined within the culturally diverse societies developing in the world today. Professor McKay remarked that "what was most impressive for me was the magnificent way in which the program was a representation of the diversity of what our profession strives to look like today. But everyone pays much lip service to diversity while most often our actions represent tokenism more than real change. This was different. The entire time that I was there I felt that the program was as it should be in real life. Now what we need to do is to work on our institutions to make the workplace—human bodies and curriculum—look just like that program." The work presented in this volume continues these discussions by exploring some of the complex issues that face us in these fields of expression and study and in the larger arena of our society as well.

Acknowledgments

The conference from which this collection has developed was made possible by support from the Ford Foundation, the University of California, Riverside, the University of California Humanities Research Institute, the Office of the President of the University of California, the Jack and Marilyn Sweeney Art Gallery, the UCR/California Museum of Photography, and the Center for Ideas and Society of the University of California, Riverside. We are most grateful to those individuals within these institutions whose contributions were invaluable: at the Ford Foundation, Allison Bernstein and Margaret Wilkerson; at the University of California Office of the President, Carol McClain and Dante Noto; at the UC Humanities Research Institute, Patricia O'Brien and her Advisory Committee; and at the University of California, Riverside, Chancellor Raymond L. Orbach, Executive Vice Chancellor David Warren, Dean Carlos Velez-Ibanez, and Georgia A. Elliott.

Many others at UCR also helped to make the project a success, including faculty members of the Conference Steering Committee: Philip Brett, Jennifer DeVere Brody, Joseph Childers, Jonathan Green, George Haggerty, Katherine Kinney, Tiffany Lopez, Kathleen McHugh, Amelia Jones, Sally Ness, Sterling Stuckey, Carole-Anne Tyler, Marguerite Waller, Katherine Warren, and Traise Yamamoto; the staff of the Center for Ideas and Society, including Marie Orillion Harker, Trudy J. Cohen, Marilyn Davis, Laura Lara, and Antonette Toney; and graduate student assistants Kwakiutl Dreher, Deckard Hodge, Deena Mauldin, Stephanie Miner, Kim Orlijan, Jasmine Payne, Jeff Rhyne, Isabelle Schaffner, Blythe Tellefsen, and Clara Wilburn.

We are grateful to Susan Chang, former editor for literature, and Elissa Morris, the current humanities editor for Oxford University Press, whose confidence and guidance made this volume possible. We also thank editorial assistants Karen Leibowitz and Jeremy Lewis and production editor Stacey Hamilton for their help. Oxford University Press Delegate Christopher Butler read the manuscript carefully and provided expert advice, and Terence Cave, also an Oxford Delegate for literature, made helpful suggestions and provided encouragement. Cathy Davidson of Duke University and two anonymous readers of the manuscript for the Press also provided valuable advice and criticism. Emory Elliott also wishes to thank Georgia Elliott for her enduring support and contributions, and Louis Caton is grateful to Delia Fisher of Auburn University for a keen eye and wise comments about an early draft of the afterword.

Contents

Contributors

JOHNNELLA E. BUTLER is Associate Dean of the graduate school and professor of American Ethnic Studies at the University of Washington. She is also adjunct professor of English and Women Studies. She has written extensively in the area of curriculum transformation and pedagogy and has conceptualized and directed numerous collaborative faculty development projects, bringing together scholarship in Ethnic Studies, American Studies, Women Studies, and the humanities, arts, and social sciences. She has taught extensively in the fields of African-American and comparative American ethnic literature and specializes on the graduate level in African-American and American ethnic literary theory and analysis. She is editor of *Color-line to Borderlands: The Matrix of American Ethnic Studies* (2001) and is currently working on a volume tentatively titled "Re-creating America: The Problem of Being and American Ethnic Literature." Professor Butler is also co-editor with John C. Walter of the American Ethnic Studies Series at the University of Washington Press.

LOUIS FREITAS CATON is Assistant Professor of English at Westfield State College. He has written for several publications on topics and authors as varied as ideology, aesthetics, Abdul JanMohamed, Don DeLillo, Jamaica Kincaid, and Leslie Marmon Silko. More recently, however, he has been concentrating on completing a book interpreting Coleridge's theories of perception in relation to the social/political issues of American multicultural criticism, especially ethnicity and literary value.

EMORY ELLIOTT is University Professor and Distinguished Professor of English at the University of California, Riverside, and the Director of the Center for Ideas and Society. From 1972 to 1989, he was on the faculty of Princeton University, where he chaired the English Department and American Studies Program. His books include *Power and the Pulpit in Puritan New England* (1975), *Revolutionary Writers: Literature and Authority in the New Republic* (1982), and *The Literature of Puritan New England* (1994). He is the editor of *The Columbia Literary History of the United States* (1988), *The Columbia History of the American Novel* (1991), and *American Literature: A Prentice Hall Anthology* (1991). He edited the *American Novel Series* for Cambridge University Press and *Penn Studies on Contemporary American Fiction* for the University of Pennsylvania Press. He has recently published a new introduction and edition of the *Adventures of Huckleberry Finn* (1999) for Oxford World Classics.

SHELLEY FISHER FISHKIN is Professor of American Studies and English at the University of Texas at Austin. Her most recent book is *Lighting Out for the Territory: Reflections on Mark Twain and American Culture* (1996). She is also the author of the award-winning books *Was Huck Black? Mark Twain and African-American Voices* (1993) and *From Fact to Fiction: Journalism and Imaginative Writing in America* (1988), as well as numerous articles, including "Interrogating 'Whiteness,' Complicating 'Blackness': Remapping American Culture" (*American Quarterly* 1995). She is editor of the 29-volume *Oxford Mark Twain* and co-editor of *Listening to Silences: New Essays in Feminist Criticism* (1994); *People of the Book: Thirty Scholars Reflect on Their Jewish Identity* (1996); *The Encyclopedia of Civil Rights in America* (1998); and the "Race and American Culture" book series published by Oxford University Press.

WINFRIED FLUCK is Professor and Chair of American Culture at the John F. Kennedy Institute for North American Studies of the Freie Universität Berlin. He studied at Harvard University and the University of California, Berkeley, and was a fellow at the National Humanities Center and a guest professor at Princeton University. He has written five books in German on aesthetics, pop culture, and American literature. He has also published widely in English language publications on genre, literary theory, and American literature—most recently, "The Search for Distance: Negation and Negativity in the Literary Theory of Wolfgang Iser," in *New Literary History* (2000), and "From Aesthetics to Political Criticism: Theories of the Early American Novel," in *Early America Re-Explored: New Readings in Colonial, Early National, and Antebellum Culture* (2000).

GILES GUNN, Professor of English and of Global and International Studies at the University of California, Santa Barbara, is author and editor of more than a dozen volumes, the latest of which is *Beyond Solidarity: Pragmatism and Difference in a Globalized World* (2001).

HEINZ ICKSTADT has been professor of American literature at the Kennedy Institute for North American Studies, Freie Universität Berlin, since 1978. He served as Chairman of the German Association of American Studies from 1990 to 1993 and President of the European Association of American Studies from 1996 to 2000. He has published widely on American literature and culture of the late nineteenth century, modernism (in poetry, painting, and fiction), and on the postwar American novel (Pynchon, Coover, DeLillo). Recent book publications include *Der amerikanische Roman im 20. Jahrhundert* (1998) and a bilingual anthology of American poetry, *Englische und Amerikanische Dichtung 4: Amerikanische Dichtung von den Anfängen bis zur Gegenwart*, which he edited, introduced, and annotated with Eva Hesse (2000).

AMELIA JONES is Professor of Art History at University of California, Riverside. She has written numerous articles in anthologies and journals and has organized exhibitions, including *Sexual Politics: Judy Chicago's Dinner Party in Feminist Art History* at the UCLA/Armand Hammer Art Museum (1996), for which she also edited and contributed to the catalog. Jones contributed to and co-edited the anthology *Performing the Body/Performing the Text* with Andrew Stephenson (1999) and has published the books *Postmodernism and the En-Gendering of Marcel Duchamp* (1994) and *Body Art/Performing the Subject* (1998). Jones has received ACLS, NEH, and Guggenheim fellowships.

PAUL LAUTER is Allan K. and Gwendolyn Miles Smith Professor of Literature at Trinity College (Hartford). Much of Lauter's work has centered on how literary canons are constructed—and changed. His book *Canons and Contexts* (1991) examines the history of the canon of American literature and the changes in it that have been generated primarily by ethnic and feminist studies. *The Heath Anthology of American Literature* (1990), of which Lauter is general editor, represents a successful effort to put canon change into practice. Earlier in his career, Lauter was active in the civil rights and anti–Vietnam War movements; he worked for a number of social cause organizations and co-authored a book about the 1960s, *The Conspiracy of the Young* (1990). His most recent book, *From Walden Pond to Jurassic Park: Activism, Culture, and American Studies* (2001), traces the development of American Studies as a discipline and a form of political discourse in the United States and overseas. Lauter served as president of the American Studies Association (USA) and has spoken and consulted at universities in almost every state and in twenty-five countries. Other recent projects include a co-edited collection called *Literature, Class, and Culture* (Longman) and a volume of Thoreau's writings for Houghton Mifflin's New Riverside Series, of which he is general editor.

KATHLEEN MCHUGH, Associate Professor of English, teaches in the Film and Visual Culture Program and the Department of English at the University of California, Riverside. She is the author of *American Domesticity: From How-To Manual to Hollywood Melodrama* (1999), which reconsiders this film genre and the feminist commentary applied to it in relation to domestic labor and its representation in the United States. She has published articles on domesticity, feminism and film theory, the avant-garde, and autobiography in such journals as *Cultural Studies, Jump Cut, Screen, South Atlantic Quarterly,* and *Velvet Light Trap*. She is currently working on a book-length study of experimental filmic autobiography.

SATYA P. MOHANTY is Professor of English at Cornell University and the author of *Literary Theory and the Claims of History: Postmodernism, Objectivity, Multicultural Politics* (1997). He works on American, British, and South Asian literatures and has cotranslated and introduced Fakir Mohan Senapati's 1897–1899 Oriya novel, *Chha Mana Atha Guntha* (Six Acres and a Third; forthcoming).

CHON A. NORIEGA is an Associate Professor in the Department of Film and Television, University of California, Los Angeles. He is the author of *Shot in America: Television, the State, and the Rise of Chicano Cinema* (2000) and editor of *Aztlán: A Journal of Chicano Studies*, as well as of seven books on film, media arts, and performance. He is also a regular curator of art exhibitions, most recently, *East of the River: Chicano Art Collectors Anonymous* (Santa Monica Museum of Art, Sept. 15–Nov. 18 2000).

DONALD E. PEASE is the Avalon Foundation Chair of the Humanities at Dartmouth College. The author or editor of nine books, Pease is the General Editor for the book series New Americanists at Duke University Press, the Founding Director of a Summer Institute for American Studies at Dartmouth, and the head of Dartmouth's Liberal Studies Program. In 2001 Pease served as the Drue Heinz Professor of American Literature at Oxford.

JOHN CARLOS ROWE teaches the literatures and cultures of the United States and Critical Theory at the University of California, Irvine. He is the author of *A Future for American Studies; Literary Culture and U.S. Imperialism: From the Revolution to World War II* (2000); *The Other Henry James* (1998); *At Emerson's Tomb: The Politics of Classic American Literature* (1997); *The Theoretical Dimensions of Henry James* (1984); *Through the Custom-House: Nineteenth-Century American Fiction and Modern Theory* (1982); and *Henry Adams and Henry James: The Emergence of a Modern Consciousness* (1976). He is the editor or co-editor of six other volumes, including the recent *Post-Nationalist American Studies* (2000).

ROBYN WIEGMAN is Margaret Taylor Smith Director of Women's Studies at Duke University. She is the author of *American Anatomies: Theorizing Race and Gender* (1995); co-editor of three anthologies, *The Futures of American Studies* (2001), *Feminism Beside Itself* (1995), and *Who Can Speak? Identity and Critical Authority* (1995); and editor of two collections, *AIDS and the National Body: Essays by Thomas Yingling* (1997) and *Locating Feminism: The Politics of Women's Studies* (2001). Her textbook, *Literature and Gender*, was published in 1999.

AESTHETICS IN A MULTICULTURAL AGE

Introduction

Cultural Diversity and the Problem of Aesthetics

EMORY ELLIOTT

When one person makes an aesthetic judgment about another in declaring that person to be physically or spiritually beautiful or, more important to our work here, in decreeing the other's cultural expression and artistic productions to possess superior qualities, the aesthetic functions as a positive bridge across the gap of difference. At the same time, however, when the person making such a judgment is in a dominant position politically, legally, or economically over the other and renders aesthetic judgments that demean and subordinate the other by pronouncing the person or his or her cultural production to be inferior, beneath consideration, or objectionable, the aesthetic may operate as a tool of divisiveness, enmity, and oppression. The critic in judgment who assumes that there are universal standards of beauty—that "we all recognize a beautiful face or a great poem when we see one"—will be likely to erase or subordinate an array of human differences and forms of creative expression as being inferior to a select few. Those who do not recognize themselves or their works of art in the features of the putative universal ideal will either feel diminished and inferior or systematically excluded and marginalized. Thus, the aesthetic is always in danger of being exploited in the service of individual prejudice or of nationalism, racism, sexism, and classism. This has always been true and remains the case today. It is the purpose of this volume to explore some of the ways in which recent global migration and the expanding ethnic diversity in the United States are affecting cultural productions and necessitating a reassessment of the nature and the role of aesthetics in our contemporary society.

Since the late 1960s, social, political, and technological changes throughout the world have accelerated the cultural diversity and synergism of many nations as people and forms of cultural expression have increasingly crossed or been crossed by altered national borders. Just as movies and popular music from the United States are distributed, broadcast, and sold in hundreds of countries, so have millions of people migrated and immigrated to the United States. While economic hardships, social tensions, and political conflict have often accompanied these population changes, the cultural production of the new immigrants often mediates the social pressures of change as people bring with them foods, styles of dress, religious practices, forms of art and expression, and perspectives on all aspects of human experience that daily transform the cultural fabric of their communities and of the United States. Although such hybrid cultures express and often allay social tensions, there are also many sources of conflict present in the clash of cultural forms, especially between generations within the immigrant communities and between those communities and their new neighbors. Still, it is almost a journalistic commonplace now to say that such forms of popular culture function as catalysts for social cohesion. Recent studies have documented the cultural blending and hybridity that have characterized the cultural expression of the Americas and have presented a more complex picture of the relation between society and cultural forms.[1]

During the last three decades, a theoretical revolution within the academic disciplines in the humanities and the arts has transformed the subject and methods of study of all forms of cultural expression. A new philosophical skepticism has questioned the epistemological foundations of judgment, arguing that all critical standards in the arts are constructed from within certain limited ideological positions. Of course, because practice does not always follow consistently from theory, many of the same critics who have challenged the foundations have also continued to make critical judgments in keeping with their own standards of taste, although their evaluations have tended to sound more tentative. What has been fairly consistent is that scholars and critics who had, in the 1960s, begun to challenge the established canons of art and literature for political reasons recognized the usefulness of theories of deconstruction as providing epistemological grounds for demonstrating how matters of class, gender, and ethnicity have always played crucial if subtle roles in decisions about artistic merit and aesthetics. Such recognition led some critics and scholars to discredit the systems of evaluation themselves, arguing that ideological, economic, and nationalist prejudices underlie and inform critical distinctions such as those between major and minor writers, sophisticated and naive art, and serious or complex works and superficial or obvious ones.

This reassessment of traditional critical standards for literature and the arts encouraged critics and scholars to work toward the formation of new and far more historically informed and politically self-aware standards for judging works of cultural production. As a result of this critical shift, assumptions upon which critical evaluations of cultural forms had been based previously have been called into question and, in many cases, discredited. Paradigms of analysis that had structured the subject matters of the disciplines—such as the distinction between high forms of artistic expression and low or popular forms—have been challenged and, in the views of many, rejected as based upon relative, political, and philosophically unsupportable distinctions.

During this period of theoretical reformulation, the growing awareness of the cultural diversity of the United States, both in the present and throughout its history, generated a remarkable expansion in the lists of texts and artifacts counted as worthy of study. On the part of artists, scholars, and teachers, a growing awareness of the cultural diversity of the United States and a corresponding new social consciousness about matters of gender equity and sexual preference began to bring more serious attention to bear on cultural productions by women and by gay and lesbian artists. Thus, for there to be fair opportunities for works of art and acts of cultural expression that had previously been rejected by the application of such narrow aesthetic standards, many of the prior aesthetic criteria needed to be re-examined and certainly the traditional hierarchies of merit needed to be challenged.

The recognition that works of art are inevitably political in some way, and that those engaged in political action nearly always employ forms of expression that are to some degree artistic, has inspired new research under the banner of "cultural studies" and has disturbed many traditionalists who still hold to the ideal of "art for art's sake." With such remarkable historical and theoretical developments occurring simultaneously, it should not be surprising that many inside and outside these disciplines have experienced a sense of disorientation and confusion; many are troubled about the current state of the academic fields and the systems of values and standards, as well as about the proper material and major research projects upon which they were formulated. At the same time, even those most convinced of the relativity of values, even to the point of rejecting the terms "art" and "literature" as class-bound and elitist, have recognized the impossibility of avoiding judgments. Thus, while academic self-critique and skeptical analysis have shaken the foundations of taste and judgment, critics and teachers are still called upon daily to make selections and judgments from among an abundant array of texts and artifacts.[2]

While in the marketplace people are purchasing music, books, films, and other cultural forms on the basis of their own individual tastes, critics and academics entrusted by society with the responsibility of deciding what is worthy of preservation and dissemination through college and university courses, libraries, museums, film and other archives have resisted making judgments. But judge they must when pressed by the leaders of institutions such as art museums and libraries to provide guidance and direction. Publishing houses, the entertainment industries, even cooking schools and ministries of tourism, seek the advice and judgments of those who are the valued experts. Indeed, cultural studies' scholars, anthropologists, art historians, and social historians address institutions besides the academy, often taking museum and archive practices or the study of the practices of contemporary communities as their research focus. It is time to end the divisive "culture war" debates that have raged on for over a decade. Now is the moment to formulate new assessments of the relationships between minority cultures and the dominant culture and of the ways that social and political upheaval and personal struggle often generate acts of cultural production and transmission through which the human experiences of transformation are expressed.

Of course, in spite of the theoretical problematic, judgment is inevitable when selecting some texts and artifacts rather than others for transmission in all its varieties—library, archival and museum preservation, scholarly and critical analysis in classrooms, publications, or display materials. In *The Ideology of the Aesthetic*, Terry Eagleton attributes the unwillingness of many recent critics to make judgments about the aesthetic qualities of art and writing not to cultural or personal bias so much as to "a loss or rejection of the dialectical habit" and to a "leap from history" by those embracing poststructuralist theories (Eagleton, 415). Without a dialectical habit, he implies, those making judgments are unable to recognize the very different aesthetic principles within which unfamiliar physical features or artistic production may be perceived not as bad or ugly but as stemming from different epistemologies of beauty and art. Without a sense of history, those positioned to evaluate the performance of others may not recognize that aesthetic values and principles are always changing and are embedded in particular cultures, or, as Eagleton puts it, fail to see that the "discourses of reason, truth, freedom and subjectivity, as we have inherited them, require profound transformation" (Eagleton, 425). In addition to this turn from history, however, there are many additional reasons for the long evasion of discussions of beauty and artistic merit in the academy in the United States.[3]

The challenges now facing scholars in the disciplines of the arts, humanities, and social sciences require thoughtful and reflective consideration. We must consider how to consolidate the breathtaking advances in theory and interpretive methods that inform our disciplines with the wealth of new knowledge and cultural materials that comprise our subjects now and compete for our judgments. Breakthrough research and extraordinary leaps in theory and knowledge are necessarily chaotic and disturbing. Once the wealth of new data is before us, however, it may be possible to formulate new terminologies, categories, and processes of assessment and to restructure the disciplines along new directions that are in accord with current theories. Such reconstitution of the disciplines will need to be accomplished in ways that will enable students, researchers, and informed citizens to find the means to express the significance of a wide array of creative and cultural productions.

In the social sciences, for the many scholars who are working on issues of migration, immigration politics, ethnicity, citizenship, and indigenous peoples, the primary concerns today are class and identity, borders and bordering, and ethnic groups and nation-states. For many of them, the political rhetoric about diversity within the United States tends to be overly celebratory of the benefits of diversity and does not acknowledge fully enough how the culturally constructed basis of much intercommunity conflict only serves the needs of oppression and exploitation. While cultural diversity is typically extolled as a desired component of modern nation-states that tends to offset what is often seen as a hegemonic monocultural dominant identity, some argue that the promotion of cultural differences and distinctions can and indeed often does have notable negative consequences. These divisive results often derive from the efforts of proponents and leaders of specific nationalist and ethnic movements and communities to construct, and indeed at times to invent, ethnic and "racially" based identities. The invention of such "imagined communities," as Benedict Anderson notes in referring to the construction of the modern nation-state, inevitably depends on the drawing of boundaries between "us" and "them." The most extreme form of such differentiation is, of course, the spurious attribution of innate biological differences to different "races." The insidious consequences that have ensued from this fallacious folk biological concept, which has no basis in human genetics, is the most extreme case of constructed diversity in the service of injustice and oppression. But comparable sociocultural and political economic dynamics often underlie the construction of ethnic and national identities and the conflicts that they enable and at times promote.[4]

From a theoretical point of view, cultural communities to one degree or another are certainly constructed, and it is important to have an understanding of these dynamics of community formation. Knowledge of the process of community development must inform any analysis of cultural expression so that the claims to cultural primacy, uniqueness, and diversity can be carefully considered and understood. The current rapid and prolific growth of transnational communities in the United States and in other metropoles are the prime examples of the most current emergence of human populations undergoing various processes of intentionality, retention, rejection, and negotiation as well. The converse, more positive side of such emergent diversity is the construction of minority ethnicity and nationalism as the necessary common cultural currency with which to build constructive political projects such as citizen advisory committees to law enforcement in the service of justice and equality.

These challenges for the social sciences and the humanities involve nothing short of the adoption of entirely new principles for evaluating cultural productions with the fullest possible understanding of the social, political, and economic conditions in which they are produced. They involve, as well, the creation of new terminologies and explanations for how and why elements of creative production affect us as they do. To do this, we need not only to study the histories of the arts in various parts of the world but also to examine the new technologies, knowledge, and human interactions around the globe that are opening new channels of communication and bringing new understandings of human expression and creativity. Beyond these issues involving the evaluation and categorization of artistic productions and close analysis of texts, we also need to consider more fully the roles of institutions of transmission—libraries, museums, publishing houses, the entertainment industry, and others, as well as the university and the public and private K–12 school system—in the preservation and dissemination of culture in a multicultural society. Such a research program must include the contributions of anthropologists, economists, sociologists, and others who might be more interested in modes of transmission than in textual analysis or production. Indeed, in terms of methodology and new knowledge, the major contribution cultural studies has made to more hermeneutically oriented disciplines such as English has been to bring literary interpretation to such issues as the processes of cultural exchange and the affective and economic relations that structure the transmission of cultural productions.

In fact, before pursuing the very specific problems of aesthetics and difference in our contemporary American situation, it is valuable to pause for a moment and to remind ourselves that the subject of aesthetics has a long history in world philosophy and criticism, going back at least to Plato and Aristotle, and to remember as well that strongly held personal opinions and widespread cultural discrimination have been very much part of that history. The ancient Egyptians, Greeks, and Romans all imposed their cultural and aesthetic values on other societies. In the East, the Chinese, Japanese, Koreans, and Thai peoples have disputed for millennia over which group is intellectually superior and whose artistic creations are superior. In modern history, Shakespeare expressed aesthetic judgments when he parodied his fellow English playwrights, as well as their Italian and French predecessors, and Scottish and Irish poets. Throughout the nineteenth century, the English and the Scottish critics belittled all aspects of American culture: "Who reads an American book?" they asked scornfully. Within the early United States, regional divisions quickly became the basis for cultural prejudice and for establishing a hierarchy of literary and artistic merit with New England at the top. Even today in the United States, among writers, critics, architects, filmmakers, artists, and museum curators, such debates often occur in relation to region, with some identifying themselves with the aesthetic values of the West Coast or Los Angeles, in contrast to others who ally themselves with the East Coast or New York.

For the present moment and for the purpose of the current discussion, issues of ethnic and racial difference are central in rethinking art and culture in the United States. At the same time, it should be recognized that a wide range of discussions of subjects related to aesthetics and culture are being carried on with little reference to multiculturalism. For example, many scholars and artists over the last three decades have been focused on the ways that many issues of gender and sexual preference affect matters of aesthetics and the critical judgments of art. This is an enormous subject that sometimes shares common ground with similar issues of ethnic identity but also reveals important gender divisions within ethnic groups. Meanwhile, other critics are passionately engaged in writing articles and books on the aesthetics of the poetry of Ovid, Dante, Li Po, and other long-established authors of the traditional Western and Eastern canons. In academic journals and on the public media, scholars of linguistics and politics are analyzing the rhetorical language and physical appeal of political candidates, while each day hundreds of reviewers produce aesthetic judgments on performances of operas, plays, television performers, rock bands, hip hop word artists, and every type of human performance that elicits aesthetic response. It is not as though the United States's ethnic diversity has suddenly resurrected a long dormant conversation about art and aesthetics. Aesthetic issues are always with us, and within various personal and social contexts, matters of beauty and taste function significantly in all dimensions of our lives.

Eagleton's *The Ideology of the Aesthetic* does provide a useful starting point for considering the issues that are the focus of this volume. Indeed, many feel that the recent theoretical revolution has made the term "aesthetic" and the cluster of ideas it contains outmoded and irrelevant. For those who believe that art itself is an elitist notion that only serves to sustain false hierarchies of expression, aesthetics is a divisive notion that does more harm than good. As long as people review and evaluate cultural expression and make choices about what to preserve, study, and recommend, however, they will seek to define standards of judgment and thereby fall back into aesthetics. The issue then is not whether we can rid ourselves of the disciplines that address the desire for beauty and art; rather, it must be how to redefine the parameters of "art" and formulate new questions for evaluating cultural expression in ways that are fair and just to all.

While Eagleton is optimistic in his affirmation of the aesthetic, he also is careful to underscore the risks of returning to it, for the aesthetic can always be used by every brand of extremist ideologue: "The left turn: smash truth, cognition and morality, which are all just ideology, and live luxuriantly in the free, groundless play of your creative powers. The right turn, . . . forget about theoretical analysis, cling to the sensuously particular, view society as a self-grounding organism, all of whose parts miraculously interpenetrate without conflict and require no rational justification" (Eagleton, 368–69). When the right embraces the aesthetic, Eagleton observes, there often develops an alliance between those intellectuals who privilege the aesthetic and the most rigid cynics concentrated in "the upper echelons of fascist organizations"; both groups share contempt for the utilitarian and an arrogant motivation to control and discipline (Eagleton, 369). Recently, in the United States, it has usually been the right, rather than the left, that has found aesthetic politics most attractive, and, when it does so, the right usually embraces a notion of the transcendence of art that tends to ignore and erase history. Such conservative uses of aesthetics also foster notions of timeless and universal appeal that ignore cultural and historical difference and seek to impose the "universal" taste and values of a cultural elite upon the rest of society. There often emerges an alliance between a conservative politics that privileges the powerful and wealthy few in politics and society and a conservative aesthetics that recognizes only a small pantheon of important writers and artists. However, there are exceptions to this general principle: many academic critics claim to hold positions that result in their being progressive in politics and egalitarian in economics while holding conservative positions in matters of the arts and culture. For example, in his *Culture of Contradictions*, Daniel Bell asserts: "I am a socialist in economics, a liberal in politics, and a conservative in culture" (361). There will always be heated debates surrounding the conscious and unconscious motives of those who claim to want equality and justice for all while also insisting that reason, taste, and learning support their view that there are only a few meritorious writers and artists.

At the same time, the continuing culture wars in the United States provide ample evidence of the continuing alliances between conservative political leaders and those intellectuals and academics who cling to aesthetics values that lead them to celebrate a mainly white, male Euro-American canon of artists and writers. Many of the conservative arguments have been characterized by their hyper-canonization of the "world classics" and by their insidious *ad hominem* attacks on what they assert to be their opponents' lack of knowledge and intelligence. There is also a strong tendency in the arguments from the right to universalize beauty and art and to judge objects and artifacts on the basis of how they measure against the ideal. Of course, what is posited as universal and essential is nothing more than the classical Western canons of art and literature, which were primarily constructed by white male anthologists, literary editors, and genteel intellectuals in the last two centuries. Such emotionally charged issues in which conflicts of identity and culture are inscribed do tend to produce extremism of the right and left and silence among those who seek to negotiate the unstable middle ground.

An example of an argument from the right that has had broad appeal appeared in a fall 1999 review in the *New York Review of Books*, entitled "The Decline and Fall of Literature." In Andrew Delbanco's call for a return to the New Critical standards of evaluation and for the literary canon of the glory years of criticism of the 1950s, he effectively tapped into the current panic that many traditional scholars feel about the erosion of the professions of literary and art criticism. Using several recent books on the "The Embattled State of the Profession" (the title of Carl Woodring's book), Delbanco writes a jeremiad chastising scholars for their failure of belief, their rush to self-destruction, and their abandonment of their divine mission to preach the word of great literature.[5]

Laced with religious terms and metaphors, Delbanco blames the current decline on the backsliding generation of scholars who have been victims to heresies from abroad and to their own carnal desires for fame and profit. He laments the passing of the patriarchs, the "respected practitioners," of English studies who "enjoyed their greatest prestige in the secular academy when they held most closely to the tradition of scriptural exegesis from which they derived." They were "primarily undergraduate teachers," he says, and "under their spell, the classroom became like a Quaker meeting" (Delbanco, 36). Delbanco calls for "a full scale revival [which] will only come when English professors recommit themselves to slaking the human craving for contact with works of art that somehow register one's own longings and yet exceed what one has been able to articulate by and for oneself. This is among the indispensable experiences of the fulfilled life, and the English department will survive . . . only if it continues to coax and prod students toward it" (Delbanco, 38).

While Delbanco writes of literature expressing transcendent universal human longings, he says very little, and certainly nothing positive, about the impact that the increasing ethnic diversity of our society has had upon responsible teacher-critics to consider the connections between the books they teach and the lived experiences of the nonwhite Americans in their classes. Indeed, Delbanco views the opening of the literary canon as one of our biggest problems. The "English department," Delbanco says, "has paid overdue attention to minority writers," and he cites a study by historian Lynn Hunt that the English department "along with the humanities in general has failed to attract many minority students." This extraordinary dismissal of unnamed writers who happen to be members of ethnic "minority" groups and college students who happen not to join English departments is quite insidious. Which of these undesirable writers are to be eliminated and why? Why should we assume that the reason more minority students do not enroll in English departments should have any relation to the number of minority writers being taught in their courses? Is Delbanco suggesting perhaps that, if a department has a small number of students of Irish, Jewish, or Italian descent, it should cut back the number of writers from those groups taught in the courses? Here is an instance in which a scholar perceives politics and aesthetics to be at odds and his responsibility to defend against those who threaten the integrity of art. Ironically, Delbanco never engages the subject of aesthetics and literary merit but merely implies that "artistic merit" and "minority writers" are mutually exclusive terms. This review, which presumes to guard some threatened artistic treasures, demonstrates why it is necessary that matters of aesthetic achievement be openly debated and that value judgments be articulated. When such claims are left unchallenged, the real debate over artistic merit is elided by presumptions that everyone already knows that T. S. Eliot belongs in the canon because his greatness is long-established, while Langston Hughes is intruding on sacred territory for political reasons. And so on.

Among the many books of the last several years on the subject of making aesthetic judgements and teaching literature in contemporary society, a few, such as Mark Bauerlein's *The Pragmatic Mind: Exploration in the Psychology of Belief* (1997) and Robert Scholes's *The Rise and Fall of English* (1998), have favored a more pragmatic approach over nostalgia and lament. These works stress the need for clar-

ity, reason, self-awareness, and demystification, and both stress the practical consequences of the choices before us. For example, Scholes does not dismiss theory
in constructing a solution but tries to employ it. He engages these issues of professional doubt and belief and constructs an argument for what should constitute the discipline of English today. In his chapter entitled "no dog would go on
living like this," he states his thesis this way:

> If there is no appeal to realities or principles beyond what we may happen to be-
> lieve at any given time, then we have no arguments either in favor of changing things
> for the better or for resisting a slide back into superstition and dogma. And we live
> in a world where we are threatened by superstition and dogma at every turn. On
> very pragmatic grounds, then, I would want to argue in favor of what Rorty calls
> a realistic position, as opposed to a pragmatic one, because it is "good" for us to
> believe. Quite specifically, it is good for us to believe that our beliefs are grounded
> in something firmer than belief itself. We need the love of truth, neither because
> we can attain ultimate truth, nor yet because it will "make us free"—but [because]
> we need a sense of a shared enterprise, to which we may contribute something. As
> educators, we need the sense that we are presenting to students and colleagues ideas,
> methods, and information that are neither false nor useless. (Scholes, 53–54)

Certainly, many teachers and scholars are motivated by these ideals of shared
intellectual goals, by a common search for truth, and by the desire to enhance
the lives of students and thus improve society in general through reading, writing, and teaching. Yet, many practitioners in the field of arts and literature are
skeptical about Scholes's plea for belief and truth. With the rise of science and
the decline of religion among major segments of our society, we have witnessed
a shift in our academic institutions. The growing importance of technology and
applied sciences has raised the value of research that yields immediate quantifi-
able results while diminishing fields that involve matters of analysis and interpretation of human actions, feelings, and ideas, such as literary and cultural studies.
Instead, many are in favor of rhetoric and composition which are presumed to
train students for the marketplace.

Such external pressures have combined with internal ones, especially the skepticism and massive psychological depression that came upon many professors of
literature in the 1970s and 80s. Scholes quotes Derrida's 1992 address at Columbia University in which he expressed his perception of the demoralized condition of humanities professors: "We feel bad about ourselves. Who would dare
say otherwise? And those who feel good about themselves are perhaps hiding
something, from others and from themselves" (Scholes, 39). Derrida went on to
argue that the reason we feel bad is that we live within a paralyzing contradiction between the realities of our institutional contexts and the values that drew
us to our calling, such as a love of language, imagination, and creativity; the desire to share our passion for reading and analyzing works of art and literature;
the satisfaction of vigorous, committed, and constructive intellectual debate over

ideas and subjects that have mattered to humanity in the past and matter still today. Derrida considered: "And who are we in the university where apparently we are? What do we represent? Whom do we represent? Are we responsible? If there is a university responsibility, it at least begins with the moment when a need to hear these questions, to take them upon oneself, is imposed. This imperative for responding is the initial form and minimal requirement of responsibility" (Scholes, 44).

The immediate and pressing problem that confronts teachers and scholars in the arts and humanities remains one of presenting the knowledge required to be a university educated person to the generation of students in today's classrooms. To approach this set of tasks as a profession, we must objectively reassess the issues of canon formation, the evaluation of works of art and literature, and the presentation of interpretations that have meaning and value for our current students. For these reasons, we must take serious notice when a scholar of the stature of Hazel Carby says in her essay, "The Multicultural Wars" in the collection *Black Popular Culture*, "As a black intellectual, I am both intrigued and horrified by the contradictory nature of the black presence in North American universities. We are, as students, as teachers, and as cultural producers, simultaneously visibly present in, and starkly absent from, university life." Regarding even the reconstructed literary canon in which writers of color are included in American literature courses, Carby observes, "From the vantage point of the academy, it is obvious that the publishing explosion of fiction of black women has been a major influence in the development of the multicultural curriculum, and I have tried to point to the ways in which the texts of black women and men sit uneasily in a discourse that seems to act as a substitute for the political activity of desegregation." (Carby, 197). She goes on to point out that the white suburbs in which such black texts are popular and the colleges in which they are taught are usually separated from urban centers by apartheidlike structures so that those who read these texts and those whose lives are written about "lack the opportunity to grow up in any equitable way with each other" (Carby, 197). Carby's observations and those of many others whose essays fill some of the recent volumes of work on multicultural America have thus far had little effect on changing those structures.[6]

Frequently, students of African, Asian, or Hispanic descent who enroll in college literature courses that include texts by writers of ethnic minorities are disappointed by how those texts are presented. They may find minority writers approached with condescension or, at best, with no recognition on the teacher's part that he or she might be ignorant of the cultural differences that have informed the aesthetic qualities of those works. Too often, teachers cover mainly the biographical, historical, and political circumstances in which the text was written and avoid discussing the formal qualities that they normally would consider in teaching established white authors. Some teachers focus only on the political and personal experiences depicted in the works and are so culturally insensitive as to ask the minority students in the class to tell others how they do or do not identify with the characters, as though they are "native informants" from a marginal society. Students recognize this variation in approach and read it as a lack of interest on the part of the professor in the work itself, or as an indication that the teacher does not respect such minoritized authors and texts as being serious art worthy of literary explication.

Ten years ago, this problem was less conspicuous than it is now. Until very recently, there was so much excitement on the part of faculty and students who were becoming newly acquainted with the writings of a wider range of American authors that the necessary contextual information for reading their works was considerable and often did not leave time for close analysis of the writing as art. But a shift has occurred, and we are beginning to see the emergence of tools for analysis of the literature itself. For example, the works on the Black Atlantic by Paul Gilroy, Joseph Roach, Joan Dayan, and others, have explored the ways that African religious and aesthetic traditions circulated through the Caribbean and in cities such as New Orleans; a wealth of research on black culture and the African Diaspora has examined the blending of African and European forms and expressions over the last three centuries. There is now also a substantial body of criticism on the Black Aesthetic so that teachers of literature today should be prepared to discuss the artistic merits of texts by African-American artists with reference to both African and European aesthetics.[7]

Now that courses and anthologies include many writers previously excluded for reasons of race, ethnicity, and gender, and now that we are taking up questions of artistic forms and methods again, we need to develop the tools that will help us to understand what those writers are doing as artists so that we can teach their works more effectively. The students, the writers, the texts are here with us, and we need to prepare ourselves and our graduate students to do a more comprehensive and accurate job of teaching the texts before us. Rejecting the texts as artistic failures or as having mere political value is not a fitting intellectual response to the major intellectual, demographic, and educational challenges we face.[8]

While it might seem attractive to some to resurrect the formalist principles of the 1950s, such a move would surely be counterproductive, for those terms and systems of analysis remain historically bound to their cultural period. This is not to assert that all art works and critical standards are entirely relative, but it is also not to say that they are universal and transcendental either. We need only to look at representations of human beauty over the centuries and across cultures to see that notions of beauty vary depending on the time and place. For this time, we need to formulate new terms and definitions and perhaps also a new system of analysis for describing the characteristics of art and literature and the feelings and intellectual pleasures they evoke in the particular diversity of the people we are today.

Indeed, as frequently happens, some artists are already ahead of us in this endeavor. In her *Playing in the Dark: Whiteness and the Literary Imagination*, Toni Morrison suggests that the "classic white American authors," even those who were conspicuously racist in their personal lives, need to be studied by readers possessing a new set of critical tools with which to reveal the Africanist presence previously hidden in many of these texts. By so doing, we not only discover how closely intertwined the lives of black and white Americans have been on this continent since the sixteenth century but how images of Africans and of African cultural elements have been integral in the formation of Euro-American history and U.S. national identity and the literature that represents them. The implications of Morrison's insights for American Studies and for rethinking a literary aesthetic are far-reaching, suggesting that we need to devote as much time and attention to the histories, cultures, languages, and artistic systems of values of the African peoples as we have been doing for hundreds of years to the contributions of cultures of the European peoples. It is not enough simply to recognize, as many critics have now, that Africanness is often present in U.S. texts by white authors even when it is disguised under various representations of otherness. We must examine more deeply the ways that structure, form, verbal rhythms, and American English have been permeated and reconstituted by cultural elements from our African heritage.[9]

Just as students of twentieth-century music of the "highest" forms could no longer approach their subject without a sound knowledge of blues and jazz, we must be able to bring to the texts we teach the degree of knowledge of African-American history, African cultures, and African-American expression needed to understand the patterns of language construction that inform those texts. As Sterling Stuckey's important historical investigations into the sources of Melville's *Benito Cereno* have shown, a critic who does not bring to that work some knowledge of Ashanti funerary customs and other cultural traditions will fail to understand important nuances of Babo's masquerade. Indeed, such critics will fall into some of the less obvious traps Melville set to catch racist readers.[10] And, of course, how could we begin to make sense of many elements of Morrison's own novels without delving into the African-American history and the African religious and spiritual traditions which so fully inform these texts. In her famous essay "Speaking Things Unspeakable," Morrison has given us a sign post, directing our attention both to Europe and to Africa when we study her works, by showing how her opening sentences function, something in the way of Shakespearean prologues, to alert readers to certain themes and major events that she will later elaborate. In that essay, she demonstrates how aspects of her literary aesthetic came down to her from the classics of the European past as well as from the forms of expression and storytelling she learned from her African heritage. Her argument is a useful demonstration of the way a process of "both/and" inclusive thinking is key in our analysis of her art as opposed to the Manichean "either/or" logic which, as Abdul JanMohamed has notably argued, is at the core of much of the racialization found in cultural critiques.

Morrison's arguments extend more broadly, of course, to the other previously marginalized and undervalued cultural influences upon U.S. writing, such as those from Latin America, Asia, and the Pacific Rim countries. It remains the case in most English departments that students who are interested in "minority literatures" are expected to take elective courses usually devoted exclusively to one or more of "those literatures." When a department has been successful in hiring, they may have a faculty member who is expert in one or more of these literatures and their many cultural contexts. Such is not always the case, and the instructor does his or her best, which may mean treating the text as if it were only within the Euro-American tradition. This situation implies to students that the relevance of these newly valorized bodies of writing to "mainstream" U.S. literature is marginal and may be short-lived. If lasting changes in the canon that result in greater cultural inclusiveness are to occur, we must be able to train all graduate students of "American" literature in the cultures and aesthetic traditions of the peoples of the world whose influence upon U.S. culture and literature is undeniable. Indeed, no serious criticism of U.S. writing can take place any longer without the critics' possession of extensive knowledge of the wide variety of recently recognized cultural influences on the United States.

Of course, works by authors who descended from non-Western and non-Anglo-European heritages present new challenges for teachers and scholars trained in the New Critical or historical schools in the United States, for the unfamiliar aesthetic systems that are inscribed in texts and artifacts are from African, Asian, and Latin-American or Hispanic cultures. In a process akin to teaching texts in translation without knowing them in their original language, teachers have been attempting to reveal to students the complexities of works by Asian-American, Latino, and African-American authors whose works are steeped in the artistic traditions of their cultures. So far the solution to this problem seems to have been mainly to wait until scholars with the same cultural heritages can bring their personal knowledge of the cultures together with their professional training in Western criticism.

The only way to approach this challenge with intellectual honesty and scholarly commitment is the same way that scholars of European Medieval and Renaissance literature have traditionally approached their subjects. By educating ourselves more fully and energetically in the languages and cultures of those parts of the world whose aesthetic contributions are now understood to be part of the culture of the United States, we will be much more competent to demonstrate to our students why texts by authors who are of African, Asian, and Hispanic descent are as rich and aesthetically pleasing as they are. Scholarly competence in the rich and diverse literature of the United States requires larger, not downsized, literature programs.

The challenges before us involve nothing short of constructing new principles for evaluating productions of art, with the fullest possible grasp of the aesthetic principles of the cultures which contributed to these works, and creating new terminologies and explanations for how and why elements of creative production affect us as they do. To do this, we need not only to study the histories of the arts in various parts of the world but also to examine our contemporary cultures and perceive how we are being changed by new technologies and evolving human interactions around the globe.

Along with the continuing emphasis on political and theoretical developments in the fields of literature and the arts, there have also been indications over the last few years of a return to an interest in aesthetics. *The Ideology of the Aesthetic* makes a good beginning in the attempt to mediate between those who argue that aesthetics is somehow independent from political ideologies and those who hold the view that aesthetics is merely a component of a bourgeois ideology to be purged from the disciplines of the arts and humanities. Eagleton enables the reconsideration of the demystification of aesthetics as ideology by rehistoricizing this contemporary confrontation within the philosophical debates of the last two centuries that have produced the current intellectual gridlock.

From a rather different angle of inquiry, a number of philosophers, psychologists, and theorists and critics of the arts have been developing new strategies to investigate what is involved in our cognitive responses to what we call art and literature. In a collection edited by Mette Hjort and Sue Laver, *Emotion and the Arts*, scholars from various fields from several countries present germinal work on issues of agency and "some of the ways in which an agent's beliefs, intentions, desires, and attitudes are constitutive of his or her emotional engagements with art" (Hjort and Laver, 5). The work of these authors participates in a broader examination of the role of the emotions and aesthetics that is found in the work of Martha Nussbaum, Michael Taussig, David Novitz, and others. Elaine Scarry's recent book, *Dreaming by the Book*, draws upon recent research in cognitive psychology to examine the processes whereby the word choices and sentence constructions of imaginative writing activate very particular responses in the reader's imagination. In this work, Scarry defines a new set of categories and terms for literary analysis. Although her work does not take up issues of cultural diversity as such, her critical methods will be likely to inspire a shift in criticism more toward close readings and thereby open up new opportunities for commentators to demonstrate the verbal skill and artistry of many writers whose works have entered the anthologies and classrooms in the last twenty years.[11]

Because of the increasingly diverse student bodies of American universities and colleges, those of us who teach language, arts, and humanities are especially well positioned to begin the formidable work of constructing a system or systems of aesthetics consistent with current theories and cultural conditions. The new fields, terminologies, methodologies, and aesthetic principles that emerge from this work and others like it will better enable scholars, teachers, and students to assess and organize the cultural expressions of the past and present and to describe and judge the cultural productions of the postnational, richly diverse community of cross-cultural global societies that already constitute the world of the twenty-first century.

Notes

1. While the focus of this volume is the United States, many of the same developments are occurring around the world. For example, global communications and the rapidly changing populations in Africa, Asia, Europe, and Latin America are producing similar cultural transformations. On the postcolonial, transnational, and postnational dimensions of these issues see Alexander and Mohanty, Anderson, Appiah, Carby, Castillo, Davidson and Moon, A. Davis, Fusco, Goldberg, Guha and Spivak, Henderson, Herra-Sobek, JanMohamed, Kaplan and Pease, Kearney and Nagengast, Lee, Lemke, Lionnet, Lowe, S. Mohanty, Patterson, Pease, Rosaldo, Roy, Sobel, Spillers, Spivak, Taussig, and West.

2. A wealth of commentary exists on the theory of political constructivism and on the problem of the inevitable expression of values and judgments in reconfiguring the critical hierarchy within the arts or redefining critical judgments of the arts and literature, see Arac, Bauerlein, Berube, Bloch, Bourdieu, Brown, Clark, Delbanco, Eagleton, Ellis, Felski, Foster, Gates, Godzich, Grossberg, N. Harris, G. Hartman, Henderson, hooks, Iser, JanMohamed, JanMohamed and Lloyd, Johnson, Kelley, Kernan, King, Lambert, Lauter, Lemke, G. L. Levine, Lipsitz, Lowe, McCormick, W. Mitchell, S. Mohanty, Morrison, Mukarovsky, C. Nelson, Novitz, Paulson, Rampersad, Redfield, J. and R. Saldivar, Scarry, Scholes, Soderholm, Steiner, Tate, Taussig, West, Woodmansee, and Woodring.

3. Eagleton posed the predicament for aesthetics in the highly self-conscious and skeptical culture that the West has become since the atrocities of the last two centuries cast a long shadow on the optimism of the Enlightenment. Several essays in the present volume attempt to negotiate some directions, different from Eagleton's neo-Marxist position, out of this bind.

4. I am grateful to my colleague Carole-Anne Tyler for her contributions to this essay, especially in these paragraphs, and to Martha Banta for her suggestions. For discussions and examples of some of the ways that the social sciences are responding to this range of subjects, see Berry, Calderon and Saldivar, A. Davis, During, Foster, Garvey and Ignatiev, Gilman, Gilroy, Goldberg, Gordon and Newfield, Grossberg, Gutierrez, N. Harris, Hoffman, Ignatiev, Kaplan, Kearny and Nagengast, L. Levine, Matthews, Patterson, Raboteau, Rosaldo, Sanchez, Sobel, Stuckey, Velez-Ibanez, Welchman, and Williams.

5. Included in the Delbanco review are Berube, Ellis, Kernan, Scholes, and Woodring. On the culture war debates, see also Arac, During, Hunt, C. Nelson, and Ohmann.

6. Representative studies of multiculturalism and the arts in the contemporary United States include Baker, Bernheimer, Berube and Nelson, Carby, Calderon and Saldivar, Castillo, Christian, Cruz, Davidson and Moon, A. Davis, Dent, Fusco, Gates, Gordon and Newfield, Gottschild, Grossberg, Guillory, Henderson, Herra-Sobek, hooks, James, Kim, King, Lauter, Lee, L. Levine, Lim and Herra-Sobek, Lim and Ling, Lionnet, Lipsitz,

Lopez, Lowe, A. Mitchell, Nelson and Gaonkar, O'Meally, Pease, Peterson, Posnock, Reed, Rosaldo, J. Saldivar, R. Saldivar, Sanders, T. Smith, V. Smith, Snead, Sollors, Spillers, Spivak, Sundquist, Velez-Ibanez, and Yamamoto.

7. For other works that have taken up issues of alterity, blackness and whiteness, Black culture, slave religion, and minstrelsy, see Allen, Andrews, Appiah, Baker, Berry, Brody, Carby, Christian, T. Davis, Diedrich and Sollors, duCille, Fisher-Fishkin, Gates, Gilman, Gilroy, Glissant, Gottschild, T. Harris, S. Hartman, Henderson, Hoffman, Holloway, hooks, James, JanMohamed, JanMohamed and Lloyd, L. Levine, Lionnet, Lott, Matthews, McKay, Morrison, D. Nelson, O'Meally, O'Meally and Fabre, Painter, Patterson, Peterson, Posnock, Roach, Roediger, Roy, Sanchez, Sobel, T. Smith, V. Smith, Sobel, Sollors, Stepto, Stepto and Harper, Stuckey, Sundquist, Tate, Thompson, Washington, West, Williams, Yamamoto, Yarborough, and Yellin.

8. In 1988, *The Columbia Literary History of the United States* presented a more inclusive account of the history of the literature the nation, and *The Columbia History of the American Novel* (1991) included within the term "American" literature the works of writers of the Americas (Elliott). In 1990, the appearance of the first edition of *The Heath Anthology of American Literature* enabled teachers to bring many of the newly included authors and texts more easily into the classroom. The anthology's general editor, Paul Lauter, led a team of scholars over several years to reconstruct the American literary canon in view of earlier discriminations and recent rediscoveries. Since the appearance of the *Heath*, other American literature anthologies have become more diverse.

9. There is an extensive scholarship on the influences of African, Asian, and Latin American cultures on Euro-American aesthetics and culture. See Alexander and Mohanty, Baker, Brody, Carby, Calderon and Saldivar, Castillon, Christian, Davidson and Moon, A. Davis, T. Davis, Dent, Diedrich and Sollors, duCille, Fisher-Fishkin, Fusco, Gates, Gilroy, Glissant, Gordon and Newfield, Gottschild, Guha and Spivak, Guillory, Gutierrez, Harris, S. Hartman, Henderson, Holloway, hooks, James, JanMohamed and Lloyd, Johnson, Kim, King, Lauter, Lee, Lemke, L. Levine, Lim and Herrera-Sobek, Lim and Ling, Ling, Lionnet, Lipsitz, Lowe, McKay, A. Mitchell, Morrison, Nelson, O'Meally, Peterson, Posnock, Pryse and Spillers, Raboteau, Rampersad, Reed, Roach, Rosaldo, Roy, J. Saldivar, R. Saldivar, Sanders, T. Smith, V. Smith, Sobel, Soderholm, Sollors, Spillers, Spivak, Stepto, Stuckey, Sundquist, Tate, Taussig, Thompson, Washington, West, Yamamoto, Yarborough, and Yellin.

10. For Stuckey's essay on Melville, see his *Going through the Storm*.

11. In addition to the established European approaches to aesthetics, recent strategies and discussions may be found in Arac, Baker, Block, Bourdieu, Brown, Clark, Cohen, Cruz, Dent, Felski, Fisher, Foster, Fusco, Gottschild, Guillory, Harris, G. Hartman, Hjort and Laver, hooks, James, Johnson, Kelley, Kernan, Kim, King, Lambert, Lemke, G. Levine, Lipsitz, Lowe, McCormick, W. J. T. Mitchell, Morrison, Mukarovsky, Novitz, Redfield, Sanders, Scarry, Scholes, Soderholm, Steiner, Thompson, and Woodmansee.

Works Cited

Alexander, M. Jacqui, and Chandra Talpade Mohanty, eds. *Feminist Genealogies, Colonial Legacies, and Democratic Futures*. New York: Routledge, 1997.

Allen, Theodore. *The Invention of the White Race.* New York: Verso, 1994.

Anderson, Benedict R. *Imagined Communities: Reflections on the Origin and Spread of Nationalism.* London: Verso, 1983.

Andrews, William L. *The Literary Career of Charles W. Chesnutt.* Baton Rouge: Louisiana State University Press, 1980.

————, ed. *African American Autobiography: A Collection of Critical Essays.* Englewood Cliffs, N.J.: Prentice Hall, 1993.

Appiah, Anthony. *In My Father's House: Africa in the Philosophy of Culture.* New York: Oxford University Press, 1992.

Arac, Jonathan, ed. *Postmodernism and Politics.* Minneapolis: University of Minnesota Press, 1986.

Baker, Houston A. *Blues, Ideology, and Afro-American Literature: A Vernacular Theory.* Chicago: University of Chicago Press, 1984.

————. *Modernism and the Harlem Renaissance.* Chicago: University of Chicago Press, 1987.

————. *Afro-American Poetics: Revisions of Harlem and the Black Aesthetic.* Madison: University of Wisconsin Press, 1988.

Bauerlein, Mark. *The Pragmatic Mind: Explorations in the Psychology of Belief.* Durham, N.C.: Duke University Press, 1997.

Bell, Daniel. *The Cultural Contradictions of Capitalism.* New York: Basic Books, 1976; rpt. 1996.

Bernheimer, Charles. *Comparative Literature in the Age of Multiculturalism.* Baltimore, Md.: Johns Hopkins University Press, 1995.

Berry, Mary Frances. *Black Resistance, White Law: A History of Constitutional Racism in America.* Englewood Cliffs, N.J.: Prentice Hall, 1971.

Berube, Michael, and Cary Nelson, eds. *Higher Education under Fire: Politics, Economics, and the Crisis of the Humanities.* New York: Routledge, 1995.

————. *The Employment of English: Theory, Jobs, and the Future of Literary Studies.* New York: New York University Press, 1998.

Bloch, Ernst. *Aesthetics and Politics.* London: NLB, 1977.

Bourdieu, Pierre. *The Rules of Art: Genesis and Structure of the Literary Field.* Trans. Susan Emanuel. Stanford, Calif.: Stanford, Calif.: Stanford University Press, 1995.

Brody, Jennifer DeVere. *Impossible Purities: Blackness, Femininity, and Victorian Culture.* Durham, N.C.: Duke University Press, 1998.

Brown, Marshall, ed. *The Uses of Literary History.* Durham, N.C.: Duke University Press, 1995.

Calderon, Hector, and Jose David Saldivar, eds. *Criticism in the Borderlands: Studies in Chicano Literature, Culture and Ideology.* Durham, N.C.: Duke University Press, 1991.

Carby, Hazel V. *Reconstructing Womanhood: The Emergence of the Afro-American Woman Novelist.* New York: Oxford University Press, 1987.

————. *Cultures in Babylon: Black Britain and African America.* New York: Verso, 1999.

Castillo, Debra A. *Talking Back: Toward a Latin American Feminist Literary Criticism.* Ithaca, N.Y.: Cornell University Press, 1992.

Christian, Barbara. *Black Women Novelists: The Development of a Tradition, 1892–1976.* Westport, Conn.: Greenwood, 1980.

————. *Black Feminist Criticism: Perspectives on Black Women Writers.* New York: Pergamon, 1985.

Christian, Barbara, and Elizabeth Abel, Helene Moglan, eds. *Female Subjects in Black and White: Race, Psychoanalysis, Feminism.* Berkeley: University of California Press, 1997.

Clark, Michael P. *The Revenge of the Aesthetic: The Place of Literature in Theory Today.* Berkeley: University of California Press, 2000.

Cohen, Ralph. *The Future of Literary Theory.* New York: Routledge, 1989.

Cruz, Jon. *Culture on the Margins: The Black Spiritual and the Rise of American Cultural Interpretation.* Princeton, N.J.: Princeton University Press, 1999.

Davidson, Cathy N., and Michael Moon, eds. *Nation, Race, and Gender: From Oroonoko to Anita Hill.* Durham, N.C.: Duke University Press, 1995.

Davis, Angela Y. *Women, Culture, and Politics.* New York: Random House, 1989.

——. *Blues Legacies and Black Feminism: Gertrude "Ma" Rainey, Bessie Smith, and Billie Holiday.* New York: Pantheon, 1998.

Davis, Thadious M. *Faulkner's "Negro": Art and the Southern Context.* Baton Rouge: Louisiana State University Press, 1983.

——. *Nella Larsen, Novelist of the Harlem Renaissance: A Woman's Life Unveiled.* Baton Rouge: Louisiana State University Press, 1994.

Dayan, Joan. *Haiti, History, and the Gods.* Berkeley: University of California Press, 1995.

Delbanco, Andrew. "The Decline and Fall of Literature," *New York Review of Books,* 4 Nov. 99: 32–38.

Dent, Gina, ed. *Black Popular Culture.* New York: New Press, 1998.

duCille, Ann. *The Coupling Convention: Sex, Text, and Tradition in Black Women's Fiction.* New York: Oxford University Press, 1993.

——. *Skin Trade.* Cambridge, Mass.: Harvard University Press, 1996.

Diedrich, Maria, and Werner Sollors, eds. *The Black Columbiad: Defining Moments in African American Literature and Culture.* Cambridge, Mass.: Harvard University Press, 1994.

During, Simon, ed. *The Cultural Studies Reader.* New York: Routledge, 1993.

Eagleton, Terry. *The Ideology of the Aesthetic.* Oxford: Blackwell, 1990.

Elliott, Emory, ed. *The Columbia Literary History of the United States.* New York: Columbia University Press, 1988.

——, ed. *The Columbia History of the American Novel.* New York: Columbia University Press, 1991

Ellis, John M. *Literature Lost: Social Agendas and the Corruption of the Humanities.* New Haven, Conn.: Yale University Press, 1997.

Felski, Rita. *Beyond Feminist Aesthetics: Feminist Literature and Social Change.* Cambridge, Mass.: Harvard University Press, 1989.

Fisher, Philip. *Wonder, the Rainbow, and the Aesthetics of Rare Experiences.* Cambridge, Mass.: Harvard University Press, 1998.

Fishkin, Shelley Fisher. *Was Huck Black?: Mark Twain and African-American Voices.* New York: Oxford University Press, 1993.

——. *Lighting Out for the Territory: Reflections on Mark Twain and American Culture.* New York: Oxford University Press, 1996.

Foster, Hal, ed. *The Anti-Aesthetics: Essays on Postmodern Culture.* Port Townsend, WA: Bay Press, 1983.

Fusco, Coco. *English Is Broken Here: Notes on Cultural Fusion in the Americas.* New York: New Press, 1995.

——, ed. *Corpus Delecti: Performance Art of the Americas.* New York: Routledge, 2000.

Garvey, John, and Noel Ignatiev, eds. *Race Traitor.* New York: Routledge, 1996.

Gates, Henry Louis, ed. *"Race," Writing, and Difference.* Chicago: University of Chicago Press, 1986.

———. *The Signifying Monkey: A Theory of Afro-American Literary Criticism.* New York: Oxford University Press, 1988.

———. *Loose Canons: Notes on the Culture Wars.* New York: Oxford University Press, 1992.

Gilman, Sander. *Difference and Pathology: Stereotypes of Sexuality, Race, and Madness.* Ithaca, N.Y.: Cornell University Press, 1985.

———. *Creating Beauty to Cure the Soul: Race and Psychology in the Shaping of Aesthetic Surgery.* Durham, N.C.: Duke University Press, 1998.

———. *Love + Marriage = Death: And Other Essays on Representing Difference.* Stanford, Calif.: Stanford University Press, 1998.

———, ed. *Jewries at the Frontier: Accommodation, Identity, Conflict.* Urbana: University of Illinois Press, 1999.

Gilroy, Paul. *The Black Atlantic: Modernity and Double Consciousness.* Cambridge, Mass.: Harvard University Press, 1993.

Glissant, Edouard. *Faulkner, Mississippi.* Trans. Barbara Lewis and Thomas C. Spear. New York: Farrar, Straus, Giroux, 1999.

Godzich, Wlad. *The Culture of Literacy.* Cambridge, Mass.: Harvard University Press, 1994.

Goldberg, David Theo. *Racist Culture: Philosophy and the Politics of Meaning.* Oxford: Blackwell, 1993.

Gordon, Avery F., and Christopher Newfield. *Mapping Multi-Culturalism.* Minneapolis: University of Minnesota Press, 1996.

Gottschild, Brenda Dixon. *Diggin: The Africanist Presence in American Performance, Dance and Other Contexts.* Westport, Conn.: Greenwood Press, 1996.

Grossberg, Lawrence, et al., eds. *Cultural Studies.* New York: Routledge, 1992.

Guha, Ranajit, and Gayatri Chakravorty Spivak, eds. *Selected Subaltern Studies.* New York: Oxford University Press, 1988.

Guillory, Monique, and Richard C. Green, eds. *Soul: Black Power, Politics, and Pleasure.* New York: New York University Press, 1998.

Gutierrez, Ramon. *When Jesus Came, the Corn Mothers Went Away.* Stanford, Calif.: Stanford University Press, 1991.

Harris, Neil. *The Artist in Society: The Formative Years, 1790–1860.* Chicago: University of Chicago Press, 1966, 1982.

———. *Cultural Excursions: Marketing, Appetites and Cultural Tastes in Modern America.* Chicago: University of Chicago Press, 1990.

Harris, Trudier. *The Power of the Porch: The Storyteller's Craft in Zora Neale Hurston, Gloria Naylor, and Randall Kenan.* Athens: University of Georgia Press, 1996.

Hartman, Geoffrey. *Minor Prophecies: The Literary Essay in the Culture Wars.* Cambridge, Mass.: Harvard University Press, 1991.

———. *The Fateful Question of Culture.* New York: Columbia University Press, 1997.

Hartman, Saidiya V. *Scenes of Subjection: Terror, Slavery, and Self-Making in Nineteenth-Century America.* New York: Oxford University Press, 1997.

Henderson, Mae G., ed. *Borders, Boundaries, and Frames: Essays in Cultural Criticism and Cultural Studies.* New York: Routledge, 1995.

Herra-Sobek, Maria. *Introduction to Reconstructing a Chicano/a Literary Heritage: Hispanic Colonial Literature of the Southwest.* Tucson: University of Arizona Press, 1993.

Hjort, Mette, and Sue Laver, ed. *Emotion and the Arts.* New York: Oxford University Press, 1997.

Hoffman, Ronald, Mechal Sobel, and Fredrika J. Teute, eds. *Through a Glass Darkly: Reflections on Personal Identity in Early America.* Chapel Hill: University of North Carolina Press, 1997.

Holloway, Karla F. C. *Moorings & Metaphors: Figures of Culture and Gender in Black Women's Literature.* New Brunswick, N.J.: Rutgers University Press, 1992.

hooks, bell. *Art on My Mind: Visual Politics.* New York: New Press, 1995.

Hunt, Lynn. "Tradition Confronts Change: The Place of the Humanities in the University," *The Humanist on Campus: Continuity and Change.* Occasional Paper No. 44, American Council of Learned Societies, 1998.

Ignatiev, Noel. *How the Irish Became White.* New York: Routledge, 1995.

James, C. L. R. *American Civilization.* Cambridge: Blackwell, 1993.

JanMohamed, Abdul R. *Manichean Aesthetics: The Politics of Literature in Colonial Africa.* Amherst: University of Massachusetts Press, 1983.

JanMohamed, Abdul R., and David Lloyd, eds. *The Nature and Context of Minority Discourse.* New York: Oxford University Press, 1990.

Johnson, Barbara, *The Feminist Difference: Literature, Psychoanalysis, Race, and Gender.* Cambridge, Mass.: Harvard University Press, 1998.

Kaplan, Amy, and Donald E. Pease, eds. *Cultures of United States Imperialism.* Durham, N.C.: Duke University Press, 1993.

Kearney, Michael, and Carole Nagengast. *Anthropological Perspectives on Transnational Communities in Rural California.* Davis: California Institute for Rural Studies, 1989.

———. *Reconceptualizing the Peasantry: Anthropology in Global Perspective.* Boulder, Colo.: Westview Press, 1996.

Kelley, Mary. *Imagining Desire.* Cambridge, Mass.: MIT Press, 1996.

Kernan, Alvin. *The Death of Literature.* New Haven, Conn.: Yale University Press, 1990.

———. *What's Happened to the Humanities?* Princeton, N.J.: Princeton University Press, 1997.

———. *In Plato's Cave.* New Haven, Conn.: Yale University Press, 1999.

Kim, Elaine. *Asian American Literature: An Introduction to the Writings and their Social Context.* Philadelphia, Pa.: Temple University Press, 1982.

———. *New Formations, New Questions: Asian American Studies.* Durham, N.C.: Duke University Press, 1997.

Kim, Elaine, and Chungmoo Choi, eds., *Dangerous Women: Gender and Korean Nationalism.* New York: Routledge, 1998.

King, Nicole. *Circles of Influence: C. L. R. James and the Idea of Creolization.* University: University of Mississippi Press, 2000.

Lambert, Craig. "The Stirring of Sleeping Beauty: After Decades in Scholarly Eclipse, Beauty Rears Its Lovely Head." *Harvard Magazine,* Sept. 1999: 46–53.

Lauter, Paul. *Canons and Contexts.* New York: Oxford University Press, 1991.

———, ed. *The Heath Anthology of American Literature.* Lexington, Mass.: Heath, 1990.

Lee, Rachel C. *The Americas of Asian American Literature: Gendered Fictions of Nation and Transnation.* Princeton, N.J.: Princeton University Press, 1999.

Lemke, Sieglinde. *Primitivist Modernism: Black Culture and the Origins of Transatlantic Modernism.* New York: Oxford University Press, 1998.

Levine, George, ed. *Aesthetics and Ideology.* New Brunswick, N.J.: Rutgers University Press, 1994.

Levine, Lawrence W. *Black Culture and Black Consciousness: Afro-American Folk Thought from Slavery to Freedom.* New York: Oxford University Press, 1977.

——. *Highbrow/Lowbrow: The Emergence of Cultural Hierarchy in America.* Cambridge, Mass.: Harvard University Press, 1988.

Lim, Shirley Geok-Lin, and Amy Ling, eds. *Reading the Literatures of Asian America.* Philadelphia, Pa.: Temple University Press, 1992.

Lim, Shirley Geok-Lin, and Maria Herrera-Sobek. *Power, Race, and Gender in Academe: Strangers in the Tower.* New York: Modern Language Association, 2000.

Ling, Amy. *Between Worlds: Women Writers of Chinese Ancestry.* New York: Pergamon, 1990.

Lionnet, Françoise. *Autobiographical Voices: Race, Gender, Self-Portaiture.* Ithaca, N.Y.: Cornell University Press, 1989.

——. *Postcolonial Representations: Women, Literature, Identity.* Ithaca, N.Y.: Cornell University Press, 1995.

Lionnet, Françoise and Ronnie Scharfman, eds. *Post/Colonial Conditions: Exiles, Migrations and Nomadisms.* New Haven, Conn.: Yale University Press, 1993.

Lipsitz, George. *Time Passages: Collective Memory and American Popular Culture.* New York: Verso, 1990.

——. *Dangerous Crossroads: Popular Music, Postmodernism and the Poetics of Place.* New York: Verso, 1994.

——. *The Possessive Investment in Whiteness: How White People Profit from Identity Politics.* Philadelphia, Pa.: Temple University Press, 1998.

Lopez, Tiffany, ed. *Growing Up Chicana/o: An Anthology.* New York: Morrow, 1993.

Lott, Eric. *Love and Theft: Blackface Minstrelsy and the American Working Class.* New York: Oxford University Press, 1993.

Lowe, Lisa. *Immigrant Acts: On Asian American Cultural Politics.* Durham, N.C.: Duke University Press, 1996.

Matthews, Donald H. *Honoring the Ancestors: An African Cultural Interpretation of Black Religion and Literature.* New York: Oxford University Press, 1998.

McCormick, Peter J. *Modernity, Aesthetics, and the Bounds of Art.* Ithaca, N.Y.: Cornell University Press, 1990.

McKay, Nellie Y. *Jean Toomer, Artist: A Study of His Literary Life and Work, 1894–1936.* Chapel Hill: University of North Carolina Press, 1984.

Mitchell, Angolan, ed. *Within the Circle: An Anthology of African American Literary Criticism from the Harlem Renaissance to the Present.* Durham, N.C.: Duke University Press, 1994.

Mitchell, W. J. T. ed., *The Politics of Interpretation.* Chicago: University of Chicago Press, 1982.

Mohanty, Satya P. *Literary Theory and the Claims of History: Postmodernism, Objectivity, Multicultural Politics.* Ithaca, N.Y.: Cornell University Press, 1997.

Morrison, Toni. *Playing in the Dark: Whiteness and the Literary Imagination.* Cambridge, Mass.: Harvard University Press, 1992.

Mukařovský, Jan. *Structure, Sign, and Function: Selected Essays.* Trans. and ed. John Burbank and Peter Steiner. New Haven, Conn.: Yale University Press, 1978.

Nelson, Cary, and Dialup Parameshwar Gaonkar. *Disciplinarity and Dissent in Cultural Studies.* New York: Routledge, 1996.

Nelson, Cary, and Stephen Watt, eds. *Academic Keywords: A Devil's Dictionary for Higher Education.* New York: Routledge, 1999.

Nelson, Dana D. *The Word in Black and White: Reading "Race" in American Literature, 1638–1867.* New York: Oxford University Press, 1992.

Novitz, David. *Knowledge, Fiction, and Imagination.* Philadelphia, Pa.: Temple University Press, 1987.

———. *The Boundaries of Art.* Philadelphia, Pa.: Temple University Press, 1992.

Nussbaum, Martha. *Poetic Justice: The Literary Imagination and Public Life.* Boston: Beacon, 1995.

Ohmann, Richard, "Historical Reflections on Accountability: Fueled by the Conservative Backlash against the 1960s and the Global Demands of Capitalism, the Current Demand for Accountability Masks a Broader Agenda," *Academe: Bulletin of the American Association of University Professors* 86 (Jan.–Feb. 2000): 24–29.

O'Meally, Robert, and Genevieve Fabre, eds. *History and Memory in African-American Culture.* New York: Oxford University Press, 1994.

O' Meally, Robert. *Lady Day: The Many Faces of Billie Holiday.* New York: Arcade Press, 1991.

———, ed. *The Jazz Cadence of American Culture.* New York: Columbia University Press, 1998.

Painter, Nell Irvin. *Sojourner Truth: A Life, A Symbol.* New York: Norton, 1996.

Patterson, Orlando. *Slavery and Social Death: A Comparative Study.* Cambridge, Mass.: Harvard University Press, 1982.

———. *Freedom in the Making of Western Culture.* New York: Basic Books, 1991.

Paulson, Ronald. *The Beautiful, Novel, and Strange: Aesthetics and Heterodoxy.* Baltimore, Md.: Johns Hopkins University Press, 1996.

Pease, Donald, ed. *National Identities and Post-Americanist Narratives.* Durham, N.C.: Duke University Press, 1994.

Peterson, Carla L. *Doers of the Word: African-American Women Speakers and Writers in the North.* New York: Oxford University Press, 1995.

Posnock, Ross. *Black Writers and the Making of the Modern Intellectual.* Cambridge, Mass.: Harvard University Press, 1998.

Pryse, Marjorie, and Hortense J. Spillers. *Conjuring: Black Women, Fiction, and Literary Tradition.* Bloomington: Indiana University Press, 1985.

Raboteau, Albert J. *Slave Religion: The "Invisible Institution" in the Antebellum South.* New York: Oxford University Press, 1978.

———. *A Fire in the Bones: Reflections on African-American Religious History.* Boston: Beacon, 1995.

Raboteau, Albert J., and Timothy E. Fulop, eds. *African-American Religion: Interpretive Essays in History and Culture.* New York: Routledge, 1997.

Rampersad, Arnold. *The Art and Imagination of W. E. B. Du Bois.* Cambridge, Mass.: Harvard University Press, 1976.

———. *The Life of Langston Hughes.* New York: Oxford University Press, 1986.

———. *Langston Hughes: The Man, His Art, and His Continuing Influence.* New York: Garland, 1995.

Redfield, Marc. *Phantom Formations: Aesthetic Ideology and the Bildungsroman.* Ithaca, N.Y.: Cornell University Press, 1996.

Reed, Ishmael. *MultiAmerica: Essays on Cultural Wars and Cultural Peace.* New York: Penguin, 1997.

Roach, Joseph. *Cities of the Dead.* New York: Columbia University Press, 1996.

Roediger, David R. *The Wages of Whiteness: Race and the Making of the American Working Class.* London: Verso, 1991.

Rosaldo, Renata. *Culture and Truth: The Remaking of Social Analysis.* Boston: Beacon, 1989.

Roy, Parama. *Indian Traffic: Identities in Question in Colonial and Postcolonial India.* Berkeley: University of California Press, 1998.

Saldivar, Jose David. *Border Matters: Remapping American Cultural Studies.* Berkeley: University of California Press, 1997.

Saldivar, Ramon. *Chicano Narrative: The Dialects of Difference.* Madison: University of Wisconsin Press, 1990.

Sanchez, George J. *Becoming Mexican American: Ethnicity, Culture, and Identity in Chicano Los Angeles.* New York: Oxford University Press, 1993.

Sanders, Mark A. *Afro-Modernist Aesthetics & the Poetry of Sterling A. Brown.* Athens: University of Georgia Press, 1999.

Scarry, Elaine. *Dreaming by the Book.* New York: Farrar, Straus, Giroux, 1999.

———. *On Beauty and Being Just.* Princeton, N.J.: Princeton University Press, 1999.

Scholes, Robert. *The Rise and Fall of English: Reconstructing English as a Discipline.* New Haven, Conn.: Yale University Press, 1999.

Smith, Theophus H. *Conjuring Culture: Biblical Formations of Black America.* New York: Oxford University Press, 1994.

Smith, Valerie. *not just race, not just gender: Black Feminist Readings.* New York: Routledge, 1998.

Snead, James A. *White Screens, Black Images: Hollywood from the Dark Side.* New York: Routledge, 1994.

Sobel, Mechal. *Travelin' on: The Slave Journey to an Afro-Baptist Faith.* Westport, Conn.: Greenwood, 1979.

———. *The World They Made Together: Black and White Values in Eighteenth-Century Virginia.* Princeton, N.J.: Princeton University Press, 1987.

Soderholm, James, ed. *Beauty and the Critic: Aesthetics in an Age of Cultural Studies.* Tuscaloosa: University of Alabama Press, 1997.

Sollors, Werner. *Beyond Ethnicity: Consent and Descent in American Culture.* New York: Oxford University Press, 1986.

———. *Neither Black Nor White Yet Both: Thematic Explorations of Interracial Literature.* New York: Oxford University Press, 1997.

———, ed. *Multilingual America: Transnationalism, Ethnicity, and the Language of American Literature.* New York: New York University Press, 1998.

———. *The Invention of Ethnicity.* New York: Oxford University Press, 1998.

Spillers, Hortense J. *Comparative American Identities: Race, Sex, And Nationality in the Modern Text.* New York: Routledge, 1991.

Spivak, Gayatri Chakravorty. *In Other Worlds: Essays in Cultural Politics.* New York: Methuen, 1987.

Steiner, Wendy. The Scandal of Pleasure: Art in an Age of Fundamentalism. Chicago: University of Chicago Press, 1995.

Stepto, Robert B., and Michael S. Harper, eds. *Chant of Saints: A Gathering of Afro-American Literature, Art and Scholarship*. Urbana: University of Illinois Press, 1979.

———. *From behind the Veil: A Study of Afro-American Narrative*. Urbana: University of Illinois Press, 1979.

Stuckey, Sterling. *Slave Culture: Nationalist Theory and the Foundation of Black America*. New York: Oxford University Press, 1987.

———. *Going through the Storm: The Influence of African American Art in History*. New York: Oxford University Press, 1994.

Sundquist, Eric. *The Hammers of Creation: Folk Culture in Modern African-American Fiction*. Athens: University of Georgia Press, 1992.

———. *To Wake the Nations: Race in the Making of American Literature*. Cambridge, Mass.: Harvard University Press, 1993.

Tate, Claudia. *Psychoanalysis and Black Novels: Desire and the Protocols of Race*. New York: Oxford University Press, 1998.

Taussig, Michael T. *The Devil and Commodity Fetishism in South America*. Chapel Hill: University of North Carolina Press, 1980.

———. *Mimesis and Alterity: A Particular History of the Senses*. New York: Routledge, 1993.

———. *The Magic of the State*. New York: Routledge, 1997.

Thompson, Robert Ferris. *Flash of the Spirit: African and Afro-American Art and Philosophy*. New York: Vintage, 1983.

———. *Face of the Gods: Art and Altars of Africa and the African Americas*. New York: Museum for African Art, 1993.

Velez-Ibanez, Carlos G. *Border Visions: Mexican Cultures of the Southwest United States*. Tucson: University of Arizona Press, 1996.

Washington, Mary Helen, ed. *Invented Lives: Narratives of Black Women, 1860–1960*. Garden City, N.Y.: Anchor, 1987.

Welchman, John C., ed. *Rethinking Borders*. Minneapolis: University of Minnesota Press, 1996.

West, Cornel. *The American Evasion of Philosophy: A Genealogy of Pragmatism*. Madison: University of Wisconsin Press, 1989.

———. *Beyond Eurocentrism and Multiculturalism*. Monroe, Maine: Common Courage Press, 1993.

———. *Keeping Faith: Philosophy and Race in America*. New York: Routledge, 1993.

Williams, Patricia. *The Alchemy of Race and Rights*. Cambridge, Mass.: Harvard University Press, 1991.

Woodmansee, Martha. *The Author, Art, and the Market: Rereading the History of Aesthetics*. New York: Columbia University Press, 1994.

Woodring, Carl. *Literature: An Embattled Profession*. New York: Columbia University Press, 1999.

Yamamoto, Traise. *Masking Selves, Making Subjects: Japanese American Woman, Identity, and the Body*. Berkeley: University of California Press, 1999.

Yarborough, Richard A. *The Depiction of Blacks in the Early Afro-American Novel*. Ann Arbor, Mich.: University Microfilms, 1980.

Yellin, Jean Fagan. *The Intricate Knot: Black Figures in American Literature, 1776–1863*. New York: New York University Press, 1972.

PART I

CHALLENGES TO AN AESTHETICS
OF DIVERSITY

Can Our Values Be Objective?

On Ethics, Aesthetics, and Progressive Politics

SATYA P. MOHANTY

Are evaluations always political? Are our efforts to make objective value judgments always thwarted by our own political interests or our cultural and social perspectives? I am interested in this question because I am interested in progressive politics and would like to believe that my values and commitments are not rigidly determined by my social background or my narrow personal interests. In this essay I would like to defend the view that objectivity is attainable in the realm of values, in such areas as ethics and even aesthetics. For the purposes of the present discussion, I shall pose the question about value in epistemological terms: Can we human beings be objective in our views and judgments about such properties as goodness, justice, or beauty?

In order to outline my position and present my argument, however, I need to first explain what I mean by objectivity, for it is clear that we live in a postempiricist intellectual world where the term has undergone substantial redefinition. Whether we work in literary studies or in philosophy, in anthropology or any of the social sciences, we have to acknowledge the deep critique of empiricist and positivist epistemologies which has emerged from related developments in the philosophies of science and language, in ethics and cultural studies. Specifically, what has been shown to be inadequate is a particular conception of observation and objective knowledge. Thus, philosophers like Quine and Putnam, Nietzsche or Heidegger, all argue that everything that science relies on— its methodology, its understanding of what "facts" are, its practices of confirmation and even observation—is always necessarily theory-dependent rather than innocent, filtered through our values, presuppositions, and ideologies, rather than unmediated and self-evident.

Where contemporary philosophers and most literary theorists disagree, however, is in their account of the implications of this antipositivist insight about the unavoidability of theory. A natural question to ask the antipositivist is this: Does the necessary ubiquity of theories and presuppositions, of biases and ideologies, lead to the conclusion that "objectivity" as such is never possible, not in values and not even in science? That conclusion, that objectivity is never possible, is endorsed by postmodernist thinkers who are influential especially in the fields of literary and cultural studies. A very different conclusion, endorsed by post-positivist thinkers in a variety of fields from philosophy of science to some new forms of literary theory, is that what is outmoded is specifically the positivist conception of objectivity, a conception based on a denial of the role of theory. This positivist view defines objective knowledge as something we achieve when we have freed ourselves from all bias and all interest; in this conception objectivity is seen as absolute *neutrality*, a complete divestiture of the thinker's subjectivity and her socially situated values, ideologies, and theoretical presuppositions. Defenders of a postpositivist conception of objectivity claim that this image of complete divestiture is profoundly flawed because such divestiture is never possible for humans. Objectivity is not neutrality. What we need to develop, such thinkers insist, is a more nuanced conception of objectivity which goes beyond the specifically positivist view of it; it is argued that this new conception can be built on an analysis of the differences between different kinds of subjective or theoretical bias or interest, an analysis that distinguishes those biases that are limiting or counterproductive from those that are in fact necessary for knowledge, that are epistemically productive and useful.

Arguing against postmodernist literary and cultural critics, I said in *Literary Theory and the Claims of History* that such an analysis of different kinds of bias and prejudice needs to focus on the role error plays in human inquiry. Our elaboration of a new, nuanced conception of objectivity in literary and cultural inquiry, I suggested, depends on the richness of our understanding of error—its sources and causes, as well as the variety of forms it takes in various contexts. Our conceptions of objectivity and error are dialectically related. Both conceptions are the product of good inquiry, inquiry that is necessarily both theoretical and empirical. The analysis of error—of the distorting role played by pernicious social ideologies for instance, or the limitations of certain methodological approaches—is unavoidably empirical, even while it involves theoretical considerations. Similarly, the analysis of what works, what is epistemically productive and useful, is also simultaneously empirical and theoretical.[1] The view I am defending is opposed to the postmodernist position that objectivity as such is impossible, for I believe that objectivity is often a realizable goal. Indeed, as I suggest later, objectivity is an epistemic ideal in the realm of values precisely because *values often refer to facts and properties that exist independently of our beliefs*. Such moral and aesthetic properties as goodness, justice, and beauty are, on this view, complex properties of objects and persons in the world, and we can be right or wrong in our attempts to detect and understand such properties. For realists (about value), the identification and analysis of error is essential for the attainment of objective knowledge.

One of my claims in this essay is that when postmodernists assume a skeptical attitude toward objectivity in an a priori way, their analysis of error often ends up being very limited in some ways and very inflated in others. An a priori skepticism makes it less urgent for us to look carefully at the variety of forms of, say, ideological error, and at the reasons for the differences among these different forms. The incomplete or inadequate empirical analysis is both supported by and seen as the support for an inflated thesis about the unavoidability of error. Error and distortion thus become a primeval epistemic condition, an original sinfulness, as it were. Instead of an explanation of error, we end up with a theology that sets unnecessarily rigid limits on the scope of social inquiry.

Foucault vs. Chomsky: Are Values Political?

The postmodernist view of error is often presented initially as an empirical caution, but the skepticism that it is supposed to lead to is deep and unwavering, ultimately amounting to an acontextual and unqualified position. What begins as an empirically grounded caution is often elevated to a rigid theoretical doctrine.[2] And nowhere is this move from methodological caution to inflexible theory as clearly evident as in the postmodernist suspicion of normativity, of values. This suspicion leads some thinkers—particularly progressive thinkers—into strange quandaries, or at least into obvious inconsistencies. Michel Foucault, for instance, in his 1971 debate with Noam Chomsky, initially raises the empirically based question about whether political activists and thinkers should rely on a substantive conception of human nature, deriving justification for their values and goals from such a conception. His initial point is a familiar one, and it is fundamentally sound: "If you say that a certain human nature exists, that this human nature has not been given in actual society the rights and the possibilities which allow it to realise itself . . . [don't you] risk defining this human nature—which is at the same time ideal and real . . .—in terms borrowed from our society, from our civilization, from our culture?" ("Human Nature," 173–74). The "risk" Foucault is talking about can be best understood in the context of the antipositivist theoretical insight I identified earlier. All knowledge is unavoidably socially situated, and it is impossible to seek the kind of objectivity that is understood as neutrality, as ideological or theoretical innocence. When we try to define human nature, we inevitably do so "in terms borrowed from our society, from our civilization, from our culture." The legitimate question, then, is: since our account of human nature is inevitably shaped by our society and culture, the context in which the account originates, how can we minimize the risk of repeating our culture's ideological errors, projecting our metaphysical blindnesses onto the ideal human nature we wish to imagine and theorize? Foucault's initial point is also a more specifically historical one: we risk error in talking about human nature, he says, because we know of so many instances in the past when we have erred, and erred seriously and egregiously. Socialists of a certain period, he points out, unwittingly used a bourgeois model of human nature even when they claimed to be going beyond such a model and its ideological implications: "The socialism of . . . the end of the nineteenth century, and the beginning of the twentieth century, admitted in effect that in capitalist societies man hadn't realized the full potential of his development and self-realization. . . . And [this socialism] dreamed of an ultimately liberated human nature. . . . What model did it use to conceive, project, and eventually realize human nature? It was in fact the bourgeois model. The universalization of the model of the bourgeois has been the utopia which has animated the constitution of Soviet society." All of this indicates, he concludes, "that it is difficult to say exactly what human nature is" and that "there is a risk that we will be led into error" (174).

Now, it is necessary to be careful here if we want to understand where exactly the disagreement lies. For few people on the other side of this debate (Chomsky, to take an obvious instance) will dream of denying that it is "difficult to say exactly what human nature is" if by that we mean that it is difficult to come up with a comprehensive account of human nature. But that is not Foucault's main point. His point about the "risk" (that "we will be led into error") cuts deeper. His antipositivist theoretical insight and his empirical caution about the historical errors in our use of the idea of human nature together lead Foucault to entertain an extreme claim: human nature as such may not exist, for what we have is entirely culture- or class-specific. He cites Mao approvingly, suggesting that there may only be a "bourgeois human nature and [a] proletarian human nature and [Mao thinks] that they are not the same thing" (174). This is a radically relativist (and historicist) position, but notice that it does not follow in a straightforward way from the earlier thesis about the erroneous and unwittingly ideological uses of the concept of human nature. From empirically grounded cautions about error, we have been led to at least two possible theses: (1) there is no such thing as human nature; and/or (2) our knowledge of human nature, even if there were such a thing, would never be reliable or objective, since everything we can say about human nature will be ideological. Now the two theses I have identified are distinct, and they call for different kinds of argument and evidence for support, but Foucault's general attitude suggests that he is drawn to (at least) the skeptical thesis (2), which denies the possibility of objective knowledge altogether. Bourgeois or proletarian, we are stuck with our own class-based views about human nature, and there is no going beyond such limited ideological views. The socialist thinkers cited earlier, Foucault would say, proved how dead wrong one can be in trying to go beyond one's culture-specific and class-specific notions and images of human nature. Their error, in other words, is symptomatic of the human condition; there is no hope of transcending such an ideology.

I believe that Foucault's attitude toward human nature cannot be adequately understood unless we see that it is accompanied by a tenacious suspicion of all normative claims as such. In fact, this suspicion strengthens the view that no objective account of human nature is possible. The problem with human nature might be that it is, as he says, simultaneously "ideal and real," and hence our thinking about it is especially vulnerable to speculative fancies. The suspicion of normative claims becomes clearer later in the discussion. Arguing for the need for the victory of the proletariat in its class struggle against the bourgeoisie, Foucault nonetheless balks at the idea that this need ought to be justified by appealing to a normative conception such as social justice. He is quite emphatic about this: "The proletariat does not wage war against the ruling class because it considers such a war to be just. The proletariat makes war . . . because for the first time in history it wants to take power. And *because* it will overthrow the power of the ruling class it considers such a war to be just. . . . One makes war to win, not because it is just" (182, emphasis added). For Foucault, this is not a psychological description (of the way the proletariat thinks); rather, it is an account of what "justifies" proletarian class struggle, which Foucault supports. The justification, he says, is not justice, since it does not exist except as tied inextricably to power (180; see the following discussion). It is power, the newly acquired power of the proletariat after its victory, that will justify its struggle. There is thus bourgeois justice and proletarian justice, with no objective conception of justice that can transcend either.

It is on this point about whether value judgments can be objectively justified that Chomsky, for the sake of clarification, presses Foucault. If Foucault could be convinced, Chomsky suggests for the sake of argument, that the victory of the proletariat will lead to terror and the permanent abuse of power and never to a better society, he would probably not support the proletariat; his support of the working people in a class war must depend on a conviction—or a vision—of something better than what exists. Foucault admits, finally, that class struggle is more than a simple logic of fighting to win: "What the proletariat will achieve by expelling the class which is at present in power and by taking over power itself, is precisely the suppression of the power of class in general" (184). "The suppression of the power of class in general"—here, clearly, is a basic conception of a more just order, where the premises are that class power (particularly in its current form) is wrong and it is only the proletariat that can use its power to get rid of class power. Here, surely, is a conception of justice, no matter how elementary a sketch it might be. But, interestingly, Foucault denies that his justification is in terms of "justice" or any other normative notion. The theoretical argument he advances is radically skeptical and relativist: "Contrary to what you think, you can't prevent me from believing that these notions of human nature, of justice, of the realization of the essence of human beings, are all notions and concepts which have been formed within our civilization, within our type of knowledge and our form of philosophy, and that as a result form part of our class system; and one can't, however regrettable it may be, put forward these notions to justify a fight which should—and shall in principle—overthrow the very fundaments of our society. This is an extrapolation for which I can't find the . . . historical justification" (187).

Here is what Foucault means by the "extrapolation" for which he can find no "historical justification": A culture's deepest evaluative concepts, like human welfare and social justice, are formed within the ideological, philosophical, and political boundaries of that culture, and people like Chomsky wish to use these concepts to justify an objective ideal, one that by definition goes beyond the bounds of this culture. How, Foucault asks, can one justify a political ideal with terms and concepts borrowed from a world that is far from ideal? How can you adequately imagine a healthy body while using the diseased and faulty organs of perception and imagination that we in fact have? I think this is a good question, and an important one, but notice that formulated in this way it is linked to the antipositivist point about the theory-dependence of observation and knowledge which I discussed earlier. Foucault's question is the same one philosophers of science, for instance, have been raising for several decades now: given that scientific methods are so radically theory-dependent, how can we use them to gain objective knowledge, knowledge that can transcend the limitations of the given theory? Different answers to this question are provided by different philosophers and historians of science, but the one point that is relevant to our discussion of the status of value is that a lot depends on precisely how we define objectivity. As may already be evident, Foucault does in fact have a conception of objective values here; it is simply that his conception of objectivity is so extreme and ahistorical that it is impossible to attain. While seeming to argue in a general way for an antipositivist view of objective knowledge, Foucault in fact *assumes* an essentially positivist conception of objectivity as absolute (ideological, theoretical, and historical) neutrality! And since this extreme and abstract notion of objectivity is impossible to attain, he ends up espousing a rigidly skeptical view about values. Let me explain how this happens.

Foucault's thesis is not that our ideas about justice and human nature are inevitably somewhat tainted by our current social ideologies and our other views about, say, morality, society, and even the nature of the universe. None of Foucault's opponents in this debate, to the extent they accept the antipositivist view we've discussed, would deny this basic claim about the social situatedness of knowledge. Foucault's real claim—the one that differentiates his position from that of someone like Chomsky—is that we cannot even distinguish between the *current* conception of justice and a *better* one. He argues against Chomsky's use of the idea of a better justice: "So it is in the name of a purer justice that you criticize the functioning of justice? There is an important question for us here. It is true that in all social struggles, there is a question of 'justice.' . . . But if justice is at stake in a struggle, then it is as an instrument of power; it is not in the hope that finally one day, in this or another society, people will be rewarded according to their merits, or punished according to their faults" (180). The thesis is this: since the notion of justice is at stake in (that is, is deployed in and hence redefined by) social struggles—a perfectly plausible empirical claim about just about every society we know—justice is *no more than* an instrument of power.

Since power corrupts our concepts and our methods of inquiry, Foucault asks, how can we use such concepts and methods to imagine a world that transcends our political framework? His own implicit answer, that we cannot legitimately justify our normative ideals, is supported by the following further specification: We cannot in principle talk about better conceptions of justice, since for such a conception to be truly better, it must not make *any* reference to any of the "fundaments of our society" (187), the society that has shaped such a conception. The underlying view is that the only conception of justice that can really—objectively—be better than what we've got is one that is entirely new, entirely free of our current social biases and ideologies, all our current knowledge—the fundaments of our society. Short of this kind of untainted and pristine conception of justice—divested of everything that can legitimately be called cultural or social—every conception becomes ideological, in the narrowly pejorative sense of the word. Objective knowledge of justice is imaginable, according to this line of argument, but only as a form of absolute theoretical and ideological neutrality. We do not know what "justice" can refer to, and it is best (on this theoretical view) to define objectivity as a purely epistemic stance—one defined by a complete shedding of all our social and political "biases," all our theoretical commitments. But of course this is the very conception of objectivity, the severely asocial and ahistorical positivist view, which we were supposed to reject![3]

This is a limiting and unproductive conception of objectivity, but why is Foucault (unwittingly) drawn to it? I suggest that it is because he subscribes to an implausible form of epistemological holism, an unnecessarily extreme version of the legitimate antipositivist thesis about the theory-dependence of all observation and knowledge. Foucault's implausible epistemological holism is not in principle limited to values, since it can have relevance for all of human knowledge, but his arguments here focus on evaluative concepts since (as we saw above) they are simultaneously "ideal and real." His initial claim is that "justice," as an evaluative notion, is tied to various other features of our social world, those features that make our world what it in fact is. In arguing against the objectivity of evaluative notions like justice, Foucault is not drawing on the familiar observation that since, when we look cross-culturally, we see a variety of conceptions of justice, our own conception must be limited and culture-specific. For this familiar observation naturally elicits the objection that the presence of variety does not preclude the possibility that one of the existing conceptions is in fact better, more accurate than the others. Recognition of variety is useful, it might be argued, to show how some cultural contexts might in fact have enabled greater accuracy and objectivity in thinking about the nature of the just society, while others have served to distort our thinking about these matters. The mere existence of cultural variety in approaches to justice does nothing, it can be objected, to establish the general skeptical or relativist thesis, the thesis that notions of justice are entirely culture- or class-specific. But Foucault's argument is not vulnerable to this objection, for at bottom he is proposing an epistemology of value. Values are always partly speculative, the claim goes, and we can never justify them since they are especially prone to social distortion. Indeed, this distortion is of a kind that undermines *any* possibility of justification. You cannot expect to eliminate distortions produced by particular relations of power, say the class system, Foucault would say, because these relations are *inextricably* dependent on various other things that make our society or culture what it is. It is this claim about *inextricability* that makes Foucault's position untenable, for it suggests that error and distortion cannot be eliminated and our critical analyses of social phenomena will always be radically compromised by the ideologies of our class or, more generally, our society. For Foucault, notions like justice are formed within overlapping structures of discourse and political power: they "have been formed within our civilization, within our type of knowledge, and our form of philosophy, and as a result form part of our class system." The type of knowledge and form of philosophy are causally related to the class system, but this relationship is so radically determined—or perhaps just so irreducibly complex—that it undermines any attempt to analyze the distortion produced by any one of them. That explains why (according to Foucault) even the search for slightly better, slightly less distorted, views of human nature or social and political justice is impossible.[4] It is this crucial thesis about the analytical inextricability of power and truth, the reduction of all analysis to ideology, that makes Foucault's epistemological holism extreme and implausible, and it on this kind of holism that the myth of an otherworldly, asocial (and always necessarily impossible) objectivity is based.

Chomsky, on the other hand, argues that we need better values, that often our social struggles are best served not only by carefully articulated critiques of what exists but also carefully elaborated visions of how the social arrangements we are criticizing could be different and better, more humane and just. His defense of the need for "better" concepts of justice is based on the view that our most valuable notions of justice are firmly grounded in a plausible (though necessarily partial) view of human nature. "Our concept of human nature is certainly limited; it's partially socially conditioned, constrained by our own character defects and the limitations of the intellectual culture in which we exist. Yet at the same time it is of critical importance that we know what impossible goals we're trying to achieve, if we hope to achieve some of the possible ones. And that means that we have to be bold enough to speculate and create social theories on the basis of partial knowledge, while remaining very open to the strong possibility, and in fact overwhelming probability, that at least in some respects we're very far off the mark" (175). Here is a view of how partly speculative notions like human nature are not only necessary but also legitimate; it outlines an epistemological approach I take for granted in the second section of this paper, where I propose an alternative to the Foucauldian (and, more generally, the postmodernist) account of values. Foucault is deeply suspicious of all evaluative concepts because, as he claims, power and knowledge are so deeply intertwined that we cannot "extrapolate" from our current ideologically tainted concepts to less ideological, more "objective" ones. This claim about the relationship of power and knowledge, as I have shown, is based on an extreme form of epistemological holism, which is an implausible version of the legitimate postpositivist thesis about the theory-dependence of all knowledge. It is this kind of implausible holism which sanctions Foucault's own view of objectivity as a kind of (absolute) epistemic neutrality, a view that mirrors the widely criticized positivist conception of objectivity. The net effect of these theses is that Foucault's skepticism about values (and perhaps all knowledge) becomes an a priori matter; notwithstanding the numerous statements about current ideologies and political arrangements, the skepticism itself is entirely independent of any empirical understanding of actually existing societies. Even though Foucault claims that he cannot find historical justification for the hope that we will be able to come up with better values and visions than what exist, his own skepticism about values is itself free of empirical support or justification. And there does not seem to be much room left open for seeking such support for it. Once we adopt this extreme thesis about values, that better values, genuinely better ones, must make no reference at all to the fundaments of our society, culture, and civilization, the skeptical position follows automatically. And the skepticism is insulated from any real empirical testing and elaboration. For there can be no genuine empirical elaboration of a claim without the possibility that the claim might itself be proved wrong. When we acknowledge such a possibility, this overly inflexible skeptical stance, this suspicion of normative theory as such, becomes untenable. In the realm of social analysis, such a priori skepticism becomes dogmatic or doctrinaire, since it leaves open no room for its own empirical or theoretical errors. Oddly enough (or, some would say, naturally enough), such a doctrinaire approach bases itself on claims about the ubiquity of ideological error and the need for a rigorous analysis of socially based distortions.

It must be evident by now that even though Foucault has been talking about political and ethical values—namely justice—the argument I have identified would extend his skeptical stance to aesthetic values as well. In fact, it is easier to see why one should be a skeptic about aesthetic values. The deeper argument against the possibility that some aesthetic values can be objective is not the empirical fact that there is a great deal of cross-cultural difference, variety, and indeed disagreement over aesthetic judgments (the purely empirical argument we often get from some multiculturalists) but rather the very one about the ubiquity of theory that I identified earlier. The deeper argument will see aesthetic value as socially situated and hence culturally subjective for the very same reasons that all values (especially ethical and political ones) are subjective; it identifies a problem with values *as such*, and how we justify them. The deeper justification for skepticism about aesthetic values must derive from a version of epistemological holism in which all value judgments are contextual and culture-specific by definition. Just as ethical and political notions like justice are inextricably tied to what Foucault calls the "fundaments of our society" (any society), so—it must be argued—are aesthetic notions, which are deeply entwined with the society's cultural and ethical notions.

The literary theorist Barbara H. Smith, who has written widely cited essays and books on value, has argued that we should define values as no more than "positive effects" ("Value/Evaluation," 180). Here is how she supports this idea:

> In recognizing the tacit assumptions built into value judgments, we can also recognize that, when we frame an explicit verbal evaluation of a text, we are usually not expressing only how we feel about it "personally" but, rather, observing its effects on ourselves and estimating its value for other people: not all other people, however, but a limited set of people with certain relevant characteristics—usually, though not necessarily, characteristics that they share with us. (183)

This is the same kind of claim as the one Foucault makes, but instead of referring to the entire civilization or culture as Foucault does, Smith refers to smaller social groups ("sets") within a culture. The underlying claim is, however, the same: the possibility of objective value judgments is ruled out in advance because values refer primarily (and perhaps even essentially) to social context. "[W]ith respect to values," Smith claims, "everything is always in motion with respect to everything else. If there *are* constancies of literary value, they will be found *in those very motions*: that is, in the relations among the variables. For, like all value, literary value is not the property of an object *or* of a subject but, rather, *the product of the dynamics of a system*" (*Contingencies*, 15–16; emphases in the original). The "system" is defined in social and historical terms, for while Smith does indeed admit to some "species-wide" features of human nature, such features are defined in highly restrictive behaviorist language. They do not point (*at all*) to deeper human needs and capacities, for instance, but instead only to "mechanisms of perception and cognition . . . as they relate to . . . verbal behavior." Such "presumably biophysiological mechanisms," Smith clarifies, "will always operate differentially in different environments . . . and, therefore, the experience of literary and aesthetic value cannot be altogether accounted for, reduced to, or predicted by them" (*Contingencies*, 15). Culture and social context determine value more than do any deep features of human nature, and thus values are no more than positive *effects*. The possibility that is ruled out in advance is that the different ways in which different social groups make value judgments may also be evaluated from a perspective that is not limited to any of these groups.

Such evaluation would partly depend, as I have been suggesting, on an analysis of different kinds of socially based error, and of the different sources and causes of these errors. Once we engage in such an analysis we have to keep open the possibility that in some instances some kinds of error can be eradicated through appropriate adjustments in our methodologies, our background assumptions and theories, or the cultural information we take for granted. Empirical inquiry becomes essential if we are to understand not only particular kinds of error but also what values are; it is the only genuine way to substantiate and test the skeptical claim Smith (and Foucault before her) wants to make about the epistemology of value. Such empirically grounded theoretical inquiry would help us see whether Smith's desire to narrowly circumscribe values as merely "positive effects" is justified or whether it tethers us to an implausible behaviorist view. An equally essential part of my theoretical proposal in the next section is a thesis about the links between value and human nature; like Chomsky, I would like to argue that values are not *only* socially determined, because often they also refer to deeper features of human nature, our species-wide needs and capacities, which set limits on how historically "contingent" legitimate evaluations can be. Our evaluations can be objective, I suggest, because they are often about features of human nature which are independent of our own socially shaped judgments and attitudes. Despite their enormous social variability, our evaluations can thus be more than merely positive effects, and more than unacknowledged political interests. One of the key challenges for any theory of value, then, is to account for *both* the social and historical variability of values *and* (simultaneously) the possibility of objectivity.

How Values Can Be Objective

I would like to outline a proposal about how to define value so that we avoid the pitfalls of the skeptical position, and in particular its a priori approach to the epistemic status of values. I propose that many of our deepest evaluative concepts, whether ethical ones or aesthetic, refer not only to the cultures and social contexts in which they were produced but also, as it were, "outward": they refer both to genuine properties of human nature and to what we know about our social and political possibilities. Such evaluative notions will naturally reflect the underlying biases and ideologies, the theoretical prejudices and empirical limitations, of our own cultural views. But they also reflect—either badly or well, reflecting degrees of error and distortion but also accuracy and objectivity—what we currently know about humankind and its possibilities. When I talk about "reference" here, I mean a process and a relation that are dynamic rather than static: our deeper evaluative notions are linked not to unique and singular objects in the world but instead to complex objects and the way we gain epistemic access to them. On this view of reference, then, as a culture acquires more accurate knowledge of, say, human potentials and capacities, its central evaluative notions and concepts will become richer. Such knowledge depends on a number of factors, from everyday practical experiments with, say, child-rearing or forms of education to more self-consciously reflexive and methodologically systematic kinds of research conducted within institutions. There is room here for both objective knowledge and error, since our deepest evaluations—regarding such things as social justice, for instance—refer not only to what we, in a given culture, know *now*, but also, necessarily, to what we may come to know later about the object of inquiry. Our values are thus "open-textured" in nature, open in the same way that any knowledge-gathering process is. Since they depend on what we know (or can imagine realistically) now, our values are historically and socially embedded. In referring outward to the object of an ongoing inquiry, they remain partial and incomplete theses or theories about something objective and transculturally valid.[5]

I submit that this way of defining value is better than the purely skeptical or relativist approaches I have identified. On this general view, the question of objectivity is raised in the context of our empirical and theoretical analyses of error. Such error arises more from cultural than from purely individual biases, for in linking values to our knowledge of our social and political possibilities, I have indicated why values are not simply inside an individual's head, reflecting merely idiosyncratic and purely subjective beliefs. They are social, even when they are refracted through an individual's beliefs and personal needs. But they should not be seen as purely internal to a given society, culture, or civilization either. At bottom, my epistemological defense of values is based on the specifically realist claim that some of our deepest evaluations refer to (properties of) objects that exist *independently* of our local social and cultural beliefs. In this context, then, "objectivity" should be understood as more than an epistemic stance or attitude (such as, say, neutrality), because *in these crucial cases* our evaluations can be right or wrong about these objects. Human nature is such an *object* about which we (entire cultures or societies) can be right or wrong. Unlike Foucault, I argue that (some of) our values track real "objects" of inquiry. It is possible to be objective in our evaluations because our deepest evaluations are often about complex objects in the world, objects which we are attempting to understand and know and which cannot be reduced to our ideological constructions.

Thus, our evaluations are necessarily shaped by answers to questions that might be asked in local cultural conditions but that are not thereby limited to the local. Here is a set of closely entwined questions that suggest how values are dependent on ongoing empirical and theoretical research and how they refer outward beyond a local culture or society; an interesting feature of the questions, you will notice, is that it is difficult to neatly separate the ethical from the aesthetic, the political from the scientific: How much fruitful cooperation and interchange are humans capable of? Are altruism and the capacity for sympathy for others fully realized in the societies with which we are familiar, or are there social forms and arrangements that might enhance, even beyond our wildest imagination, these traits and capacities? To what extent are human cognitive powers dependent on the affective dimension of our lives, and how does affective growth expand even our theoretical imagination? And finally, is the imagination one underlying cognitive faculty, with deep connections and interdependencies among its various activities—in the realms of, say, science, ethics, and aesthetics—or would it be legitimate to talk about various faculties, various kinds of imagination—moral, aesthetic, and so on? Answers to such questions cannot be purely speculative but will need to be empirically grounded as well, and so such answers will entail the possibility of our being wrong at times and right at times, of both error and distortion on the one hand and of knowledge on the other (or at least of a better account, a less distorted one). It also seems clear that our accounts of both what we consider error and what we consider objective knowledge will themselves involve both empirical and theoretical considerations. Judgments about error or knowledge will, quite typically, arise out of complex negotiations among competing theories and even bodies of theory, including normative theory. In this way, even such basic judgments will be socially embedded, tied to ideologies and the social practices of our own cultures. But notice, once again, that on the realist view I am advocating here, the pursuit of such questions (at least in these crucial cases) has to be shaped by "objects" that are not purely cultural or ideological. The thesis here (going back to contrast the claim with what Foucault says) is that even though there is a bourgeois conception of human nature and a proletarian conception of human nature, there is a human nature that may well not be accurately and adequately depicted by either conception, and it is this that is *also* the subject of inquiry. The implication of this thesis is that even though, say, the bourgeois view of the human capacity for cooperation will be limited and shaped by the ideology and experience of the bourgeoisie, to ask questions about such a capacity for cooperation is to inquire, in a way that transcends any particular ideology, about a property that is shared by all humans, both members of the bourgeois class and the proletariat. So it would be unnecessarily limiting to consider the questions themselves to be purely ideological, open only to intracultural descriptive analysis.

Let me develop my claim that many of our deepest evaluative notions—moral and political, as well as aesthetic—refer to relevant features of human nature and to genuine social and historical possibilities that are available to us. I distinguish these deep notions (social equality, say) from more superficial and variable ones, even though the latter pervade our daily lives and make up the stuff of our everyday existence. My preference that the walls of my study be a certain color is quite possibly of much consequence to me, but there is no need to see such a preference as any more than an individual's taste or a culturally determined value. My marginal preference that all my friends have an environmental consciousness may seem a bit more significant, but even in these kinds of choices or evaluations a great deal of human variety is possible and perhaps even desirable. Things are not entirely different with our partiality toward certain kinds of novels or toward certain choices in lifestyle. These choices and evaluations may not be purely arbitrary and capricious, and one may allow that there can be considerable inter-subjective agreement about which of these evaluations are objectively justified (after sustained reflection, extensive experience, and relevant comparison among various genres and types of novels or of various lifestyles). But it is unlikely that such intersubjective agreement reveals anything essential about humans as such, about the way we happen to be constituted, our species-specific traits and capacities.

Many of our deepest evaluative notions, I am claiming, do indeed point to such traits and capacities. Take equality, for instance. It is clearly a normative notion, and it is used in a variety of ways in our everyday lives as we evaluate our work situations or even our personal relationships. But in the modern sense in which it becomes the basis for social and political struggles against despotism or slavery, equality rests firmly on notions about what human beings are like across cultural and historical differences. The modern conception of equality is based on a rather complex metaphysical idea (formulated most clearly in eighteenth-century Europe) that all humans have in principle a capacity for rational agency, defined as the capacity to reflect upon their own thoughts and actions and hence to guide and determine their own lives. Equality as a moral and political ideal would mean very little, for instance, if it denoted or implied merely sameness of, say, social opportunities or economic resources; indeed it would generate a rather uninspiring social vision. The real content of equality as an evaluative notion comes from what is implicit in the metaphysical claim that humans, all of us, across class-, gender-, or cultural lines of division, are capable of governing our lives and, in fact, that our welfare consists partly in the exercising of this capacity. To the extent that inequalities in access to material resources inhibit or impede such exercise, they are seen as morally objectionable, even when they might have the weight of cultural tradition behind them. Underlying this moral conception, then, is a substantive claim about human nature which cannot be valid only within particular cultures. If it is, everything in modern culture that is based on such a claim—the notion of inalienable human rights, for instance, or the very idea of a genuine democracy—would become untenable.

The claim about human nature, specifically about the capacity for rational self-determination, is at the basis of related notions about individual human worth or dignity. Sharply at odds with claims about worth based on social prestige, power, or dignity, this notion of worth grounds our modern political vision of all humans as belonging to a single community to which each of us is morally accountable. The idea is this: individual human worth (in this sense) is not a product of one's social standing and is not even tied to one's meritorious actions or one's moral standing in the community. In fact, the notion of inalienable rights as an ideal is based on a radically egalitarian notion that there is nothing a human individual *needs to do* in order to earn his or her worth (in this sense). Personal merit of even the most admirable kind is irrelevant in this regard; all that matters for this rather extraordinary moral status to be awarded to a person is that he or she exist. It is, as Gregory Vlastos puts it, like the most traditional kind of caste status and privilege acquired at birth. But the difference is crucial: there is only one unique caste—the human species!

> In one fundamental respect our society is much more like a caste society (with a *unique* caste) than like [a society that distributes privileges and worth according to merit]. The latter has no place for a rank of dignity which descends on an individual by the purely existential circumstance (the "accident") of birth and remains unalterably for life. To reproduce this feature of our system we would have to look not only to caste-societies, but to extremely rigid ones, since most of them make some provision for elevation in rank for rare merit or degradation for extreme demerit. In our legal system no such thing can happen: even a criminal may not be sentenced to second-class citizenship [under which one is "deprived of rights without any presumption of legal guilt"]. And the fact that first-class citizenship, having been made common, is no longer a mark of distinction does not trivialize the privileges it entails. It is the simple truth, not declamation, to speak of it, as I have done, as a "rank of dignity" in some ways comparable to that enjoyed by hereditary nobilities of the past. To see this one need only think of the position of groups in our society who have been cheated out of this status by the subversion of their constitutional rights. (46–47; emphasis in the original)

This status, thus, does not exist in degrees. One does not, because of one's actions, acquire more of this kind of status, and neither can one trade it away at will. This radical thesis about human worth does not, however, prescribe sameness and uniformity to humans, for it is not a comprehensive account of human creatures. In fact, it is compatible with there being cultural and even individual differences among such creatures; part of the argument for the notion of human worth, as might be evident by now, is that individual self-determination, individual choice, is held to be a genuine good, and such self-determination leads naturally to the flowering and exploration of differences in how human lives are lived, human capacities realized.

Now, on the realist view I am outlining, the complex and rich moral notion we call "equality" rests on properties of human nature which are discovered and formulated in and around the eighteenth century, but that does not mean that such discovery was entirely unanticipated. Indeed, momentous moral "discoveries" are rare, and rarely "punctual" or easily localizable. It is not hard to see how earlier claims, made in a variety of cultures and societies, about the soul, or the divinity that resides in each human breast, were anticipations of the modern idea, but they brought with them theological and ideological baggage that needed to be discarded. Moreover, while such theological claims about the soul have indeed been used in progressive ways, in particular in the fight against slavery, the crucial claim that is missing until the eighteenth century is that the notion of human dignity or worth is not a utopian idea but can be worked out in terms of a realistic and critical social and political theory.

What explains, then, the emergence of this critical account in (roughly) the eighteenth century? This is where the other dimension of values that I mentioned earlier becomes relevant. The notion of equality refers also to (our knowledge of) genuine social and political possibilities. It depends ultimately on concrete historical conditions and what is possible within them, for they shape our moral and theoretical imagination. My view is thus historicist rather than abstract. While my realism about value leaves open room for progress toward greater moral objectivity, it grounds its account of the development of morality and moral knowledge (following Hegel and Marx) in historical and social conditions. As socioeconomic forces develop and mature enough so that we can realistically imagine going beyond entrenched inequalities, moral notions like equality become less utopian and airy, more grounded in our increasing knowledge of the social and natural world (and of humans as a part of that world). In addition, organized social struggles of previously subjugated and subordinated classes and groups open up the imagination (of even an original thinker like a Rousseau or a Kant) to see how freedom, or the power to live and make one's life without chains, is not the province of the socially privileged but of all humans. Moral knowledge thus depends on historical and social factors, as does error or ignorance. In the absence of the right social conditions, in which social equality can be imagined realistically and genuine human features and traits can be detected or accurately intuited, accounts of equality (such as those produced by the classical Greek philosophers) remain limited and provincial. What this kind of realist view of values can offer, then, is an explanation of error as well as of reliable knowledge. Its dual orientation—toward human nature, on the one hand, and toward social and political conditions of the possibility of knowledge—enables us to see how values can be both historical and objective.

Objectivity and Aesthetic Values

To some readers, the claim that objectivity is possible in ethical and political matters may be easy to grant, but the realm of aesthetic value would appear to be fundamentally different. In the aesthetic sphere, in our judgments about colors and flavors and landscapes and poems, it would seem, to argue for objectivity is to ignore the genuine variety there is in individual and group tastes. It might even be said that a realist who argues for the possibility of objective judgment in aesthetic matters will be blind to the role pernicious social ideologies play in shaping our notions of beauty and ugliness, what pleases and what repels. Now my defense of objectivity in the realm of aesthetics acknowledges that both these points are important. What I propose to do, in sketching a general account of some of how our deepest aesthetic notions (say, beauty) refer outward, beyond a culture's boundaries, is to draw on thinkers like Hume and Dewey to show how basing aesthetics partially in human nature can be liberating for aesthetic inquiry, and how a nonreductive naturalistic view of deep aesthetic values can be perfectly compatible with our desire to account for the innocent differences in individual taste as well as the not-so-innocent (ideological) distortions that are the result of social conflicts and prejudices. My thesis about objectivity in aesthetics is, however, independent of the thesis I have already presented about ethics, even though my argumentative strategy is similar. My primary goal here is to show that such arguments for objectivity can succeed. Thus, except for a few suggestions, I do not intend to make any substantive claims about how aesthetics in general is related to ethics.

Influential studies of aesthetic ideology have appeared during the last few years arguing that the realm that is currently called "the aesthetic" is defined in an idealist way and that our primary task should be to demystify such idealism and reveal its hidden political agenda (see, e.g., de Man, Bourdieu). I agree partly with some of these analyses but would like to suggest that we should first acknowledge that what we call the aesthetic might answer to some genuine needs we have as human creatures, some of which we in fact share with other creatures in the natural world. As John Dewey suggested, the experience of making or responding to artworks provides a profound pleasure in many instances, but this pleasure—or more generally the experience itself—should be understood in the context of other areas of human life where similar responses are elicited from us. He argued that we misunderstand our experience with artworks if we do not see the continuity between it and other similar (sometimes less intense) experiences—responding to flowers and sunsets, engaging in warfare, and rearing children. Like all natural creatures, we engage in creating and procreating, satisfying our various desires and needs and attempting to survive against odds. An adequate account of art, Dewey suggested, needs to guard against relegating it to "a separate realm, where it is cut off from that association with the materials and aims of every other form of human effort, undergoing, and achievement" (3). What would such an "association" achieve? Dewey's argument is that it will show us how, notwithstanding its grander and more ethereal flights, art is also based in our connections to the rest of nature, and acknowledging these connections can help us discern some of the roots of the formal and rhythmic qualities that move us so deeply:

> Art is . . . prefigured in the very processes of living. A bird builds its nest and a beaver its dam when internal organic pressures cooperate with external materials so that the former are fulfilled and the latter are transformed in a satisfying culmination. We may hesitate to apply the word "art," since we doubt the presence of directive intent. But all deliberation, all conscious intent, grows out of things once performed organically through the interplay of natural energies. . . . The distinguishing contribution of man is consciousness of the relations found in nature. . . . Apart from the relations of processes of rhythmic conflict and fulfillment in animal life, experi-

ence would be without design and pattern. . . . The primeval arts of nature and animal life are so much the material, and, in gross outline, so much the model for the
intentional achievements of man, that the theologically minded have imputed conscious intent to the structure of nature—as man, sharing many activities with the
ape, is wont to think of the latter as imitating his own performances. (24–25)

Dewey's attempt to naturalize aesthetics is thus partly an attempt to detheol-
ogize it. The connections among social and biological rhythms on the one hand,
and the more developed aesthetic ones on the other, Dewey suggests, are open to
complex empirical verification, and what these connections will show us is the extent
to which aesthetic experiences are also based in our nature, our species-specific
history and our biological endowment. This will not debase the higher moral or
spiritual aspirations many glimpse in our deeper aesthetic experiences; it will, rather,
help us understand ourselves more fully, as natural creatures with propensities, needs,
and desires which often make us reach toward the starry skies above.

This naturalist account helps make sense of my realist claim that some of our
deepest aesthetic notions (like beauty) refer in part to human nature. On this
account, what gives an object (a painting, a landscape, even a meal) aesthetic value
is that it provides deep and abiding satisfaction (rather than simply pleasure) to
us, given our needs as humans. The kind of objectivity we are talking about, then,
is not completely aperspectival: indeed, there is no (aesthetic) value without basic
reference to what we are like as humans, to the way we happen to be constituted,
contingently. We might have been built differently, with a different range or register of responses. It is quite possible that extraterrestrials—say, Martians—will
have a different set of sensory responses and will find aesthetic value in things to
which we do not respond. All that is not only possible but quite likely, given the
naturalist account Dewey provides and the one some have derived from David
Hume's writings on taste. Peter Railton, developing the kind of naturalist account I have been suggesting here, puts this very vividly:

> Might there be something deserving the name "Martian beauty" even if it were
> quite different from what we recognize to be beauty? How would we understand
> this? How would we interpret "This image leaves us cold, but it possesses true
> Martian beauty"? Such a remark need not mean that Martians find it to have the
> distinctive qualities *we* identify as beauty-making—for example, particular struc-
> tures, symmetries, harmonies, and palettes. For we can understand well enough that
> Martians might be sufficiently dissimilar from us that they would not find excite-
> ment or delight in the forms or palettes that please us. Martians might even have
> quite different senses. Yet don't we understand what it would be for them to have
> a distinctively aesthetic practice of *evaluating beauty*? It would be (inter alia) for them
> to have a practice using distinctive terms, which they take to be normative, for those
> objects that have a general, robust match with *their* sensory and cognitive capacities
> for experiences *they* intrinsically desire. (84)

Railton points out, for instance, that the preference humans seem to display cross-culturally for bilateral symmetry can be explained naturalistically, and it may not be shared by Martians, who (given their "radially symmetric, intelligent subterranean life" (85) may be (*typically*) left cold by the "front elevations of our great pyramids, cathedral, totems, stately houses, tombs, and burial mounds" (85), which we find so moving. They may, instead, prefer "our hot mud springs and our undersea manganese nodules" (85). Railton asks: "Does our aesthetic discourse depend for its interest and authority on a claim that Martian beauty is at best only Martian beauty, while human beauty is beauty itself?" (85) Our deepest aesthetic values are clearly relational, grounded in what we humans happen to be like contingently. But to say that what constitutes aesthetic value for us is not part of the architecture of the extra-human cosmos is not to deny it objectivity. It may not hold for all sentient creatures but if it holds (potentially) for all humans because of our common genetic endowment, it is objective enough! To claim that only completely universal and invariable values are objective is to reify objectivity and to have an inaccurate picture of what values are.

I have been pointing to a level at which our aesthetic responses are shaped by human nature. No doubt, there are other major influences on our complex responses to television sit-coms and designer clothes, to Kalidas and Homer. The point of this naturalistic redefinition of aesthetics is to open up the possibility that there is, as Railton puts it, an "infrastructure" for the field of aesthetic value (67ff.). The basic claim derives from Hume, who suggested in his famous essay "Of the Standard of Taste" how "Some particular forms or qualities, from the original structures of the internal fabric are calculated to please, and others to displease," especially a human creature with "sound" organs of perception and cognition (140). "Though it be certain that beauty and deformity, more than sweet and bitter, are not qualities in objects, but belong entirely to the sentiment . . . ," Hume argued, "there are certain qualities in objects which are fitted by nature to produce those particular feelings" (141). To call such a match between the sensory-cognitive capacities of humans and aspects of their world the "infrastructure of value" is to point to causal connections and to suggest where fruitful empirical hypotheses can be formulated. Dewey's suggestion about the need for rhythmic structures, about the ground on which narrative pleasures are based (see also 37–38), or Railton's Humean theses about what kinds of symmetry please us and why, provide organizing hypotheses or frameworks for inquiry.

What the thesis about value's infrastructure cannot do, and what it was never meant to do, is explain all our evaluative judgments in a deterministic way. But if this naturalist thesis is plausible, it provides an interesting account of how human solidarities can be grounded not only in common beliefs and historical struggles but also in our animal-like nature, our in-built propensities and capacities for deep emotional and cognitive response. Cathedrals and temples, sunsets and deserts, even horrific spectacles that we cannot tear our eyes away from, all have formed the bases for social cohesion. If we understand why we need circuses (and not just bread), what exactly it is in us that fuels this need, we would be better prepared to imagine what a truly progressive (say, democratic and antiauthoritarian) cultural pedagogy would be like. If the aesthetic points to a dimension of our lives that is genuine but susceptible to ideological manipulation, we need to understand how and why this is so.

Unless we do so, we may learn to demystify the dominant ideology, but we— progressive critics and teachers—will not be able to propose powerful alternatives to that ideology. Alternatives to the dominant ideology cannot succeed if they are based on unrealistic idealizations of (say, rational) human behavior; such ideologies need to grounded in our genuine capacities for powerful feeling and emotional response, capacities which can be harnessed for both good and evil. If this naturalistic thesis about the aesthetic is sound, we have to recognize the limited power of ideas—of *only* ideas—to shape a critical and reflexive subjectivity; like Aristotle, we need to explore (against the Socratic view that knowledge, by itself, constitutes virtue) how and why we learn and act in new ways, what *nonideational* bases there might be for changes in character, in our habits and our stable dispositions. To identify the "infrastructure" of value is thus not to advocate a determinist view of our evaluative practices but rather to explain the range of options that are *typically* available to us. It is not to reduce history to nature but instead to see how history and nature together produce the environment through which we perceive our selves and we create our lives.

It might be useful, then, to consider how even some of the deeper aesthetic notions (like beauty) are inevitably social and historical, constrained as I said earlier by what we know and can imagine about our social and political possibilities. While such notions can refer accurately to some central features of human nature, such features are discovered only through the kind of sustained practice and contact with aesthetic experience which only a certain amount of leisure and independence from everyday responsibilities makes possible. Thus it would not be surprising if members of societies that are engaged primarily in warfare or in all-consuming labor for basic survival cannot experiment enough with aesthetic experiences (that are in principle always available to them) so as to be able to realize the significance of such experiences in their lives. It would be almost impossible for them to elaborate rich aesthetic notions, which are always products of sustained intellectual and practical work. In societies where such possibilities for leisure exist (because of the development of sophisticated social negotiation to avoid warfare or of efficient distribution of resources to satisfy basic material needs), "inquiry" into and discovery of genuine aesthetic needs and values becomes more likely.

It is an unfortunate fact of human history that such a realm of aesthetic practice (and implicitly aesthetic inquiry) has almost always existed by virtue of oppressive and unjust systems in which only a few can enjoy and practice what we might call aesthetic "goods." Even in such limited and unjust settings, however, real aesthetic discovery has been possible. One can argue that fuller exploration of such "discoveries" and the elaboration of aesthetic notions are more likely in less unjust social organizations, when those possibilities of aesthetic experience are available to a wider range of people. When new social relations become imaginable, aesthetic notions are sometimes revised and extended. In nineteenth-century Europe, for instance, when ideas about equality deepened in response to genuine possibilities of the extension of democracy (no matter how limited the existing reality), visionary writers like George Eliot were able to extend the notion of beauty (say, beautiful human features) to include much that was earlier left out of it: namely, the coarser features of peasants, which are the result of years of backbreaking labor, or even the humdrum features of ordinary people who were not born looking like heroes and heroines of romantic novels. Consider, in this famous passage from *Adam Bede*, how beauty itself is in the process of being redefined. The narrator's discursive gesture is not unlike that of a bold and innovative critic urging us to read and appreciate a neglected body of writing, inviting us to go beyond our limited aesthetic response to a fuller one. Indeed, the "discovery" of new kinds of beauty is predicated on the development and refinement of the reader's innate responsive, appreciative, consciousness:

> All honor and reverence to the divine beauty of form! Let us cultivate it to the utmost in men, women, and children—in our gardens and in our houses. But let us love that other beauty too, which lies in no secret of proportion, but in the secret of deep human sympathy. Paint us an angel, if you can, with a floating violet robe, and a face paled by celestial light; paint us yet oftener a Madonna, turning her mild face upward and opening her arms to welcome the divine glory; but do not impose on us any aesthetic rules which shall banish from the region of Art those old women scraping carrots with their work-worn hands, those heavy clowns taking holiday in a dingy pot-house, those rounded backs and stupid weather-beaten faces that have bent over the spade and done the rough work of the world—those homes with their tin pans, their brown pitchers, their rough curs, and their clusters of onions. In this world there are so many of these common coarse people, who have no picturesque sentimental wretchedness! It is so needful we should remember their existence, else we may happen to leave them quite out of our religion and philosophy, and frame lofty theories which only fit a world of extremes. Therefore let Art always remind us of them; therefore let us always have men ready to give the loving pains of a life to the faithful representing of commonplace things—men who see beauty in these commonplace things, and delight in showing how kindly the light of heaven falls on them. (224)

What I want to emphasize is that Eliot is introducing a thesis about beauty here, and this thesis can be challenged. The claim that there is an "other beauty," with its basis in "the secret of deep human sympathy," is not self-evidently true and it should not be treated as such. In other words, it is perfectly possible for someone to counter Eliot's thesis by saying something like the following: what Eliot's narrator is doing is to confuse our appreciation of beauty in human features with moral considerations (sympathy). It is the fact of the matter, this person would argue, that only "proportion" points to the beautiful, and disproportion does not. But that does not mean (Eliot's adversary in this debate would go on) than we should not care about—feel for, sympathize with, and even love—individuals whose physical features are disproportionate. We would, however, be doing so for reasons other than aesthetic ones. Beauty is proportion; although of course we can, and should, love disproportionate features.

On the interpretation I am offering, however, Eliot (like several others around that time) is proposing that the criteria for detecting beauty be extended and that at least as far as the beauty of human form is concerned our ideas about social equality and about the moral desirability of forming social bonds with (potentially) all humankind can transform our conception of beauty. In particular, these ideas can radically alter our conception of how central the "secret of proportion" is to "beauty"; when we choose to live in a world that is not of "extremes," of unrealistic idealizations, we shall come to perceive physical beauty as consisting not only in "proportion" but also in those new attributes we detect through our feelings of solidarity with our fellow creatures, whose "coarse" features are transfigured as "the light of heaven falls" on them. This is, then, a thesis about beauty and about the human capacity to respond to our world. Eliot would argue with her critic by raising metacritical issues; beauty, she would be saying in effect, is much more complex than our traditional criteria (like "proportionality") indicate, and that is so in part because our human capacity to respond "aesthetically" is dependent on (or at least tied to) our affective responses in the nonaesthetic realms. Here, then, is room for genuine disagreement. It may well be that Eliot is right, and that the way her critic would come to see this is by looking at the alternative definition of beauty Eliot is proposing—the definition implicit in the metaphysical claim about the complex interactions among our (human) aesthetic and moral responses. Such a claim refers to human nature as such, and should be treated like any such claim ought to be, instead of being dismissed outright as a confusion of beauty with morality, the aesthetic with the extra-aesthetic. The connection among these different domains is exactly what is being redefined, and Eliot's thesis invites both theoretical and empirical testing and elaboration.

But then doesn't this discovery, that our ideas about beauty, one of the deep aesthetic notions, can change and be improved, contradict the naturalist claim that aesthetic notions refer to human nature? Shouldn't the objectivity of "human nature" underwrite one (and no more than one) stable conception of beauty, to which our aesthetic notions could refer? The simple answer to both questions is No. A naturalist-realist grounding of aesthetic value in human nature implies that there are kinds of response that are typical of human beings, but this does not mean that such responses are easy to detect or define. If the debate as I have staged it between George Eliot and her more traditional adversary is a plausible one, it suggests how—to argue for Eliot's position, which is close to my own— aesthetic responses are not simple but complex, and even the accurate detection of beauty is itself dependent on feelings and ideas that are in themselves not aesthetic. That means that if Eliot is right, the traditional aesthetic isolation of (at least the perception or detection) of beauty blinds us to the objective nature of beauty, beauty as it is (as it can ideally be) for human creatures. Beauty, as we saw above, is a human phenomenon, but not thereby purely arbitrary or subjective; of course we can be wholly or partially wrong about it. Such error will not, however, be a simple error of observation, a mere misperception of beautiful objects or beauty-making properties. Rather, the error is often (as it is in this case) theoretical—that is, it arises from our mistaken notion that criteria of the beautiful (proportion, symmetry, etc.) are always applicable in a similar way, no matter what the object under consideration: skyscrapers, landscapes, or human faces. Eliot's point would be that such a context-free notion of beauty is defective, mainly because (to consider her example here) our aesthetic perception of fellow humans is never narrowly aesthetic in the traditional sense indicated above. What this disagreement between Eliot and her adversary in this debate would indicate to a realist is that there is meaningful disagreement precisely because both sides share a common point of reference: the beauty of the human form, especially in the context of what beauty is (more generally) for us humans. On the view I am sketching, then, aesthetic inquiry is inevitably dialectical and open-ended partly because it is grounded in our historically contingent knowledge about (human) nature.

Now it would be extravagant to claim, on the basis of one passage from one of her novels, that George Eliot is a naturalist-realist about aesthetic value. But my point here is not about Eliot's beliefs: I am using a view articulated by the narrator of *Adam Bede* as an example of how, if such a narrator held the kind of view about aesthetics I have defended above, she might believe in the objectivity of aesthetic values without agreeing with the current definition of what such values consist in. She would, like other realists about value, look not only for alternative and more supple criteria for identifying beauty, but also attempt to explain (for instance) how we come to misperceive beauty because of social prejudices against peasants and laborers. In providing such an explanation, she would be looking at the role pernicious ideologies play in distorting our understanding of aspects of ourselves and our world. Whether or not the distortion or misperception of value is the result of social prejudice, realists would be more generally interested in understanding how our ideas about aesthetic value originate and how they function in the social realm; because they are interested in objectivity, they would see evaluative claims (such as the one about the centrality of the cri-

terion of "proportion") as *corrigible* formulations, open to revision and improvement. Such formulations include their own theses about beauty, which they would
present as unavoidably fallible theses about the nature of human (aesthetic and
moral) response. Such theses about objective beauty do not point to ideal Forms
but rather to key properties of human nature, which we come to discover in highly
mediated, historically contingent, ways. As I have been indicating in discussing
how values refer outward, such theses and insights would be shaped by our ongoing negotiations with the wider world—by political struggles, for instance,
which allow us to see how class or gender relations can be restructured more
equitably.

Objectivity and the Multicultural Curriculum

The epistemic defense of value I have outlined here is, then, a strong alternative
to the postmodernist argument, which depends on implausible theses about the
relationship between power and knowledge and an intransigent skepticism about
objectivity as an epistemic ideal. If, as the realist account suggests, our ethical
and aesthetic evaluations are indeed historical and social, and they (in many crucial cases) also refer outward to human nature, then the kind of skepticism I
identified may not be a reasonable position. Moreover, for defenders of multiculturalism, the realist view would be attractive because it provides a nonrelativist
defense of the need for cultural and social diversity. Since our deeper ethical and
aesthetic concepts are necessarily theory-laden, ideological, and culturally inflected,
the realist can argue that the best form of inquiry into the nature of value, aesthetic or ethical, will need to be comparative and cross-cultural. Error and knowledge are both thrown in sharper relief when the theoretical and experimental field
is widened; and cross-cultural inquiry becomes necessary because we wish to avoid
cultural parochialism and provincialism. On this view, then, multiculturalism itself
becomes in part a kind of comparative *epistemic* project; it represents a social and
political ideal to be defended because of the objective knowledge—about human
nature and human welfare—that it can enable us to achieve. If cultural practices
are implicitly forms of inquiry, then a healthy multicultural society becomes a
model for the best kind of epistemic cooperation; it becomes an ideal laboratory
for inquiry about values.[6]

The subject of multiculturalism brings me to a few practical considerations
about the literature curriculum at universities and colleges that are grappling with
the need for comparative and cross-cultural studies. What I propose follows both
from my thesis about the objectivity of value and from what I have suggested
about the relation between ethics and aesthetics. I have argued against a purely
skeptical attitude toward aesthetic value, but I am not convinced that while aesthetic concepts like beauty can be based in objective features of human response
they ought—at least for now—to be reintroduced by progressive critics as self-

evidently valuable, to be detected by trained students of art and literature. For one thing, if George Eliot's thesis is plausible, we need to pay much more attention to those moments in the history of a culture when the traditionally accepted ideas about what constitutes beauty in a given domain are challenged in a principled and sustained way. When someone (like, say, Eliot's narrator) who believes that beauty might be objectively detected has serious doubts about the adequacy or accuracy of the criteria for detecting beauty that are currently dominant in her society, such doubts themselves provide the best testing ground for discussion of aesthetic evaluation. That is because they will force us to look at relevant historical and ideological considerations, while keeping open the possibility that we might be on to something genuinely "aesthetic," genuinely valuable across ideological and cultural divisions.

Second, since it is overwhelmingly likely that the dominant views about literary and aesthetic value in most American universities (to take one example) are for the most part informed by mainly the Western traditions, discussion of the objectivity of value will tend to be ethnocentric and ideological even with the best of intentions. One way out of this problem, if you take the realist view seriously, is to make every such course on aesthetic value into one where the primary emphasis is comparative and cross-cultural. A thoughtfully planned, team-taught course on comparative aesthetics may in fact help make students (and their teachers) less smug about their own cultural categories and more open to an objective assessment of the difficulty of particular judgments about aesthetic value.

But it may be that the greatest challenge to such a course or curriculum (not considering, for the moment, the practical difficulties of accurately representing the views of oral cultures) is that not every culture has assigned the same role to (aesthetic) beauty that the modern West has. Thus, while many traditional societies may have a view that the response to beauty is a deep and universally valid one, in principle available to all humans, they often also argue (anticipating George Eliot's views) that to isolate such a response would be to grossly misperceive the nature of the more complex response of which it is a (limited) part. To take merely one instance, Abhinavagupta, commenting on Bharata's *Natyashastra* and contemporary Indian aesthetics and metaphysics in his tenth- to eleventh-century treatises, can be read as suggesting that even our full response to beauty ("aesthetic relish") is only a small part of a more complex and meaningful meditational-contemplative response to the world. The latter response, it can be argued, should inform all aesthetic inquiry as well, since to see the aesthetic response as autonomous would be (according to this tradition) to make a serious error about the nature of human beings and their welfare. It would not be hard to imagine other, more radical interlocutors, who would question the central role ascribed to beauty itself. While arguing that it exists as a human phenomenon, they could go on to claim that it plays only a minor role in human lives since its value is merely instrumental: it is valuable because it is one of *several* ways that humans gain access to a deep aspect of themselves. Aesthetic experiences point beyond themselves to other, fuller experiences and possibilities—like those available now only to, say, a seer or a mystic (on this last subject, see Murdoch). On this view, genuine aesthetic experiences are unavoidably linked to ethical and metaphysical values and perspectives, and they can enlarge our conception of what it means to be more fully human—that is, they can radically deepen and alter our existing conceptions of human flourishing.

From the vantage point of such cross-cultural challenges, one can see more clearly why George Eliot's thesis as I presented it in a purely intracultural debate can be both unsettling and liberating. Not only can it improve the traditional criteria Eliot seems to be criticizing, it can also open up for investigation more basic questions about the relationship between the aesthetic and the ethical. My central proposal, then, is that (at least for now) we make more of our courses comparative and cross-cultural, and focus centrally on *the complex relationship between ethical and aesthetic values.* Instead of deciding in advance which of these kinds of value is more basic, it might be best to take the relationship itself as the theoretical and historical question to be examined, a question that other cultures have explored (and sometimes settled) in different ways. The belief that values can be objective, combined with relevant and complex cross-cultural knowledge, will enable students to deal maturely with uncertainties and the absence of resolution of *some* issues, without (to borrow Keats's words) the "irritable reaching after fact and reason." It will prepare them to be better judges of their own lives, as well as of the world around them. In fact, they might learn from such sustained inquiries into value that what the world and our own nature demand of us is both an attitude of honest, open appreciation of the value there is around us and an attitude of humility as we make our own judgments, as we shape and remake ourselves as human agents. It will enable them to be such judges and agents by exposing them to the potential riches of a genuinely multicultural world, in which historically entrenched inequalities do not limit us to ethnocentric views of ourselves and our futures, and liberating cross-cultural contact is sought for epistemic and moral reasons rather than merely sentimental ones.

Notice, then, that this view of multiculturalism is fundamentally nonrelativist, that is, it does not depend on extreme arguments about the radical alterity of other cultures. This realist definition of multiculturalism suggests why cultural diversity should not be merely tolerated, but rather defended in its best forms for good epistemic reasons, the same reasons we draw on to demand the democratization of any kind of intellectual research or inquiry. But what are the best forms of multiculturalism? Clearly, answers to that question will not follow self-evidently from the theoretical arguments I have advanced here. These answers will be themselves shaped by the empirical variety we face in different social contexts, and so, naturally, the answers will depend on the details. But acknowledgment of such contextual variety and complexity is a necessary part of all reflexive and rigorous inquiry, and it becomes especially important when we are dealing with the kind of social-theoretical questions that any discussion of multiculturalism raises.

What I have tried to suggest in this final section is that a strong defense of multiculturalism becomes available to us when we go beyond the postmodernist skepticism about value. In the course of this essay I hope to have clarified my proposal that values should be defined in this realist way, emphasizing both their social embeddedness and their epistemic dimension. My proposal was built on my account of one of the deepest arguments for the postmodernist's skepticism and relativism about value, which I identified as an extreme form of epistemo-logical holism. I showed why this argument is unsatisfactory and outlined an alternative view, a more nuanced and plausible *realist* view, that while there is no hope of attaining a completely neutral and bias-free view of values, a richer con-ception of theory-dependent objectivity is essential for productive human inquiry, particularly inquiry into values. Central to the alternative view I sketched is the rejection of a priori accounts of the place of (social and ideological) error in human evaluation and the counterproposal that such questions be opened up to empiri-cal investigation. I suggest that the skeptical thesis has now become doctrinal, rather than an open-ended intellectual claim or hypothesis, since it is asserted and repeated more often than it is defended or examined. But if a theoretical doctrine appears to shut off more doors for cautious and responsible human inquiry than it leaves open, it might suggest the need to reexamine it and to con-sider alternative accounts and explanations. In my defense of the objectivity of value, I hope to have proposed one such alternative.

Notes

This essay was presented to audiences at the Universities of Wisconsin–Madison, Cali-fornia–Riverside, and Rome, as well as at Cornell, Rice, NYU, and Harvard. Early drafts were read by Linda Alcoff, Michael Hames-García, Andrew Galloway, Terry Irwin, Dominick La Capra, Paula Moya, Ramon Saldivar, Paul Sawyer, and Harry Shaw, and I thank them for their helpful responses. A slightly different version of this chapter ap-pears in *New Literary History* (Autumn 2001).

1. For an elaboration of these ideas, see Mohanty, *Literary Theory and the Claims of His-tory*, Chapters 6 and 7; see also Moya's introduction and the essay by Caroline Hau in Moya and Hames-García, eds., *Reclaiming Identity*.

2. See, in addition to the discussion that follows, the brief discussion of Donna Haraway's notion of error in Mohanty, *Literary Theory and the Claims of History*, Chapter 7, note 19 (pp. 215–16).

3. Many postmodernist thinkers implicitly assume such impossible views of objec-tivity or truth when they make their epistemological arguments against objectivity. See, e.g., the discussion of Paul de Man in Mohanty, *Literary Theory and the Claims of History*, Chapter 1, esp. pp. 39–42. See also the discussion of Laclau and Mouffe's critique of the notion of objective social interests in Chapter 7, note 16 (pp. 212–13).

4. Foucault says, "I admit to not being able to define, nor for even stronger reasons to propose, an ideal social model for the functioning of our . . . society" (170–71). But his underlying arguments about power and knowledge apply not just to "ideal" (in the sense of "perfect") social models but also, as I have pointed out, to "better" ones (than what we have now)—cf. his suspicion of the idea of a "purer justice." So it is not clear how we can criticize existing institutions to reveal their ideological distortions, which is part of what Foucault clearly wants to do: "It seems to me that the real political task in a society such as ours is to criticize the workings of institutions, which appear to be both neutral and independent; to criticize and attack them in such a manner that the political violence which has always exercised itself obscurely through them will be unmasked" (171). How can we talk about the "political violence" of existing institutions without drawing on normative notions, as well as on some conception of how such institutions can be "better," more "just"? There is a basic confusion here. For a discussion of this kind of confusion more generally, see Taylor.

5. In both ways, however, they represent more than simply empirical information: that is, they include hunches and guesses, drawing on the imagination to make rational conjectures. This feature of values does not make them epistemically suspect, however, but rather—as the postpositivist philosophy of science tells us—fundamentally akin to any legitimate area of human inquiry: simultaneously empirical and theoretical, dependent for its progress not only on the right methodologies but also on social ideologies and practices (see Boyd; Kitcher). On reference, see Boyd, and the references in Mohanty, *Literary Theory and the Claims of History*, Chapter 2.

6. The following discussion is best read in conjunction with Mohanty, *Literary Theory and the Claims of History*, Chapter 7, "Universalism, Particularism, and Multicultural Politics," esp. pp. 234–51.

Works Cited

Boyd, Richard. "How to Be a Moral Realist." *Essays on Moral Realism.* Ed. Geoffrey Sayre-McCord. Ithaca, N.Y.: Cornell University Press, 1988. 181–228.

De Man, Paul. *Aesthetic Ideology.* Minneapolis: University of Minnesota Press, 1996.

Dewey, John. *Art as Experience.* New York: Minton, Balch, & Co., 1934.

Eliot, George. *Adam Bede.* New York: Penguin, 1985.

Foucault, Michel, and Noam Chomsky. "Human Nature." *Reflexive Water: The Basic Concerns of Mankind.* Ed. Fons Elders. London: Souvenir, 1974.

Hume, David. *Selected Essays.* Ed. S. Copley and A. Edgar. New York: Oxford University Press, 1993.

Kitcher, Philip. "The Naturalists Return." *Philosophical Review* 101 (Jan. 1992): 53–114.

Mohanty, Satya P. *Literary Theory and the Claims of History: Postmodernism, Objectivity, Multicultural Politics.* Ithaca, N.Y.: Cornell University Press, 1997.

Moya, Paula M. L., and Michael Hames-García, eds. *Reclaiming Identity: Realist Theory and the Predicament of Postmodernism.* Berkeley: University of California Press, 2000.

Murdoch, Iris. *Metaphysics as a Guide to Morals.* New York: Penguin, 1993.

Railton, Peter. "Aesthetic Value, Moral Value, and the Ambitions of Naturalism." *Aesthetics and Ethics: Essays at the Intersection.* Ed. Jerrold Levinson. Cambridge: Cambridge University Press, 1998. 59–105.

Smith, Barbara Herrnstein. *Contingencies of Value.* Cambridge, Mass.: Harvard University Press, 1988.

———. "Value/Evaluation." *Critical Terms for Literary Study.* Ed. Frank Lentricchia and Thomas McLaughlin. Chicago: University of Chicago Press, 1990. 177–85.

Taylor, Charles. "Foucault on Freedom and Truth." *Philosophy and the Human Sciences: Philosophical Papers, 2.* New York: Cambridge University Press, 1985.

Vlastos, Gregory. "Justice and Equality." *Social Justice.* Ed. Richard B. Brandt. Englewood Hills, N.J.: Prentice-Hall, 1962. 31–72.

The Pragmatics of the Aesthetic

GILES GUNN

She would take him to faraway lands to observe foreign ways, so he
could get closer to the strangeness within himself.
Fatima Mernissi on Scheherazade

The correlation between the aesthetic and the pragmatic has been problematic
ever since William James first hijacked—as Peirce later felt he had—the term
pragmatism in his lecture on "Philosophical Conceptions and Practical Results"
at the University of California at Berkeley in 1898. Indeed, despite recent work
by various critics and scholars, conventional wisdom about pragmatism's sensi-
tivity to the aesthetic remains pretty much where Lewis Mumford left it in *The
Golden Day* in 1926.[1] "The Pragmatic Acquiescence," as he termed it, represented
a particularly sorry moment in the history of American creative thought. Instead
of effecting "an overturn in philosophy," as James himself had hoped, pragmatism simply "killed only what was already dead" (Mumford, 93). Amounting to
no more than a bit of antifoundationalism here, a bit of social constructionism,
relativism, and radical empiricism there, some individualism here, and some
multicultural pluralism there, pragmatism betrayed the practical aesthetic mission of all genuinely innovative thinking: "to gather into it all the living sources
of its day, all that is vital in the practical life, all that is intelligible in science, all
that is relevant in the social heritage and, recasting these things into new forms
and symbols, to react upon the blind drift of convention and habit and routine"
(Mumford, 83).

While irony abounds in the fact that James himself could easily have accepted
this definition of creative thought as the aesthetic mission of pragmatism itself—
Mumford could have been parroting James when he said, "Life flourishes only
in this alternating rhythm of dream and deed; when one appears without the other,
we can look forward to a shrinkage, a lapse, a devitalization" (Mumford, 83)—
Mumford's judgment at the same time reflects the depth of misapprehension from
which pragmatism's interest in the aesthetic has suffered ever since. This misapprehension becomes only the more surprising if one remembers that the ultimate
aim of Charles Sanders Peirce's "marvelously intricate universe," as Joseph Brent
once described it (Brent, 203), was not merely to display the dependence of logic

on ethics but also the dependence of ethics on aesthetics, and to demonstrate along the way how all logical inquiries require something like an aesthetic leap of faith to bring them to conclusion, as when we say "This fits" rather than "This is correct." It also disregards the fact that James himself installed the aesthetic at the very center of epistemological operations by reconstruing all mental calculations as a kind of art in which the "inferential" and the "possible" play at least as large a part as the "practicable." It entirely ignores the fact that George Herbert Mead subsequently constructed out of pragmatism a philosophy of the act in which thinking is undertaken and selves constructed by means of epistemological traffic in what Mead called "significant symbols." And, finally, it slights the all-important fact that Dewey later went further, perhaps, than all of his fellow pragmatists with his claim that, by permeating all experience, the aesthetic thus succeeds in making all experience potential art.

To stay with several of the founders of pragmatism for a moment and draw this out somewhat further, it is worth recalling that James not only identified the meaning of ideas with outcomes and consequences; he also insisted that many of these outcomes and consequences cannot be verified and confirmed before we must act on them. We act for the most part not on the basis of confirmed facts but on the basis of surmises and conjectures. Thus, for James the imagination assumed a role in the operations of the intellect that was far from accidental or secondary, since so much of the life of the mind is devoted to determinations whose results we can never substantiate in advance but can only guess at or speculate before we have to respond. Dewey then took this same conception of the pragmatic method one step further in *Experience and Nature* by identifying what he called the "critical," by which he meant the intellectual, with a double movement that of necessity operates aesthetically in two directions at once. While one of the aesthetic movements of critical reflection inevitably carries inquiry back into the past to determine the probable, as opposed to certain, conditions from which something presumably emerged, the second inevitably carries inquiry forward by trying to figure out the potential, as opposed to the predictable or assured, outcomes in which something may issue.

In *Art as Experience*, Dewey ratcheted up still further his claims for the primacy of the aesthetic, arguing that, as the potential form and destiny of every experience, it is not merely one category among others but in fact the most basic category of all. Dewey had already stated as early as 1920 that "reconstruction in philosophy"—as he entitled the seminal lectures he delivered the year before in Japan—depends on relinquishing the search for an absolute and immutable reality and replacing it with an effort to enhance experience by exploring its possibilities for richer fulfillment. This meant abandoning what he later called, in his Gifford lectures, "the quest for certainty" and supplanting it with a new philosophical practice in which "the creative work of the imagination" is understood to be merely the obverse of the "negative office" performed by philosophy's "criti-

cal mind": Where the latter is directed against the domination exercised by prejudice, narrow interest, routine custom and the authority which issues from institutions apart from the human ends they serve," the former points "to the new
possibilities which knowledge of the actual discloses" and projects "methods for
their realization in the homely everyday experience of mankind" (Dewey, 1929,
311–12). It was but a short step from thus reintegrating the imagination within
the new practice of philosophy to reconceiving experience as itself a form of art
in *Art as Experience* and then reformulating the purpose of art, in terms not unlike
those that Nietzsche had invoked earlier, as the continuous revaluation and aug-
mentation of life itself.

In the remainder of this essay I wish to press these claims for the conjuncture
between the pragmatic and the aesthetic still further. Let me begin by noting that
insofar as the aesthetic can, at least under certain circumstances or conditions,
be conceived as constituting, if not a realm apart, then at least a realm that is
discriminable and distinctive, it has often been held to carry within itself practical dimensions with markedly ethical overtones. Support for this belief initially
comes from a tradition that in America goes back at least to Ralph Waldo
Emerson, Margaret Fuller, and Walt Whitman and that has its sources in Europe in the thinking of everyone from Giambattista Vico, Johann von Herder,
and Madame de Staël to Edmund Burke and Samuel Taylor Coleridge. Variously described most recently by Raymond Williams and Richard Rorty, this
tradition possesses as one of its chief interests the meaning of culture itself when
the chief business of culture now is to take over and reshape from theology and
philosophy the task of deciding what is worth keeping in such various departments of contemporary experience as science, art, politics, social thought, literature, morality, humor, and religion.

In recent years, this same tradition has itself come under severe attack, where
it has not been simply dismissed, for being no more than a reinscription of the
traditional Arnoldian, or, if you prefer, Genteel American, theory of culture. Much
of this attack has seemed by turns short-sighted and self-serving, since it could
be plausibly argued that instead of having thoroughly broken with this theory of
the work of culture, much less having successfully superseded it, we have merely
decided in the present historical moment to reconceive what it is that culture
actually seeks to repossess and reshape, how this is effected, who in fact may be
said to participate in or contribute to it, and why it is that this project is deemed
important in the first place.

Consistent with our more democratic, or at least less elitist, racist, or sexist
views of such matters, we are now more likely to say that culture seeks to appropriate and redescribe what any given people have, if you will, learned from their
experience. This is reflected not only in the specialized forms of their science,
philosophy, religion, and so forth but also in their tales, songs, aphorisms, jokes,
dances, riddles, oratory, and manners—in short, the strategies they have devised

to answer, or at least to symbolically encompass, the questions put to them by the problematics of their own existence. We still maintain, however, that one of the principal mediums in which such reflections occur is the realm of the aesthetic, which in alliance with its chief instrument, the imagination, provides the motive force for all those symbolic stratagems by which a culture's wisdom or ignorance is refracted and transmitted. We assume that the people who deserve most credit for contributing to and advancing this process are not simply those who, in response to questions posed by the problematic forms of their existence, have produced the most sophisticated symbolic answers to them, but also any individuals, far more numerous, who have had a hand in turning those answers into modes of ritual re-enactment and ceremonial self-realization for other people and later times. And, finally, we now take such cultural work to be important not alone because it reveals, as was once assumed, an essential unity of being underlying all its expressions but also because it suggests—or can suggest—something of the greater diversity of life forms that can now be comprehended and accepted as at once recognizably human and also ethically significant.

Culture in this sense, then, has in the interests of its own explication developed a kind of reading and writing—actually a kind of writing about reading—that we call criticism, a kind of writing that from the time of Goethe, Carlyle, and George Eliot to that of Hannah Arendt, Ralph Ellison, and Jacques Derrida has neither been, as Richard Rorty has put it, "an evaluation of the relative merits of literary productions, nor intellectual history, nor moral philosophy, nor epistemology, nor social prophecy but all these things mingled together in a new genre" (Rorty, 66). While the idioms in which this form of writing expresses itself have clearly changed over the last several decades, thanks in no small measure to the importation of a variety of new discourses from the Continent, the kind of task that this "new" genre of critical reflection has set for itself has remained more or less consistent. That task might be described as determining what to make of our customary ways of making sense when there is no longer any universally authoritative vocabulary in which to describe those ways, much less any universal agreement within such a vocabulary about how to evaluate their comparative advantages and disadvantages.

Here, again, the aesthetic is alleged to hold the key, a key that is both practical and ethical at the same time. As attested by a host of witnesses from Hans-Georg Gadamer, Paul Ricoeur, Wolfgang Iser, E. H. Gombrich, Annette Baier, and Clifford Geertz to Barbara Herrnstein Smith, the aesthetic emerges for this tradition at the point where, as Hayden White once put it, "our apprehension of the world outstrips our capacities for comprehending it, or, conversely, where canonized modes of comprehension have closed off our capacities for new experience." Either way, the aesthetic acquires a critical relation to what E. H. Gombrich refers to as a culture's mental set by appearing to breach, to return to White, "the conventional hierarchies of significance in which experience is presently ordered" and to project a new imagination or sense of things "which previously existed only as a perceptual possibility" (White, "Point of It All," 179–80).

While retaining the same practical and ethical mission for the aesthetic, Paul Ricoeur has expressed this somewhat differently by associating the aesthetic with the power texts possess to project a world of potential meaning and implication beyond the range of their own ostensive reference. In other words, texts become more aesthetic the less their range of potential meaning and implication is constrained either by the hierarchies of significance that define their wholeness or by the semiological and tropological mechanisms that determine their distinctiveness, and the more it depends on the vectors of sense they propel outward beyond themselves. It is these trajectories of meaning they project beyond themselves—and which can then be actualized and appropriated in any number of ways—that give to aesthetic as opposed to other kinds of texts the appearance of transcending themselves, of being able to invoke, or at any rate to insinuate, worlds of import not fully amenable to representation by their own expressive materials. But they transport us in imagination to distant places, to foreign topographies of the mind, to follow Scheherazade, only so that we may become better acquainted with the strangeness within ourselves.

Barbara Herrnstein Smith explains the capacity of the aesthetic, or, as she prefers to call it, the "fictive," to enable this kind of flight and return in relation to the peculiar cognitive needs that it serves. On the one hand, human beings are unable to express or communicate everything they know, or feel, or desire, because, as she puts it, the motives, reasons, and necessities for human expression are far more plentiful than the opportunities for it. We all long for occasions to talk and be talked to that our society can never adequately provide, whether because the saying of it would expose us to contempt, hostility, danger, embarrassment, or incrimination, or because the persons with whom we would and must speak are, like dead relatives, absent friends, estranged lovers, divine beings, or jars in Tennessee, inaccessible to us, or because what we have to say is too complicated, subtle, ambiguous, self-contradictory, or offensive to put into words. Consequently, Smith notes, there are always sentiments we could express, ideas we would explore, and desires we might acknowledge if there were suitable occasions on which to do so, appropriate audiences to hear them, and available styles and forms in which to render them. On the other hand and at the same time, human beings are constantly subject to potential experiences, as Smith calls them, that pass them by, either because these experiences don't serve their most immediate cognitive needs or because, for whatever reason, human beings suppress them. Whichever the case, "much that is potentially knowable to us, because it is part of what has, in some sense, happened to us, slips by apparently unknown or at least unacknowledged" (Smith, 144–45). Without some reason for acknowledging such prior experiences—"a perception never before quite articulated, an emotion we had sustained on the periphery of consciousness, a sense, barely grasped, of the import of some incident" (Smith, 145)—they slip away from us, depriving us of what we didn't even know we knew.

Aesthetic or fictive texts seem eminently suited to help address these two problems by simultaneously furnishing occasions, with their necessary audiences and appropriate styles, when the unspeakable may be spoken, the potentially lost retrieved. However, inasmuch as aesthetic texts utter the unutterable not by actually bringing the dead back to life, rendering God visible, or recovering lost experiences, but rather by creating a re-presentation or imitation of such things, or at least by creating situations that trigger such memories and actions, there is much that is in danger of being missed, blocked, or misinterpreted in aesthetic transactions. If all the meanings of any text are at least potentially inferable, in aesthetic texts more of them are interpretively indeterminate and unstable, which is why aesthetic texts encourage, and indeed often compel, a greater degree of speculative play than other kinds of texts. In fact, that play itself constitutes a considerable part of their meaning. Not that the play is, as some poststructuralists believe, wholly speculative and free-form, encouraging readers to begin anywhere in a text and simply let their imaginations roam. Even the most experimental and nonconventional texts shape and direct such activity while at the same time provoking it: "Even as certain possibilities of interpretation are opened, they are also directed, lured, and redirected by the poet through the verbal structure he has designed" (Smith, 145).

Perhaps the simplest way of explaining how the verbal structures of literary forms stimulate as well as direct the speculative play they encourage is by reminding us that they are generally constructed like conditional contrary-to-fact or "as-if" statements. Typically addressing aspects of human subjectivity that otherwise tend to be glossed, ignored, discounted, shunned, or mystified, aesthetic texts cast these aspects in forms that allow the feelings as well as the intellect to interrogate them. These forms are structured and motivated in such a way that within their confines we can accept as plausible, though not necessarily as inevitable, both the actions and the responses into which their initial situations— what Henry James called "the donnée"—are imagined to unfold. Grant me my initial assumptions, the aesthetic or fictive text states, assumptions that we can all accept as given with, or at least possible for, experience itself—in *King Lear*, let us say, that all fathers want gratitude from their children; in *Uncle Tom's Cabin*, that all mothers want to keep their families together; in *Moby-Dick*, that injustice perceived as divine must be answered for—and I will show you where those assumptions can lead.

As a suppositional or conjectural structure, then, what the aesthetic text takes from life are not its conclusions but rather the terms and substance of its original premise, which it then selects, rearranges, and develops to produce a purely hypothetical or speculative outcome, that is, a set of events that are not given at all with the original premise but which nonetheless follow from it as one set of alternatives within a variable range of conditions (Van Ghent, 3). Aesthetic texts, we thus say, are less interested in confirming or interpreting the known than in extending the realm of the knowable. But the realm of the knowable they potentially extend is not one whose contents can be defined apart from the figures of its expression, and the figures of its expression allow for—and indeed invite—speculation as to their meaning precisely because of their critical relation to their own medium. And when literature reflects on its own discourses, it creates within those reflections an "internal distance" that ultimately results from what Pierre Macherey calls "the non-adhesion of language to language, the gap that constantly divides what we say from what we say about it and what we think about it." If this is "the void, the basic lacuna on which all speculation is based" (Macherey, 234), it not only prevents all speculation from becoming fixed on a single content but enables us, finally, to think and feel differently than we normally do. Constituting an ironic relation between the aesthetic object and its own materials, this void or lacuna makes it possible for the aesthetic object "to erect a larger context of experience within which we may define and understand our own by attending to the disparity between it and the experience of others" (Cunningham, 141).

In this conception, then, the heuristic value of the aesthetic is closely associated with its pragmatics, and its pragmatics are both critical and emancipatory. Aesthetic texts are critical just insofar as they submit actual conditions and their presumed consequences to the contrasting prospect of potential experiences whose outcomes are merely plausible. On the other hand, aesthetic texts are emancipatory just insofar as the contrast they probe, or at any rate presuppose, between the actual and the potential leads to an extension, however minimal, of our sense of the knowable, just insofar as their technologies of projection alter, at least temporarily, how we think and feel.

From the perspective of contemporary critical fashions, this conception of the aesthetic and its heuristic potential may appear to concede too little to such recent nostrums as the "death of the author," the self-deconstruction of the text, the intertextualization of culture, the relativization of cultural perspectives and standpoints, and the subsumption of all such processes in the struggle for power. Furthermore, each of these critical approaches amounts to a further erosion in the coherence, effectuality, or relevance of the category of the aesthetic itself. Its real vulnerability, however, may come from the greater likelihood that the aesthetic, far from being delegitimated, eviscerated, or extirpated in this postmodern moment, has now apparently breached all textual and nationalist boundaries and begun to circulate freely as, if you will, the main solvent of culture as a whole.

This last describes the altogether new efficacy and centrality attributed to the aesthetic by, among others, Arjun Appadurai. Appadurai attributes this alteration in the fortunes of the aesthetic to the development of a postelectronic world, together with recent, unprecedented movements of people worldwide, that have created new opportunities for the making of imagined selves and invented worlds:

> Thus, to put it summarily, electronic mediation and mass migration mark the world of the present not as technically new forces but as ones that seem to impel (and sometimes compel) the work of the imagination. Together, they create specific irregularities because both viewers and images are in simultaneous circulation. Neither images nor viewers fit into circuits or audiences that are easily bound within local, national, or regional spaces. Of course, many viewers may not themselves migrate. And many mass-mediated events are highly local in scope. . . . But few important films, news broadcasts, or television spectacles are entirely unaffected by other media events that come from further afield. And few persons in the world today do not have a friend, relative, or co-worker who is not on the road to somewhere else or already coming home, bearing stories and possibilities. (Appadurai, 4)

Nonetheless, even if technological advances in the global reach of communications and the increased movement of peoples have now somehow altered the role of the imagination, and with it the practical work of the aesthetic, it seems on the face of it a bit exaggerated to claim that this has fundamentally altered the role of the imagination in the modern world. Ever since the age of print capitalism, as Benedict Anderson pointed out some time ago, the imagination has been busy creating—and revising—collective senses of identity among people lacking any personal knowledge of each other, people defined by boundaries other than geographical or territorial, boundaries that can nowhere be accurately or adequately represented, even through the instrumentalities of the law. These same collective senses have also always been reinforced for people in the age of print capitalism by an unsubstantiable belief in the sovereignty or integrity of what those boundaries mark, a sense of sovereignty that has in turn afforded them a feeling of solidarity with others that is more or less self-validating (Anderson, 6–7). And long before the age of printing, as everyone from the brothers Grimm, Max Mueller, and Sir James Frazer to Jane Harrison, Northrop Frye, and Italo Calvino has reminded us, narrative structures that were originally transmitted orally, such as myth, legend, folktale, and even anecdote, accomplished roughly similar feats.

Appadurai's point, however, is that this is the first age when, as he puts it, "the imagination has broken out of the special expressive space of art, myth, and ritual and has now become a part of the quotidian mental work of ordinary people in many societies." The imagination has not only, as he says, "entered the logic of ordinary life from which it had largely been successfully sequestered" but in its role as the producer and reinforcement of fantasy work has now also acquired a new and more collective sense of agency (Appadurai, 5). Whether as catalyst or as intoxicant, the imagination helps potential young freedom fighters and their antagonists dream, so to speak, in "Rambo"; at the same time it enables women separated by oceans as well as cultures to share with their sisters all over the world a common sense of oppression and empowerment. In instances such as these, the imagination is more than a place of escape; it is also an inducement to action and a site of contestation.

While much of his analysis is persuasive, Appadurai's claim that until very recently the imagination has been largely sequestered from the logic of ordinary life—and thus presumably unable to perform its role in the pragmatics of daily existence—is quite possibly overstated. Even if the scope of the imagination—and perhaps as well its ethical governance, or at least its ethical influence—has never extended wider than it now does in our new digital era, it has always been deeply sedimented in the logics—and what Ralph Waldo Emerson called the "precincts"—of the ordinary. Let me turn to two somewhat different accounts of how the aesthetic has found its way into the precincts of the ordinary, the first social and political, the second epistemological and ethical.

The first account comes from the writings of Hannah Arendt and in certain respects parallels the thinking of John Dewey. Arendt's theory about the ethical dimensions of the aesthetic emerges from her discussion of Kant's *Critique of Judgment*, particularly the first part, entitled "Critique of Esthetic Judgment." In this section, Kant tries to distinguish between the kind of thinking we associate with pure reason, which requires that the thinker be in agreement with him- or herself, and the kind of thinking called judgment, which requires that the thinker come to some kind of agreement with, as it were, everyone else. Assuming that the positions of all others are at least potentially open to inspection, this second kind of thinking is decidedly social, even political:

> The power of judgment [as of interpretation] rests on a potential agreement with others, and the thinking process which is active in judging [or interpreting] something is not, like the thought process of pure reasoning, a dialogue between me and myself, but finds itself always and primarily, even if I am quite alone in making up my mind, in an anticipated communication [or conversation] with others with whom I know I must finally come to some agreement. (Arendt, 1961, 220)

The thinking known as judgment, then, is made possible by the imagination and seeks insofar as possible to liberate itself from purely personal or subjective factors and enter into the place from which others think, thereby achieving what Kant called an "enlargement of the mind" (Quoted in Arendt, 1978, 257).

But this raises a serious question as to just what "thinking in the place of others" amounts to. As Arendt clarifies in her "Excerpts from Lectures on Kant's Political Philosophy"—which are attached as an appendix on "Judging" to the second volume, called *Willing*, of her *Life of the Mind*—it does not amount to thinking what others think. Complete empathy is neither desirable nor possible, since it would prevent one from thinking for oneself even as one tries to move into a space that is more public than private, a space, as Arendt describes it, "open to all sides"

(Arendt, 1978, 258). Kant says at one point that thinking in the place of others entails "comparing our judgment with the possible rather than the actual judgment of others, and by putting ourselves in the place of any other man" (Quoted in Arendt, 1978, 257); Arendt says at another point that it "means you train your imagination to go visiting" (Arendt, 1978, 257). In either case, the object is to move toward a perspective that is more general without being abstract. As the thinker moves from standpoint to standpoint, his or her thinking expands. But this expansion is not achieved at the expense of subsuming all of the particular standpoints that the thinker encounters along the way: "It is on the contrary closely connected with particulars, the particular conditions of the *standpoints you have to go through* [italics mine] in order to arrive at your own 'general standpoint'" (Arendt, 1978, 257).

As it happens, Kant's reflections on judgment would have proved less interesting to Arendt if he had not made these discoveries while examining the subject of taste. For Arendt, this remained a relationship of the greatest significance because it demonstrated that taste, which has always traditionally been thought of as the most private and idiosyncratic of senses, is in fact the most public and political of human faculties. Arendt elucidates its public as well as political dimensions by pointing out that if arguments about taste cannot, as she believes, be adjudicated, much less resolved, without appeal to the sentiments and sensibilities of others, such disputes also possess the inevitable effect of drawing individuals out of themselves and into a wider world of meanings that they can share, or at least contest, with their fellows.

The effect of the exercise of taste, then, is to extend the public world of meaning, of interpretation, of significant experience we share with others by compelling us to join with them in a debate about what things are most worth valuing and what attitudes shall be taken with respect to them. Without the constant and relatively free exercise of taste, Arendt believed that this world of publicly acknowledged and variously interpreted meanings and values we call culture would eventually disappear. With it, on the other hand, she felt that this public world of culture could be continuously expanded and enriched, because questions of taste, like all other matters of individual judgment, can never be resolved through coercion or the appeal to authority, but only through moral argument, or, as Arendt was fond of quoting Kant to say, "by wooing the consent of everyone else" (Quoted in Arendt, 1978, 222).

In this view, taste is not, as proverbial wisdom has it, the one thing that is altogether beyond dispute but rather almost the only thing, as Dewey noted, about which we ever do dispute. Dewey's statement is worth quoting entire:

> The word "taste" has perhaps got too completely associated with arbitrary liking to express the nature of judgments of value. But if the word be used in the sense of an appreciation at once cultivated and active, one may say that the formation of taste is the chief matter wherever values enter in, whether intellectual, esthetic or moral. . . . Instead of there being no disputing about tastes, they are the one thing

worth disputing about, if by "dispute" is signified discussion involving reflective inquiry. Taste, if we use the word in its best sense, is the outcome of experience brought cumulatively to bear on the intelligent appreciation of the real worth of likings and enjoyments. There is nothing in which a person so completely reveals himself as in the things which he judges enjoyable and desirable. Such judgments are the sole alternative to the domination of belief by impulse, chance, blind habit and self-interest. The formation of a cultivated and effectively operative good judgment or taste with respect to what is esthetically admirable, intellectually acceptable and morally approvable is the supreme task set to human beings by the incidents of experience.

To complete the circle with Arendt, all that Dewey omits to say here, but expressed elsewhere, is that by being formed in relation with, and always in dialogue with, other people, taste, which is but the handmaiden of the aesthetic, not only presupposes community but actually generates it.

The second account of the sedimentation of the aesthetic in the precincts of the ordinary comes from what philosophers like Martha Nussbaum and Mark Johnson have taught us about the role of the imagination in ethical reflection and understanding. Nussbaum's models come almost entirely from fiction, particularly from Henry James's view of the novel as a moral form devoted to showing us how to live and Marcel Proust's conviction that certain truths can only be examined and expressed in the form of stories. Her central point is that literary forms evoke certain kinds of practical moral reflection that cannot be evoked in any other way. She asserts that this practical thinking is most adequately expressed in complex narrative structures, by which she means everything from Samuel Beckett's novels to classical tragedy:

[W]e can say provisionally that a whole tragic drama, unlike a schematic philosophical example making use of a similar story, is capable of tracing the history of a complex pattern of deliberation, showing its roots in a way of life and looking forward to its consequences in that life. As it does all of this, it lays open to view the complexity, the indeterminacy, the sheer difficulty of actual human deliberation. If a philosopher were to use Antigone's story as a philosophical example, he or she would, in setting it out schematically, signal to the reader's attention everything that the reader ought to notice. He would point out only what is strictly relevant. A tragedy does not display the dilemmas of its characters as pre-articulated; it shows them searching for the morally salient; and it forces us, as interpreters, to be similarly active. Interpreting a tragedy is a messier, less determinate, more mysterious matter than assessing a philosophical example; and even when the work has once been interpreted, it remains unexhausted, subject to reassessment, in a way that the example does not. To invite such material into the center of an ethical inquiry concerning these problems of practical reason is, then, to add to its content a picture of reason's procedures and problems that could not readily be conveyed in some other form. (Nussbaum, 1986, 14)

If one of the reasons narrative deserves to be invited into formal ethical inquiry is because of the contribution it can make to our understanding of "reason's procedures and problems," a second is because aesthetic forms put the emotions to uses they are usually not given in nonaesthetic, more discursive forms. As Nussbaum says with particular reference to narratives (though I don't see why this doesn't apply to all forms of the aesthetic), the practical utility of the emotions as an aid to reflection is a direct result of the way they not only stimulate cognitive activity but also represent it. Indeed, far from merely arousing emotion in the reader, narratives—and, I would argue, other aesthetic forms—exist in themselves, Nussbaum rightly notes, as models, paradigms, examples, archetypes of what, in certain instances, feeling or emotion actually is. Hence the emotions are not sensational only but also cognitive, and the ideas they represent are so closely related to various of our beliefs and opinions about the world that when we change the one we alter the other.

Nussbaum's claims for the moral validity of the study of stories rests a good deal of its own validity on the belief "that the concrete judgments and responses embodied in stories are less likely to lead us astray, in the sense that they will contain what is deepest for us, most truly expressive of our moral sense, and most pertinent to action, by comparison with the abstractness of theory" (Nussbaum, 1988, 237). Yet at the same time, she admits that this does not overlook the fact that stories originate from the same fields of experience as do our other theories and beliefs and they therefore deserve to be treated with the same kind of suspicion, or interpretive skepticism and wariness, that we bring to our study of any other social constructs. This admission seems to render her argument for the moral utility of the aesthetic somewhat circular, but its circularity may simply be a function of how closely she ties the moral dimension of the aesthetic to the supposed inherency of narrative as a structure of the human mind itself. In point of fact, Nussbaum never veers very far from a notion of narrative associated with the nineteenth-century European and English novel; she has little to say about forms where such notions have been challenged (Sterne, Diderot, Broch, Musil, Kafka, Gombrowicz) or where narrative has itself been mixed with and transmuted into other forms, such as music, painting, architecture, industrial design, even fashion.

Mark Johnson seeks to back his own claims for the imaginative structure of moral understanding—and hence for the ethical implications of the aesthetic— by seeing narrative as only one of five components of moral reasoning, each of which contains a figurative component. Employing second-generation cognitive science, Johnson argues that the exercise of the moral imagination requires the ability not only to construct and interpret narratives but also to recognize and be able to think with the help of prototypical structures, to employ and manipulate semantic frames, to develop and extend conceptual metaphors, and to identify and reflect on "basic-level experience."

To think at all requires that we employ categories and concepts, but categories and concepts do not reflect, as is popularly supposed, sets of properties belonging to things in the world; rather, they describe what cognitive science thinks of as resemblances between things that seem to be of a similar type no matter what their properties or features. Thinking prototypically rather than strictly categorically thus enables reflection to become more ambulatory and less rigid, just as, according to cognitive science, our terms and concepts acquire much of their referentiality and specificity by means of the larger frames or schemas within which we understand them. While such frames or schemas are not infinitely variable, they provide much of the scaffolding and orientation for thought that is then free to undertake more precise mappings with the help of the tropological operations afforded by metaphors.

Metaphor contributes to the moral reflection in several ways, according to Johnson. In addition to generating different ways of conceptualizing particular situations, metaphor furnishes "different ways of understanding the nature of morality as such (including metaphorical definitions of the central concepts of morality, such as will, reason, purpose, right, good, duty, well-being, etc.)," and it provides a mechanism or technology "for analogizing and moving beyond the 'clear' or prototypical cases to new cases" (Johnson, 10). However, there may well be experiences which have no known prototypes, which disrupt, break through, or simply recompose our traditional frames and schemas, and defy metaphorical comparisons or analogies. Johnson calls these "basic-level experiences" because they refer to such elemental phenomena as pain, fear, harm, pleasure, and humiliation, phenomena that may, or may not, be universal but that nonetheless put great pressure on the felt legitimacy or effectuality of all the other imaginative or aesthetic components of moral reflection.

At the end of this series, Johnson situates narrative itself, not because he views it as any less important than the other components of the moral imagination but rather because he seems to believe that its operations can only be understood in relation to them. If narrative is the way we organize the other components of moral reflection into a meaningful structure, it is also the way we make sense of these other ways of making sense. While no one of these modes of thinking is by itself capable of enabling the imagination to overcome the protocols of reason in moral reflection, working together they help the imagination to transform morality from a rational search for immutable laws to guide our life into a continuously aesthetic and, at the same time, practical exploration of possible solutions to the problems with which life confronts us.

If this turns culture itself into what Satya Mohanty calls "a moral testing ground," that moral testing ground is for Arendt, Nussbaum, and Johnson something more than, or at least something different from, the almost infinitely fluid, changeable, and redescribable medium that it becomes for Appadurai, where the global movement of people and information now permits the imagination to infiltrate and inflect even the most routine structures of daily life. Appadurai's view of culture bears a strong resemblance to the readily familiar postmodernist image, where aesthetics tends to subsume all other categories, including ethics, in a realm in which everything is presumed to be constructed and thus contingent, relative, and redescribable. But if everything is constructed, and hence susceptible to redescription, including our discriminations and judgments, then no matter how diverse its elaborations, aesthetic or otherwise, there is no way of explaining, as Mohanty reminds us, "what difference different kinds of construction make" (231). Diversity then exists, or at least exists for us more and more in contemporary life, not as a heuristic instrument but merely as a theatrical entertainment or a source of diversion. Hence, whether we phrase the ethical question in Dewey's terms, as which life would be better to live, or in Mohanty's terms, as why the oppressed may know something the rest of us need to understand, we cannot learn anything necessary to, or propaedeutic for, the reform of conduct or the revision of practice from any theory that severs the aesthetic from the pragmatic, that divorces the imaginary from the empirically consequential.

This leads Mohanty back in the direction of Kant in the belief that the only way that we can secure the lessons that aesthetics, among other disciplines, teaches us about cultural diversity is by grounding them in a limited kind of moral or humanistic universalism. Yet such a move is not without its difficulties. The problem is not that such a moral universal inevitably leads to an idealization of Enlightenment reason or freedom—to my mind, Mohanty successfully shows that it does not, and, in any case, belief in the dignity of reason and an autonomous human agent capable of a measure of free choice is not, as Amartya Sen has recently demonstrated with great eloquence, either an invention of the French Enlightenment or a Western bias (Sen, 33–40)—but rather that it raises a specter of one of the more invidious forms of essentialism, one where the definition of humanity in all its inconceivable variety is reduced to a set of shared and sharable traits.

Mohanty is by no means unmindful of this difficulty and therefore bases his claims for such universalism not on the positive features that human beings exhibit in all cultures and at all times—who could know such things?—but rather on those needs that human beings have revealed over the course of human history, needs that are inscribed, at least negatively, in the world's various declarations of human rights. These rights constitute what might be thought of as the world's estimate of the minimal requirements for human welfare that no culture or society should be permitted to deny its members. Elsewhere Mohanty associates those features "which are not purely cultural or conventional but are shared by all humans across cultures" more positively with people's ability to determine their own lives (Mohanty, 248).

If this still sounds like too Western a sense of universalism—isn't it, really, the disputes we have about which rights to call human rights, and how far such rights extend into the life around us, and not the consensus we ever reach about how many such rights there actually are, which reveal our commonalities, or at least our resemblances, as human beings?—the conclusion that Mohanty draws from this assertion is unassailable: "It is from such radical claims that all anti-colonial movements of our times have drawn their best arguments, and it is these universalist moral and political positions that have been behind the demands for socialism, for the equality of women or the abolition of slavery—in short, behind so many of the struggles to extend and deepen democracy which constitute our modernity" (Mohanty, 248). It is also difficult to believe that any theory of aesthetics or ethics grounded on something very much less general, or, at any rate, less widespread than this kind of humanism can provide a sufficiently convincing explanation either for how aesthetics can render diversity educative or for how consciousness can thereby be altered.

Note

1. In this connection, see, among others, John J. McDermott, *The Culture of Experience: Philosophical Essays in the American Grain* (New York: New York University Press, 1976); Richard Poirier, *The Renewal of Literature: Emersonian Reflections* (New York: Random House, 1987); Poirier, *Poetry and Pragmatism*; Hans Joas, *The Creativity of Action*; Richard A. Hocks, *Henry James and Pragmatist Thought: A Study in the Relationship between the Philosophy of William James and the Art of Henry James* (Chapel Hill: University of North Carolina Press, 1974); Joseph Brent, *Charles Sanders Peirce: A Life*; Ross Posnock, *The Trial of Curiosity*; Posnock, *Color and Culture*; Ann Douglas, *Terrible Honesty*, 129–43; Henry Samuel Levinson, *Santayana, Pragmatism, and the Spiritual Life*; Richard Shusterman, *Pragmatist Aesthetics*; Thomas Alexander, *John Dewey's Theory of Art, Experience, and Nature: The Horizons of Feeling* (Albany: State University of New York Press, 1987); Steven Mailloux, *Reception Histories*; and Jonathan Levin, *The Poetics of Transition*.

Works Cited

Anderson, Benedict. *Imagined Communities*. Revised Edition. London: Verso, 1991.

Appadurai, Arjun. *Modernity at Large*. Minneapolis: University of Minnesota Press, 1996.

Arendt, Hannah. *Between Past and Future*. London: Faber and Faber, 1961.

———. *The Life of the Mind*, Vol. 2: New York: Harcourt Brace Jovanovich, 1978.

Baier, Annette. *Moral Prejudices: Essays on Ethics*. Cambridge, Mass.: Harvard University Press, 1994.

Brent, Joseph. *Charles Sanders Peirce, A Life*. Bloomington: Indiana University Press, 1993.

Burke, Edmund. *Reflections on the Revolution in France*. World Classics Edition. London: Oxford University Press, 1950.

Burke, Kenneth. *The Philosophy of Literary Form*. Berkeley: University of California Press, 1973.

Coleridge, Samuel Taylor. *On the Constitution of Church and State*. London: Pickering, 1839.

Cunningham, J. V. *Tradition and Poetic Structure*. Denver, Colo.: Swallow, 1960.

Dewey, John. *Reconstruction in Philosophy*. New York: Holt, 1920.

———. *Experience and Nature*. 1925. La Salle, Ill.: Open Court, 1971.

———. *The Quest for Certainty*. 1929. New York: Putnam, Capricorn Books Edition, 1960.

———. *Art as Experience*. 1934. New York: Putnam, Perigree Books Edition, 1980.

Douglas, Ann. *Terrible Honesty: Mongrel Manhattan in the 1920s*. New York: Farrar, Straus & Giroux, 1995.

Emerson, Ralph Waldo. *Selected Essays*. Ed. and introduction by Larzer Ziff. New York: Penguin, 1982.

Fuller, Margaret. *Women in the Nineteenth Century*. New York: Norton, 1997.

Gadamer, Hans-Georg. *Truth and Method*. New York: Seabury, 1975.

Geertz, Clifford. *Local Knowledge*. New York: Basic Books, 1983.

Gombrich, E. H. *Art and Illusion*. New York: Pantheon, 1960.

Herder, Johann Gottfried. *J. G. Herder on Social and Political Culture*. London: Cambridge University Press, 1969.

Iser, Wolfgang. *The Implied Reader*. Baltimore, Md.: Johns Hopkins University Press, 1974.

James, William. *Pragmatism and The Meaning of Truth*. Cambridge, Mass.: Harvard University Press, 1978.

———. "Philosophical Conceptions and Practical Results," *William James, Writings 1878–1899*. New York: Library of America, 1992. 1077–97.

Joas, Hans. *The Creativity of Action*. Chicago: University of Chicago Press, 1996.

Johnson, Mark. *Moral Imagination: Implications of Cognitive Science for Ethics*. Chicago: University of Chicago Press, 1993.

Kant, Immanuel. *Critique of Judgment*. Oxford: Clarendon, 1964.

Levin, Jonathan. *The Poetics of Transition: Emerson, Pragmatism, and American Literary Modernism*. Durham, N.C.: Duke University Press, 1999.

Levinson, Henry Samuel. *Santayana, Pragmatism, and the Spiritual Life*. Chapel Hill: University of North Carolina Press, 1992.

Mailloux, Steven. *Reception Histories: Rhetoric, Pragmatism, and American Cultural Politics*. Ithaca, N.Y.: Cornell University Press, 1998.

Mead, George Herbert. *Selected Writings*. Ed. Andrew Reck. Indianapolis, Ind.: Bobbs-Merrill, 1964.

Mohanty, Satya P. *Literary Theory and the Claims of History*. Ithaca, N.Y.: Cornell University Press, 1997.

Mumford, Lewis. *The Golden Day*. 1926; Boston: Beacon Paperback, 1957.

Nussbaum, Martha. *The Fragility of Goodness: Luck and Ethics in Greek Tragedy and Philosophy*. New York: Cambridge University Press, 1986.

———. "Narrative Emotions: Beckett's Genealogy of Love," *Ethics* 98 (Jan. 1988): 225–54.

Peirce, Charles Sanders. *Philosophical Writings of Peirce*. Ed. Justus Buchler. New York: Dover, 1955.

Poirier, Richard. *Poetry and Pragmatism*. Cambridge, Mass.: Harvard University Press, 1992.

Posnock, Ross. *The Trial of Curiosity: Henry James, William James, and the Challenge of Modernity*. New York: Oxford University Press, 1991.

———. *Color and Culture: Black Writers and the Making of the Modern Intellectual*. Cambridge, Mass.: Harvard University Press, 1998.

Putnam, Ruth, ed. *The Cambridge Companion to William James*. New York: Cambridge University Press, 1997.

Ricoeur, Paul. *Interpretation Theory: Discourse and the Surplus of Meaning.* Fort Worth: Texas Christian University Press, 1976.

Rorty, Richard. *Consequences of Pragmatism.* Minneapolis: University of Minnesota Press, 1982.

Sen, Amartya. "Human Rights and Asian Values." *New Republic,* July 14 and 21, 1997: 33–40.

Shusterman, Richard. *Pragmatist Aesthetics: Living Beauty, Rethinking Art.* Oxford: Blackwell, 1992.

Siegfried, Charlene Haddock. *Pragmatism and Feminism.* Chicago: University of Chicago Press, 1996.

Smith, Barbara Herrnstein. *On the Margins of Discourse.* Chicago: University of Chicago Press, 1978.

Staël, Madame de. *An Extraordinary Woman: Selected Writings of Germaine de Staël.* Ed. Vivian Folkenflik. New York: Columbia University Press, 1987.

Van Ghent, Dorothy. *The English Novel, Form and Function.* New York: Harper, 1961.

Vico, Giambattista. *The New Science of Giambattista Vico.* 3rd Edition. Ed. and trans. Thomas Goddard Bergin and Max Harold Fisch. Ithaca, N.Y.: Cornell University Press, 1968.

White, Hayden. "The Point of It All." *New Literary History* 2 (Autumn 1970): 173–85.

———. *Tropics of Discourse: Essays in Cultural Criticism.* Baltimore, Md.: Johns Hopkins University Press, 1978.

Williams, Raymond. *Culture and Society, 1780–1950.* New York: Columbia University Press, 1958.

Aesthetics and Cultural Studies

WINFRIED FLUCK

It has become one of the starting moves of recent revisionist scholarship in literary and cultural studies to emphasize the historical relativity of all aesthetic judgments and to stress their function not only as cultural but also as political acts. This argument can be traced back to one of the founding texts, if not *the* founding text, of cultural studies, Raymond Williams's *Culture and Society*. In order to defend his own extension of literary studies to cultural studies against the then dominant views in British and American English departments, Williams introduced an astute argument about the historical situatedness of cultural and aesthetic values that had appeared self-evident and universal up to this point: "The organizing principle of this book is the discovery that the idea of culture, and the word itself in its general modern uses, came into English thinking in the period which we commonly describe as that of the Industrial Revolution" (ix). Williams then applies this perspective to the idea of art and describes the emergence of the term aesthetic as a response to an alienating division of labor between artist and artisan. In *Marxism and Literature*, he goes one step further and characterizes aesthetic theory as a form of evasion, that is, as an instrument of obfuscation: "Art and thinking about art have to separate themselves, by ever more absolute abstraction, from the social processes within which they are still contained. Aesthetic theory is the main instrument of this evasion. . . . Thus we have to reject 'the aesthetic' both as a separate abstract dimension and as a separate abstract function" (154–56).

The passage shows Williams both at his best and his worst. On the one hand, he illustrates the typical strength of his approach by discussing aesthetics not merely as a philosophical problem but also as a cultural practice. On the other hand, this shift of focus also has its price: seen from a preindustrial, artisanal, and idealized vision of practice, in which different activities and faculties are still united, aesthetics appears to have no other function than that of evasion. A long philosophical tradition and a rich cultural history in which aesthetics has taken on entirely different forms, including the task of philosophically grounding emancipated art, is thus ignored. The reason for Williams's neglect of this tradition lies in certain unacknowledged premises of his own position. In arguing against the separation of art and life, the case Williams makes is, in the final analysis, not necessarily one against aesthetics per se but against its separation from other forms of social practice. He is not arguing against the theoretical description and justification of art or aesthetic experience (in fact, he is engaging in it himself), but against a conceptualization of the aesthetic as a separate sphere. His position is "anti-aesthetic" only in rejecting a particular historical manifestation of aesthetics, namely one in which, according to his view, the division of labor is uncritically reproduced. Consequently, his argument is made in support of another role of the aesthetic, elaborated more fully in books like *The Long Revolution*, in which culture and reality are reunited as social practice in order to overcome capitalism's division of labor—a version and variant of Marxist aesthetics based on a concept of *Entfremdung* that has its source in philosophical idealism. Thus, Williams's case against the concept of aesthetics is really a case made in the name of a more meaningful role of art in life.

This unacknowledged "conflation of aesthetics *in toto* with a discredited concept of aesthetic value" (Guillory, 271) is one of the recurrent shortcomings of the present-day rejection of the concept of the aesthetic. As I shall argue in the following essay, there are, in fact, three basic reductions that make the current dismissal of the aesthetic possible: (1) the equation of the aesthetic with art or beauty and the reduction of the question of aesthetics to a philosophy of art or a philosophy of beauty; (2) the conflation, sometimes confusion, of aesthetic function and aesthetic value, so that the whole question of aesthetics is reduced to the problem of evaluation; (3) the recurring identification of aesthetics with a particular, discredited historical version of it, so that the question of aesthetics can be "abbreviated as the thesis of the transhistorical or transcendental value of the object, the work of art" (Guillory, 275) and the dismissal of aesthetics as a discourse of "universal value" can be justified. However, as Guillory points out: "We should not expect that a critique of aesthetic discourse in its historical forms can proceed by rejecting the category of the aesthetic any more than a critique of political economy would have to deny the reality of specificity of the economic domain" (282). Nevertheless, Williams's rejection of the term aesthetic as "an instrument of evasion" has become commonplace in the new revisionist literary and cultural studies after the linguistic turn. Since the social and political functions of cultural practices are often obscured in the process of discussing their aesthetic dimension, so the argument goes, the "real" function of the aesthetic is that of an ideology, and the critic who still insists on the importance of the category must be seen as someone who is trying to turn back the clock for whatever sinister purposes.[1] Fittingly, a contemporary German critic starts an essay on the issue of aesthetic experience by saying: "Whoever deals with aesthetics nowadays, dissects a corpse."[2]

The problematization of the unquestioned authority of the category of the aesthetic stands at the beginning of the new revisionism in literary and cultural studies. Explicitly or implicitly, Williams's argument became one of the starting premises of revisionist approaches for which the discourse of aesthetics is merely a screen for unacknowledged ideological interests. In the struggle against the dominance of the New Criticism and its insistence that the literary critic should focus on intrinsic, specifically literary values (as against the so-called extraliterary or extrinsic values), it became almost commonplace to point out that the apparently innocent categories of the "literary" or the "aesthetic" are by no means exempt from history or politics. In fact, the New Criticism itself provides a good example, for its theory of literature and its definition of specifically literary values are "historical" in at least three ways. To start with, they do not reflect a superior insight into the true nature of literature that is gained by disciplined close reading; rather, their source is the elevation of the aesthetic premises of a certain historical period or school, for example the aesthetics of modernism, to the level of a general principle. Second, the idea of "intrinsically literary" values itself is historical in the sense that it has emerged in specific historical contexts and reflects particular interests.[3] From this perspective, it is not just a certain canon that has specific historical origins but the idea of canonicity itself. Third, the new critical categories of the literary and the aesthetic were not, as was claimed, "disinterested" categories. They reflected the, in the broad sense of the word, political interests of a certain group by functioning as social and professional strategies of self-empowerment. Recently, Jonathan Arac has provided a fine example of this type of analysis by pointing out how Lionel Trilling's hypercanonization of *Huckleberry Finn* as a literary masterpiece and especially his praise of Chapter 31 as a moral struggle for independence served the needs of Trilling's anti-Stalinist agenda and his search for an independent stand against conformist pressures.

Arac's example confirms my own findings in an analysis of the history of *Huck Finn* criticism which was written at the height of the dominance of the New Criticism and directed against the seemingly self-evident authority of a strictly formalist approach to literature. At the time, *Huckleberry Finn* had finally been canonized as one of *the* masterpieces of American literature and was discussed almost exclusively in terms such as literary craftsmanship or organic unity. However, a critical analysis of the plausibility of these claims for formalist mastery or organic unity led to the result that these claims were mere rhetorical constructs which disregarded contradictory evidence almost at will, despite a claim to base critical assessments on a close reading of the literary text. In fact, it was striking to see how little resistance was offered to the absurd claim of *Huck Finn's* organic unity by the methodological criterion of a "close reading": at a closer look, a "specifically literary analysis" was what the critic wanted a literary analysis to be. Consequently, the assessment of the aesthetic value of the novel was not the result of a close reading but actually its starting premise, which was then to be confirmed in the act of interpretation. In order to justify the study of a book like *Huckleberry Finn*, it had to be classified as a literary masterpiece. For this, it had to meet criteria that were derived from certain literary models but then applied as norms to all literature indiscriminately, because only in this way could a literary text be described as possessing literary value.[4] Hence my conclusion, then, that in their effort to treat literature as specifically literary, critics tended to confuse the literary with its definition by the New Critical contextualists. This definition, however, represents an unwarranted generalization of one type of literary structure and results in the interpretation of many texts according to principles by which they patently were not written. Its basic shortcoming is the identification of literary structure with the idea of organic unity or a coherent whole which is usually found in a dualistic pattern or metaphor. The "specifically literary" interpretation practiced by New Critics and those trained in their approach can thus be seen as a form of self-deception, for, given his or her tacit acceptance of New Critical premises, the critic is bound to discover exactly those qualities in the text which the theory has already codified as valuable. Ironically, the moment of the greatest influence of the New Criticism was thus also a moment in which the idea of the aesthetic was strongly discredited by its conventionalized and schematic application.

The following problematization of the categories of the "intrinsically literary" and "the aesthetic" in the sense of New Critical formalism has gone through several stages. In the earliest stage, which was Marxist in Europe and vaguely leftist in the United States, it was not aesthetics per se but a special version of it that was attacked in order to replace it with a more relevant or "truthful" form of aesthetics. After all, Marxism had its own elaborate aesthetics influenced by the philosophy of German idealism.[5] The situation changed with the arrival of poststructuralism and its replacement of the idea of the specifically literary with concepts such as writing, rhetoric, textuality, discourse, or representation. The crucial theoretical move of this new cultural radicalism in contrast to older forms of political radicalism lies, as I have argued elsewhere, in a shift in the definition of political power from the repression thesis, in which power is still enacted through agents and institutions of the state, to cultural forms or discursive regimes as the actual source of power, because these cultural forms constitute the very ways in which we make sense of the world before we are even aware of it.[6]

Inevitably, this redefinition of power must also change the view of the aesthetic: as long as power is located in agents of the state or institutions of society, the realm of the aesthetic can still be conceptualized as a counterrealm, if only for the articulation of a utopian impulse or a negation of systemic closure. Where, on the other hand, power is "everywhere," including in cultural forms, the claim of aesthetic transcendence or even a negative aesthetics in the manner of the Critical Theory of the Frankfurt School can no longer be upheld. In his discussion of the work of Henry James, Mark Seltzer has used a neat neo-historicist chiasm to describe this fundamental reorientation by transforming the New Critical trust in the power of art into "the art of power." Aesthetics thus becomes only another power game, which is, by and large, its theoretical status in the current cultural radicalism. As a consequence, it appears no longer necessary to deal with the dimension of the aesthetic and to employ it as a point of reference in the analysis of cultural material. On the contrary, to do so carries the immediate suspicion of an attempt to distract from the real issues.

The current dominance of cultural studies is one result of these developments. The emergence of cultural studies as a new version of the field that used to be called philology and then literary studies can be seen as the logical outcome of the story I have traced. It is, of course, notoriously difficult to define cultural studies, because cultural studies is what you get when some of the more traditional criteria for defining the field are taken away. However, even in its most diffuse form, cultural studies reflects two major changes: (1) If nothing else, cultural studies is a field of programmatic dehierarchization. It breaks down the barriers between high culture and popular or mass culture and says that both— that all cultural practices—are worth studying. What distinguished post–World War II literary studies from philology was that it was based on certain aesthetic norms. Not all works qualified for serious professional consideration, and a crucial, if not *the* crucial, task of the critic was to determine what works were legitimate objects of study. To be sure, literary studies also dealt with so-called inferior works but only in order to characterize them as such. This definition of the field as constituted by aesthetic norms, and more specifically, by the search for specifically literary values, explains why this form of literary studies had such a hard time extending the discipline to other cultural forms such as film or, even worse, television. There simply wasn't any way in which the concept of specifically literary values could be convincingly applied to a medium like film.[7] In contrast, there are no real canon wars within cultural studies (although cultural studies is, of course, very much at the center of the canon debates), because there is no longer a canon. In principle, "anything" goes. Cultural hierarchies are rejected as the foundation of the field, though their historical and cultural sources may be studied in investigations such as Raymond Williams's.

(2) If the aesthetic dimension is no longer the explicit or implicit point of reference in cultural studies, then the definition of the object to be studied must change. In postwar literary studies this object was the form or structure of the literary work—although one has to add that these seemingly neutral "technical" terms were already value-laden in characteristic ways. Structure, for example, was not any kind of formal organization but only a *gestalt* with certain regular patterns. In the formalist approach of the New Criticism, the starting premise is that the literary work distinguishes itself by its artful, organic structure, because only such a type of structure can constitute an object that is ontologically different from other, everyday discourses. In current cultural studies, the starting premise is that the text is part of a discursive network or regime which should become the object of study, because it exerts power by means of classification, representation, and exclusion. Consequently, power resides in rhetoric, or, more broadly, in representation (in the broad semiotic sense of the word).

When texts can no longer be distinguished by whether or how they transcend power effects, or whether they are good or bad according to certain aesthetic premises, they must be constituted as objects on the basis of a new premise about their relevance and function. This assumption is now political. What makes the literary text an important object of study is no longer its power of transcendence but the fact that it exerts power. This power is not exerted through a particular form or structure (so that only some texts would exert power) but through the one aspect all objects of cultural studies have in common, namely that they are all representations. Representation is the most neutral, the most "dehierarchized" term one can find to describe the form in which the object (and its ideology) appear, and it has thus become one of the key words of analysis in cultural studies. Yet, the important thing to note here is that, inevitably, the concept of representation has its own normative base and thus, in a way, functions like aesthetic premises did in the New Criticism, that is, as a premise that guides all subsequent interpretive acts. If I have an aesthetic premise, that is, a premise about what constitutes value in the object, then I will search out those qualities and characteristics in my textual description and interpretation. Similarly, if I have a premise about why representation should be studied, namely because it is a manifestation of systemic power effects, then I will pay attention to features of the text in which power manifests itself in exemplary fashion, for only in this way can I describe the text as relevant choice, for example, by arguing, that the text is complicit with the social system or not.

This point—that there are premises and normative concepts at work in any interpretation of cultural material—may, in fact, be granted by a revisionist critic, who would then argue, however, that in the new revisionism, the founding premise has undergone a welcome transformation from aesthetic to politics. This seems to confirm the claim that it is no longer useful or necessary to deal with the concept of the aesthetic and to make it a point of reference for critical practice. However, I want to claim that the new revisionism has systematically misunderstood and misrepresented the issue of aesthetics, because it has conflated the New Critical version of aesthetic value with the issue of aesthetics in general.[8] One may suspect that this conflation has two reasons. First, the New Critical aesthetics was the only one the new revisionists ever encountered in their academic socialization (while Marxist aesthetics, for example, was subsumed under the rubric "Critical Theory"). And secondly, they have done so because they could not hope for a better version of aesthetics in order to justify their own project of an historical and political criticism. But in conflating the question of aesthetics with its New Critical version, the new revisionism has disregarded other and different conceptualizations of the aesthetic, much, as I want to show, to its own disadvantage. For it is one of the unfortunate consequences of this conflation that the new revisionists seem to act on the completely mistaken assumption that they have to choose between either aesthetics or politics, while, in reality, I shall claim, the two are inseparable and, in fact, mutually constitutive.

One of the striking and puzzling aspects of the revisionist's rejection of the aesthetic is its ahistorical approach to the issue. Although Fredric Jameson's dictum "Always historicize!" (Jameson, 9) has become something like the first commandment of the new revisionism, Jameson's advice seems to be entirely forgotten as soon as the question of aesthetics is addressed by the new revisionists. Because of a crude opposition between the political and the historical on the one side and the aesthetic on the other, the aesthetic appears to have only one function, namely the evasion of political views and historical explanations. As such, it always remains the same and always functions in the same manner. While everything else is subject to historical change, the meaning of the word aesthetic seems to stay the same. However, the New Critical conceptualization of aesthetic value is still a traditional aesthetics in the sense that the aesthetic is considered a quality of the text or object itself. The aesthetic is identified with a specific formal aspect of the work, so that the analysis of the work's structure can also determine the nature of aesthetic experience. With this approach, New Criticism gave a scholarly, professionalized version to a long philosophical tradition.[9] The names for the intrinsic qualities change—a change that is in itself an interesting part of cultural history—but the idea that the aesthetic experience resides in intrinsic qualities of the work of art remains the same.

This approach is self-defeating, however, for if it can be shown that these aesthetic values are not universally valid but instead are particular historical manifestations of the aesthetic, and that, moreover, they are read into the text rather than residing in it, or, they are created, even "invented" by certain cultural discourses, then the idea of the aesthetic seems to be thoroughly discredited. This happened to New Criticism when its contextualist version of organic unity was questioned in its universal applicability by pointing out that many so-called masterpieces, from *Hamlet* to *Huck Finn*, did not meet the criterion of organic unity and had to be submitted to a rather violent reinterpretation in order to save them as so-called literary masterpieces. Clearly, as long as one identifies the aesthetic with the assumption of an intrinsic quality, such reinterpretations are essential, for only if the object possesses an inherent quality described as aesthetic, will it be able to qualify as a legitimate object for literary studies.

But the equation of the aesthetic with an inherent quality, structure, or *gestalt* is by no means plausible. It is certainly not the only way in which we can speak about the aesthetic dimension of cultural objects. In fact, it presents a profound misunderstanding. In contrast, a number of different approaches such as pragmatism, Czech structuralism, and the reception theory of the Constance School have argued, each in its own way and with different emphases, that the aesthetic is not an inherent property of a text or object, so that an object either possesses aesthetic qualities or does not. Instead, it is argued that the aesthetic is constituted by the attitude we take toward an object and that it is hence not a word for a particular formal quality but for a distinct communicative mode and function.[10] The point is illustrated in John Dewey's *Art as Experience* where Dewey evokes the scene of a number of men approaching the Manhattan skyline on a ferry. Toward this object of perception the men on the ferry's attitudes might range from practical matters of orientation or an assessment of the real estate value of the buildings to an aesthetic appreciation of the skyline:

> Some men regard it as simply a journey to get them where they want to be—a means to be endured. So, perhaps, they read a newspaper. One who is idle may glance at this and that building identifying it as the Metropolitan Tower, the Chrysler Building, the Empire State Building, and so on. Another, impatient to arrive, may be on the lookout for landmarks by which to judge progress toward his destination. Still another, who is taking the journey for the first time, looks eagerly but is bewildered by the multiplicity of objects spread out to view. He *sees* neither the whole nor the parts; he is like a layman who goes into an unfamiliar factory where many machines are plying. Another person, interested in real estate, may see, in looking at the skyline, evidence in the height of buildings, of the value of land. Or he may let his thoughts roam to the congestion of a great industrial and commercial centre. He may go on to think of the planlessness of arrangement as evidence of the chaos of a society organized on the basis of conflict rather than cooperation. Finally the scene formed by the buildings may be looked at as colored and lighted volumes in relation to one another, to the sky and to the river. He is now seeing esthetically, as a painter might see. (140)

The aesthetic, here, is not a word for the intrinsic property of an object. Nor is it identical with art. Hence aesthetics, as a philosophical discipline, is not only and not necessarily a philosophy of art. Nor is it restricted to the study of beauty. Experiences of the sublime, the uncanny, the grotesque, even the ugly have produced their own powerful and influential aesthetics. As a branch of philosophy, aesthetics has a much broader range than the beautiful. Historically, it emerged as a "science of sensuous knowledge" ("sinnliche Erkenntnis").[11] As Dewey implies, such a mode of perception is a part of daily experience and hence, potentially, an everyday occurrence.[12]

Similarly, the Czech structuralist Jan Mukařovský argues that any object of the life-world can, in principle, be viewed (and interpreted) from a number of different perspectives. A building or a dress serves a practical function, but we can also, at the same time, look at them as aesthetic objects and we may even reflect upon the possible relations between the two aspects.[13] An aesthetic function is, in this view, not the property or inherent quality of a privileged object we can then call a masterpiece.[14] On the contrary, we can, in principle, look at any object of perception or experience as an aesthetic object.[15] Take a subway map of Berlin, for example. At one moment, we may regard it as purely referential and rely on its truth-value; at the next moment, we may bracket the referential function for the time being and look at the pattern of subway lines as an aesthetic object that reminds us of an Egyptian hieroglyph; in a third moment, we may reflect on what this strangely irregular pattern can tell us about the historical growth patterns of Berlin's subway system, including the possibility that it may have been designed by an artist for the purpose of illustrating or dramatizing this fact. In other words: referential and aesthetic dimensions do not occupy ontologically different planes. They interact with and complement one another. In even more radical fashion than Dewey, for whom aesthetic experience marks a culminating moment in which fragmented elements of daily experience are successfully reintegrated, the aesthetic, for Mukařovský, is created by a temporary and, possibly, fleeting shift in a hierarchy of functions that is in constant flux, so that each of the functions remains present and can, at every moment, regain dominance.[16] Consequently, the aesthetic cannot be defined as separate sphere.[17] Neither does it present a counterworld, nor does it come into existence by an act of transcendence or a retreat from reality. While looking at the subway map as an aesthetic object, we cannot completely suppress our awareness that it is a subway map. In fact, only on this background does the hieroglyphic pattern take on significance as an aesthetic object. It is not that we find hieroglyphic patterns pleasant or interesting in themselves. On the contrary, without reference to that which has been turned (temporarily) into a hieroglyphic pattern, the transformation would be pointless.[18] In order to be able to bracket a referential function, we first have to have a referential function. Many forms of recent art, such as, for example, pop art, junk art, or abject art, therefore set out by declaring everyday objects or, increasingly, thoroughly "profane" objects to be art objects in order to dramatize the redefining power of shifting attitudes that can transform even the "lowest"—the most vulgar, junkiest, or most repulsive—materials into aesthetic objects.[19] Similarly, to take another extreme example from literature, in Donald Barthelme's experimental postmodern story "The Glass Mountain" the dogshit on the streets of Manhattan, in its subtle color shadings, can take on an almost sublime aesthetic quality.[20]

This is an important point, because it helps to underline the fact that taking an aesthetic attitude toward an object does not mean, or, at least, does not necessarily mean, that we disengage the object or ourselves from reality. By conceding that the object may not be identical with reality, we do not have to assert that it is autonomous or that it has nothing to do with that reality. In changing our attitude toward an object, the aesthetic function may become dominant, but it is not becoming exclusive. What exactly does it mean, then, to take an aesthetic attitude? The concept refers to the capacity of any system of signification to draw attention to itself as a form of expression and to refer to itself as a sign, thus drawing our attention to the organizing and patterning principles by which the object is constituted.[21] For this purpose, the object is temporarily depragmatized and dereferentialized. We no longer insist that reality be truthfully represented by our subway map, because only in this way can we concentrate on the object itself. This temporary bracketing of reference is useful and often gives pleasure, not because it allows us to escape, if only temporarily, from reality but because it opens up the possibility of a new perspective on the object and, by implication, on reality.[22] We discover aspects of the object which we have missed in our exclusive concentration on the referential function.[23] At the same time, the dominance of the aesthetic function does not mean that the reference is cancelled. On the contrary, the temporary change in perspective only makes sense (and is only meaningful) as long as the reference to reality is not lost. The referential and the aesthetic function always coexist.[24] The new perspective on the object can only be experienced in its various possibilities of revelation, criticism, intensification of experience or pleasure as long as the reference is kept in view, so that we are constantly moving back and forth between the newly created world and the reference that has served as a point of departure for this reinterpretation.[25] In this sense, the aesthetic object can be described as repetition with a difference which links the real and the imaginary in a new constellation. The temporary bracketing of the referential and practical function of the object does not mean that the object's relation to reality is erased. On the contrary, it is put on new grounds, and the clarification of this new relation is one of the major tasks of literary criticism and art criticism. The aesthetic mode opens up the possibility of a new interpretation of the world.[26] It draws attention to aspects that have been overlooked, ignored, or suppressed. We may not approve of this new interpretation and may criticize it, but in order to criticize it meaningfully, we first of all have to acknowledge it in its own right.

Dewey's and Mukařovský's description of what it means to take an aesthetic attitude has a crucial theoretical advantage over traditional forms of aesthetics: it allows us to distinguish between two aspects that have been continuously conflated and confused in recent attacks on the concept of the aesthetic, namely the aspects of aesthetic function and aesthetic value.[27] *Aisthesis* means both the ability to perceive and the power to judge. For most contemporary revisionist critics of the aesthetic, however, aesthetics appears to be synonymous with evaluation and, more specifically, with a suspect hierarchy of values.[28] In contrast, Dewey and Mukařovský claim that the taking of an aesthetic attitude only constitutes a different object by setting the aesthetic function dominant. When, in looking at the Manhattan skyline or the Berlin subway map, we take an aesthetic attitude, it opens up the possibility of perceiving these objects as, in Dewey's words, a set of "colored and lighted volumes", or, in my example of the subway map, as a hieroglyphic pattern.[29] However, whether we consider these colored and lighted volumes or the hieroglyphic pattern of the subway pleasing or an especially impressive manifestation of its kind, is quite another matter and logically distinct from constituting the object of perception as an aesthetic object. Logically distinct, but not separate. Clearly, the two categories and aspects are interdependent. Inevitably, my consciously or unconsciously held values will influence my constitution of the aesthetic object, just as, on the other hand, my—often tacit—assumptions about the function of literature will shape my aesthetic value judgments. A critic may argue, for example, on the basis of certain premises of what constitutes a work of art, that objects in which single parts blend harmoniously may be best suited to invite the observer to take an aesthetic attitude, just as, on the other hand, taking an aesthetic attitude may mean for a particular observer to focus on certain characteristic features that constitute aesthetic value for him or her. And yet, it is precisely because of this interdependence that it is necessary to keep the two aspects logically apart. We have to keep them apart in order to be able to grasp the ways in which these assumptions shape and determine our interpretations of literary texts and cultural practices. Before we can assess the aesthetic value of an object, we have to constitute it as an aesthetic object. Taking an aesthetic attitude means constructing an aesthetic object on the basis of a guiding assumption about the function of art or the aesthetic.[30] This founding assumption will in turn influence my judgment of the aesthetic value of the object. The reception history of many artistic works demonstrates that, even when critics agree that a literary text such as, for example, *Huckleberry Finn*, is a masterpiece, they will still disagree on the specific reasons why, because they hold different notions about the function of art and, consequently, different views about what constitutes aesthetic value.[31] Aesthetic evaluations thus have their often unacknowledged base and justification in their tacit premises about what constitutes an aesthetic function. This also means, however, that they are open to rational dispute at this point.[32]

Let us go back for a moment to our subway map. In principle, I said, any object can become an aesthetic object if an aesthetic attitude is taken toward it and its aesthetic function is made dominant. The object itself, however, can also encourage us to take such an attitude. This is especially obvious in the case of fictional texts (in the broadest sense of the word as any form of "invented" representation). Once we classify a representation as fictional, we can no longer regard the object as predominantly referential. Because a fictional text does not merely replicate reality but embodies it in new shape and form, understanding a fictional text cannot simply be a mimetic act of recognition. Rather, we have to create the object anew. Since we have never met a character named Huckleberry Finn and do, in fact, know that he never existed, we have to come up with our own mental representation of him. Inevitably, we invest our own emotions, draw on our own associations and form our own mental images in imagining characters like Huck Finn or Isabel Archer and make them come alive so that we can become interested in their fate. These imaginary elements can only gain a *gestalt*, however, if they are based on discourses of the real.[33] Thus, a character like Huck Finn emerges as a combination of a Victorian local-color discourse of a figure of the bad boy on the one hand, and our imaginary complementation of the figure on the other.[34] If it weren't for the bad-boy discourse, there would be no reference and thus no common object of debate, while, on the other hand, the imaginary elements are the reason for the puzzling and often frustrating phenomenon that we can come up with ever new interpretations of one and the same book.

Fictional forms of representation bring an object into our world but they are not identical with this object. They create an object that is never stable and identical with itself. Fictional representation is thus, to use Wolfgang Iser's words, a performative mode: "Representation can only unfold itself in the recipient's mind, and it is through his active imaginings alone that the intangible can become an image" (*Prospecting*, 243). Taking an aesthetic attitude thus becomes the source of non-identity, and it is this non-identity, in turn, which can be seen as a source of aesthetic experience, because it allows us, for example, to be inside and outside of a character at the same time.[35] We can look at ourselves from the outside and, in doing so, create another, more expressive version of ourselves. Fiction is an especially potent and heightened means of taking the role of the other and of looking back at oneself from that perspective. As Wolfgang Iser puts it: "In this respect the required activity of the recipient resembles that of an actor, who in order to perform his role must use his thoughts, his feelings, and even his body as an analogue for representing something he is not. In order to produce the determinate form of an unreal character, the actor must allow his own reality to fade out. At the same time, however, he does not know precisely who, say, Hamlet is, for one cannot properly identify with a character who has never existed. Thus role-playing endows a figment with a sense of reality in spite of its impenetrability which defies total determination. . . . Staging oneself as someone else is a source of aesthetic pleasure; it is also the means whereby representation is transferred from text to reader" (244).

Non-identity, in other words, is that element of an aesthetic experience which makes it possible to review and reexperience reality. If aesthetic representation is characterized by non-identity, however (which is something entirely different from "autonomy"), then interpretation is also always a transfer and a role-play, the creation of another self, the staging of a new identity, or the articulation of a socially otherwise stigmatized impulse.[36] In Trilling's case it is clearly the first. Trilling, however, was not the last critic who described a moral struggle on the basis of his own experiences and needs, or, to put it in hermeneutical terms, in terms of his own horizon. To be sure, his interpretation of *Huckleberry Finn* was a role-play, with Huck cast in the role of nonconformist postwar liberal and the slave-holding South in the role of Stalinism, real or imagined. But if this is true for the past, then it must also be true for the present. The practice continues. There is a tendency in current revisionist criticism to imply that critics may have enacted such critical role-plays in the past for ideological reasons, but that the current historical and political criticism is no longer in need of such "disguises," because it expresses its own interests and politics openly. In contrast, I have argued that such processes are inescapable because of the radicalized form of non-identity on which aesthetic representation is based. In other words: even political criticism cannot help but create an aesthetic object when it interprets a fictional text. Or, to put it differently, and in a sufficiently polemical manner: politics, if articulated via literary or cultural representations, becomes an aesthetic phenomenon. This appears to be most obvious to me in the current interest in the racially other, e.g. in the massive self-racialization or self-ethnicization which characterizes not only American and European culture at large, as, for example in the movies of Quentin Tarantino, but literary and cultural studies as well. Such role plays are not only at work in cultural crossovers, however. They are also at work in identity politics, for clearly the racial or ethnic identity a critic affirms through a literary text is also a creation, the construct of an imaginary identity which does not exist in this form in the real world. It is true that the nation is an imaginary community, but it is not the only one.

This, in fact, is where cultural studies comes in again and where it can draw on the original insights of Raymond Williams. What I have described so far affects cultural studies in three ways: (1) For a number of reasons, cultural studies are especially tempted to use the concept of representation in a mimetic rather than a performative sense. However, the performative mode of cultural material is not restricted to deliberately self-referential works. It is a characteristic of all fictional texts and aesthetic objects. (2) The processes of transfer and critical role-playing which are inextricably linked to descriptions and interpretations of aesthetic objects do not only occur, of course, in literary studies. They may be even more prominent in cultural studies. In fact, one explanation for the popularity of cultural studies may be that it facilitates such processes, because its objects often invite role-play more easily than, let us say, experimental texts. Responding to popular culture, for example, one can shake off the burdensome role of the complex intellectual and go back to "immediate experience," to use Robert Warshow's words, that is, to a relatively direct, immediate expression of strong emotions. (3) What may be even more important in this context is that cultural studies were generated by the crucial insight that critical analyses, including value judgments, are also always cultural acts of self-definition and self-empowerment in which readers, audiences, or critics make use of the nonidentity of aesthetic objects in order to articulate their own needs and interests. The history of literary criticism is usually written as that of theoretical and methodological progress. It has yet to be written as a history of changing acts of self-fashioning.[37] I think that the current revisionism is wonderfully perceptive in analyzing critical role-plays of the past, but strangely disinterested in acknowledging the elements of transfer and role-play in its own critical practice. Perhaps, one reason for this omission is the belief that such an analysis would undermine its own politics. In contrast, I believe that it makes for a better politics, because it adds a needed dimension of self-awareness and self-reflexivity.

The current rejection of the aesthetic and its displacement with the political is in itself a cultural act, that is, an act of self-definition and self-empowerment which can be seen in a larger historical context. The reason why Raymond Williams characterized the aesthetic as a form of evasion lay in what he saw as its separation from social processes. His critique of the concept had the purpose of overcoming this separation: if, in a particular stage of the division of labor, "art and thinking about art have to separate themselves . . . from the social processes within which they are still contained," then "we have to reject 'the aesthetic' both as a separate abstract dimension and as a separate abstract function" (154–56). This project of overcoming the separation between the aesthetic and the social sphere is by no means new, however. It reenacts the avant-garde's ongoing attempts, starting with dadaism and surrealism, to erase the separation of art and life by destroying the aura of the work of art. In reaction to idealist aesthetics, the modern avant-garde has authorized and defined itself by ever renewed attacks on the aesthetic as a realm of special, transcendent values. This has resulted in increasingly radical attempts to dissociate the practice of art from aesthetics, and has finally led to a programmatically antiaesthetic stance.[38] The development is analyzed in a number of "post-aesthetic" theories about an ongoing process of "de-aestheticization" (H. Rosenberg), the "delimitation of the aesthetic sphere" (D. Wellershoff), or the "disenfranchisement of art" (A. Danto).[39] In fact, Mukařovský's revision of aesthetic theory can already be seen as an important stage in this development.[40]

The search for a radical delimitation of the aesthetic sphere has had two major consequences. One is a far-reaching cultural dehierarchization; the other, surprising and unforeseen, consequence, is what could be called a pan-aestheticization.[41] Both, seemingly contradictory, developments can be seen as two sides of the same coin.[42] If art and life no longer occupy different planes of cultural hierarchy, then art is no longer a transcendent realm but another social practice. As a result, it has to establish new sources of authority. This leads to an interesting trajectory: (1) because the aesthetic is said to mask power, the authority of the aesthetic has to be unmasked, deconstructed, or subverted; (2) to counter the potential loss of cultural distinction resulting from the radical dehierarchization, art (as well as the institutions of criticism and academic scholarship) need a new marker of significance; (3) this new marker of significance can only come from one of the remaining areas of cultural authority such as the realm of political commitment.[43] Ironically, however, this extension of the sphere of the political cannot leave the political unaffected. It is contaminated, so to speak, by the aesthetic and this, in turn, leads to an aestheticization of politics. Aestheticization of politics means that politics is no longer authorized by a systematic analysis of the political, social, or economic system but by privileged forms of cultural representation. The attempt to overcome the separation between aesthetics and politics thus has a paradoxical effect. Since both aesthetics and politics are delimited, the boundaries between them become permeable. The political extends into the aesthetic dimension but the delimitation also works the other way round: the aesthetic dimension also extends into the sphere of the political and transforms it into cultural performance, that is, into an aesthetic object.

The major reason for the new revisionism's reluctance to consider questions of aesthetics is not merely a disagreement over aesthetic values. If it were, one only would have to replace one set of values with another. The actual disagreement is one about the function literary texts or other aesthetic objects have (or should have) in society. To accept aesthetics as a central term would mean to accept the premise of non-identity, while the whole point of the revisionist project is to erase the difference between politics and aesthetics, so that literary texts can have a direct political function and the profession of literary criticism can be redefined as political work. In contrast, I have argued (1) that the difference between the two realms cannot be erased and that attempts to do so only lead to exactly the opposite result: not to a politicization of aesthetics but to an aestheticization of politics, a restaging of politics through imaginary role-plays of self-empowerment, and (2) that it is a case of muddled thinking to assume that an object can only have "progressive" political functions, if it is "de-aestheticized." Instead, I would argue that the only meaningful way in which aesthetic objects can have social or political functions is as aesthetic objects that make use of the special communicative possibilities created by the taking of an aesthetic attitude. If the new revisionism is beginning to rediscover and reclaim aesthetics, as some recent developments seem to indicate, then I would therefore strongly support this attempt. Such a recovery is to be supported on professional grounds, because the concept of the aesthetic, as I have tried to argue in this essay, must be seen as an indispensable category for cultural studies. But, if one wants to, it is also to be supported on political grounds, for only in this way can the growing aestheticization of politics be grasped, which is one consequence of the current conflation of the political and the aesthetic.

Notes

1. Two recently published handbooks illustrate the matter. The second edition of *Critical Terms for Literary Study*, edited by Frank Lentricchia and Thomas McLaughlin, contains 28 entries on such terms as representation, writing, discourse, unconscious, rhetoric, ideology, diversity, race, class, gender, and ethics, but none on aesthetics. *The Columbia Dictionary of Modern Literary and Cultural Criticism*, edited by Joseph Childers and Gary Hentzi, contains more than 450 entries but, again, none on aesthetics. In its stead, we find an entry on "Aesthetic Ideology." In the same line, Donald Pease states categorically: "As Terry Eagleton has observed, the aesthetic should be understood as ideological in the Althusserian sense that it produces a subject for ideology" (144). As Eagleton himself makes clear, however, he only deals with a certain—idealist—tradition within aesthetics, just as he leaves no doubt on the other hand that he is also arguing against the reduction of the

aesthetic to nothing but a bourgeois ideology. In this sense, the title of the German trans-lation—*Ästhetik. Die Geschichte ihrer Ideologie* (Aesthetics: A History of its Ideology)—is more fitting than that of the English original, *The Ideology of the Aesthetic*. Generally, the broaden-ing of Eagleton's argument to a generalized dismissal of "the aesthetic" must be seen as reductive even in the light of Eagleton's own argument.

2. Ulrich Schödlbauer: "Wer heute Ästhetik betreibt, seziert einen Leichnam" (33).

3. See, for example, Richard Brodhead's excellent study of the redefinition of Ameri-can literature through the idea of specifically literary values in the nineteenth century in his *The School of Hawthorne*. As Brodhead argues convincingly, this redefinition was actively supported by the publisher James T. Fields, who looked for an argument to sell Ameri-can literature on the basis of new value assumptions.

4. The dissertation, submitted in 1972, has the title *Ästhetische Theorie und literaturwissen-schaftliche Methode* ("Aesthetic Premises and Literary Interpretation"). In the field of American Studies, it was one of the first books that questioned the seemingly self-evident authority of New Critical literary and aesthetic norms and drew attention to their historical relativity.

5. This raises the interesting question of the relation of current critical theory and a rich, sustained tradition of Marxist aesthetics. Rightly, John Guillory reminds us: "In the context of critical theory, however, it may be surprising to some that the concept of the aesthetic was never rejected within the Marxist tradition, the very body of theory which cultural conservatives are likely to blame for the current critique of aesthetics" (273). Thus, "the arguments for dismissing the aesthetic do not derive from Marxist theory" (274). However, since Guillory does not have a concept for distinguishing the politics of tradi-tional Marxist theory from that of the current cultural radicalism, he can only register the fact "that the refusal of the aesthetic is an epistemic feature of current critical practice, constituting a consensus powerful enough to enlist in an alliance of 'left' critiques even the form of left critique—Marxist theory—historically sympathetic to aesthetics" (274).

6. A note on terminology: In the following discussion, I shall use the term "new revi-sionism" as a broad umbrella term for the description of the movement toward a revision of literary and cultural history, including canon revision, whereas the term "cultural radical-ism" refers to a radical analysis of Western societies, shared by various approaches from New Historicism and Cultural Materialism, to race, class, and gender studies and post-colonial studies in which the primary source of power is no longer seen as political insti-tutions but cultural forms. For a more detailed analysis of cultural radicalism, see my essay on "The Humanities in the Age of Expressive Individualism and Cultural Radicalism."

7. Thus, for a long time, to deal with film usually meant to compare the literary source and filmic version—a comparison that always led to the same result, namely the claim that the film failed to match the complexity of the literary text. Again, the result con-firmed the starting premise.

8. Other instances of such a confusion of the aesthetic with a particular historical manifestation of it include the equation of the aesthetic with taste or refinement, its re-duction to aestheticism or the superficial equation of aesthetics with elitism—superficial, because, obviously, working-class culture or popular culture also have an aesthetic dimen-sion and, hence, their own aesthetics.

9. Cf. Barbara Herrnstein Smith's characterization of this tradition: "This special value, often referred to as the text's 'essential *literary* value,' or its 'value *as* a work of literature,'

is sometimes said to reside in the text's purely 'formal' as opposed to 'material' qualities, or in its 'structure' as opposed to its 'meaning,' or in its 'underlying meaning' as opposed to any obvious 'theme,' 'subject,' or ostensible 'message'" ("Value/Evaluation," 179).

10. The pragmatist premises of the concept of aesthetic attitude are clarified by Jerome Stolnitz: "An attitude is a way of directing and controlling our perception. We never see or hear everything in our environment indiscriminately. Rather, we 'pay attention' to some things, whereas we apprehend others only dimly or hardly at all. Thus attention is selective—it concentrates on some features of our surroundings and ignores others" ("The Aesthetic Attitude," 78).

11. It is hard to provide an adequate translation of the philosophical concept of "sinnliche Erkenntnis." "Sensory" is too empiricist and downplays the aspect of a meaningful, transformative experience in which a synthesis of sense impressions leads to a form of knowledge not to be gained through reason; "sensuous" bears connotations of sensuality which are not intended at all, in fact, are considered a perversion of aesthetic experience. For a succinct summary of the emergence of the concept of the aesthetic see Jürgen Peper: "The history of this concept begins, as is well known, with Alexander Gottlieb Baumgarten's book *Aesthetika* (1750). The Greek term *aisthetike* (*téchne*), which means the study of sensuous perception, designates for Baumgarten a newly planned branch of epistemology. Alongside the traditional *cognitio intellectiva*, he places a newly defined *cognitio sensitiva*. While maintaining its previous function of supplying the rational faculties of cognition with sensuous data, it now gains an intrinsic value as the source of a prerational grasp of reality, ascribed by Baumgarten especially to art and poetry. This emphasis on art and poetry determined today's use of the term 'aesthetic.' It is important, however, to keep in mind the epistemological core" (294). "Baumgarten's specification of *cognitio sensitiva* as aesthetic signals the disintegration of the Platonic ideal unity of the true, the good and the beautiful. In fact, poetry and the fine arts now preclude the intellectual grasp of reason (*cognitio intellectiva*). Kant's three *Critiques* provide us, then, with a systematized expression of this division of classical Reason into the spheres of science, morality, and art" (295).

12. Consequently, it makes no sense to be "against" aesthetics, since the aesthetic attitude is part and parcel of daily life. Implicitly, Dewey's pragmatist shift from a philosophy of art or beauty to a view of the aesthetic as everyday social practice also undermines the equation of the aesthetic with the idealist project of subjectivation which forms one of the bases of the current radical critique of the ideology of the aesthetic. If the aesthetic is part of everyday life, it is also part of a conflictual, open-ended negotiation and staging of identity-formation that is marked by inherent instability.

13. Raymond Williams therefore praises Mukařovský as "the best representative" (152) of an approach in which the aesthetic is seen as a function of practice. One of the reasons for the evasive nature of bourgeois aesthetics which Williams deplores ("Aesthetic Theory is the main instrument of this evasion") is that the potential of Mukařovský's approach has been disregarded: "Mukařovský's important work is best seen as the penultimate stage of the critical dissolution of the specializing and controlling categories of bourgeois aesthetic theory. Almost all the original advantages of this theory have been quite properly, indeed necessarily, abandoned" (153). Williams calls this process "necessary," because as a form of social practice, aesthetics is reenacting a growing division of labor.

14. In his essay on functions in architecture, Mukařovský claims that wherever other functions, for whatever reasons, are weakened, dropped, or changed, the aesthetic function may take on an increased importance; he then insists that, in principle, "there is not an object which cannot become its vehicle or, conversely, an object which necessarily has to be its vehicle. If certain objects are produced with the direct intention of aesthetic effectiveness and are adapted formally to this intention, it by no means follows necessarily that they cannot lose this function partially or entirely, for example, because of a change in time, space, or milieu" ("On the Problem of Functions in Architecture," 244). The passage demonstrates that Mukařovský's aesthetic theory, in contrast to other forms of aesthetics, has no problem accounting for changes in the critical assessment and evaluation of an aesthetic object.

15. Cf. Mukařovský: "The aesthetic is, in itself, neither a real property of an object nor is it explicitly connected to some of its properties" (Aesthetic Function, 18).

16. Cf. the summary of Mukařovský's position by Raymond Williams in *Marxism and Literature*: "Art is not a special kind of object but one in which the aesthetic function, usually mixed with other functions, is *dominant*. Art, with other things (landscapes and dress, most evidently), gives aesthetic pleasure, but this cannot be transliterated as a sense of beauty or a sense of perceived form, since while these are central in the aesthetic function they are historically and socially variable, and in all real instances concrete. At the same time the aesthetic function is 'not an epiphenomenon of other functions' but a 'codeterminant of human reaction to reality'" (153).

17. Cf. Mukařovský's description: "The limits of the province of aesthetics, therefore, are not provided by reality itself, and are exceedingly changeable. . . . We have all encountered people for whom anything can acquire an aesthetic function and, conversely, people for whom the aesthetic function exists only to a minimal degree. Even from our own personal experience we know that the borderline between the aesthetic and the extra-aesthetic . . . fluctuates for each person according to his age, changes in health, and even momentary moods" (Aesthetic Function, 3). In his essay on architecture, Mukařovský employs images of extreme plasticity in order to determine the shifting relations between aesthetic function and other functions. He describes the aesthetic function in terms of air and darkness which creep into a room and fill out the spaces that have been vacated by the taking away of an object or the turning off of the light.

18. Or, to draw on Mukařovský's argument: as an—in comparison with other functions—"empty" function, the aesthetic function depends on other functions to manifest itself.

19. The recent exhibition "Sensation: Young British Artists From the Saatchi Collection" at the Brooklyn Museum of Art, which created such heated public debates, is only the latest illustration of this project of contemporary art to transform the conspicuously profane into art. However, without a sacred or other reference still implied, this "profanization" would make no sense and would be pointless.

20. Harold Rosenberg was one of the first critics to describe this development. Cf. his description of the movement toward the "de-aestheticization" of art in the 1960s: "Ideally, art *povera* strives to reach beyond art to the wonder-working object, place ("environment"), or event. It extends the dada-surrealist quest for the revelatory found object into unlimited categories of strange responses. Redefining art as the process of the artist

or his materials, it dissolves all limitations on the kind of substances out of which art can be constructed. Anything—breakfast food, a frozen lake, film footage—is art, either as is or tampered with, through being chosen as fetish" (37). As Rosenberg indicates, de-aestheticization paves the way for re-aestheticization. It does not do away with aesthetics, it paves the way for a new aesthetics.

21. In his essay "Die Bedeutung der Ästhetik" (The Importance of Aesthetics), reprinted in the collection *Kunst. Poetik, Semiotik*, Mukařovský gives the example of gymnastics. As long as our perception of physical exercise is dominated by practical functions (gaining strength, strengthening certain muscles, etc.), we will focus on the aspects that help achieve those goals and will judge the single exercise by how well it helps to realize the desired result. Once the aesthetic function becomes dominant, on the other hand, the exercise takes on interest in itself as a performance or spectacle. The various movements, the sequence of movements, and even the "useless" details of the periods between different exercise may now become objects of attention for their own sake. The significatory dimension of reality is foregrounded and the sign is of interest *sui generis*. Even the "wrong" movements may now be of interest as movements, not just as "wrong" movements.

22. Jürgen Peper therefore describes the aesthetic function as "experimental and experiential epistemology" (296). Thus, if an aesthetic object has a political function, then on communicative, "experimental" conditions of its own.

23. In this sense, the aesthetic function becomes dominant when the referential function is bracketed. There are two main reasons why this may occur: (1) the gradual loss of other functions, such as, for example, in the gradual aestheticization of objects of material culture which have lost their practical function, and (2), at the other pole, the possibility that the referential function is still being explored, which can also result in the dominance of the aesthetic function. In his essay on architecture, Mukařovský describes these possible forms of relation with reference to the aesthetic and the practical function. The aesthetic function, he argues, not only becomes dominant when practical functions disappear. It accompanies a process of constant shifts in the hierarchy of practical functions and, thus, can also have the effect of anticipating future practical functions by providing a possibility of articulation before these functions are able to gain any cultural or political acceptance. (In Critical Theory, this would be called the utopian function of art.) In this way, the aesthetic function plays an important role in historical development and can be seen as one important manifestation of it.

24. From this perspective, claims for the autonomy of art are heuristic claims (e.g. for a temporary bracketing of the referential or practical function) in order to allow art to do its cultural work on conditions of its own. Often, discussions of the "autonomy" or "disinterestedness"-premise ignore this heuristic dimension, "mistaking the possibility of a specific experience called 'aesthetic' by a temporary bracketing of exoteric purposes for an ontological claim of autonomous existence" (Grabes, 1995, 160). In order to emphasize the heuristic dimension of the temporary bracketing of referential or other functions, Peper redefines autonomy as the "free play" of reason in a specific sense: "Thus, the pre-rational cognitive powers could not obtain free play (autonomy) except through the bracketing of reason (*cognitio intellectiva*)" (297). This "free play" is an *epoché* [in the phenomenological sense of a temporary bracketing of cognition and knowledge] for a limited time, prompted by scepticism about the higher, generalizing faculties of cogni-

tion, and motivated heuristically" (299). It may be used for purposes of subjectivation and even subjection but, as many examples of contemporary art demonstrate, also to subvert such subjectivation. Cf., for example, Jon Simon's chapter "Transgression and Aesthetics" in his book on Foucault, in which the aesthetic is discussed as a form that can promote new modes of subjectivity. This refutes the argument, employed by Pease and others, that the aesthetic is per se a mode of subjection or ideological subject formation: "Moreover Foucault's support for the new social movements of marginal groups such as women, gays and radical ecologists is said to rest on 'an aesthetic subject' which highlights those aspects of subjectivity excluded by modernity, i.e. 'pre-rational embodied otherness,' as well as 'spontaneity and expressiveness'" (79).

25. Peper thus states that "aesthetic effects can only unfold against and into the non-aesthetic. . . . The aesthetic pleasure in the free play of cognitive powers is most intense where—far from empty arbitrariness—it has to be gained within a given conceptual structure, making us aware of this level of cognition as the reflexive play of forces" (314–15).

26. It should be added, however, that "new" interpretation does not necessarily mean politically advanced. It is part of the freedom opened up by art that the disagreement with reality can also come from the opposite side of the political spectrum. Thus, art is neither "progressive" by definition, nor reactionary. As Robert Hellenga points out in his essay "What Is A Literary Experience *Like*?", it merely opens up new possibilities of articulation. The term "aesthetic function" refers to a specific condition of communication ("Wirkungsbedingung"). It does not yet tell us anything about "real" functions art may have had in history (something only a detailed historical analysis can clarify), only about the specific communicative conditions for these functions.

27. When I first presented this paper in the United States, one of the defensive reactions was that Mukařovský has long been known and was now considered "old hat." Obviously, however, his significance and potential contribution to current debates has not been fully grasped by this form of "cutting edge" criticism, for otherwise it would not be understandable how the traditional conflation of aesthetic function and aesthetic value can continue. By disregarding the concept of aesthetic function and conflating it with aesthetic value, the current revisionism can claim that aesthetics, by concepts such as "disinterestedness," denies that the aesthetic has a function. The absurd consequences are pointed out in Guillory's discussion of Barbara Herrnstein Smith's counterargument in her *Contingencies of Value*: "For Smith the refutation of the traditional denial by aesthetics of the utility of the artwork is surprisingly simple: one only has to reassert the artwork's purpose or 'use'; but that use turns out be [sic] nothing less than all the *uses* to which the work may be put as an object not generically different—with respect to use—from any other object. And of course, one cannot predict or limit the uses to which any object may be put" (291). Interestingly enough, Smith has a footnote in her *Contingencies of Value* in which she acknowledges Mukařovský only to dismiss him: "Monroe Beardsley's 'instrumentalist' theory of aesthetic value in *Aesthetics: Problems in the Philosophy of Criticism* (New York, 1958), pp. 524–576, and Mukařovský's otherwise quite subtle explorations of these questions in *Aesthetic Function, Norm and Value as Social Facts* (Prague, 1936), trans. Mark E. Suino (Ann Arbor, Mich., 1970), do not altogether escape the confinements and circularities of formalist conceptions of, respectively, 'aesthetic experience' and 'aesthetic function'" (192n.). It would be interesting indeed to learn more

about what aspects of Mukařovský's argument Smith considers "subtle" and how this is related to Mukařovský's concept of aesthetic function.

28. This, in fact, may provide a possible explanation for the striking absence of the term aesthetics in Frank Lentricchia's representative handbook, *Critical Terms for Literary Study.* Most likely, the editors Lentricchia and Thomas McLaughlin assumed that the phenomenon of the aesthetic was covered by the entry "Value/Evaluation." Similarly, in his introduction to the volume *Aesthetics and Ideology,* George Levine undermines his own laudable project of—to quote the title of his introduction—"Reclaiming the Aesthetic" and regaining a sense of its "central importance" (17) by equating the aesthetic with "questions of literary value" and fighting contemporary criticism's "reluctance to engage the question of literary value" (13).

29. To avoid a possible misunderstanding: these two descriptions—skyline as lighted and colored volumes; subway map as hieroglyphic pattern—are, of course, not the only possible ways in which the object can be seen aesthetically. Depending on different aesthetics, different aspects will be emphasized. Dewey's description, for example, clearly reflects his own latently organicist aesthetics which I have analyzed in more detail in my essay on "Pragmatism and Aesthetic Experience."

30. This tacit assumption about the function of the aesthetic will, in turn, be embedded in a specific view of society and interpretation of history. Every aesthetic judgment therefore implies overt or covert assumptions about society, and every aesthetics is at the same time also a philosophy of history *in nuce.*

31. For a detailed discussion of the logical dependence of every interpretation of an aesthetic object on underlying concepts of reality, society, and the specific role of literature within this concept, see my study of the constitutive role of aesthetic premises in *Huck Finn* criticism (*Ästhetisches Vorverständnis und Methode*). For a discussion of the theoretical dilemma produced by the unwillingness of the new revisionism to openly discuss the issues of aesthetic function and aesthetic value, see my review of Jonathan Arac's otherwise excellent book, *"Huckleberry Finn" as Idol and Target,* "'Huckleberry Finn': Liberating an American Classic from Hypercanonization."

32. The canon debate which has brought the issue of aesthetics on the agenda again is really a debate about different concepts of what constitutes an aesthetic object.

33. Cf. Rachel Brownstein's description of the doubleness of a novel's heroine: "In one sense this doubleness of a novel heroine is perfectly obvious. Every good reader recognizes a heroine as a representation of an actual woman and, at the same time, as an element in a work of art. She does not regard a woman in a novel as if she were one of her acquaintances; she experiences how the context of the fiction limits a character's freedom and determines her style. . . . The reader identifies with Elizabeth, and as she does so accepts the rules involved in being Elizabeth, and at the same time she sees how the rules determine that Elizabeth be as she is—not merely the rules of the society Jane Austen's novel represents, but also the rules that govern the representation of it, the novel" (xxiii).

34. In his entry on "representation" in the critical handbook *Critical Terms for Literary Study,* W. J. T. Mitchell speaks of "the complex interaction between playful fantasy and serious reality in all forms of representation" (12).

35. In summarizing prior work on the psychology of reading, J. A. Appleyard speaks of "the double state of mind we experience by immersing ourselves in a work of literature; we are both 'participants' and 'spectators'" (39) at the same time.

36. On the complex and complicated processes of transfer that are set in motion by the perception or reconstitution of an object as aesthetic see my essay on "Pragmatism and Aesthetic Experience."

37. Such a history would have to include, especially in view of recent developments, instances of a homogenization, if not essentializing, of imaginary communities not only on the basis of "constructed" identities but, even more so, desired identities.

38. For a theoretical debate of this movement, see Hal Foster's anthology "The Anti-Aesthetic."

39. Fittingly, a recent German anthology of cutting-edge comments on aesthetics by leading poststructuralists and postmodern thinkers is called *Aisthesis: Wahrnehmung heute oder Perspektiven einer anderen Ästhetik* (Aisthesis: Perception Today, or, Perspectives of a Radically Different Aesthetics), emphasizing the purely physical and sensory dimension against the traditional idea of "sensuous knowledge."

40. Cf. the introductory justification of his approach in his essay on Aesthetic Function, Norm, and Aesthetic Value: "Modern art, beginning with Naturalism does not ignore an area of reality when choosing its subject matter and, beginning with Cubism and similar movements in other branches of art, no restriction is placed on the choice of materials or technique. All of the foregoing provides sufficient evidence that even those items which, in the traditional aesthetic view, would not have been credited with aesthetic potential, can now become aesthetic facts" (Aesthetic Function 2). Reflecting the fact that Mukařovský's approach was decisively influenced by the aesthetic revolution ushered in by the art of modernism, Raymond Williams writes, "Mukařovský's important work is best seen as the penultimate stage of the critical dissolution of the specializing and controlling categories of bourgeois aesthetic theory," and then adds, "Mukařovský, from within this tradition, in effect destroyed it" (153–54). The close, inextricable link between the history of art, modernity, and the history of aesthetics is also the subject of Luc Ferry's study *Homo Aestheticus*.

41. In fact, one might claim that, far from being discarded, the aesthetic, at present, has had something of a comeback in contemporary thought: "From the closeness of deconstruction's affirmative 'freeplay' to the 'free play of the imagination' in traditional aesthetics, to the aestheticization of the ethical in postmodern philosophy; from the revival of the sublime to the aestheticising of the 'Lebenswelt'; from the recourse to modernist collage in New Historicism, and to modernist temporality in *post-histoire* anti-utopian visions, and from the poetic quality of pre-symbolic women's writing to the recent notion of culture as a self-deconstructive text—postmodernism and anti-foundationalism has, wittingly or unwittingly, come extremely close to the sphere that traditionally bears its foundation within itself: the aesthetic" (Grabes, 1995, 297).

42. This can explain the, at first sight, puzzling and seemingly contradictory fact that a contemporary philosopher of art such as Richard Shusterman can, to quote the titles of two of his essays, speak of the "The End of Aesthetic Experience" and, at the same time, draw attention to an "aesthetic turn" in contemporary thought in his essay "Postmodernism and the Aesthetic Turn."

43. For a more detailed analysis of this process see my essay "Radical Aesthetics." As Shusterman points out in his essay "Postmodernism and the Aesthetic Turn," in contemporary philosophy aesthetics takes the place of reason. He then goes on to ask "whether aesthetics or politics will inherit the primacy that philosophy has lost" (620). Actually, however, this is not an either-or issue. As a result of the delimitation of the aesthetic, the two are converging in unforeseen ways.

Works Cited

Appleyard, J. A. *Becoming a Reader: The Experience of Fiction from Childhood to Adulthood.* New York: Cambridge University Press, 1991.

Arac, Jonathan. *"Huckleberry Finn" as Idol and Target: The Functions of Criticism in Our Time.* Madison: University of Wisconsin Press, 1997.

Barck, Karlheinz et. al. *Aisthesis. Wahrnehmung heute oder Perspektiven einer anderen Ästhetik.* Leipzig: Reclam, 1990.

Barthelme, Donald. "The Glass Mountain," *City Life.* New York: Pocket Books, 1976. 67–74.

Brodhead, Richard H. *The School of Hawthorne.* New York: Oxford University Press, 1986.

Brownstein, Rachel M. *Becoming a Heroine: Reading about Women in Novels.* New York: Penguin, 1982.

Childers, Joseph, and Gary Hentzi, eds. *The Columbia Dictionary of Modern Literary Cultural Criticism.* New York: Columbia University Press, 1995.

Danto, Arthur C. *The Philosophical Disenfranchisement of Art.* New York: Columbia University Press, 1986.

Dewey, John. *Art as Experience: The Later Works, 1925–1953.* Volume 10. 1934. Carbondale: Southern Illinois Press, 1987.

Ferry, Luc. *Homo Aestheticus.* Paris: Éditions Grasset et Fasquella, 1990.

Eagleton, Terry. *The Ideology of the Aesthetic.* London: Blackwell, 1990.

————. *Ästhetik. Die Geschichte ihrer Ideologie.* Stuttgart: Metzler, 1994.

Fluck, Winfried. *Ästhetische Theorie und literaturwissenschaftliche Methode. Eine Untersuchung ihres Zusammenhangs am Beispiel der amerikanischen Huck Finn-Kritik.* Stuttgart: Metzler, 1975.

————. "Radical Aesthetics." *REAL: Yearbook of Research in English and American Literature.* Vol. 10, *Aesthetics and Contemporary Discourse.* Ed. Herbert Grabes. Tübingen: Narr, 1994. 31–47.

————. "The Humanities in the Age of Expressive Individualism and Cultural Radicalism." *Cultural Critique* 40 (1998): 49–71.

————. "Pragmatism and Aesthetic Experience." *REAL. Yearbook of Research in English and American Literature.* Vol. 15, *Pragmatism and Literary Studies.* Ed. Winfried Fluck. Tübingen: Narr, 1999. 227–242.

————. "'Huckleberry Finn': Liberating an American Classic from Hypercanonization." *Annals of Scholarship* 13 (1999): 123–26.

Foster, Hal, ed. *The Anti-Aesthetic. Essays on Postmodern Culture.* Port Townsend, Wash.: Bay Press, 1983.

Grabes, Herbert. "Errant Specialisms: The Recent Historicist Turn Away From Aesthetics." *REAL. Yearbook of Research in English and American Literature.* Vol. 11, *The Historical and Political Turn in Literary Studies.* Ed. Winfried Fluck. Tübingen: Narr, 1995. 159–72.

————. "Introduction to New Developments in Literary Aesthetics," *Anglistentag 1994 Graz.* Ed. Wolfgang Riehle and Hugo Keiper. Tübingen: Niemeyer, 1995. 297–98.

Guillory, John. *Cultural Capital. The Problem of Literary Canon Formation.* Chicago: University of Chicago Press, 1993.

Hellenga, Robert R. "What Is a Literary Experience *Like?*" *New Literary History* 14 (1982–1983): 105–115.

Iser, Wolfgang. "Representation: A Performative Act." *Prospecting: From Reader Response to Literary Anthropology.* Baltimore, Md.: Johns Hopkins University Press, 1989. 236–48.

Jameson, Fredric. *The Political Unconscious. Narrative as a Socially Symbolic Act.* Ithaca, N.Y.: Cornell University Press, 1981.

Lentricchia, Frank, and Thomas McLaughlin, eds. *Critical Terms for Literary Study.* Chicago: University of Chicago Press, 1990.

Levine, George. "Introduction. Reclaiming the Aesthetic," *Aesthetics and Ideology.* New Brunswick, N.J.: Rutgers University Press, 1994. 1–28.

Mitchell, W. J. T. "Representation." *Critical Terms for Literary Study.* Ed. Frank Lentricchia and Thomas McLaughlin. Chicago: University of Chicago Press, 1990. 11–22.

Mukařovský, Jan. *Kapitel aus der Ästhetik.* Frankfurt/M.: Suhrkamp, 1966.

————. "Aesthetic Function, Norm and Value as Social Facts." Trans. and ed. Mark E. Suino. *Michigan Slavic Contributions,* No. 3. Ann Arbor: University of Michigan, 1970.

————. "On the Problem of Functions in Architecture." *Structure, Sign, and Function: Selected Essays by Jan Mukařovský.* Trans. and ed. John Burbank and Peter Steiner. New Haven, Conn.: Yale University Press, 1978. 236–250.

————. "Zum Problem der Funktionen in der Architektur." *Zeitschrift für Semiotik* 5 (1983): 217–28.

————. *Kunst, Poetik, Semiotik.* Frankfurt/M.: Suhrkamp, 1989.

Pease, Donald E. "*Martin Eden* and the Limits of the Aesthetic Experience," *boundary 2* 25 (1988): 139–60.

Peper, Jürgen. "The Aesthetic as a Democratizing Principle." *REAL: Yearbook of Research in English and American Literature.* Vol. 10, *Aesthetics and Contemporary Discourse.* Ed. H. Grabes. Tübingen: Narr, 1994. 293–323.

Rosenberg, Harold. "De-aestheticization." *The De-definition of Art. Action Art to Pop to Earthworks.* New York: Horizon, 1972.

Ross, Stephen David, ed. *Art and Its Significance. An Anthology of Aesthetic Theory.* 3rd ed. Albany: State University of New York Press, 1994.

Schödlbauer, Ulrich. "Ästhetische Erfahrung." *Erkenntnis der Literatur. Theorien, Konzepte, Methoden der Literaturwissenschaft.* Ed. Dietrich Harth and Peter Gebhardt. Stuttgart: Metzler, 1982. 33–55.

Seltzer, Mark. *Henry James and the Art of Power.* Ithaca, N.Y.: Cornell University Press, 1984.

Shusterman, Richard. "Postmodernism and the Aesthetic Turn." *Poetics Today* 10 (1989): 605–22.

————. "The End of Aesthetic Experience." *Working Paper, J.F. Kennedy-Institut für Nordamerikastudien, No. 91.* Berlin: Freie Universität Berlin, 1996.

Simons, Jon. "Transgression and Aesthetics." *Foucault and the Political.* London: Routledge, 1995. 68–80.

Smith, Barbara Herrnstein. *Contingencies of Value. Alternative Perspectives for Critical Theory.* Cambridge, Mass.: Harvard University Press, 1988.

——. "Value/Evaluation." *Critical Terms for Literary Study.* Ed. Frank Lentricchia and Thomas McLaughlin. Chicago: University of Chicago Press, 1990. 177–185.

Stolnitz, Jerome. "The Aesthetic Attitude." In: *Aesthetics: The Big Questions,* ed. Carolyn Korsmeyer. Oxford: Blackwell, 1998. 78–83.

Warshow, Robert. *The Immediate Experience.* New York: Doubleday, 1962.

Wellershoff, Dieter. *Die Auflösung des Kunstbegriffs.* Frankfurt/M.: Suhrkamp, 1976.

Williams, Raymond. *The Long Revolution.* Harmondsworth, U.K.: Penguin, 1961.

——. "Aesthetic and Other Situations." *Marxism and Literature.* New York: Oxford University Press, 1977. 151–57.

——. *Culture and Society, 1780–1950.* 1958. New York: Harper, 1996.

The Resistance to Cultural Studies

JOHN CARLOS ROWE

> It is a recurrent strategy of any anxiety to defuse what it considers
> threatening by magnification or minimization, by attributing to it
> claims to power of which it is bound to fall short.
>
> Paul de Man, "The Resistance to Theory"

We have done a great deal over the past thirty years to establish the theoretical
and practical contexts for exciting multidisciplinary work in the humanities and
social sciences, then denounced these aims by reducing them to a single school
or movement that many fear threatens accepted epistemologies. I am talking about
the "cultural studies" that many scholars criticize, condemning its impossible
scope, failure to define its key terms, lack of theoretical self-consciousness, historical ignorance, the "easiness" of its topics for teaching and research, obsession
with "relevance," reflex treatment of "race, class, and gender," and refusal to read
carefully. What I propose in this essay is a treatment of each of these complaints,
in order to define better "cultural studies" and to interpret the various ideological motives behind these criticisms. My definition of cultural studies is intended
to serve as a model or ideal, rather than as a defense of any specific example of
work that identifies itself with cultural studies.

It is true that cultural studies sets its practitioners the impossible task of
articulating those conditions whereby cultural conventions and values are accepted. Freud used the term "reality-principle," Althusser used "ideology," and
Foucault the "episteme" to refer to the complex processes and systems whereby
people in a given time and place agree to certain demonstrably relative truths.
What constitutes "culture" or "society" for Freud, Althusser, and Foucault is
never something that any of these theorists presumes to define but rather what
manifests itself in the social practices of people who accept the term; for instance, nineteenth-century U.S. culture, the Victorian Age, the Second Empire, fin de siècle, and so forth.

For these theorists, "culture" or "society" is the horizon of interpretation. It
is the ability of these theorists to go beyond specific disciplinary practices to
understand the demonstrable, working cohesiveness of culture that makes them
continuing influences on our work in the humanities and social sciences, and they

105

are certainly important predecessors for many contemporary cultural critics. But it is also fair to say that Freud, Althusser, and Foucault were products of modern European cultural practices, which according to their respective analyses were often structured around bourgeois individualism. And although each contributed importantly to the critique of the coherent philosophical subject and attendant myths, each was celebrated, along with many other modern intellectual "geniuses" as a singular font of cultural knowledge. Cultural studies abandons the impossible notion that any single intellectual, however unusual and brilliant, can possibly command the many different knowledges necessary to analyze basic conditions for prevailing cultural phenomena. Cultural studies must be a collaborative scholarly project or suite of different projects. Such collaborative scholarly practices are still very difficult for many of us in the humanities and some of the social sciences to understand in practical terms, but cultural studies is not calling for every one of its practitioners to comprehend "culture" in a comprehensive and transdisciplinary manner. Cultural studies does ask us to think of our different scholarly projects in relationship to each other by way of the larger "horizon" of the specific "cultural" reality it helps us understand.

Another frequently heard complaint is that cultural critics fail to "define their terms" and therefore lack intellectual foundations. In recent years, I have attended several lectures in which those critical of cultural studies have offered their own, usually philologically oriented, accounts of the historical and social vagaries of the term "culture."[1] The customary point is that "culture" is so relative to its sociohistorical circumstances as to be impossible to define, which leads these critics to the conclusion that "cultural study" is thus impossible. The model for "study" is, of course, the analytical tradition of modernity, in which epistemic value depends upon transhistorical truth and universal validity. But cultural critics aren't as interested in providing a categorical and totalized definition of "culture" as they are in understanding how this term designates certain practices and values for a specific society. In other words, "culture" may well refer to a totality for those nineteenth-century British who accept the designation "Victorian culture," but the cultural critic wants to look primarily at the social, human, and natural consequences of that assumption, avoiding totalizing assumptions in his or her own work. Defining the term "culture" is beside the point; "culture" is whatever people happen to take it to be at a particular time and in a particular place. What matters is how that term works to organize diverse experiences and information.

The complaint that cultural critics do not "define their terms" is linked with the charge that they "lack" theoretical "self-consciousness," or a "metatheory." After all, if cultural critics knew what they were studying, they would know it as a consequence of processes that are articulable as "theory." Therefore, cultural studies should respect the "higher" authority of critical theory, whose transhistorical perspective enables it to adjudicate historically and culturally disparate claims.[2] Some cultural critics have responded to this charge by claiming that cultural studies is an eclectic, hybrid, unsystematic approach—indeed, it must have this improvisational quality because it claims to encompass such an enormous set of different subjects. I think this defense is mistaken because it reinforces complaints that cultural studies lacks a "proper object of study" and is primarily responsible for the "lack of a metatheory."

Jean-François Lyotard argued that one of the distinguishing characteristics of the "postmodern condition" is an "incredulity with respect to metanarratives." This is a corollary of his notion that postmodernity is marked by the breakdown of the "Grand Narratives" of Enlightenment and Emancipation that distinguished modernity.[3] Contemporary cultural studies, especially as it has been influenced by recent movements in the United States and Australia, differs from 1960s British Cultural Studies (of the sort done in Birmingham and Manchester, for example) by virtue of its incorporation of crucial concepts from poststructuralist theories. Cultural studies is not deconstruction, but it draws on such poststructuralist concepts as: the social construction of reality, the discursive construction of society, the "textualist" position generally, and thus the irreducibility of the signifier. As de Man puts the matter, "The resistance to theory is a resistance to the use of language about language."[4] Another instance of de Man's famous *doubles entendres*, this aphorism does not mean that the resistance to theory is a resistance to metalanguages in general. De Man means the opposite: the resistance to "theory" depends on the repression of the full consequences of the "linguistic condition"—that the "use of language about language" means there can never be a proper "metalanguage." It might be argued that these ideas constitute in their own right a "grand narrative" of postmodernity or poststructuralism.[5] Derrida's effort to substitute strategic interpretive terms—trace, differance, supplement, écriture, spectre—for foundational concepts or Kantian a prioris convinces me that he is using "non-concepts," as he terms them, despite claims by critics of deconstruction that such departures from Enlightenment rationality render such thought irrational or illogical.

Cultural studies also imagines its work taking place within a chain of signifiers whose "interruption" is itself part of the historical and social process.[6] Like "defining terms," theoretical self-consciousness in the sense of "stepping outside" that historical and semiotic process is just not possible, not because cultural critics are unself-conscious.[7] It is the postmodern condition, Lyotard argues, that is characterized by "little narratives," none of which can be made convincingly to "stand" as the governing narrative under which other little narratives might be ruled and/or generated. This is not the fault of "cultural critics," who are themselves products of such "postmodern" conditions; it is a consequence of the prevailing historical conditions for representation and interpretation. Under such circumstances, any claims made by cultural critics must be justified by a certain pragmatics of effect: What will this interpretation *do*, rather than: What does this interpretive schema explain? Whether this "action" takes place in an academic or wider social context, it is always *political*, so that there can be no "theory" or "metanarrative" apart from the action cultural critics take in conjunction with their ideas.[8] In response to the criticism that the "postmodern condition" refers only to very restricted historical circumstances and thus does not apply to the M'ing Dynasty in China, Milton's England, pre-Columbian North America, or Goethe's Germany, for example, the cultural critic's appropriate response should be that any of these eras or movements that preceded postmodernism are interpretable only within our present hermeneutic conditions.

The irreducible historicity of cultural studies is thus at considerable odds with what critics often term its supposed "historical ignorance." There are really two different issues in this criticism. On the one hand, scholars call attention to cultural studies' emphasis on the contemporary flotsam-and-jetsam of a thoroughly superficial (and very postmodern) world: comic books, women's fashion, grade-B movies, porno, sports, Harlequin romances, etc. On the other hand, these critics attack what Lauren Berlant terms the "tinny archive," by which phrase she refers to a prevailing sense that cultural studies isn't "serious" about its scholarship or the history behind its interpretive objects.[9]

Ranging from Jameson's characterization of postmodernity's retro-effects, its *faux* history, and irreducible "superficiality" to Neil Postman's complaint that we have lost a coherent public sphere and civic virtue, criticism of postmodernity's or cultural studies' "historical ignorance" often depends on nostalgia for Enlightenment rationality and its conception of "history" as a grand narrative.[10] Sometimes the archive the scholar must draw upon is "tinny," because other well-trained scholars haven't visited that library very often, if ever. When I started writing in the 1970s on U.S. cultural responses to the Vietnam War, there was virtually no serious scholarship on the topic. Today there is substantial work, but in those days I relied on popular journalism, bizarre historical and first-person accounts, gossip, and archives ranging from the Borgesian—taped testimonies of demobilized veterans stored "alphabetically" in a Navy Yard archive that measured the collection in miles—to the "classified."

Fashion and fad-driven as their phenomena often are, popular and mass culture may be even more crucially historical than other cultural products. Interestingly, it is often those scholars who elsewhere defend the "universal" values of canonical texts, ideas, or events who also criticize the "ahistorical" qualities of cultural studies. The "literary history" I was taught as an undergraduate and graduate student was primarily that of literary influences, literary movements, and the "intellectual history" that linked literature with other philosophical and aesthetic activities. My complaint about that education is that it was not sufficiently *historical*, in large part because it failed to take into account the larger political, social, and economic forces involved in such cultural production.[11]

One motive for criticizing cultural studies' lack of historical consciousness is to distinguish between important and fashionable historical phenomena. In "The

Resistance to Theory," de Man clearly valorizes literature as a linguistic modality that foregrounds the "rhetorical or tropological dimension of language," but he hedges his bets by claiming that this "literature (broadly conceived)" may only make more manifest linguistic functions "which can be revealed in any verbal event when it is read textually."[12] At the very moment de Man deconstructs the hierarchies of linguistic representation that the poststructuralist theory of signification topples, he reinstates new hierarchies, perhaps because of a proleptic resistance to cultural studies. Many scholars justifiably fear the ever-widening scope of the humanities and social sciences; the absence of criteria for "selecting" literary texts, historical events, philosophical problems, and sociological data is cause for alarm. But are we talking about an absence of such criteria or a *change* in the criteria themselves? As I suggested above, cultural critics must sometimes rely on archives drastically different from those consulted by scholars in nominally the same "periods" or "disciplines." In other cases, traditional prejudices against popular or mass cultural evidence prevent some scholars from recognizing its historicality. In work I completed recently on John Rollin Ridge's (Yellow Bird's) 1854 popular novel about the legendary California bandit, Joaquín Murieta, I found myself swamped with historical legends, texts, and data from several different historical registers: the history of the Cherokee tribe, its relations with the U.S. government, California in transition from Mexican to U.S. rule, the Gold Rush, Spanish and Latin American recyclings of the Murieta legend, and so forth.[13]

For these very reasons, my principles of historical and literary selection were crucial matters for me, uppermost in my mind from the moment I selected Ridge's text to understand better the cultural reception of the Mexican-American War. By contrast, the selection of an indisputable literary classic for interpretation— Henry James's *Portrait of a Lady* or *The Wings of the Dove*, for example—raises far fewer problems of basic selection, no matter what I am planning to do with the classic text. In writing about Ridge's *Life and Adventures of Joaquín Murieta*, I have to be constantly attentive to the larger historical and cultural purposes served by what I might term this cultural synecdoche than I would be in treating one of those novels by James because I know that my readers are likely to be complaining, "What's the point of reading about this old pot-boiler?" In short, the noncanonical text often places greater demands on the scholar to justify studying it. And since that justification rarely can be made in terms of the "universal value" of noncanonical or popular/mass market texts, then the argument must be profoundly, irreducibly historical.

The preceding remarks about the historicality of cultural studies allow me to treat quickly but effectively two other common objections: that the topics cultural critics choose to research and teach are easy and superficially relevant. There is nothing easy in trying to explain how and why Ridge's story of the Sonoran bandit, Joaquín Murieta, appealed both to Latin American miners, who were persecuted in and driven from the California goldfields, and to U.S. citizens eager to impose their cultural values in the new state of California. Although Ridge's text is lexically easier to understand than a novel by Henry James, its cultural and political contexts are at least as difficult to interpret. The cultural implications and origins of many popular and mass-audience texts are considerably *more difficult* to comprehend than those of canonical texts. In contemporary literary criticism, we often write about the intentional fallacy and about a textual unconscious that cannot be commanded by any author or even described in the most comprehensive account of the text's author-function, but we nevertheless have some confidence that a writer working in an established literary tradition possesses a high degree of self-consciousness regarding his or her sense of that tradition and how his or her work should ideally be situated in it. Such a general description applies as well to avant-garde, politically radical, and socially marginalized writers who wish to challenge fundamentally the terms of such a literary tradition.

Such "literary history" as Paul de Man once viewed as constituted by the dialectics of "Literary History and Literary Modernity" seems quite restricted (and restrictive) when measured against the theoretical and practical problems facing the cultural interpreter interested in explaining how and why *Titanic* was the largest grossing film of all time, Sylvester Stallone's "Rambo" character should have so captivated global audiences in the aftermath of the Vietnam War, or the social, ideological, and economic work done by the Book-of-the-Month Club or Harlequin romances.[14]

Then try *teaching* such materials to students who have been accustomed since grade school to distinguish between high and low cultural materials in terms of their relative seriousness and value. Students are often horrified, embarrassed, or downright angry to be studying texts that they otherwise consume happily and willingly but feel should not be part of the university's curriculum. Yet once they accept the immodest proposal that they should interpret seriously what they watch, read, listen to, not necessarily for its intrinsic or enduring value but for what it tells them about their culture and themselves, these students are excited, energized by literary, historical, philosophical, or social studies, often for the very first time.[15]

To be sure, this sounds much like the arguments made for teaching "relevant" materials that we used in challenging the curricula defended by our teachers in undergraduate and graduate programs around the country in the late 1960s. Another common criticism of cultural studies is: "We tried that in the Sixties, and it didn't work." Despite a handful of courses, often taught by graduate TAs, that experimented with new texts and topics, most humanities curricula in U.S. colleges and universities from 1965 to 1975 focused on traditional topics and texts. The exceptions were emerging feminist, ethnic, and some American Studies programs, almost all of which were institutionally marginalized and underfunded (which may be the same thing), and whose curricular and scholarly work we ought to recognize today as foundational for contemporary cultural studies.[16]

A broadly multicultural, multimedia, multidisciplinary curriculum in the humanities was not attempted until many associated with cultural studies (and other intellectual methods as well) proposed major redefinitions of "Western Civilization" introductions and other influential undergraduate and graduate courses in the humanities. What is often behind the claim that "It's been done and doesn't work" is profound anxiety regarding changes in familiar curricula, methods of teaching, and texts. "Relevance" is a code word, as it was in the 1960s, for "what the students want," and for that very reason is somehow suspect or corrupt. Actually, undergraduate students are not the primary voices urging faculty to teach popular and mass cultural materials, to broaden the "humanities" to include non-European cultures and histories, to respect the many different and often competing traditions within virtually any "national" culture. Fortunately, there is probably no generalization that can be used today to describe what students "want" or "don't want." Students are too politically, culturally, sexually, ethnically, regionally, and socioeconomically diverse.

It is just this extraordinary diversity of students that argues in favor of the topics, interdisciplinary methods, and collaborative intellectual spirit of cultural studies, and it is this very diversity of the student population that troubles many of the critics of cultural studies. The disappearance of the homogeneity of those student bodies should be a matter of pride to those of us who believe that much of the promise of postwar America depended on extending opportunities for higher education to a much wider and thus more diverse segment of the population. In other words, cultural studies *does* have *relevance* for today's students, and thus interests them, because it addresses questions of self-evident importance for those students' daily lives and experiences.

The same may be said for complaints that cultural studies relies on formulaic or predictable considerations of race, class, gender, and sexual orientation. These categories are important precisely because they help map so many social fields and because so many people have something to say about them. They thus have the advantage of providing us with very useful points of reference for comparative interpretations and understanding. Race, class, gender, and sexual orientation also have the advantage of bringing together economic status and social affiliations, potentially avoiding the Marxist overdetermination of economic factors and the exclusive focus on identity politics that has sometimes limited feminist, gay, and ethnic studies approaches.

The ideology behind the criticism of "race-gender-class critics," as John Ellis reductively terms many cultural critics, is an older assimilationist ideal, founded on Enlightenment models of a single type of "rational human being."[17] What such critics cannot understand is that many scholars committed to cultural studies do not share these modernist notions and are committed instead to articulating a spectrum of identities, beings, subjectivities, community affiliations more appropriate to the different peoples and cultures today studied by the humanities and social sciences. In this case, many of the humanist critics of cultural studies are right to be nervous; cultural studies calls for reconceptualizations of the singular models for humanity, reason, civic virtue, and domestic responsibility outlined in the synthetic modern theories of Kant, Hegel, Marx and Engels, and Freud.

Finally, let me deal with the complaint that cultural studies fails to "read closely" enough. It is a significant complaint because it is often made by deconstructive critics with whom many cultural critics share the poststructuralist model for language and cultural semiotics. Jacques Derrida's work has complicated enormously the task of cultural interpretation because it requires us to recognize the always arbitrary boundaries for any specific act of interpretation. Taking into account the full range of retentions and protentions involved in any utterance, however trivial, involves the interpreter theoretically in a recapitulation of a history and potential reception that exceeds the hermeneutic command of any particular interpreter, even team of interpreters. Given this textualist situation, which cultural studies generally accepts, "close reading" in the formalist sense of a thorough *explication de texte* is impossible, and every textual occasion demands scrupulous attention to the complex intertextuality it involves, whether that occasion is nominally an effect of popular, mass, or high culture.

Yet virtually all the complaints regarding cultural studies' lack of attention to textual complexity come from scholars interested in canonized texts and authors. If Kant is criticized for contributing to an Enlightenment model for humanity, Kantian defenders complain that these critics haven't "read closely enough" to discover just how postmodern Kant is. Ditto for Hegel, the "New" Nietzsche, Marx and Engels in the wake of Baudrillard, Freud in the wake of Lacan, Lacan in the wake of Zizek, Derrida in the wake of Cixous and Irigaray, and so on. Now I have no objection to historically revisionist interpretations of major figures and texts, as long as the interpreter makes clear why he or she is recontextualizing that figure. All acts of reading are limited and limiting; every interpretation establishes an arbitrary hermeneutic "frame." Every reading is also a misreading—of "original" intentions, of cultural norms, of implied reading dynamics, and so on.

Behind the demand for "close" and "careful" reading there is also a profoundly conservative impulse to keep us focused on familiar texts recognized as "difficult" and "serious." But too often these criteria are left unarticulated or defended. How important is William Shakespeare, John Keats, Karl Marx, Henry James, or Sigmund Freud today? Some will insist that these great Western intellectuals hardly need to be justified. Others will more carefully explain, defend, locate, justify, and argue about the contemporary relevance of these figures, thereby participating in just the sort of intellectual debate that makes for valuable teaching, useful scholarship, and historically vital intellectual exchanges.

In the course of these arguments about canonical figures, there will inevitably be efforts to situate them with respect to claims made for Mary Wollstonecraft,

Mary Shelley, Margaret Fuller, Frederick Douglass, Lydia Maria Child, Harriet Jacobs, Harriet Beecher Stowe, Nick Black Elk, Frantz Fanon, Alejo Carpentier, Ngugi Wa Thiong'o, Salman Rushdie, and Toni Morrison. That sort of comparative reading strikes me as closer to the poststructuralist model of intertextuality and unlimited interpretive horizons than the ideal of "close" and intricate reading of discrete texts often advocated by those complaining of cultural studies' failure to "read," such as Richard Rorty's passionate appeal for "The Necessity of Inspired Reading."[18] The textualist position teaches us that everything is reading and interpretation, that students are surrounded always, already by a massive onslaught of signs demanding their attention. They must read on the run, make new loops and connections, all without hope of reaching an end or proper conclusion.

I do not mean to argue that we represent only this sort of postmodern echolalia in our classrooms and formal interpretive acts. Training in close reading of texts can be valuable as long as we teach our students that it can be learned by reading *any* text. Are some texts more important than others? Why? How? When? Our students should learn how to ask such questions, and we must provide them with the means to formulate their own answers. Shakespeare and Henry James will not survive in the twenty-first century simply because of their self-evident and undeniable literary virtues. They will be read by successive generations of students because they are interpreted in ways relevant to the historical and social contexts in which they are received.

I did not include in my initial list of complaints about cultural studies the commonest of them all: "Cultural Studies politicizes knowledge, which should remain neutral and value-free in our contemporary political debates." My reason for not treating this objection until the very end of this essay is that we cannot comprehend the irreducibly political character of cultural studies without investigating these other predicates of cultural studies: its commitment to understand the nontotalizable relations of different cultural forces in the determination of human meanings and values; the relativity of these forces to their specific historical and social circumstances of usage and acceptance; the impossibility of understanding such circumstances in the terms of any universal or general theory or model; the need for helpful terms of comparison, such as race and class and gender and sexual orientation, to pursue comparative interpretations of different historical and cultural situations while avoiding the temptation to essentialize such terms. Reviewing these parts in the definition of cultural studies, we should conclude that cultural critics cannot imagine "knowledge" that is separable from its political and social functions, even when such knowledge is presented as politically neutral, value-free, or scientifically universal (or essential). Even if we wish to stand outside the framework of "cultural studies" by insisting upon the possibility of knowledge free from its political and social significance, the cultural critic would reply that his or her interest centers on how such apolitical knowledge functions within specific social, political, and historical circumstances. To the challenge of its critics, "Why must all knowledge be political?" cultural studies replies, "If knowledge is *not* political, then what social function does it perform?" Phrasing the criticisms in this way, we may begin to recognize that the heated debates regarding the politicization of the academy may hinge upon different interpretations of what we mean by "politics." For the cultural critic, the term refers generally to social governance and the intellectual abilities of subjects and groups within democratic societies to assume their responsibilities for such governance. Everything is political in liberal education because liberal education prepares students to become good, thinking, critical citizens.

I have tried to analyze some of the ideological reasons behind the contemporary resistance to "cultural studies," arguing along the way that this criticism involves more embedded resistance than the demands for better scholarship, theoretical self-consciousness, and careful reading suggest. Paul de Man concluded "The Resistance to Theory" by dramatizing the rhetorical deconstruction he had advocated in the essay, cleverly arguing: "Nothing can overcome the resistance to theory since theory *is* itself this resistance."[19] Cultural studies may also be said to offer a critical resistance that negates and demystifies its critics. But cultural studies or cultural *criticism* must accomplish this work in a variety of "linguistic moments," including those institutional, curricular, pedagogical, and public situations where rhetoric involves more than a simple change of name or witty turn of phrase. The resistance to cultural studies masks a more profound conservatism in the academy that clings to canonical texts and figures, established curricula, and disciplinary divisions in an historical period and institutional circumstances when intellectual, pedagogical, and scholarly changes are necessary for our very survival.

Notes

Epigraph to this chapter from "The Resistance to Literary Theory," *Yale French Studies* 63 (1982), 3–20, and revised as the title essay of *The Resistance to Theory*, ed. Wlad Godzich (Minneapolis: Univesity of Minnesota Press, 1986), p. 5.

1. Brook Thomas's lecture on "subaltern" for the Critical Theory Institute and Wolfgang Iser's Wellek Library Lectures, May 1994, forthcoming from Columbia University Press.
2. J. Hillis Miller, "Literary and Cultural Studies in the Transnational University," in *"Culture" and the Problem of the Disciplines*, ed. John Carlos Rowe (New York: Columbia University Press, 1998), p. 63, argues that "the acceptance by the university of cultural studies has been suspiciously rapid and easy," especially when cultural studies contributes to an "antitheoretical turn" among contemporary intellectuals. Miller's point is that critical theory is more "radical" and "challenging" to traditional university structures than "cultural studies," which in its untheorized versions reinforces "an antitheoretical return

to mimetism." Miller implies here that cultural studies is far more subject to a naive "reflection theory"—wherein cultural texts merely reflect distortedly more profound social, economic, and political conditions—and can thereby relegitimate critical theory as more sophisticated in its interpretation of the relationship between culture and ideology. His position is in several instances clearly defensive: "Theory of the sixties, seventies, and eighties has gone on being effective," for example (p. 63).

3. Jean-François Lyotard, *The Postmodern Condition*, trans. Geoff Bennington and Brian Massumi (Minneapolis: University of Minnesota Press), pp. 31–34.

4. De Man, *The Resistance to Theory*, p. 12.

5. I refer here to interview questions sent to me (and other Western theorists) by Fengzhen Wang (Beijing University) and Shaobo Xie (University of Calgary) addressing a wide range of issues in contemporary theory. My answers to those questions are included in "Cultural Studies Today," an interview for *Cultural Studies*, ed. Fengzhen Wang and Shaobo Xie (English ed., Alberta: University of Calgary Press, 2002; Chinese ed., Beijing: Foreign Languages Institute, 2001).

6. De Man, *The Resistance to Theory*, p. 8: "Contemporary literary theory comes into its own in such events as the application of Saussurean linguistics to literary texts." But for de Man this application does not result in the subordination of "literature" to its "linguistic" infrastructure; instead, literature as the best site for the "thinking" (substitute here "reading") about language affirms and distinguishes itself. It is a clever argument, but in the retrospect of more than fifteen years an argument haunted by its own internal logic, lack of historical demonstration (language is nothing if not its historical enactment), and its author's apparent ignorance of the rapid developments of "rhetoric" and "tropology" in popular and mass media even in the 1980s (actually, long before that!).

7. In "The Resistance to Theory," De Man makes a similar point about the rhetorical deconstruction he proposes as an alternative to structuralist semiotics, New Critical aesthetic categories, and philosophical a priori in general. De Man's affirmation of "reading" as the interpretive practice of following rhetorical paths, teasing out their implications and signifying potentials, rather than drawing conclusions about "meaning," is his own version of the impossibility of a metalanguage. In the place of metalanguage, de Man frequently offers "literature": "Literature involves the voiding, rather than the affirmation, of aesthetic categories" (10). Elsewhere he asks rhetorically: "What is meant when we assert that the study of literary texts is necessarily dependent on an act of reading, or when we claim that this act is being systematically avoided?" (15). For de Man, "reading"—that is, the deconstructive mapping of rhetorical possibilities—takes the place of "systematic," "grammatical," and "logical" modes of analysis, all of which are mystified by their assumption of a metatheoretical model.

8. Such pragmatics differ significantly from de Man's distinction in "The Resistance to Theory" of the "linguistic moment" from "historical and aesthetic considerations," which for him are illusions when understood apart from their linguistic conditions of appearance (7). For de Man, such a distinction enables him to trivialize the "historical" and the "aesthetic," which are coded terms that refer respectively to Marxists (none is mentioned in the essay) and Formalists (either New Critics or *Rezeptionsaesthetik* theorists, like Hans Robert Jauss and Wolfgang Iser, who are specifically mentioned). Cultural

criticism is not, then, anything like the "theory" or "literary theory" so celebrated by de Man in "The Resistance to Theory," because cultural criticism refuses the distinction de Man makes between interpretation as the determination of "meaning or value" (an illusion for de Man) and interpretation of "the modalities of production and of reception of meaning and of value prior to their establishment" (what his version of rhetorical deconstruction accomplishes) (7). According to the very "non-concepts" of a poststructuralist theory of language, the distinction cannot be maintained in any effective, pragmatic, systematic, even functional way.

9. I am grateful to Lauren not only for this helpful phrase, but also for her public lecture and discussion in the Spring of 1998 at the University of California, Irvine, during which many of these resistances to cultural theory were discussed.

10. Fredric Jameson, *Postmodernism, or the Cultural Logic of Late Capitalism* (Durham, N.C.: Duke University Press, 1991), and Neil Postman, *Amusing Ourselves to Death: Public Discourse in the Age of Show Business* (New York: Viking, 1985).

11. Cary Nelson, *Manifesto of a Tenured Radical* (New York: New York University Press, 1992), pp. 13–28, also points out the limitations of "English as it was." Nelson and I are exactly contemporaries, as far as our undergraduate and graduate educations are concerned.

12. De Man, *The Resistance to Theory*, p. 17.

13. John Carlos Rowe, *Literary Culture and U.S. Imperialism: From the Revolution to World War II* (New York: Oxford University Press, 2000), pp. 97–119.

14. Paul de Man, *Blindness and Insight* (New York: Oxford University Press, 1971), pp. 148–150; John Carlos Rowe, "'Bringing It All Back Home': American Recyclings of the Vietnam War," *The Violence of Representation: Literature and the History of Violence*, ed. Leonard Tennenhouse and Nancy Armstrong (New York: Routledge, 1989), pp. 197–218; Susan Jeffords, *The Remasculinization of America: Gender and the Vietnam War* (Bloomington: Indiana University Press, 1989); Janice Radway, *A Feeling for Books: The Book-of-the-Month Club, Literary Taste, and Middle-Class Desire* (Chapel Hill: University of North Carolina Press, 1997); Tania Modleski, *Loving with a Vengeance: Mass-Produced Fantasies for Women* (Hamden, Conn.: Archon, 1982).

15. When asked in the early 1990s to give a series of lectures to high school seniors at Tustin High School that would simulate a lower-division university lecture course, the English teachers proposed that I lecture on Herman Melville's *Moby-Dick*. I suggested instead that we screen *Rambo: First Blood, Part II*, on the grounds that the AP English teachers at Tustin were perfectly capable of teaching *Moby-Dick* to their students but that the treatment of mass-market texts might involve less familiar theoretical and practical concerns. The lectures were successful, especially when measured by the excellent papers written by the students—papers I read and graded, with the help of Krista Walter, then a Ph.D. candidate at UC, Irvine (working on a dissertation under my direction), and the students were excited and challenged by the subject matter. But there was considerable initial resistance among them to viewing, much less writing about, such low-cultural material. That, too, was part of the learning experience for all of us.

16. See Nelson, *Manifesto of a Tenured Radical*, especially chapters 1 and 4.

17. John M. Ellis, *Literature Lost: Social Agendas and the Corruption of the Humanities* (New

Haven, Conn.: Yale University Press, 1997). See my review of Nelson's and Ellis's very different books in *Academe: Bulletin of the A.A.U.P.* (May-June 1998), 76–77.

18. Richard Rorty, "The Necessity of Inspired Reading," *Chronicle of Higher Education* (Feb. 9, 1996); see my response in "Letters to the Editor," *Chronicle of Higher Education* (Mar. 8, 1996), B4.

19. De Man, *The Resistance to Theory*, p. 19.

PART II

REDEFINING CATEGORIES OF VALUE AND DIFFERENCE

Desegregating American Literary Studies

SHELLEY FISHER FISHKIN

In a survey of forty university and college literature departments conducted between 1986 and 1988, Alan Wald found that "students across the country who enroll in courses called 'The Modern Novel' or 'Modern Poetry' read and discussed works almost exclusively by elite white men that were interpreted through the prism of the British tradition" (quoted in Katterman, 14–15). It went without saying that if the authors on the reading lists in courses called "The Modern Novel" or "Modern Poetry" were almost exclusively white, their counterparts on the reading lists in courses called "The African-American Novel" or "Afro-American Poetry" were all black. During the years since this survey, a handful of black writers have indeed made it onto the core literature and poetry syllabi. In the twenty-first century, will black and white writers who find themselves next to each other on those syllabi enter into a rich and complex cultural dialogue, or will they remain divided from one another by the essentialist paradigms that are the inheritance of a segregated curriculum?

This important question deserves to be at the forefront of debate and discussion in the academy today. I do not pretend to be able to answer it, or even address it as it deserves to be addressed, in an essay of this length. Rather, I will explore some aspects of that question by probing the fate of transgressive texts in late–twentieth-century culture—texts in which black writers create serious white protagonists, and white writers black ones. These texts challenge us to produce criticism that goes beyond the old binaries and identity politics.[1]

For much of the twentieth century, literary studies have been characterized by a segregated set of assumptions: white writers write books focused on white protagonists (where issues of race, if present, remain relatively peripheral); meanwhile black writers write books focused on black protagonists (where issues of race are omnipresent and central). Contemporary scholarship, however, is demonstrating the inadequacy of these assumptions to do justice to American literary history and to the work of authors writing today.

Take the case of Mark Twain. In the 1990s, revisionist critics, myself included, increasingly argued for the centrality of Twain's black protagonist in his most famous novel, *Adventures of Huckleberry Finn*. Emory Elliott, Jocelyn Chadwick-Joshua, Ralph Wiley, and I have all suggested that although *Huck Finn* is, on the surface at least, "Huck's book" (he is its ostensible author), the hero of the book may well be Jim, who is clearly at the top of the moral hierarchy of characters in the novel, and whose superiority is thrown into sharp relief by virtually every episode in the book. The idea that Twain respected Jim, took him seriously, and meant us to take him seriously—an idea David Lionel Smith eloquently articulated in the mid-1980s—still meets opposition among readers who are (1) thrown by Jim's speech (refusing to entertain the idea that the author actually admired—and meant the reader to admire—someone who speaks so ungrammatically); (2) disturbed by what they see as resonances of minstrelsy (but is it minstrelsy? or does careful reading show Jim manipulating minstrel masks?); (3) forgetful of the fact that the book is narrated through Huck's limited vision (a vision not congruent with Twain's); or (4) troubled by the fact that most readers in Twain's day did not interpret the book this way (is there no such thing as "progress"?). Could it be that the bright glare of Twain's whiteness got in the way? Could readers in late twentieth-century America still be too blinded by racist assumptions to recognize Jim for what he is?[2] *Huckleberry Finn*, I suggest, is a transgressive text, a text in which a white writer violates reigning paradigms of what a white writer should be writing. Those paradigms interfere with our understanding Twain's achievement. Parallel assumptions about what black writers should be doing can interfere with our appreciation of their achievements as well.

If a white writer like Twain is mistrusted when he crafts a major black character—Jim—and when he ventures into the murky morass of the dynamics of racism, black writers have tended to be considered suspect when they wander away from that same terrain or when they create white protagonists. Books by black writers as famous as Richard Wright or Zora Neale Hurston in which virtually all the characters are white came to be not even read, let alone analyzed or taught. Until very recently, for example, Wright's 1954 novel *Savage Holiday* was deemed unworthy of attention by most critics. In books devoted to Wright's fiction it would receive a one-line dismissal: "A curiously incoherent little potboiler," one critic said (McCall, quoted in Tate, 87). The book languished out of print and out of favor. Also missing from print and from critical discussion was Zora Neale Hurston's 1948 novel *Seraph on the Suwanee*, a book that came out of what Hurston once referred to as her "hopes of breaking that old silly rule about Negroes not writing about white people" (quoted in Carby, x). Hurston and Wright mounted direct challenges to the convention that black writers should concern themselves only with black protagonists.

But what was Richard Wright actually doing when he wrote *Savage Holiday*, a book whose main character is a middle-aged white insurance agent forced into early retirement? I suggest that the book may have begun, at least in part, with Wright asking himself the question: What would it take to turn a middle-class, church-going white man into a Bigger Thomas? What vagaries of fate, chance, and human psychology could lead a pillar of the community to commit a savage murder? Margaret Walker was one critic who fairly early on took such questions

seriously. "Despite his white skin," Walker writes, Erskine Fowler (the protagonist of this novel) "is the same persona as Bigger Thomas in *Native Son,* Jake Jackson in *Lawd Today,* Cross Damon in *The Outsider,* and Richard Wright in *Black
Boy*" (quoted in Tate, 92). As Gerald Early recently observed, *Savage Holiday* can
be seen as "yet another expression . . . of [Wright's] intense, lifelong, and unsen-
timental interest in exploring the human soul, the position of women in modern
western culture, and the pathological aspects of various forms of repression" (223).

From its initial appearance to the present, *Savage Holiday* was dismissed by almost everyone but Walker for being too "Freudian"—as if a Freudian work by
a black writer were a priori preposterous. But as Claudia Tate argues in her 1998
book *Psychoanalysis and Black Novels,* "psychoanalysis can tell us much about the
complicated social workings of race in the United States and the representations
of these workings in the literature of African-Americans" (5). Focusing on *Savage
Holiday* allows Tate to understand the dynamics of Wright's entire body of work
in a new way. Tate finds in this neglected novel a key to a deeper understanding
of his most famous works—including *Native Son.*

In February 1991, in an article on Black History Month, the *Bergen Record* referred to the novel *A Different Drummer* as being written by "the late William Melvin
Kelley" (Chollett, E4). But Kelley isn't dead; he is just so obscure he might as
well have been; in fact, he is alive and well and teaching at Sarah Lawrence. In
1996 the *New York Times* ran a curious correction notice in which it apologized
for confusing William Melvin Kelley with William Kennedy in an article published the day before ("Corrections," 4 Nov. 1996). The author of *A Different
Drummer* had been hailed by the *New York Times* when the book came out in 1962
as "a bitter fabulist worthy of the Nathanael West Tradition" (Lyell, 24). However, three decades later he was erroneously listed as dead, or confused with the
white writer William Kennedy. What did Kelley do to deserve such obscurity?
The answer is that this innovative African-American writer wrote a brilliant but
transgressive *tour de force* in which the startling actions of the novel's only black
character take place offstage, before the novel begins, and are recounted and interpreted throughout the book through the eyes of *white* characters. "Shifting
narrators, time frames and points of view" were the same techniques that helped
win William Faulkner lasting fame (Bradley, xxvii).[3] But they earned William
Melvin Kelley lasting oblivion. Kelley deserves better.

Toni Morrison's 1998 novel *Paradise* rejects the idea that obviously black characters and issues of race, per se, must be the central focus of a black writer's text.
Morrison begins the book with the sentence, "They shoot the white girl first" (1).
But race is never mentioned again as directly throughout the entire book, and
only the most careful and discerning reader, after much rereading, could deci-
pher which of the five central characters is white. Responding to a journalist's
question about her intentional ambiguity on this point, Morrison said, "The
tradition in writing is that if you don't mention a character's race, he's white.

Any deviation from that, you have to say. What I wanted to do was not erase race, but force readers either to care about it or see if it disturbs them that they don't know. Does it interfere with the story? Does it make you uncomfortable? Or do I succeed in making the characters so clear, their interior lives so distinctive, that you realize (a) it doesn't matter, and (b), more important, that when you know their race, it's the least amount of information to know about a person" (quoted in Streitfeld, B01).

Morrison's comments about her artistic strategies in this book show a determination to force the reader to abandon essentialist thinking. At one point in the book, for example, a male character observes, "He had been warned about the consequences of marrying outside his own people, and every warning had come true: Dee Dee was irresponsible, amoral; a slut if truth be told" (quoted in Streitfeld, B01). Morrison has not specified whether Dee Dee was black or white. This is intentional. Morrison notes in an interview, "I had to be careful in carving that sentence, so it both acknowledges the fact that he felt he had married someone alien to him, but at the same time that alienness was not necessarily race. They could both be black, or both be white. I was making it deliberately fuzzy, so that the reader has to give up and do the thing we all say we do, or say we want to do, which is not to judge people on their race" (quoted in Streitfeld, B01).

During the last few years, Wright's *Savage Holiday*, Hurston's *Seraph on the Suwanee*, and William Melvin Kelley's *A Different Drummer* have all come back into print with forewords, respectively, by Gerald Early, Hazel Carby, and David Bradley. In addition, critics including Claudia Tate, Ann duCille, and Lawrence Hogue have made critical discussions of these works central to books published in the mid-1990s or forthcoming shortly. Does this work, combined with the publication of Morrison's *Paradise*, signal that the walls of the essentialist literary ghetto are cracking? Perhaps. But there are other signs that they are still firmly in place.

What happened to Ralph Wiley when Random House published his 1996 book, *Dark Witness*, is a case in point. Wiley, a mordant and hard-hitting black social and cultural commentator and satirist, had published books previously with titles like *Why Black People Tend to Shout* and *What Black People Should Do Now* and had also co-authored with Spike Lee the book about the making of the film *Malcolm X*. But although *Dark Witness* explored many of the issues related to race and racism that Wiley had focused on in earlier volumes, he did something different here: in addition to including a long, thoughtful chapter on Mark Twain in the book, and quoting profusely from Twain in epigraphs, Wiley styled virtually every chapter as a reworking of or response to a specific piece by Twain, a writer he acknowledges as the master from whom he learns the most. When Random House insisted that the book needed a subtitle, the one Wiley submitted was "In Homage to Mark Twain." Random House wouldn't hear of it. They suggested instead "When Black People Should Die." Wiley had already spent his advance, and Random House was unyielding. Finally, reluctantly, he agreed to the sub-title, "When Black People Should Be Sacrificed Again" (personal communication, 1997–1998). But when Wiley gives his book to friends, he discards the dust jacket and crosses out Random House's subtitle on the title page and writes in his own.[4]

Random House accomplished several things by refusing to allow Wiley to embrace Twain as his literary father in the subtitle of his book. First of all, they helped ensure that his book would be walled off from the world of Twain criticism that it could have helped transform had it entered it as brazenly and boldly as Wiley had wanted it to. And secondly, their misguided marketing decisions—shaped by a form of essentialist typecasting of both authors and book buyers that Wiley finds reductive, offensive, and demeaning—helped prevent a larger audience from responding to the originality and power of this transgressive text.

If black fiction writers are expected to focus on African-American life in the United States as seen through the eyes of black characters, white writers are expected to focus on the lives of white people in the United States as seen through the eyes of white characters. And while black novelists are expected to focus on issues of race and racism and are considered suspect when they do not, white novelists are expected *not* to focus on issues of race and racism and are considered suspect when they do. Transgressive texts—books that violate these norms—are, as often as not, ignored.

Take, for example, the fate of Sinclair Lewis's novel *Kingsblood Royal*. When the novel begins, white midwestern banker Neil Kingsblood has a fine job, a wife and child he adores, and an attractive suburban home that is almost paid for. Then, by chance, he discovers that he is part-black. The book centers on his response to this news and the responses of those around him. What begins as a suburban idyll ends in a race war. The book is nearly forgotten today by all but a handful of scholars. This is unfortunate, since it represents more than the bold and controversial efforts of a canonical, white, Nobel Prize–winning American author to understand the dynamics of racism in American society: it provides a window on a critical period in American race relations, illuminating the historical moment that shaped it in dramatic, compelling ways.

Published in 1947, on the eve of the desegregation of the Armed Forces, Lewis's novel appeared during the same year that Jackie Robinson entered Major League baseball and the same year that the President's Commission on Civil Rights attacked racial injustice in the United States in its formal report, *To Secure These Rights*. The reactions of ordinary readers who wrote scores of letters to Lewis, which I have examined, were extraordinary.

One correspondent from Sacramento, California, for example, who began *Kingsblood Royal* "with the anticipation of enjoyment in its pages which I had experienced in reading 'Main Street,' 'Babbitt' and several of your former books" wrote that "I finished it with nothing but disgust and wonderment that such could ever have come from your gifted pen! . . . Negroes were glorified at the expense of the white people in a ridiculous 'Much ado about nothing tale.'" She found the book "too inflammatory and dangerous," adding: "You might be interested to know that so far, not one of our second-hand book stores in this city, and there are several fine ones, will even buy it—and people out here are pretty broad-minded. I am burning my copy for I do not want it in our library nor would I care to pass on such to others" (Hayes). An anonymous correspondent from Dallas who signed himself "a real friend," demanded, "How could a man of your reputation dare to write a book such as Kingsblood Royal? You couldn't possibly need money that badly." A correspondent from Oklahoma who scribbled "(white)" under her signature wrote, "The question upermost [*sic*] in my mind is this: Is this your announcement to the world of your 'coming out'? Are you a negro, Mr. Lewis? Indeed, I can not imagine anyone but a negro having such a deep love and admiration for the colored race" (Cox).

A black beautician from Chicago posed the same question but from a different angle: "Tell me, Did you turn to a 'man of color' and live as such while writing this Book??? As I gaze at your photo on the back flap, I can read your thoughts and they go like this: 'Now I've done it and I don't give a damn whether you like it or not.'" . . . More Power to you Mr. Lewis if you could use it" (Phillips). One black correspondent reported that "Negro circles in New Orleans are discussing the book, favorably of course, and with some wonder at its penetrating insight concerning the attitudes Negroes have toward whites. . . . You have done a service to society" (Quarles).

A white correspondent from Toronto who admitted that he had "been guilty (even as your hero was before he discovered his ancestry) of treating colored people quite differently than I would any of the other races," not "considering them as 'people' at all, but as something quite separate and almost—I am ashamed to admit it—not human," wrote:

It was strange that yesterday, just after finishing your book, I should interview a man whose advertisement had appeared in the morning paper soliciting work painting walls, polishing floors, etc. I telephoned the number given in the paper and a very soft woman's voice answered, evidently the advertiser's wife, and I made an appointment with her to have him call at my home last evening to give me an estimate. When I answered the door, there stood a handsome young Negro over six feet tall. He was well spoken, well mannered and very clean. Before reading your book I would never have invited him into my apartment, my reaction to his race being so unreasonable and unfair, but I did with no self-consciousness on my part or his. I had a very interesting talk with him and enjoyed it too. He is a perfect stranger to me but I was so impressed with his straightforwardness in dealing with him in regard to the work that I engaged him and will do my best to see that he gets more work in our apartment building. What's more I did feel him very much my equal and I am sure that I am permanently cured of my snobbishness. . . . Thank you for the moral pointed in your very excellent book. Perhaps it may prove to be another "Uncle Tom's Cabin." (Coskeran)

Others saw the parallel to "Uncle Tom's Cabin," as well. Reiterating views he expressed in a personal letter to Lewis, Albert Deutsch in *PM* called it "A stinging, ringing, tingling attack on the 'White Supremacy' myth. From the social standpoint, it is in some ways the most important race relations novel since *Uncle Tom's Cabin*. It is as blistering an attack on current Jim Crow as was Harriet Beecher Stowe's novel against slavery nearly a century ago" (quoted in "First Reactions"). A similar comment was made by Michael Carter, special correspondent to the Afro-American Newspapers, in a letter to Lewis: "I personally think that your *Kingsblood Royal* is the 'Uncle Tom's Cabin'—in social impact—of the 20th Century" (Carter). In the same vein, a reader from Madera, California, wrote FBI director J. Edgar Hoover that the novel was "the most incendiary book" since *Uncle Tom's Cabin* (quoted in Mitgang, 30).

The chairmen of Chicago Citizens Committee against Lynching, an alliance of representatives of fifty religious, fraternal, trade-union, and civic organizations, wrote Lewis that the book gave his group "new impetus" and "new allies" (Stephens and Gray). And the head chief of the St. Regis Mohawk Reservation in New York wrote Lewis detailing the positive reactions of his community to the book and offering to help Lewis write "an Indian book along similar lines" (Cook).

While these readers were busy writing to Lewis with their responses to the book, J. Edgar Hoover was busy compiling a file on the book's author. The F.B.I., which had started a file on Lewis in 1923 and had added to it continuously over the years, was besieged in 1947 with letters from readers outraged by *Kingsblood Royal*. One F.B.I. report said the book was "very inflammatory due to its references to the question of Negro and White relations," while another said that "the book was stated to be propaganda for the white man's acceptance of the negro as a social equal"; by the time of Lewis's death four years after *Kingsblood Royal* was published, the F.B.I. had collected more than a hundred references to him (Robins, 99–101). The F.B.I. considered *Kingsblood Royal* so subversive that it even stamped "SECRET" a book review about the book included in Lewis's file (Mitgang, 22).[5]

Given the extraordinary social change that would follow in the years immediately after the publication of this novel, the obscurity to which this book plummeted is all the more puzzling. Why did this book sink like a stone after becoming an instant bestseller? Why is it virtually unknown today? The novel itself is highly readable. But what it brings to the table is nothing short of astonishing. That the first American to win the Nobel Prize for literature decided to make the paradoxes, ironies, and tensions of racism, American-style, the center of a major novel, and that he embarked on painstaking research to get the story "right" is extraordinary to begin with. But that he could do all that—*and* write a bestseller to boot—only to turn up missing from the canon in an era when issues of race and identity have risen to the surface with unprecedented urgency is truly remarkable. This book is not just not in the American literary canon—and it's not even in the Lewis canon—the handful of books by Lewis that get discussed when Lewis makes it onto the syllabus or onto the table. *Kingsblood Royal* has been out of print for decades.

What do we lose when we typecast Lewis as the author of *Main Street* and *Babbitt*—but not of *Kingsblood Royal?* We bury an intriguing chapter in American literary history, and in the history of American race relations; and we keep from our students the knowledge that Toni Morrison is not the only American winner of the Nobel Prize for literature who thought deeply and provocatively about the ways in which racism stained and continues to stain American society.

To move to our own time, right now, let's look for a moment at the work of the contemporary fiction writer Susan Straight, whose luminous, lyrical, and powerful portraits of black life in the California town she calls Rio Seco have been enlivening the literary landscape since 1990. Some of the most moving scenes of black life in contemporary literature—and some of the most dramatic—appear in her first book, *Aquaboogie*, and in her most recent novel, *The Gettin' Place*. But Straight's books don't tend to get reviewed in *Essence* or *Ebony* or the *African-American Review* or *Callaloo* despite the fact that they would be likely to appeal greatly to their readers. Why? I have a hunch. Susan Straight is white. Never mind that she spent virtually her entire life in the black community from which she draws the inspiration. Never mind that Straight is raising her black daughters in that community. Never mind that her characters are vivid and compelling, and that her craft is sharp and finely honed. Where is it determined that by definition she can't write "African-American literature?"

We are all hurt by the implicit assumption that Susan Straight's stories told through black eyes and William Melvin Kelley's stories told through white eyes are immediately suspect and undeserving of our attention. By the same token, we are all hurt by an identity politics that assumes that only black writers may be relied upon to write truthfully about African Americans, or that only white writers may be depended upon to tell the truths about whites.

Sterling Stuckey has argued (in a lecture in 1994, and more fully in an article published four years later) that Melville knew more about Africa and African-American life than most of his contemporaries, black and white ("Keynote" and "Tambourine"). Should Stuckey, one of the country's leading black historians, *not* study Melville because Melville was white? (At the 1994 conference at the University of Pennsylvania where Stuckey initially voiced these ideas, a white scholar argued precisely that point, only to have Stuckey argue against it with a passion I'll never forget.)[6]

White Americans going back to Thomas Jefferson and beyond had written about black Americans with a glib confidence that masked supreme ignorance; white views of blacks, however inaccurate, had been readily published, purchased, and believed by readers for generations. Indeed, the field of African-American studies developed in part as an effort to counter the often arrogant, ignorant, and offensive "white gaze." Meanwhile, black Americans had offered insights into white Americans for just as long—but since they had less power and fewer of the publishing perks that accompany it, those views did not circulate as widely. (A wonderful corrective on that front is David Roediger's brilliant new anthology *Black on White: Black Writers on What It Means to Be White*.) I do not claim that we need not remain vigilant regarding this familiar asymmetry. Nonetheless, maintaining segregated American literary studies today strikes me as a bad idea. As long as black writers are safely ensconced in an African-American literature ghetto, the core American literature courses need not really deal with them in any but token ways. Do we do justice to their impact on mainstream American oratory, prose, and poetry and the impact of that oratory, prose, and poetry on them if we maintain separate intellectual wings? And isn't keeping white writers who dare to write about blacks out of the cultural conversation about African-American literature shortsighted as well?

The walls won't crumble by fiat or exhortation. They'll disintegrate as a result of writing that renders them pointless and obsolete. Jane Marcus's groundbreaking research on Nancy Cunard and Danzy Senna's beautiful first novel, *Caucasia*, are two cases in point.

To oversimplify a very complicated case of intellectual redlining, Cunard is not a part of the narrative of African-American literary history because she was white; she's not part of mainstream American literary history because she was British; the left distrusted her upper-class origins too much to incorporate her into histories of the left, and feminists distrusted her often male-identified and very public erotic life too much to give her a place in women's history. But to focus for a moment on just the first of these pigeon-holes, Jane Marcus's research demonstrates that ignoring Cunard's innovative contributions to the Black Atlantic and African American literary world has distorted our understanding of that world. Cunard researched, organized, and edited the 800-page *Negro Anthology*, bringing together in one massive volume an impressive array of black and white writers on both sides of the Atlantic concerned with issues of racial justice. For its contributors and for its readers, the anthology mapped the Black Atlantic as no other work had, presaging the late twentieth-century research of scholars like Robert Farris Thompson and Paul Gilroy. Cunard, Marcus tells us, was an important intellectual influence on C. L. R. James, who reportedly carried a copy of the *Negro Anthology* with him wherever he went to teach and lecture. In addition to bringing writers together in this book, Cunard helped bring many writers together in person, making introductions that would shape African-American literary history. As Marcus's forthcoming book, *White Looks*, will show, Cunard is much too intriguing a figure to neglect any longer, and any paradigm that requires us to ignore her is a limited and faulty one.

Danzy Senna's lyrical and gripping coming-of-age novel, *Caucasia*, is told in first person through the eyes of Birdie, the light-skinned daughter of Deck Lee, a black college professor, and his wife, Sandy, a white woman active in radical politics who is a descendant of Cotton Mather. Birdie and Sandy are the two central figures in the novel (Deck and Sandy separate shortly after the book begins). When Sandy is persuaded of the necessity of going underground, she and Birdie decide that Birdie should pass as "Jesse Goldman," the daughter of Sandy and (an invented) deceased Jewish intellectual. Sandy, a messy mix of competence and confusion, good intentions, fierce attachments and pervasive paranoia, is a beautifully drawn character. Birdie, a smart, sensitive child who spends the book struggling to come to terms with who she is, is equally compelling. Will the loving attention that the author lavishes on this blueblood W.A.S.P. mother— or the fact that her central "black" character passes as white and Jewish for most of the novel—redline this book from discussions of contemporary "African-American Literature"? Or alternatively, will the centrality of issues of race and racism push this book onto the "African-American Literature" shelves and dissuade readers of all races from recognizing it as a coming-of-age novel that engages the great American tradition of self-invention? What do essentialist paradigms do to characters whose every breath involves confounding essentialist labels? Danzy Senna has crafted rich and complicated characters negotiating real and imaginary color lines every day of their lives, on every page of her novel, in technicolor that refuses to be reduced to black and white. Our challenge as critics is to open our paradigms to this kind of complexity, to break down the habits of thought that would flatten it into anything less fertile and less interesting than it is.

In conclusion, I'd like to throw out some rather provocative statements suggested by the examples I've discussed in this essay: American literary studies will not be desegregated until we learn to value transgressive texts that refuse to be contained in the critical pigeon-holes of the past, until students and teachers and publishers and the public come to value the writings produced by writers of African-American descent like Wright and Kelley and Morrison and Wiley and Senna not just for their "black" protagonists, but also for their "white" ones; and not only for what they have to say about race and racism and African-American life but also for what they reveal about artists struggling to forge a form to contain their vision; about the dynamics of human agency, of friendship, of love; for what they teach us about the suppleness of the creative mind; the mastery of language itself. And American literary studies will not be desegregated until teachers and students and publishers and the public come to value books by white writers like Twain and Melville and Lewis and Straight not only for their "white" protagonists, but also for their "black" ones; not only for their narrative gifts but also for their insights into race, racism, and African-American life—and until books by both groups of writers are featured in publishers' African American Studies *and* American literature catalogs, shelved in both the Literature and African American Studies sections in bookstores, and taught in both American Literature and African-American Literature classes in colleges.[7]

In sum, American literary studies will not be desegregated until we open our scholarship and our classrooms to impertinent questions and to the subversive answers that may well follow.

Notes

I presented versions of this essay at the American Studies Program of the University of Minnesota, the Graduate Center of the City University of New York, the Aesthetics and Difference Conference at the University of California at Riverside, the American Studies Association Annual Convention in Montreal, and the American Studies Program of Hebrew University, Jerusalem. I am grateful to all of the friends and colleagues whose responses shaped my thinking in such constructive ways. In particular, I would like to thank David Bradley, Emily Budick, Joel Dinerstein, Chiyuma Elliott, Emory Elliott, the late Milton Fisher, Jane Marcus, Elaine Tyler May, Carla Peterson, Riv-Ellen Prell, Lillian Robinson, David Roediger, Jeffrey Rubin-Dorsky, Viola Sachs, Siva Vaidhyanathan, Todd Vogel, Ralph Wiley, and Richard Yarborough.

1. This essay is intended to raise more questions than it answers. It is fueled by the energy of recent scholarship on American culture across a range of disciplines, and by the challenges that scholarship poses for us in the future. I suggest that the issues I will raise here may well apply not only to so-called "black" and "white" authors, but also to writers from other ethnic groups—Asian-American and Chicano, for example. Although other groups are not the primary focus here, I believe that the kinds of arguments I make regarding the inadequacy of the current black-white binary will be increasingly made in the future about their work, as well.

2. In a 1999 re-examination of the book's racial dynamics, for example, Louis J. Budd expressed the view that Twain never went beyond "empathetic paternalism" in his characterization of Jim.

3. Bradley's brilliant essay notes further parallels between *A Different Drummer* and Faulkner's last work, *The Reivers*, which appeared the same year, 1962. Bradley notes that both writers used these techniques "to precisely the same end: to humanize and sympathize characters whose points of view readers might have ignored. One striking similarity between *A Different Drummer* and *The Reivers* is the use of a child's uncomplicated, uncomprehending—and nonracist—point of view." Bradley further notes that "Kelly is able to do both what Faulkner could and what Faulkner could not. He creates Faulknerian characters as sympathetically as Faulkner himself, and at the same time creates a powerful black character—so powerful that (unlike Faulkner's blacks) he can liberate himself and other blacks without white intervention. Indeed, so powerful that he can liberate white people too . . ." (xxvii).

4. Copy of clothbound edition thus corrected (in pink highlighter) in possession of the author. I also own a copy of the paperback edition of this book, in which Wiley has used a yellow post-it note to replace the subtitle his publisher foisted on him with the one he originally chose.

5. I am grateful to David Armstrong for his help in locating this material.

6. The exchange between Stuckey and Eric Cheyfitz, one of the conference organizers, took place during the question-and-answer period following Stuckey's keynote talk at the symposium on "The Question of Race in the Americas" at the University of Pennsylvania in September 1994.

7. Eventually these ways of dividing publishers' catalogs or the curriculum in colleges or the floor space in bookstores may prove obsolete; but it is difficult to imagine their disappearance any time soon.

Works Cited

Anon. ["A real friend"] to Sinclair Lewis, 20 Nov. 1947. Sinclair Lewis Collection, Beinecke Library, Yale University.

Anon. "Corrections." *New York Times.* 4 Nov. 1996, section B3.

Anon. "Corrections." *New York Times.* Westchester Weekly Desk. 1 Dec. 1996, section B3 [Lexis Nexis].

Anon. "FIRST REACTIONS: *Kingsblood Royal,* by Sinclair Lewis." Typed sheet of excerpts from reviews. n.d. Sinclair Lewis Collection, Beinecke Library, Yale University.

Bradley, David. "Foreword." William Melvin Kelley, *A Different Drummer* [Reprint edition]. New York: Anchor Books, Doubleday. 1989.

Budd, Louis J. "Mark Twain and the Sense of Racism." Talk presented at the American Literature Association Convention, Baltimore, Md., May 1999.

Carby, Hazel. "Foreword." Zora Neale Hurston, *Seraph on the Suwanee.* New York: HarperPerennial, 1991.

Carter, Michael, to Sinclair Lewis, 26 May 1947. Sinclair Lewis Collection, Beinecke Library, Yale University.

Chadwick-Joshua, Jocelyn. *The Jim Dilemma: Reading Race in Huckleberry Finn.* Jackson: University Press of Mississippi, 1998.

Chollett, Laurence. "A Category and a Chorus" [Book Reports column]. *Bergen Record,* 10 Feb. 1991, E4 [LexisNexis].

Cook, Julius, to Sinclair Lewis, 8 July 1947. Sinclair Lewis Collection, Beinecke Library, Yale University.

Coskeran, Jean, to Sinclair Lewis, 12 Sept. 1947. Sinclair Lewis Collection, Beinecke Library, Yale University.

Cox, Reba, to Sinclair Lewis, 28 May 1947. Sinclair Lewis Collection, Beinecke Library, Yale University.

Cunard, Nancy. *Negro Anthology.* London: Nancy Cunard/Wishart, 1934.

Deutsch, Albert, to Sinclair Lewis, 5 May 1947. Sinclair Lewis Collection, Beinecke Library, Yale University.

DuCille, Ann. *The Coupling Convention: Sex, Text, and Tradition in Black Women's Fiction.* New York: Oxford University Press, 1993.

Early, Gerald. "Afterword." Richard Wright, *Savage Holiday* [Reprint edition]. Jackson: University Press of Mississippi, 1995. 223–235.

Elliott, Emory. "Introduction." Mark Twain's *Adventures of Huckleberry Finn.* Oxford World's Classics. Oxford: Oxford University Press, 1999.

Fishkin, Shelley Fisher. *Was Huck Black? Mark Twain and African American Voices.* New York: Oxford University Press, 1993.

———. *Lighting Out for the Territory: Reflections on Mark Twain and American Culture.* New York: Oxford University Press, 1997.

———. "New Perspectives on 'Jim' in the 1990s." *Mark Twain Review* (Korea). Winter 1999.

Gilroy, Paul. *The Black Atlantic: Modernity and Double Consciousness.* London: Verso, 1993.

Hayes, Hettie F., to Sinclair Lewis, 1 Oct. 1947. Sinclair Lewis Collection, Beinecke Library, Yale University.

Hogue, Lawrence. *Race, Modernity and Postmodernity: A Look at the Literatures of People of Color Since the 1960s.* Albany: SUNY Press, 1996.

Hurston, Zora Neale, to Carl Van Vechten, Nov. 2, 1942. Carl Van Vechten Papers, James Weldon Johnson Memorial Collection, Beinecke Library, Yale University.

———. *Seraph on the Suwanee* [Reprint edition]. Foreword by Hazel Carby. New York: HarperPerennial, 1991.

Katterman, Lee. "In Search of an 'American' Literature: UM [University of Michigan] Scholar Argues That Emphasis on the British Tradition Creates Damaging Myths." *Research News* [University of Michigan] 41:1–2 (Jan.–Feb. 1990): 14–15.

Kelley, William Melvin. *A Different Drummer* [Reprint edition]. New York: Anchor Books, Doubleday, 1989.

Lee, Spike, and Ralph Wiley. *By Any Means Necessary: The Trials and Tribulations of the Making of Malcolm X.* New York: Hyperion, 1992.

Lewis, Sinclair. *Kingsblood Royal.* New York: Random House, 1947.

———. *Main Street & Babbitt.* New York: Library of America, 1992.

Lyell, Frank H. "The Day the Negroes Left." Review of *A Different Drummer* by William Melvin Kelley *New York Times Book Review,* 17 June 1962: 24–25.

Marcus, Jane. "White Looks." Unpublished manuscript.

McCall, Dan. *The Example of Richard Wright.* New York: Harcourt, Brace and World, 1969.

Mitgang, Herbert. *Dangerous Dossiers: Exposing the Secret War against America's Greatest Authors.* New York: Ballantine, 1988.

Morrison, Toni. *Paradise.* New York: Knopf, 1998.

Phillips, Constance, to Sinclair Lewis, n.d. Sinclair Lewis Collection, Beinecke Library, Yale University.

President's Committee on Civil Rights. *To Secure These Rights: The Report of the President's Committee on Civil Rights.* Washington, D.C.: U.S. Government Printing Office, 1947.

Quarles, Benjamin, to Sinclair Lewis, 22 May 1947. Sinclair Lewis Collection, Beinecke Library, Yale University.

Robins, Natalie. *Alien Ink: The FBI's War on Freedom of Expression.* New York: William Morrow, 1992.

Roediger, David R., ed. *Black on White: Black Writers on What It Means to Be White.* New York: Schocken, 1998.

Senna, Danzy. *Caucasia.* New York: Riverhead, 1998.

Smith, David Lionel. "Huck, Jim and American Racial Discourse." In *Satire or Evasion? Black Perspectives on* Huckleberry Finn, ed. James S. Leonard, Thomas A. Tenney, and Thadious M. Davis. 103–20. Durham, N.C.: Duke University Press, 1991.

Stephens, Milas S., and John M. Gray to Sinclair Lewis, 31 May 1947. Sinclair Lewis Collection, Beinecke Library, Yale University.

Straight, Susan. *Aquaboogie: A Novel in Stories*. Minneapolis, Minn.: Milkweed Editions, 1990.

———. *The Gettin' Place*. New York: Hyperion, 1996.

Streitfeld, David. "The Novelist's Prism; Toni Morrison Holds Race Up to the Light and Reflects on the Meaning of Color." *Washington Post*. 6 January 1998, Style section: B01 [Lexis Nexis].

Stuckey, Sterling. [Keynote Talk]. Symposium on "The Question of Race in the Americas" sponsored by the Women's Studies Program of University of Pennsylvania. Philadelphia, Sept. 1994.

———. "The Tambourine in Glory: African Culture in Melville's Art." In Robert S. Levine, ed. *The Cambridge Companion to Herman Melville*. 37–64. Cambridge: Cambridge University Press, 1998.

Tate, Claudia. *Psychoanalysis and Black Novels: Desire and the Protocols of Race*. New York: Oxford University Press, 1998.

Thompson, Robert Farris. *Flash of the Spirit: African and Afro-American Art and Philosophy*. New York: Random House, 1983.

Walker, Margaret. *Richard Wright: The Daemonic Genius, a Portrait of the Man: A Critical Look at His Work*. New York: Amistad, 1988.

Wiley, Ralph. "Spike Lee's Huckleberry Finn." Unproduced screenplay, c. 1977.

———. *Why Black People Tend to Shout: Cold Facts and Wry Views from A Black Man's World*. Secaucus, N.J.: Carol Publishing, 1991.

———. *What Black People Should Do Now*. New York: One World/Ballantine, 1993.

———. Personal interviews, fall 1997 and spring 1998.

Wright, Richard. *Native Son*. Ed. Arnold Rampersad. New York: Library of America, 1991.

———. *Savage Holiday* [Reprint edition]. Afterword by Gerald Early. Jackson: University Press of Mississippi, 1995.

Zafar, Rafia. *We Wear the Mask: African Americans Write American Literature, 1760–1870*. New York: Columbia University Press, 1997.

Difference and Disciplinarity

ROBYN WIEGMAN

This essay began as a deliberation on "Canons, Hierarchies, and the Profession of the Critic," the opening session at the Aesthetics and Difference Conference that was the inaugural occasion for the essays collected in this volume. It focuses on issues central to contemporary academic feminism by turning to Susan Gubar's "What Ails Feminist Criticism?," which registers its lament over the seeming decline of feminist literary criticism by tracing the textual rhetorics and aesthetics of feminist ethnic studies and poststructuralist theory. By exploring the way Gubar miscasts disciplinary issues by articulating them as generational ones, I hope to restage academic feminism's discussion of transforming not simply individual disciplines, but the institution, its organization of knowledge, and the way in which we understand difference within the intellectual composition and history of feminism.

Such a conversation contributes to the agenda of this collection by demonstrating how the aesthetic, as the *value* term of certain disciplinary modes of literary judgment, is currently formed against interdisciplinary identity projects and their theoretical imperative to transgress normative models not simply of racial, national, or gendered belonging, but of the epistemological and methodological practices of traditional disciplines. That the opposition between difference and disciplinarity is not an essentialist one is certainly a major tenet of papers in this volume. But rather than pursuing the collection's promise to marry difference to the aesthetic, my paper forwards the possibility that "difference"—gendered, sexual, racial—does not need the aesthetic as such. I say this in order to transfer the value of judgment from the question that the aesthetic poses for literary study to the kinds of judgments that difference might make were it to be understood not as a specifying container for culture and its diversity, but as a metacritical project that transforms the theoretical and methodological knowledge practices of the university itself.

Murderous Beginnings

In "Murder without a Text," Amanda Cross (better known to academics as Carolyn Heilbrun) offers a tale of feminist generational fury and murder that foregrounds the kind of antithetical relationship between disciplinary knowledge and social difference I hope to explore in this essay. Cross's murder mystery features a seasoned feminist scholar accused of bludgeoning a student to death. The murder takes place during a highly contentious women's studies senior thesis class in which Professor Beatrice Sterling, an early Christian history specialist, has difficulty convincing students of the importance of archival research and canonical texts. To these students, as Sterling explains, "All history, all previously published research, was lies. They would talk to real sex-workers, real homeless women, real victims of botched abortions. . . . When I suggested some academic research, they positively snorted" (131). The students' refusal of the kind of scholarly apparatus most familiar to Sterling constitutes within the narrative a generational betrayal: "They spoke about early feminists, like me, as though we were a bunch of co-opted creeps . . . they never talked to me or asked me anything . . . It was the kind of rudeness that is close to rape. Or murder" (130). This generational dysfunction is finally solved by a third party—a detective named Kate Fansler—who learns that the dead coed's roommate had interviewed, on the day in question, an aging homeless woman. This woman is proven guilty and so ends Professor Sterling's incrimination. As the detective ruminates about the case, "It could well take an undergraduate to send even the most benign homeless person over the edge" (135).

And what of the Women's Studies seminar? "I have urged Beatrice," says the detective, "to write a calm letter to the director of women's studies suggesting an entire revamping of the senior thesis seminar. They must require texts. Under the circumstances, it seems the least they can do" (135). The disruption of generational conflict can be addressed, if not cured, by returning to the sanctity of the text, where traditional humanistic methodologies can center the students' inquiries on what the professor has been trained to know. This solution absolves Professor Sterling of her own murderous desire toward the unruly coed (and the responsibility of learning oral history methodologies) while shifting the problem of generational tension to the middle-class domain of appropriate manners. "The young are rude today," Professor Sterling says. "The odd part of this is that the most radical students, who talk of little but the poor and the racially oppressed, are, if anything, ruder than the others, courtesy being beneath them" (130).

In defining the affective register of feminist institutional relationships as rudeness, and implicitly positing an ethnographic approach to race and class analysis as unrigorous and nonacademic, Cross's short story raises a set of issues important for academic feminism to entertain.[1] How much, in fact, have the questions of difference, understood as both social and methodological, worked to challenge the disciplinary practices through which feminism has been most legible in the contemporary academy? What does it mean for feminism in general and Women's Studies in particular that a disciplinary structure of knowledge serves as the primary institutional form for producing feminist scholars? How does the political imperative of feminism work in tension, if not contradiction, with the critical and methodological demands of discipline? And further, how have academic practices of social discipline forwarded an aesthetic ideal of proper manners that manages difference by defining courtesy as the normative affect for social belonging?

Susan Gubar's "What Ails Feminist Criticism?" offers a critical entry into these questions, even as its narrative of feminist literary criticism's fall from mirthful unity to spirit-murdering factionalism tends to repeat Cross's reduction of the knowledge politics of identity to a generational tale of bad manners. "I hope to show," writes Gubar, "that a number of prominent advocates of racialized identity politics and of poststructuralist theories have framed their arguments in such a way as to . . . hinder the tolerance and understanding needed for open dialogue" (880).[2] In her view, feminists of color have used "a curiously condemnatory vocabulary," directing a "barrage of diatribes . . . against white feminists" (888, 886). They have been "censorious about white thinkers engaged in purportedly antiracist and feminist meditations" (888). They have "disparage[d] any feminist theory grounded on equality" (889). They have falsely and negatively essentialized white women, contaminating "feminist prose with self-righteousness" and using the language of antiracism, in Janet Todd's words, "'to denigrate the feminist enterprise'" (891). Poststructuralists, on the other hand, have created a "language crisis," which not only obstructs affiliations with women outside the academy, but performs a disservice to "libertarian politics and pedagogies" (881, 900). "Churlish or cultish, its political or theoretically correct jargon stifles rather than nurtures thoughtful interchange" (901). Taken together, postcolonial, U.S. ethnic, and poststructuralist feminisms are "debilitating rhetorics" that have made "*women* an invalid word" (902, 886).

Where Gubar's first version of this paper, delivered as a talk, featured these advocates as the culprits of feminism's murder, the kinder version of the story, published in *Critical Inquiry*, casts postcolonial, U.S. ethnic, and poststructuralist criticism as life-draining carnivores intent on consuming feminism's historically robust flesh. As Gubar tells it, feminist criticism begins in the 1970s, where, in a "paradise of . . . roused, indeed, 'raised,' consciousness," it flourished "as female academics brought the women's movement into such departments as English and history" (881). From the first stage of "critique" to the second of "recovery" to the third of "engendering differences," feminist critics, Gubar writes, exposed the normative masculinity of traditional disciplines, uncovered women's unique literary traditions, and brought "gender to bear on other differences: sexual and racial differences primarily, but also economic, religious, and regional distinctions" (884). By the end of the 1980s, however, the tone began to change as the fourth stage of "metacritical dissension" emerged. Here, the category of *women* that made possible the first three stages was dismantled from two sides: African-American and postcolonial feminist critics who interpreted it as "universalizing a privileged, white womanhood" and poststructuralists who found *any* claim to identity fundamentally essentialist and unsophisticated (886). While acknowledging the "subtle methodologies provided by African American, postcolonial, and poststructuralist studies," Gubar devotes her essay to diagnosing the unpleasant "linguistic practices these approaches have occasionally sponsored" (886). Her assessment of the bad rhetorical manners of bell hooks, Hazel Carby, Chandra Mohanty, Gayatri Spivak, Julia Kristeva, Judith Butler, and Donna Haraway is intended to demonstrate feminist criticism's "bad case of critical anorexia": "for racialized identity politics made the word *women* slim down to stand only for a very particularized kind of woman, whereas poststructuralists obliged the term to disappear altogether" (901).[3]

By shifting from murder to illness as the reigning metaphor for the interruption of feminist criticism's institutional domain by national, ethnic, and theoretical differences, Gubar attempts to soften her tale's explosive emotional condemnation in order to promise hope not simply for feminist criticism's eventual rehabilitation, but for that of the women's movement as well. "I find myself echoing the words of [Rosi] Braidotti," Gubar writes, "who understands the word *women* as 'a general umbrella term' and who exclaims, 'I wish feminism would shed its saddening, dogmatic mode to rediscover the merrymaking of a movement that aims to change life' . . . What should be tried are not only nutritious but also delicious linguistic practices so that we can heal feminist discourses of the infirmities that made us cranky with one another" (902). In thus calling for "more mirthful scholarly lexicons," Gubar ends her essay by re-privileging those aspects of the first three stages that generated, in her narrative, their critical coherency: their mutual participation in a model of feminist criticism that relied upon, indeed extended, the textual aesthetics and critical idioms of literary study as a distinct disciplinary practice. By the fourth stage, however, new disciplinary discourses and their methodologies emerged to make a claim on academic feminism, and what I would call an extradisciplinary project gained critical hegemony: the problematic of *women* as both an object of study and as feminism's referent for politicized knowledge. While Gubar reads the metacritical rendering of difference as the wrong turn in the road for feminist criticism, we might understand women's incoherence as the condition of possibility for producing a feminist academic project that can rethink not simply the liberal understanding of difference as inclusion, but the politics and organization of knowledge as well.[4]

It is precisely in the relation between disciplinarity and metacritical difference that I want to locate a set of persistent problems for contemporary academic feminism, for it seems to me that Gubar is quite right to register the anxiety over metacritical difference as a matter of disciplinarity.[5] I say this not simply because as a director of a women's studies program I feel the force of the antagonism between interdisciplinary identity-based studies and disciplinary departmental domains in an everyday sense. More crucially, it is because feminism's institutionalization in the academy is just one instance of a larger academic project that used identity—most prominently racial, ethnic, gendered, and sexual—to inaugurate an epistemological critique of knowledge production by foregrounding the problem which embodiment and subjectivity present to objectivist method-ologies and to the segregation of culture (the humanities), nature (the sciences), and the state (the social sciences) that the university as an institution both pro-duces and defends. To the extent that the project of identity has been transformed into a liberal discourse of difference—and difference has been reduced to proper political manners—the metacritical potential of difference has been quite effec-tively displaced. In that displacement, difference functions as the centerpiece of a rhetoric of democratic inclusion, which is to say that it contributes mirthfully to the humanities' traditionally affirmative production of culture.

Here I attempt to sketch some of these issues, in part as a cautionary response to the prospect that the way to rehabilitate the humanities in general or English in particular in this period of their quite confounding crisis is by linking the question of difference to the aesthetic. This is not to say that the literary and artistic productions of the historically minoritized should not be retrieved from the sociological approach that has most often accompanied their critical evalua-tion.[6] African-American criticism in particular has discussed the problem of black literature's function as social documentary throughout the twentieth century, and anyone currently working in an English department in the United States knows that the study of so-called minority literatures never fully escapes the shadow of the "minor" that their identity-based inclusion continues to cast. This is the case in part because the challenge to the canon has not undermined the sense that traditional canonical texts were defined as such not as a consequence of an iden-tity politic of their own, but precisely because they were considered to be the most significant aesthetic feats of human culture. Where the center has indeed held—and vigorously so—the challenge to the canon must be regarded as its own project of national expansion whereby territory for identity is annexed to the original state (of affairs) and students are allowed to vacation in difference as long as they continue to know by heart their Shakespeare or early Melville.

From this perspective, then, difference and the aesthetic do need to engage in conversation, but it is my contention that it is not urgent *for the knowledge project of difference* that they do so. Rather, as I hope to demonstrate in this essay, the ques-tion of difference needs to be deployed metacritically as a means of examining larger questions about the university and its organization of knowledge. For this reason I am going to delve further into "What Ails Feminist Criticism?" to ana-lyze the loss of the literary that underlies Gubar's interpretation of feminist criticism's academic sojourn. That discussion serves as a kind of preamble to my closing consideration of the interdisciplinary institutional sites that have come in the past thirty years to represent radical claims for democratic inclusion, but whose representation as such now works to undermine their metacritical chal-lenge to knowledge production.

Bad Manners, Lost Objects

It is perhaps no overstatement to say that feminist scholars in the 1990s have been preoccupied with narrating the history of feminism as both a political movement and intellectual discourse. For those of us, junior and recently tenured faculty, who benefited from the ascendancy of feminist knowledge in our undergraduate and graduate training, the fact that feminism could be a legitimate object of study has had a transformative effect not only on the ways in which scholarship can be imagined, but on the meaning of the university as a site of political intervention. To speak of generation, as both "What Ails Feminist Criticism?" and "Murder Without a Text" rightly suggest, is not simply to produce an essentialist discourse about age and life cycle so much as to describe the historical institutional conditions under which feminism attained and has sustained its status as knowledge. This is not to say that the contestatory status of feminism in the academy has been superceded by its wholesale acceptance, but it is to explain why both fictional and academic narratives about the history of feminism bring so much generational anxiety and tension into play.[7]

In "What Ails Feminist Criticism?" the anxieties that accompany generational transformations in feminist knowledges collectively link U.S. ethnic studies, postcolonial theory, and poststructuralism as the "after" generation—after the initial heady days of feminism's radical incursion into the university. This critical linkage provides a new twist on the now familiar story of academic feminism's contemporary fall by creating a collective of knowledge formations that have rarely been cast together. More frequently, poststructuralism's tie to European philosophical traditions engenders a narrative of its white and first world complicities, thereby setting postcolonial and U.S. ethnic studies in opposition to the domain of so-called high theory. How, then, do these critical discourses come together to undo academic feminism in "What Ails Feminist Criticism?"

The answer to this question is found in Gubar's focus on affect and proper manners. As she writes, "prominent advocates of racialized identity politics and of poststructuralist theories have framed their arguments in such a way as to divide feminists, casting suspicion upon a common undertaking that remains in dispute at the turn of the twentieth century" (880). Thus, the epistemological and disciplinary, not to mention political, differences between and among the scholarly archives of postcolonial, U.S. ethnic, and poststructuralist feminisms are diminished as "debilitating rhetorics . . . that made us cranky with one another," unpleasant idioms that ruined feminism's good mood (902). Writing of two essays by Chandra Mohanty and Hazel Carby, for instance, Gubar discusses how their critical analysis questioned "reductive images of 'the' Third World woman, but the way in which they did so explains why white feminists began to feel beleaguered by blatantly imperative efforts to right the wrong of black female instrumentality" (889). Emphasizing other feelings of white feminists—their fear of "saying the wrong thing, of sounding racist"—Gubar argues that the attack on *women*'s categorical cohesion undermined the equality feminism sought; indeed, she writes, "the politics of racial authenticity . . . [threatened] feminism's endorsement of all women's right to self-expression" (891).

In reading race-based critique as a matter of manners, "What Ails Feminist Criticism?" lacks a systematic consideration of race as a mode of domination. Carby becomes a suspect in essentializing white women, for instance, because of "her conviction that 'white women stand in a power relation as oppressors of black women'" (889). What precisely is essentialist about Carby's claim? She is not saying that white women are naturally, primordially oppressors; rather she is identifying a structure of power, a "power relation," that for her necessarily conditions feminist thought and social movements. Her "conviction" is therefore a contextualization, but in the rhetoric of "What Ails Feminist Criticism?" it becomes a lament that feminists of color, "though they sought to serve the interests of women of color . . . promoted consternation among white women" (890). The shift here—from the intentions of women of color to speak for themselves to the effects of their discourse on white women—demonstrates the inability of "What Ails Feminist Criticism?" to divorce its analysis of race from white women's emotional centrality. Even a sentence that begins with the acknowledgment of the interests of women of color has "white women" as its critical destination.

The consequence of this analytic strategy is far reaching, since it produces the divide between feminist criticism's first three stages and its "quarrelsome" (900) fourth as one that hinges, quite explicitly, on the now injured feelings of white women.[8] Each of the first three stages, let's recall, features scholarship by feminists of color: Toni Cade Bambara, Barbara Christian, and Mary Helen Washington are presented as part of the critical power of academic feminism's early emphasis on women's literary traditions, and Nellie McKay, Hortense Spillers, Deborah McDowell, and Gloria Hull contribute to the important construction of a black female literary "subtradition."[9] Hence it is not accurate to say that Gubar dismisses the significance of difference altogether. Rather, her narrative pinpoints feminist criticism's fall as the metacritical turn in which scholars of color refuse feminism's historical "dependence on the word *women*" (899). In this narrative construction, where difference escapes the disciplinary boundaries of its third-stage place as a subtradition, "What Ails Feminist Criticism?" offers only a negative assessment of the intellectual implications of *women*'s fall into epistemological contingency.[10] Thus judging the theoretical work of racial deconstruction in terms of its ill-mannered effect, Gubar contains the epistemological challenge that difference might, metacritically speaking, represent. Most crucially, her essay demonstrates that disciplinary identity, no less than social identity, is a powerful form of attachment, so much so in fact that it provides the discursive structure on which her genealogy of feminist criticism ultimately depends.[11]

But why, readers may ask, do I keep pointing to Gubar's devotion to the literary as if this devotion has to be proven? Her essay, after all, does not disguise the fact that a "specifically literary context . . . is my subject" (882). She quite overtly addresses her reader as a member of "our discipline" (880), and the "feminist criticism" of the title is obviously a shorthand for the scholarly work that now constitutes the tradition of feminist literary criticism. Further, Gubar's emplottment of the first three stages foregrounds major figures in English as a field: Kate Millett, Toni Cade Bambara, Lillian Robinson, Carolyn Heilbrun, and Barbara Christian. She is, in this regard, pointedly invested in diagnosing feminist literary criticism's decline—a decline brought on in her tale by a number of scholarly figures (Mohanty, Butler, and Haraway) most notable for their disciplinary divergences from literary study (more on this later). What interests me is how porous the boundaries of literary study are in this essay, so much so that at times feminist literary criticism comes to stand for the entirety of feminist critical work in the academy: "The first stage of feminist criticism, which Elaine Showalter has called 'critique,' undercut the universality of male-devised scripts in philosophy as well as science, in intellectual as well as social history" (881, 882). The second stage of recovery, Gubar writes, has produced major publications in "East Asian and Middle Eastern Studies, in Spanish and German departments, as well as in English and in American Studies," at the same time that two of the most important of the French feminist thinkers, Helene Cixous and Luce Irigaray, relied on "comparable strategies of critique and recovery" (883). When, at essay's end, Gubar cites Rosi Braidotti on the need to return to the merrymaking of the "women's movement," we encounter the double register in which "feminist criticism" has been evoked: it is not simply a referent for feminist literary study; feminist literary study is itself the microcosm, if not centerpiece, of academic feminist criticism.[12] "How paradoxical," she thus writes in the conclusion, "that during the time of feminist criticism's successful institutionalization in many academic fields it seems to be suffering from a sickness that can end in suicide" (901).[13]

There are a number of ways to interpret Gubar's unacknowledged representation of an overlap between and critical exchange of feminist literary criticism for academic feminism. Readers might expect me to accuse her of disciplinary chauvinism which, like all such chauvinism, mistakes one's own disciplinary home for the complex critical agencies at work in the entirety of an intellectual apparatus. A more interesting interpretation, however, takes Gubar's word for it, conceding the historical significance of literary study as one of—if not *the*—primary disciplinary locations for academic feminism's early flourish.[14] How and why literary study would serve this particular function is not the focus of my discussion here, though one might surmise that the undermining of the sanctity of the discipline's object of study, inaugurated in the 1970s via the contradictory forces of continental theory and cultural studies, helped to produce the kind of porousness that Gubar's essay represents. Such porousness is, it seems to me, both symptom of the loss of the literary object's critical hegemony within English and the welcoming sign of the field's own ability to house postdisciplinary inquiry. But for Gubar, the porousness operates without explanation, which has the effect of rendering feminism's critical trajectory errant in literary study, the academy, and the public realm of the "women's movement" as well. Gubar can thus simultaneously use feminist literary criticism to speak about feminism's transit from the street to the university (thereby aligning it with social movement, the most powerful discourse of the political to operate in the twentieth century) *and* blame the breakup of the discipline-based project of feminist literary criticism on the faulty rhetorics of academic feminism itself.

In her attention to faulty rhetorics, Gubar establishes a methodological practice that yearns for textual pleasure, substituting issues of grammar and trope—mainstays of literary study as a discipline—for the content of feminist criticism's political concerns.[15] The bad manners of Judith Butler's work, for instance, are evidenced by "the preponderance of subject-verb disagreements"—twenty-two in all—that Gubar reads as characteristic of "the tensions continually at play in efforts to combine poststructuralism with feminism" (896). When Butler writes in *Gender Trouble*, for instance, that "The totality and closure of language is both presumed and contested within poststructuralism" (40), Gubar refuses to concede the possibility that this formulation is, as she puts it, "a legitimate extension of the rule that a singular verb may be used when nouns form a compound word or convey a singular notion" (898). Instead she argues that the pattern of mistakes "demonstrates how often the most vigilantly anti-totalizing theorist of poststructuralism relies on stubborn patterns of totalization (two treated as one)" (898). As a syntactical error for the feminist critical project, poststructuralism transforms feminist commitments to multiplicity (stage three's formulation of difference) into metacritical dissension, privileging "recondite abstractions" (896) over the human being's proper grammatical place in the English language, all of which is said to discount the truths of corporeal existence and pre-discursive reality (899, note 45).[16]

As if this were not enough to indicate how fallen is a poststructuralist feminism from effectivity, clarity, and political coherency, Butler's bad prose is also evidence of the star system and its negative effect on all humanities scholars today. As Gubar writes in a lengthy footnote:

> Where was the copyeditor when her manuscripts arrived at the publisher's or journal's office? Have economic pressures on publishers caused them to withdraw this important safety net from writers? Or has the star system so dismantled the normative manner of refereeing that anything goes for an elite group of academicians? If so, should we count as one of the problems facing feminist criticism the effects of this star system on a depressed marketplace? For, at the institutional level, marked disparities . . . between the few at the top and those laboring in what we

tellingly call the trenches have contributed to a divisive atmosphere that affects all practitioners in the humanities at the present time. (897)

Grammar here morphs into economics, offering a totalizing (if you will) interpretative strategy for understanding the complexities of power and hierarchy in both the publishing industry and the contemporary university. In this way, one of the most powerful and distinctive disciplining modes of English as a formal field of study becomes the only methodology offered to read Butler's theoretical prose, thereby establishing not only Butler's difference and distance from English as a normative professional culture, but poststructuralism as a syntactical refusal of "feminism's dependence on the collective word *women*" (899).

Gubar is not unaware that she has brought a discipline-based reading tactic to the work of a philosopher or that a great deal of work outside the poststructuralist feminist tradition similarly abandons faith in *women*'s collectivity. This is, rather, her very point: bad grammar, itself a form of bad manners, demonstrates feminist criticism's fateful fall from the literary, and the refusal of the literary's unit of meaning—the *word* women—indicates feminism's failure to produce a political self. Hence, the various betrayals that Butler comes to represent—of grammar, feminist politics, humanism, and the humanities—turn on feminist criticism's lost relation to the hegemony of the literary:

> The consequence for criticism of a linguistic model deriving from philosophy has been to divorce feminist speculations from literary texts or to subordinate those texts to the epistemological, ideological, economic, and political issues that supplanted literary history and aesthetic evaluation as the topics of writing about women. Given poststructuralist assumptions . . . it is not surprising that the aesthetic got marginalized and the first three stages of feminist criticism sidelined. (896)[17]

This passage is Gubar's only overt articulation of the way that the status of the aesthetic guides her entire history of feminist criticism. In this statement, interdisciplinary developments and the transformations in critical lexicons they inaugurate have—let me emphasize her word—"divorced" the feminist critical project from an aesthetic model of literary inquiry, betraying feminism's hard-won marriage to the disciplinary tradition of English. Hence the scholarly turn to "epistemological, ideological, economic, and political issues" is cast as central to feminist criticism's intellectual decline, and a critical strategy that focuses on the grammatical becomes the essay's sole means to account for economic, ideological, epistemological, and political concerns.

But let me not linger further over Gubar's deployment of the textual aesthetics of literary study as a disciplinary mode, since I want my readers to take for granted the content but not the interpretation of her larger point: that there indeed has been a profound shift in the reigning production of feminist criticism in the United States and that this shift has introduced for feminism the possibility of an extradisciplinary project of its own. That this shift is less the demise of one kind of feminist inquiry than the emergence of another is how I mark my difference from Gubar. What she decries as "metacritical dissension" can be understood to represent the institutional transformation of feminism from the status of disciplinary based critiques of the knowledge formations of "man" to the possibility that the incoherence of *women* can serve as an object of study for feminism's own academic enterprise. This is not to say that Gubar's concern for the specific project of feminist literary criticism is not an interesting or important one, but it is to argue against the decontextualizing narrative production of the literary as the singular register in which we assess the vitality and future of feminist knowledge in the contemporary academy.[18]

From the perspective of the interdisciplinary project of Women's Studies, it is perhaps necessary to argue that feminism in the academy has for too long been owned by the disciplines and thereby disciplined, especially in the humanities, by the nationalist rubrics that identify Western European, British, and U.S. culture as the center and substance of inquiry.[19] "Other" geopolitical sites of knowledge may be included, but these are "area" studies appended to a seriously truncated and idealized version of the West. That this idealized West is currently under assault on many campuses because of decreased student enrollments often means a reinvigorated claim to the historical hegemony of western knowledges, not their rearticulation in the context of new migrations of capital, people, and cultures. To hunker ourselves down in the disciplines, to cast a nostalgic gaze at a past that now finds comfort in the sanctity of discipline-as-home, to reject the compelling possibility for academic feminism of a new knowledge formation: these critical positions abandon academic feminism to an institutional framework that lags behind the kinds of issues that such a political project must confront. By engaging the antidisciplinary and postdisciplinary implications of metacritical dissension, we "make good" on academic feminism's long-time goal to transform not simply individual disciplines, but the institution, its organization of knowledge, and the ways in which we understand both the intellectual composition and possible histories of feminism itself.

Difference against Disciplinarity

The kind of metacritical challenge that Gubar's essays strenuously negates has been articulated in politically positive terms by Lisa Lowe in her important essay, "The International within the National: American Studies and Asian American Critique." Here Lowe extends discussions begun in *Immigrant Acts* concerning the interplay of Asian immigration, U.S. nationalism, and racialized democracy to address the question of the university and its disciplinary role in the production of the citizen-subject. By reading Asian immigration as an effect of empire and empire as the disavowed engine of transnational capitalism, Lowe argues that the mobilization of "identity" in interdisciplinary study is far more significant than the liberal model of cultural diversity and subtradition conferred on it would suggest. She writes:

> The traditional function of disciplinary divisions in the university is to uphold the abstract divisions of modern civil society into separate spheres for the political, the economic, and the cultural. The formation and reproduction of the modern citizen-subject is naturalized through those divisions of social space and those divisions of knowledge. The historical exclusion of Asian immigrants and Asian Americans from the political and cultural spheres continues, and is reproduced, in the relative invisibility of that history of racialization within the modern university . . . Let us understand, then, that student activism for Asian American studies in our contemporary moment is not an "identity" movement in search of cultural "roots," it is a voicing of racial consciousness that seeks to bring this history into the university, that seeks to refuse this disavowal. (12)

And again, she writes, "the force of Asian American studies is not the restoration of a cultural heritage to an identity formation, but rather the history of Asian alterity to the modern nation-state" (2). While Lowe's insistence on the critical redeployment of racialized identity is figured around the production of "Asian Americans," she expressly argues against rendering this group "exceptional" in counternarratives of national formation and empire. In doing so, she emphasizes "the history of Asian American racialization *as* a critique of national history" (17) and seeks to understand the epistemological challenge to the university that considerations of identity might hold.

My interest in Lowe's piece for this discussion arises from her desire to redeploy understandings of identity as the sedimented logic of cultural difference in the contemporary university. But while she is optimistic that the radical meaning of identity studies can register its challenge to the organization of knowledge, I am less so. This is not to say that identity studies have failed; certainly they have intervened in the logic of the university's social reproduction by critiquing the practices of exclusion on which national subjects have long been defined and produced. But they have been less successful in establishing the study of identity as a knowledge project that distinctly challenges the identitarian form of the university's intellectual reproduction in the disciplines. This is the case even though every identity-based studies program in the country initially organized itself as an interruption into disciplinary practices by generating an imperative for interdisciplinary study. Through an interdisciplinary approach to gendered or ethnic identity, such programs hoped to overcome the professionalized illegibility between knowledge domains in the university, between, say, the study of literature and language on one hand and political economy on the other. In Women's Studies, for instance, "woman" has been the vehicle for the collaborative enterprise of interdisciplinary study, and the many facets of "her" existence are thought to be illuminated by the combined interrogations of literary specialists, sociologists, anthropologists, historians, musicologists, and so on. The problem of disciplinarity has been cast more often, then, as its partial account of women—to the extent that any specific discipline provided an account at all. Forging such accounts and critiquing the methods by which the racial or gendered subject was rendered marginal or absent in the disciplines motivated identity studies as a curricular project and provided the collaborative engine for sustaining faculty involvement from diverse parts of the academy. While traditional units thus collated faculty by disciplinary expertise, identity studies have functioned more often according to a politicized convergence with the object of study (i.e. women study women, Asian Americans study Asian Americans, queers study queers). It is this convergence between subject and object that has shaped the dynamics of disciplinarity and difference in the academy today.

Belonging to identity studies has thus been a compelling, at times confounding affair: their predication on the disciplines has garnered them intellectual legibility and credibility, but the intellectual foundations of disciplines and their own identity structures (in which one comes to *be* a historian, literary scholar, or sociologist) have impeded the ability of identity studies to signify beyond the corporeal logics that they have simultaneously critiqued and rearticulated. More often than not, interdisciplinary identity projects function as solo engines for undergraduate education, providing multicultural diversity credits for students who will not encounter the larger critique of identity embedded, if at all, in upper division course work. While scholars from traditional disciplines may find interdisciplinarity liberating for certain kinds of nontraditional scholarly work, interdisciplinarity is still very much tied to the disciplines where the critical work of reproducing academic intellectual subjects continues to take place.[20] (Most scholars in interdisciplinary sites have been trained in disciplines and need to maintain their disciplinary identity in order to signify as an agent of knowledge in the academy.) The distinction I am drawing between the recognition of identity as a requirement for undergraduate education and the current impossibility of producing scholars from interdisciplinary sites occludes those divisions of knowledge—the political, economic, and cultural—described by Lisa Lowe within the institutional space of interdisciplinarity, consigning its object of study to the realm once again of cultural difference as supplementary diversity. Even attempts by identity projects to develop the doctorate degree have tended to reiterate this supplemental logic by installing difference as a form of identification and affect on one hand and cultural subtradition on the other.

The tension produced here—between the political mobilization of bodies under identitarian signs and the politicized interrogation of the problematic of identitarian social forms and formations, what I am calling metacritical difference—constitutes the primary fault line on whose sides scholars within identity studies now assemble. This fault line is riven with gendered, racial, and/or national discourses of contestation, as the identitarian production of gendered and ethnic subjects that now constitutes objects of study bears the trace of their late twentieth century U.S. production. Asian American Studies, for instance, is currently split over the question of its national belonging: is it a project of reclamation within American Studies, the racialized consciousness of the U.S. nation's racist disavowal of Asian Americans? Or is it a postnational knowledge formation, one with productive linkages to Asian area studies whose critique of national identity inaugurates its interrogation of transnational racial identity production? More crucially, through what discourses, institutional affiliations, and curricular projects will these national and postnational problematics be solved? Is Women's Studies a field formation whose political guarantee must be generated by the productive reiteration of its origin as a social movement as both the political and subjective paradigm for approaching its object of study? Is it, in other words, a location for identification in a historical, political, or corporeal sense? Or must its constitution of an identity object be strenuously deferred in order to suspend the epistemological violence that has accompanied *woman*'s intellectual viability as a specifically U.S. national discourse? If this binary is unsatisfactory, on what intellectual grounds will Women's Studies negotiate its institutional relation to knowledge, given the field's emergence within U.S. social movements? How, in short, will it resolve the unproductive opposition that has accompanied its identitarian imperative: that between the academic and the political or, in more telling language, activism and critical thought?

These questions are important not simply because of the different trajectories of analysis they project, signifying identity and difference either within or against U.S. national horizons, but because they forge distinctly different conceptions of identity's status as a proper object of study on one hand and its proper function as a knowledge formation on the other hand. It is not too much to say, in fact, that the tension I am defining here, between an object of study given coherence by its circumscription in the nation and a knowledge formation that functions in contradistinction to the hegemony of nation, brings into visibility, if not crisis, the very logic on which most of the human sciences as a coherent set of disciplinary units now depends. Certainly in the humanities, which has been the domain most receptive to and productively challenged by identity studies, it is the nation that serves as the primary structure of knowledge, with literature and language, along with history, classics, art history, film, and philosophy—not to mention area studies—organized according to national domains. In the social sciences, sociology makes its break from anthropology precisely by studying the United States, the national entity occluded by anthropology's early ethnographic emphasis on "elsewhere," and political science and economics take their macro shape via the determinations of international organizations of people and processes. The consequences of disciplinary logics on identity studies are multiple, especially when considered in the context of the academy's own political economy of knowledge production. In their underresourced and mainly programmatic status in the institution, identity studies regularly rely on faculty both trained and located in traditional disciplines, which means that intellectual subjective formation as well as intellectual belonging are predicated on the identity and authority conferred by disciplinary structures. This is not to say that scholars experience no abjection in their relation to disciplinary structures, but it is to foreground the fact that knowledge identity is today disciplinarily based, which often has the powerful effect of rendering identity studies as domains of belonging in a corporeal identitarian sense.

What would it mean for feminism (or any interdisciplinary identity site) to forge a recognition of the way that the modern university has been constructed on the grounds of identitarian logics, those that have not only refused to think about the relation between corporeality and knowledge but that have opposed corporeality and knowledge via the power of disciplinarity as the primary form of the university's identitarian politics? To the extent that practitioners in identity-based studies maintain the priority of the disciplines as uninterrogated sites of identity construction, they tacitly reproduce the minoritizing modalities within which identity studies are deprived of the status as knowledge formation and hence repeatedly reiterated as cultural diversity. Indeed, the crisis narrative of academic feminism that Gubar produces indicates most profoundly that we have not yet responded to the implications of constructing a knowledge project in the afterlife of identity's political mobility as a discourse of intervention in state practices and institutions. Rather than directing our attention to those political and intellectual origins in the disciplines that cannot be sustained in the present as a vehicle for unwriting the future of difference, we might consider what it is that thinking within identity studies as the institutional domain of difference can do. This will entail not only a rigorous explication of the nationalist contours of identity politics but also a far more extensive consideration of the relationship between disciplinary and difference in the history and politics of knowledge production. It is this approach that would constitute a metacritical deployment of difference, as it would proceed from and not against the deconstruction of categories that has simultaneously interrupted the diversity model of racialization within feminist criticism and challenged the disciplinary vocabularies that have functioned to contain *women* as a referent for themselves.

My purpose in shifting from Gubar's history of feminist criticism to the organizational strategy for interdisciplinarity is to forestall the familiar move in feminist discourse of heralding interdisciplinarity as the critical answer to the limitations of disciplinary formations of knowledge. Instead, I want to foreground how the current difficulty facing those of us who want to think difference against the disciplines requires a critical stance toward interdisciplinarity, one that can assess its "domestication" by disciplinary authority and its ongoing entanglements with the corporate forces of both capitalism and the nation-state. This is where the work of the culprits that Gubar cites—U.S. ethnic, postcolonial, and poststructuralist theory—might meet up in an intellectually productive way, to deliver to feminism an intellectual imperative that simultaneously refuses the supplementary logic of disciplinary "diversity" and the current domestication of interdisciplinary "identity." This is, at the very least, the centerpiece of my argument here, which hopes to rescue difference from the performative function of providing for the institution a good mood.

Notes

1. One might argue here that the academic institutional and critical analytic questions I am raising through "Murder without a Text" are just that: academic questions that have no discursive relation to the genre of the short story in general or the murder mystery in particular. But while Gubar's essay and Cross's short story are different kinds of discursive engagements, they share a mutual interest in academic feminism, which is either the topic or the background against which their narratives about relationships among women play. Such a confederacy, if you will, makes possible (if not wholly predictable) *this* essay's examination of the way that disciplinary authority trumps the epistemological value of difference in certain contemporary feminist discourses.

2. Gubar's organization of U.S. ethnic and postcolonial feminist thought into a composite category of "racialized identity politics" is problematic in a number of ways. It condenses the intellectual histories and social conditions from which ethnic and postcolonial studies have been generated, eclipsing the differing constructions of U.S. national identities and their contradictory relation to postcolonial frameworks. Racialization is not a uniform or universal process of economic and social disenfranchisement, as various scholars writing on issues of immigration, colonialization, and national identity currently explore. George, for instance, investigates the way that a racialized identity based on color is routinely resisted by South Asian immigrants to the U.S., even as the history of South Asian immigration must be understood as a phenomenon of both British colonialism and first world transnational capital flows. Other recent scholarship forges a conversation about the applicability of postcolonial studies to American Studies (Cherniavsky; King) in general and Asian American studies in particular (Chuh).

3. Schor echoes in a different vein some of Gubar's concerns. In her introduction to *Bad Objects*, she laments how cultural studies has meant "being drawn away from the literary text" and links it to the conditions of the present in which "academic feminism [has] bec[o]me a victim of its own success" (xiv). Such success is described explicitly in the context of social constructionism's theoretical challenge to woman and to the subsequent "rise of a growing number of identitarian communities spawned to a large extent by feminism," communities which have

> weakened what many of those of my generation of feminists had treasured about feminism: a sense of commonality, of participating even as a footnote in perhaps the most successful peaceful revolutionary movement of our era. Anguished and legitimate claims to difference cannot, however, mask the perils of particularism and the dangers of separatism that are beginning to show through. . . . I remain a feminist, and I feel myself going back to literature as a feminist, but differently

so. . . . The question for me is: will a *new* feminist literary criticism arise that will take literariness seriously while maintaining its vital ideological edge? (xiv)

4. Does this mean that Gubar dismisses difference altogether or that we can read her as being an opponent of critical interrogations of differences among women? The answer is clearly no. Her first three stages each feature scholarship by feminists of color: Toni Cade Bambara, Barbara Christian, and Mary Helen Washington are presented as part of the critical power of academic feminism's early emphasis on women's literary traditions, and Nellie McKay, Hortense Spillers, Deborah McDowell, and Gloria Hull signal the significance of difference to a history of subtraditions. It is not social difference, then, but difference as a metacritical challenge to literature as a disciplinary domain that threatens to undo feminist criticism's good health.

5. My discussion here of Gubar's "What Ails Feminist Criticism?" is a revised version of a response published in *Critical Inquiry*. I want to thank Susan for subsequent conversations about the issues raised in our exchange in *Critical Inquiry* and for her continued contribution to my thinking about academic feminism, difference, and the problem of disciplinarity. See Wiegman, "What Ails Feminist Criticism: A Second Opinion."

6. By "minoritized" I want to mark the production of a social group as discursively and historically minor even as some groups—women for instance—are numerically a majority. Certainly a postnational perspective would demonstrate the numerical minority status of whites globally.

7. On the question of generations in academic feminism, see Looser and Kaplan and Christian et al.

8. In describing white women as injured by the "debilitating rhetorics" of racialized identity discourses, Gubar participates in the rhetorical transformation that now marks the popular public sphere where discourses of injury and white minoritization have come to characterize the postsegregationist white subject. As Wendy Brown has discussed in *States of Injury*, injury is at the end of the twentieth century the governing grammar of American democracy, which means that political power and redress are defined by a group's ability to demonstrate its identity status as an injured one. In this context, white identity has been renarrated as injured via those civil rights projects that arose historically to challenge it, to such an extent that, in academic feminism, as Gubar puts it, "the politics of racial authenticity may be experienced as an attack on feminism's endorsement of all women's right to self-expression" (891). Since Brown's book was published in 1995, the grammar of injury has had its more significant conservative deployment in California, where Proposition 209 succeeded in outlawing affirmative action in public education and services. This application of injury to defend and extend the rights of the racially dominant group is spreading to other states and "marks," quite literally, a historical shift in the way that white racial identity is rhetorically defined. Whiteness, so often the universal norm of the generic citizen, has been particularized as a consequence of both civil rights reform and the post-segregationist move to multiculturalism, with the result that whites throughout the United States are finding it increasingly difficult to isolate themselves from some kind of awareness of their own racial status. See Wiegman, "Whiteness Studies and the Paradox of Particularity."

9. Gubar places works by both Bambara and Washington in a list of texts, including Lillian Robinson's *Sex, Class, and Culture* and Tillie Olsen's *Silences*, that "were based on

Simone de Beauvoir's insight into women's alterity and spawned numerous analyses of the images and stereotypes of 'the second sex' in male-authored literature" (6). While one does not doubt that de Beauvoir had wide influence on feminist literary critics in the 1970s, it is a reduction of the critical contribution of *The Black Woman: An Anthology* and *Black-Eyed Susans* to jettison both U.S. racial conditions and the African-American Studies movement in situating their projects historically. This is not to say that one must make "black" (and hence particular) every utterance by African-American feminist scholars; rather I am pointing to the asymmetry in the critical history offered by "What Ails Feminist Criticism?" in which the issue of racial specificity is absent in the first two stages, while it oversaturates the third and fourth stages, where it functions as symptomatic error.

10. By responsibility, I am referring to the necessity of disarticulating the history and meaning of academic feminism from the prototypical plot of white women's subjectivity.

11. For a discussion of the ways in which disciplinary identity operates in relation to other contemporary critiques of academic feminism in general and Women's Studies in particular, see Wiegman, "Feminism, Institutionalism, and the Idiom of Failure."

12. Fraser's "Multiculturalism, Antiessentialism, and Radical Democracy" offers an importantly broader history of feminist scholarship since the 1970s than the focus on literary criticism provided in "What Ails Feminist Criticism?" Explicating the shift in the early 1990s from a focus of differences (racial, sexual) among women to an analysis of "multiple intersecting differences," Fraser writes, "What had appeared at first to be a turning inward (instead of focusing on our relation to men, we would focus on the relations among ourselves) seemed instead to invite a turning outward (instead of focusing on gender alone, we would focus on its relation to other crosscutting axes of difference and subordination). In this way, the whole range of politicized differences would become grist for the feminist mill" (180). By placing her discussion in the context of a clear articulation of the political field in which feminism for her necessarily struggles (radical democracy), Fraser is able to mount a critique of culturalist understandings of social change without simultaneously creating a narrative of feminism's fall. Such a method enables feminism to exist in a contradictory historical present, with no overarching nostalgia or reverse teleology. For critical conversations about the broad implications of feminism's self-reflective turn in the 1990s to narratives of its own historical becoming, see Elam and Wiegman, eds., *Feminism Beside Itself*, especially the essays by Susan Stanford Friedman and Deborah McDowell. For a consideration of the lesbian as the figure around which feminist critical history turns, see Dever.

13. Gubar is not alone in lamenting the course of academic feminism. Modleski's *Feminism Without Women: Culture and Criticism in a "Postfeminist" Age* opened the decade with a lament about the undoing of feminism, leveling the charge against feminist poststructuralism on one hand and gender studies on the other. But where Modleski saw the poststructuralist evacuation of the category of woman as the "latest ruse of white middle-class feminism" (21), Gubar sets poststructuralism in league with postcolonial and U.S. ethnic feminisms, indicting the way "racialized identity politics made the word 'women' slim down to stand only for a very particularized kind of woman, whereas poststructuralists obliged the term to disappear altogether" (901). For a counter to Modleski, from the perspective of lesbian studies, see Jagose.

For Bordo, postmodernism has been the culprit and deconstruction the weapon in battering feminism into docility, so disconnected has feminism seemingly become from its earliest political urgency. For an important counter to the view that postmodernism is incompatible with feminism, see Flax. For a more positive view of the relationship of deconstruction to feminism, see Elam's *Feminism and Deconstruction*.

14. It seems to me that the field of history would most closely vie with English as the domain for early academic feminism's proliferation as, much like English, it has been profoundly transformed by feminist scholarship. But I would argue that it is English's own definitive position as the university's largest humanities unit—and that it is the relationship between subjectivist methodologies and humanistic inquiry—that has made the difference, so to speak, in how feminism has fared in the academy. Further, once literary studies is no longer securely ensconced in a Cold War understanding of a homogeneous national culture, once its role in the production of citizen-subjects is de-emphasized by the globalizing imperatives of a transforming nation-state, its porousness becomes the symptom of its social devaluation. When this devaluation is read as the consequence of feminism's theoretical waywardness, and when this waywardness is couched in the language of manners, it becomes difficult to consider how the porous nature of the discipline of English today might be a sign of its ability to entertain a certain productive undisciplining of its own traditional knowledge.

15. Feminist theory's interest in poststructuralism has created a now lengthy discussion concerning the use and abuse of "jargon," the elitism of theory, the irony of feminist engagement with white male European thinkers, and theory's seeming displacement of the feminist commitment to politics outside the academy. See, for instance, Hartsock; and Christian, "The Race for Theory." For a defense of poststructuralist influences on feminism, see the essays collected in Butler and Scott. Much of this critique of poststructuralism is propelled by the general public attack on the humanities, which continue to undergo radical reconfiguration by the corporate imperative for instrumental knowledge. From this perspective, then, Gubar's explanation of the language crisis—that "economic forces . . . escalated the pressure always exerted on humanities scholars to produce a reputation by engaging in arcane, agonistic maneuvers or by feverishly finding innovative vocabularies" (900–901)—actually misunderstands the way the critique of philosophical language from within the humanities further *undermines* the tradition of humanistic inquiry she elsewhere defends by requiring uniform intellectual vocabularies. In a similar way, much of the current conversation about the declining role of the public intellectual positions itself as defending the threatened humanities while tacitly supporting the imperative to reduce critical fluencies by creating for the humanities a monodisciplinary discourse, one that can stand on its own in the mass-mediated commodity sphere.

16. Signaling "a conflict between what Butler seeks to argue and the terms available to her," Gubar reads Butler's antigrammatical strategy as a violation of both feminist and poststructuralist commitment, totalizing a multiple subject by transforming it into one (897). But a second look at Butler's pattern of disagreements yields a different story: in all of the examples cited in the text Butler reverses grammatical logic, refunctioning the predicate as the controlling subject of the sentence and thereby subordinating the grammatical

subject. In so doing, Butler challenges, in rigorous poststructuralist fashion, the foundational logic of the subject so firmly ensconced in the structure of the English language.

17. In an implicit counterargument to the one advanced by Gubar, Miller's "Philoctetes' Sister" argues that the aesthetic and the racial/political are not divisible elements of the literary text. "[W]e need a revisionary 'morality of the aesthetic' that would produce a reading capable of interpreting . . . the marks of race and gender in the text as intrinsic to literariness itself" (113).

18. English as the institutional location from which we assess the impact of postcolonial theory—also part of Gubar's fourth stage of metacritical dissension—is nothing if not ironic, given the incongruence of wagering feminism's effectiveness from within a knowledge formation so finely tuned to the exigencies of the first world nation. "English" is after all the culmination and preservation of a distinct history of literature's privileged citation as "culture," defining, as David Lloyd and Paul Thomas have recently observed, the nationalist discourse of the educated person in the consolidation of the modern state. To the extent that postcolonial studies sees its intellectual project as a political engagement with decolonization, not only in terms of state practices and historical memories but also disciplinary formations, it is striking that so few departments devoted to literary study have been able to register what the postcolonial might mean to their disciplinary configurations. Even the hiring of postcolonial theorists tends not to inaugurate a reconsideration of departmental organizations of research and teaching, as Irish, South Asian, and Native Indian studies, to take only three examples, are forced to remain uncomfortably within the nation-bound rubrics of the U.S. and British literary traditions. For feminism to wed its academic worldview to the perspective of literary study, with the discipline's contested but nonetheless continued commitment to British intellectual and geopolitical colonialism, is to limit feminism as a project that critically interrogates the institution's disciplinary management of culture, gender, and knowledge. I have been a member of one department of English that used the insights of postcolonial theory to decolonize the conceptual structures governing undergraduate instruction, producing a course rubric for the major that replaced national and period specifications with the categories of History, Theory, and Politics. While this new rubric has problems of its own, it is nonetheless significant that the department's organization of itself as a discipline tried to work against the inscription of English as the overarching signature for the study of literature and other textual objects. For more about Syracuse University's curriculum, see Mailloux.

19. For an important conversation about the circumscription of Asian literary studies in the United States, see Chow.

20. Indeed, the reproductive logic of a discipline—its ability to reproduce both practitioners and the legitimacy and knowability of its object of study—is the most essential characteristic of disciplinarity, and not even interdisciplinarity can come close to threatening this, for interdisciplinarity merely proliferates the disciplinary investment in an object by making it available to each discipline's mode of mastery. This is why feminist studies, for instance, has been far more successful in finding a place in the disciplines than it has been in establishing Women's Studies as a disciplinary entity in its own right. Women's lack of status as an epistemological object, their "additive" difference to man enables history departments and literature programs to expand their canons while the counter-possibility—the study of men within the Women's Studies curriculum—is met even by

feminist faculty with great alarm. Interdisciplinarity often protects the disciplines by guaranteeing their proliferation at the site of an object—today so often a minoritized identity—whose social rebellion has engendered it as an object to be known. Belonging to a discipline and the disciplining of belonging are crucial parts, then, of the reproductive logic of disciplines.

Works Cited

Barrett, Lindon. "Identities and Identity Studies: Reading Toni Cade Bambara's 'The Hammer Man.'" *Cultural Critique* 39 (Spring 1998): 5–29.

Bordo, Susan. *Unbearable Weight: Feminism, Western Culture, and the Body*. Berkeley: University of California Press, 1993.

Brown, Wendy. *States of Injury: Power and Freedom in Late Modernity*. Princeton, N.J.: Princeton University Press, 1995.

Butler, Judith. *Gender Trouble: Feminism and the Subversion of Identity*. New York: Routledge, 1990.

Butler, Judith, and Joan W. Scott, eds. *Feminists Theorize the Political*. New York: Routledge, 1992.

Cherniavsky, Eva. "Subaltern Studies in a U.S. Frame." *boundary 2* 23.2 (Summer 1996): 85–110.

Chow, Rey. "The Politics and Pedagogy of Asian Literatures in American Universities." *differences* 2.3 (Fall 1990): 29–51.

Christian, Barbara. "The Race for Theory." *The Nature and Context of Minority Discourse*. Ed. Abdul JanMohamed and David Lloyd. Oxford: Oxford University Press, 1990. 37–49.

Christian, Barbara, Ann duCille, Sharon Marcus, Elaine Marks, Nancy K. Miller, Sylvia Schafer, and Joan W Scott. "Conference Call." *differences* 2.3 (Fall 1990): 52–108.

Chuh, Kandice. "Perfecting the Union: Asian Americanism and the Politics of the Transnational." Dissertation. University of Washington, 1997.

Cross, Amanda. "Murder without a Text." *A Woman's Eye*. Ed. Sara Paretsky. New York, 1991. 114–134.

Dever, Carolyn. "Obstructive Behavior: Dykes in the Mainstream of Feminist Theory." *Cross-Purposes: Lesbians, Feminists, and the Limits of Alliance*. Ed. Dana Heller. Bloomington: Indiana University Press, 1997. 19–41.

Elam, Diane. *Feminism and Deconstruction: Ms. en Abyme*. London: Routledge, 1994.

Elam, Diane, and Robyn Wiegman, eds. *Feminism Beside Itself*. New York: Routledge, 1995.

Flax, Jane. "The End of Innocence." *Disputed Subjects: Essays on Psychoanalysis, Politics and Philosophy*. New York: Routledge, 1993. 131–147.

Fraser, Nancy. "Multiculturalism, Antiessentialism, and Radical Democracy." *Justice Interruptus: Critical Reflections on the "Postsocialist" Condition*. New York: Routledge, 1997. 173–188.

Friedman, Susan Stanford. "Making History: Reflections on Feminism, Narrative, and Desire." *Feminism Beside Itself*. Ed. Elam and Wiegman. New York: Routledge, 1995. 11–53.

George, Rosemary. "'From Expatriate Aristocrat to Immigrant Nobody': South Asian Racial Strategies in the Southern Californian Context." *Diaspora* 6.1 (Spring 1997): 31–60.

Gubar, Susan. "What Ails Feminist Criticism?" *Critical Inquiry* 24.4 (Summer 1998): 878–902.

Hartsock, Nancy. "Rethinking Modernism: Minority vs. Majority Theories." *Cultural Critique* 7 (Fall 1987): 187–206.

Jagose, Annamarie. "'Feminism without Women': A Lesbian Reassurance," *Cross-Purposes: Lesbians, Feminists, and the Limits of Alliance*. Ed. Dana Heller. Bloomington: Indiana University Press, 1997. 124–35.

King, Richard, ed. *The U.S. Postcolonial*. Urbana: University of Illinois Press, 1998.

Lloyd, David, and Paul Thomas. *Culture and the State*. New York: Routledge, 1998.

Looser, Devoney, and E. Ann Kaplan, eds. *Generations: Academic Feminists in Dialogue*. Minneapolis: University of Minnesota Press, 1997.

Lowe, Lisa. *Immigrant Acts*. Durham, N.C.: Duke University Press, 1997.

———. "The International within the National: American Studies and Asian American Critique." *Cultural Critique* 40 (Fall 1998): 29–47.

Mailloux, Steve. "Rhetoric Returns to Syracuse: The Reception of Curricular Reform." *Reception Histories: Rhetoric, Pragmatism, and American Cultural Politics*. Ithaca, N.Y.: Cornell University Press, 1998. 151–181.

McDowell, Deborah. "Transferences: Black Feminist Discourse: The 'Practice' of 'Theory.'" *Feminism Beside Itself*. Ed. Elam and Wiegman. New York: Routledge, 1995. 93–118.

Miller, Nancy K. "Philoctetes' Sister: Feminist Literary Criticism and the New Misogyny." *Getting Personal: Feminist Occasions and Other Autobiographical Acts*. New York: Routledge, 1991. 101–120.

Modleski, Tania. *Feminism without Women: Culture and Criticism in a "Postfeminist" Age*. New York: Routledge, 1991.

Schor, Naomi. *Bad Objects: Essays Popular and Unpopular*. Durham, N.C.: Duke University Press, 1995.

Wiegman, Robyn. "Feminism, Institutionalism, and the Idiom of Failure." *differences* 11 (Fall 1999/2000): 107–136.

———. "What Ails Feminist Criticism? A Second Opinion." *Critical Inquiry* 25.2 (Winter 1999): 362–379.

———. "Whiteness Studies and the Paradox of Particularity." *boundary 2* 26.3 (Fall 1999): 115–150.

Doing Justice to C. L. R. James's
Mariners, Renegades and Castaways

DONALD E. PEASE

Just Phrasing

William E. Cain contributed an essay to the 1995 volume *C. L. R. James: His Intel-lectual Legacies* entitled "The Triumph of the Will and the Failure of Resistance: C. L. R. James's Readings of *Moby-Dick* and *Othello.*"[1] He represented the essay as in part an effort to redress the failure of Melville scholars to acknowledge the significance to their archive of James's *Mariners, Renegades and Castaways: The Story of Herman Melville and the World We Live In.* James had written the book in 1953 on Ellis Island where he had been detained by the state for his "subversive activities." "Melville scholars said little about *Mariners, Renegades and Castaways* when it ap-peared in 1953," Cain mentions as an example of this interpretive neglect, "and it continues to be absent from nearly all of the bibliographies and critical studies devoted to Melville" (261). To document this latter claim Cain entered into evi-dence the following footnote:

> Stanley T. Williams, in *Eight American Authors*, an important reference book pub-lished in 1956, dismisses James's book in three sentences (235). Incredibly, it is nowhere cited in John Bryant's nine-hundred-page *Companion to Melville Studies.* Nor is it cited by Kerry McSweeney or Martin Bickman ("Introduction"), both of whom provide overviews of the novel and its place in modern criticism. It is also absent from all the anthologies of criticism devoted to Melville in general and to *Moby-Dick* in particular. Richard Brodhead mentions it in passing ("Introduction" 19), but inappropriately links it to D. H. Lawrence's chapter on Melville in *Studies in Classic American Literature* (1923) and Charles Olson's *Call Me Ishmael* (1947). Lawrence's and Olson's commentaries have been widely read and have informed scholarship on *Moby-Dick.* Melville specialists, as well as historians of American literature and criticism, either have not known about, or have ignored, James's work. (270–271)

In the wake of these observations, Cain's readers might have expected him to right this injustice with an account of the difference the inclusion of James's project within the Melville archive would make. But in place of either arguing the case for the addition of James's text to the Melville archive, or providing a commen-tary of it that would compare its interpretive claims with those of other Melville scholars, Cain instead enumerated the several critical shortcomings of James's reading of Melville.

Cain's criticisms of James were broad gauged. They ranged from the observation that James's project "shuns (the) academic decorum" expected of literary exegesis to the accusation that James had willfully reimagined the events of Melville's novels and the meanings they declared (261). "But this truth is one that James himself extrapolates from, indeed creates in, the texts bringing to light and affirming not what the text contains but, rather, his vivid reimagination of it" (260–261). The differences in the tone and reference of Cain's judgments might be understood to derive from the different registers in which Cain applied the key phrases from the title of his essay.

Throughout "The Triumph of the Will and the Failure of Resistance: C. L. R. James's Readings of *Moby-Dick* and *Othello*," Cain deployed the two phrases from his title within linked but separable genres of discourse. This double-voiced reading enabled him to articulate an interpretive as well as a juridical accounting of James's work. The key phrase in Cain's title, "the triumph of the will," is a quotation of the famous title of Leni Riefenstahl's Nazi propaganda film. In his usage of it in the interpretive aspect of his essay, Cain proposed that this phrase be construed as the encompassing theme that would explain the effect of Melville's representation of Ahab's rhetorics of persuasion. But when Cain linked "the triumph of the will" to "the failure of resistance," he meant for the latter phrase to refer to the crew's incapacity to withstand the debilitating effects of Ahab's rhetoric.

When he thereafter applied these identical phrases to his assessment of James's reading of Melville's crew, however, Cain reinvested them with the quasi-legal power of juridical verdicts. In the first of the following sentences Cain accused James of exercising the totalitarian will that Melville had condemned; in the second, Cain described Melville's text as unable to resist James's willful misrepresentations: "James's book is a fateful meeting between James and another man, Melville, whom he refuses to become—and whom he overcomes by transforming into his own likeness. James misconstrues and, thus, seeks to vanquish Melville's language about Ahab, the crew and the implications of the ship's manic quest" (266).

These examples would suggest that James's revisionistic reading of the *Pequod's* crew has provoked in Cain a transformation in his essayistic stance from the representative of more or less agreed upon interpretive norms to the arbiter of a juridical matter. "James honors Melville and acts as his representative but he also edits and contains him," Cain judiciously observes, "providing a selection of passages and commentary that substitute for *Moby-Dick* and the other primary works themselves" (261). In stipulating that James's programmatic championing "of the creativity of the masses and the resolve and resourcefulness of workers" resulted in his "over-honoring the men and dissociating them from Ahab," Cain has transferred Ahab-like control onto James's commentary.

Cain has exercised the juridical authority tacitly invested in the phrases of his title, that is to say, in order to charge James with inflicting interpretive harm on Melville's narrative. James has not read Melville's novel, Cain concludes, but bent it into conformity with his own ideology, and thereafter recreated it to make it "serve his own social, political and historical purposes and affirm his goals" (270).

As Cain's idiom has vacillated back and forth between hermeneutic and juridical registers, its juridical phrases have transformed its interpretive assumptions into decisive judgments. This crossing over from the interpretive into the juridical sphere became most evident when Cain characterized James's commentary as "subversive" of Melville's text. The term "subversive" produced an homonymy which deserves further elaboration between a judgment Cain arrived at concerning James's literary practices and the state's reclassification of his political activities as posing a clear and present danger to the Cold War state.

Moby-Dick was not for scholars of American literature merely an object of analysis. It provided the field itself with a frame narrative that included the norms and assumptions out of which the field was organized. The action that *Moby-Dick* narrated was made to predict the world-scale antagonism of the Cold War. The narrative provided the state with an image of itself as overcoming the totalitarian order to which it defined itself as opposed, and it supplied the literary sphere with an image of itself as exempt from the incursions of the state. Overall, this frame narrative helped structure the constitutive understanding of the society that it purported to represent.

This frame narrative has continued to accumulate cultural capital through scholarly readings of Melville's novel that have reproduced, transmitted, and distributed its normative assumptions. The literary protocols which Cain has invoked to regulate James's reading of this text were tied to cultural axioms and interpretive norms that lay sedimented within this frame narrative. The difference between readings of the novel that had reproduced the assumptions of the state and the very different assumptions organizing James's commentary emerge at the site of the difference between the two phrases in his title—"the story of Herman Melville" and "the world we live in."

The first of these phrases referred to the interpretive aspect of James's book as a commentary on Melville's project. But the second phrase designated the place from which James wrote as the locus for his juridical appeal of the state's decision to deport him. In place of linking the juridical phrase in his title to the interpretive norms that regulated the field of American Studies, James connected it to the injustice the "mariners, renegades, and castaways" had suffered in Melville's novel. After James associated his plight with that of the mariners, renegades, and castaways, he transformed his commentary into a witness against the aestheticization of the social injustice they shared.

Doing Justice; Aesthetic Judgment

I have turned to Cain's criticisms of the interpretive liberties James took with Melville's crew because the clarity with which Cain has described the dilemma James's reading of Melville posed for scholars trained in the field of American literature constituted the first truly responsible reading of James's book. Cain elucidated the difference between James's writing practice and the aesthetic ideology that prevailed in the field of American literature when he provided determinate aesthetic criteria for the exclusion of James's work from the field of American literature.

Cain found *Mariners, Renegades and Castaways: The Story of Herman Melville and the World We Live In* guilty of having violated the scholarly field's aesthetic rules on the following three counts: James had not written a disinterested interpretation; James had reimagined the canonical work which the field of American literature had elevated into its frame narrative; and James had substituted a narration of the crew as collective movement that aspired to social change in place of Melville's representation of them as wholly subordinated to Ahab's will. Instead of an interpretation of Melville's novels, James had written an allegory of his own subjection.

Cain derived the authority for each of these negative judgments concerning James's commentary from aesthetic criteria which ratified the belief that the subordination of the interpreter's will to the author's transcendent imagination would result in a truly disinterested interpretation of the work. Cain's dispute with James over the appropriate interpretation of Melville's crew resulted from their different understanding of the relationship between aesthetic and juridical criteria. It originated with the question that James asked of Melville's novel and that Cain believed violated its aesthetic integrity: "Why, in Melville's *Moby-Dick*, don't the crew members aboard the *Pequod* rebel against their diabolical captain?" (260) Cain states that in answering this question, James championed "the creativity of the masses and the resolve and resourcefulness of workers." This interpretive tack resulted in James's "over-honoring the men and dissociating them from Ahab." James had not read Melville's novel, Cain concluded, but bent it into conformity with his own ideology, and thereafter recreated it to make it "serve his own social, political and historical purposes and affirm his goals" (270). But the idiom in which Cain proceeded to articulate his dispute with James over the question of the mariners could not accommodate within its vocabulary the injustice that James believed them to have suffered.

When James bore witness against the injustice in Melville's narrative, he did so by way of an idiom that was in only one of its aspects an interpretation of *Moby-Dick*. In another it was a juridical appeal of the state's decision to deport him. The difference between James's writing practice and the aesthetic ideology that prevailed in the field of American literature might become clearer if we consider James's rationale for refusing to abide by the several interpretive norms of which Cain found him in violation.

Cain construed Melville's representation of the crew as a narrative theme whose significance, while open to different interpretations, was nevertheless restricted to a horizon of expectations circumscribed by the already archivized readings of it. But James's account of the crew was neither cognitive in its aims nor mimetic in its means. James did not arrive at the significance of the crew by submitting their experiences to a range of already determined concepts. He believed that a strictly thematic reading of their predicament would silence the mariners by turning them into the mute referent for an interpretive discourse that was alone authorized to speak of and for them.

In addressing the question of the crew's right to revolt to *Moby-Dick*, the frame narrative of U.S. culture, James had shifted the register of his commentary from that of interpreting a secondary theme within an American masterwork to that of acting upon the social injustice that he found within the narrative. Whereas Cain believed that aesthetic criteria alone were required to do justice to a literary work, James's commentary questioned Melville's having adjudicated questions of social injustice according to strictly aesthetic criteria.

Cain's disagreement with James over the appropriate interpretation of Melville's crew becomes an indissoluble double bind: Cain could not redress the wrong Melville scholars had done to James's work without providing them with the aesthetic criteria they required to justify their having ignored it. But James could not adhere to the field's interpretive norms without legitimating a political wrong. Cain invoked aesthetic criteria to overrule James's "reimagination" of Melville's crew. But James rewrote Melville's text to bear critical witness against an injustice that Cain's strictly aesthetic criteria could not acknowledge: namely, the horror of Melville's failure to provide the crew with the power to revolt against their monomaniacal captain.

By way of the observation that after Ahab "stated that the purpose of the voyage was different from that for which they had signed, the men were entitled to revolt and to take possession of the ship themselves,"[2] James fashioned Ahab as a prefiguration of the national security state's emergency powers. He also described the crew as the internal limit to Ahab's totalitarian governance. The crew held the place of the rule of law, and, as such, they were comparably empowered by this "higher" law to overthrow Ahab's totalitarian rule.

It was because they owed "no allegiance to anybody or anything except the work they have to do and the relations with one another upon which that work depends" (20) that the mariners in *Moby-Dick* produced a discontinuity with the oppressive conditions that prevailed under Ahab. Thus reimagined, Melville's castaways enabled James to talk back to the power of the Cold War state through figures who were likewise extrinsic to its forms of governance.

Upon remarking the parallel between Ahab's illegal change of the contract and the emergency powers claimed by the Cold War state, James replaced the Ishmael–Ahab opposition, which establishment Americanists had proposed as the narrative's thematic center, with the unacknowledged knowledge that the "meanest mariners, renegades and castaways" constituted alternatives to both forms of totalitarian rule. In drawing upon this subaltern knowledge to focus his reading, James also disclosed the state's interest in its disqualification.

In complaining that these aspects of James's text transgressed against the range of acceptable substitutions ratified by the field, Cain also, as we have seen, verged on legitimating the state's decision to deport James.[3] This correlation between the state's political judgment and American literature's aesthetic judgment suggests a relationship between the ideology of the aesthetic and the reason of state and the pertinence of that relationship to C. L. R. James's *Mariners, Renegades and Castaways: The Story of Herman Melville and the World We Live In* that requires some brief explanation.

Cain's critical judgments were finally authorized by criteria derived from what Terry Eagleton has called the "ideology of the aesthetic." Eagleton has conceptualized the aesthetic as ideological in the Althusserian sense that it supplied a universal subject for ideology. The category of the aesthetic regulated and described at once the agent responsible for the production of the aesthetic work, as well as its medium and its interpreter.[4] As the space in the social order defined as exempt from the incursions of power common to the realm of realpolitik, the aesthetic sphere was construed as at once a utopia resistant to politics and the site for the reproduction of the regulatory norms that are prerequisites for the modern liberal state to function.[5] The aesthetic sphere supplied properties—disinterest, impartiality, taste—which comprised the ideal conditions for consent to the processes of subjectivization and reproduction of the liberal state.

The state exercised its juridical power by representing its laws as the enforcement of the sovereign rights its citizens had subjectivized. Aesthetic judgment produced the illusion of autonomy for the individual citizen's sovereign rights by linking them with the universal subject of aesthetic ideology rather than the state. In its restaging of subjection to state rule, the aesthetic fostered belief in the individual's capacity to create the laws that the state enforced. Redescribed as the artist's sensuous revelation of the laws that the state enforced, the aesthetic ideology reconciled, in the form of a "lawfulness without a law"[6] its subjects to the regulatory power of the state. Artistic expression was subsequently recharacterized in terms of freedom from state regulation.

The aesthetic sphere thereby magically transformed the state's sovereign power of governance into laws that it encouraged free subjects to believe they had "created" and then given themselves. In representing the law as the outcome of a subject's freely exercised creative activity (a lawfulness without a law), the aesthetic ideology mystified the site wherein the state integrated individual subjects within its order.

When construed as the means whereby the field has regulated itself, the ideology of the aesthetic permitted Cain to conduct what Pierre Bourdieu has described as a kind of "structural censorship."[7] Rather than appealing to protocols specifically empowered to isolate and thereafter punish James's transgression of the field's norms and expectations, Cain presupposed the structuring norms of the field itself as the final authority for his critique of James.

As an instance of this structural censorship, consider Cain's judgment that James has written "interpretive commentary on them that substitute for *Moby-Dick* and the other primary works themselves." The force of this judgment derived from the assumption that the literary interpreter should occupy the position of the universal subject of aesthetic ideology whose capacity to interpret was drawn from the attitude of disinterested interest in the imaginative work. In thus reconstituting the autonomy of the literary sphere out of the exclusion of such questions, Cain reinscribed his aesthetic judgments within the logic of the reason of state.

But Cain's arbitration of the dispute between Melville and James over the crew's right to revolt ignored the condition under which James wrote. James's position was identical with that of Melville's mariners, renegades, and castaways, who lacked the social enfranchisement that was the prerequisite for having their values recognized in the arena of aesthetic representation. In advancing their rights at the borderline between aesthetic universalism and the matters it could not subsume, James repudiated the transcendental aesthetic in the name of their contingent social needs. He refused to ratify art's autonomy in order to disclose the social inequalities—the differences in privilege, taste, access, and legitimation—that the political ideal of autonomous expression covered over. James's refusal entailed changing the criteria by which aesthetic practices were evaluated. His scrutiny of its processes of eligibility revealed the fact that the aesthetic was interested behind its "universalist" guise in who would and who could not be given access to the standard of judgment.

Whereas Cain's judgments were fully authorized by the aesthetic ideology, James wrote his book on Melville after the state had derecognized his claim to occupy the universal subject position presupposed within that ideology. In writing about Melville's mariners while detained on Ellis Island, awaiting a court's decision on his appeal of the state's order that he be deported, James numbered himself among the mariners, renegades, and castaways whose exclusion constituted the limit as well as the precondition for the aesthetic realm.

C. L. R. James's Scene of Writing

In the following scene James explains how officials from the Immigration and Naturalization Services removed from him the rights and liberties that the aesthetic subject presupposed:

> I had lectured on Melville for three seasons, in many parts of the United States, to audiences of all kinds, putting forward many of the ideas contained here. What

stood out was the readiness of every type of audience to discuss him and sometimes very heatedly as if he were a contemporary writer. I had long contemplated
a book on Melville, had decided to write it in the summer of 1952, and was busy
negotiating with publishers. What form it might have taken had I written it according to my original plans I do not know. But what matters is that I am not an
American citizen, and just as I was about to write, I was arrested by the United
States government and sent to Ellis Island to be deported.

My case had been up for nearly five years. It had now reached the courts, and
there would be some period before a final decision was arrived at. I therefore actually began the writing of this book on the Island, some of it was written there, what
I did not write there was conceived and worked over in my mind there. And in the
end I finally came to the conclusion that my experiences there have not only shaped
the book but are the most realistic commentary I could give on the validity of
Melville's ideas today. (132)

As warrant for his internment, state agents cited the McCarran-Walter Act,
which, despite the fact that it was passed two years after James had completed
the examinations qualifying him for citizenship, would nevertheless ultimately
become the juridical instrument invoked by the state to justify James's detain-
ment.[8] The bill authorized I.N.S. officials to apply different combinations of rules
and norms for the purpose of sorting immigrants into economic and political
classifications. The phrases whereby the bill distinguished immigrants the state
could exclude on political grounds from migrants whose labor it could exploit
included within the former category "any alien who has engaged or has had purpose to engage in activities 'prejudicial to the public interest' or 'subversive to
the national security.'"[9] In addition to granting the state the right to expel sub-
versives, the bill also called for a careful screening of persons seeking to reside in
the United States and installed cultural literacy as one of the criteria whereby
the state might determine whether or not "they" were adaptable to the American
way of life. Although the state had kept James under scrutiny from the time of
his formal application to become a legal resident in 1938, its designation of him
as a subversive brought about a drastic change in his juridical relationship to the
category of U.S. citizenship.

United States citizenship was grounded in the legal fiction whereby an individual citizen was construed as both legislator, the "I" who was the sender of the
law, and subject, the "you" who was its addressee. By way of its derecognition of
James's personhood, the state denied him the first person pronominal powers necessary to support and defend his civil and political liberties. After the state pronounced him a security threat, James's legal subjectivity underwent demotion to
the status of "you." As its secondary addressee, James was subject to the law's powers
of enforcement, but he was no longer recognized as the subject of its norms.[10]

James's loss of the power to speak as "I" also deauthorized the testifying phrases
through which he could convey his claims before a court and invalidated his in-

terlocutory privileges within the civil society. The state's restriction of his pronominal identifications to the "you" who must obey the law had also disallowed
James membership in the "we" of "we the people" whose sovereign will the state
was understood to represent. "You" could never become "we" because "you"
named the subversive whom the state had refused the rights of dialogue with or
as an "I."[11]

Jean-François Lyotard has proposed the term "differend" to describe the kind
of juridical dilemma in which James was thereby embroiled. Lyotard defines a
differend as a "case of conflict between at least two parties, that cannot be equitably resolved for lack of a rule of judgement applicable to both parties."[12] Because
the damage for which James sought legal remedy originated with the legislation
whose rules the courts were required to render applicable to their decisions, the
judgment James sought exceeded the appellate courts' juridical authority. James
could not appeal the state's ruling without calling for the repeal of the McCarran
bill. But James could neither organize nor participate in a movement calling for the
repeal of the McCarran bill without providing the state with an example of the
activity for which he was accused. Moreover, any United States citizen who came
to James's defense was liable to prosecution for collaborating with a subversive.

In an effort to supply a rule of judgment that the courts lacked. James produced an interpretation of *Moby-Dick* underwritten by a juridical standard by which
he intended to define the illegality of the McCarran legislation and to represent
as well the wrong against him which the state had perpetrated on McCarran's
authority.[13]

Moby-Dick in an Expanded Field

Throughout his essay, Cain criticized James for substituting his "reimagination"
of *Moby-Dick* for the narrative Melville had written. But in lodging this critique,
Cain failed to read the following passage from *Moby-Dick* from which James had
derived the authority for his reading:

> If, then, to meanest mariners, and renegades and castaways, I shall hereafter ascribe
> high qualities though dark; weave round them tragic graces; if even the most mourn-
> ful, perchance the most abased, among them shall at times lift to the most exalted
> mounts; if I shall touch that workman's arm with some ethereal light; if I shall spread
> a rainbow over his disastrous set of sun; then against all mortal critics bear me out
> in it, thou just Spirit of Equality, which has spread one royal mantle of humanity
> over all my kind! (16–17)

Rather than continuing the narrated action, this scene represents the site from
within which the narrator construes himself as still in the process of composing
Moby-Dick. The passage opens onto a scene that involves the narrator in a deliberation over the means of its narration as if this scene were locatable within the

narrative proper. As the representation of a scene of writing in which the narrating "I" is still deliberating over how to do narrative justice to his book's actions, characters, and events, the scene alludes to the novel's surplus eventfulness, the possible shape of the narrative that has not yet settled into Melville's novel. The representations that Melville finally decided upon lie within the published text. But the scene whereon Melville wrote the novel must perforce remain outside of the completed narrative as the locus for the alternative narrative Melville may have wanted to narrate but did not.[14]

Rather than representing an event within the narrative, the passage inscribes the scene from within which the author wrote the narrative that must remain extraneous to the narrated action. This scene is not determined by propositional logic but addresses a question of narrative pragmatics: it concerns the relationship between the narrated "I," the narrating "I," and the characters and events that each "I" shall narrate.

The time in which this scene takes place is not continuous with the action as narrated or with the narrating instances of the subject of narration. Rather than continuing the narrated action, this passage represents a scene that involves the narrator in a deliberation over the means of its narration. It represents the narrator's process of deciding upon the narrative before the narrating "I" has become committed to what shall be written. The passage stages the difference between the manner in which the narrating "I" is predisposed to narrate the crew's actions and the constraints that the narrator-protagonist, Ishmael, has imposed. It gives expression to the possible enunciations of the narrating subject who aspires to accomplish a narration that has not yet been narrated and that Ishmael will not narrate.

The "If I shall" clauses constitute quasi-promises whose primary addressee is the spirit of equality. But they are secondarily addressed to the members of the crew concerning the possible outcomes of their narratives. The promise involves the narration of the ship's mariners', castaways', and renegades' enactment of heroic deeds as the conditions of its accomplishment.

The "I" within this scene splits into two narrating aspects: the "I" who confidently intends what "I shall hereafter" narrate and the "I" whose capacity to narrate is a function of whether or not the addressee of the apostrophe "thou just Spirit of Equality" will supply the imaginative wherewithal ("bear me out in it") necessary to accomplish the narrative project. The "If I shall" clauses tether the former "I" to an already intended course of narrative action. But the latter "I" enunciates these clauses as conditional or possible acts of narration still in need of a decision. The former "I"'s phrasing of the "If I shall" clauses as intentionals is not compatible with the latter "I"'s phrasing of them as conditionals.

Each of these narrating "I"'s (the intentional and the conditional) is involved in an imaginary dialogue with the spirit of equality. Each "I" apostrophizes this spirit as at once the source of the order that he do narrative justice by these men, the locus of the narrator's authority to invest them with these virtues, and the harbinger of the social norms that would ratify the narrator's having accomplished this order. Acted upon by the spirit of equality that would actualize itself through what "I shall narrate," the narrating "I" aspires to be borne up by that spirit through the communication of its animating gifts in and through, but also as the mariners, renegades, castaways. The just spirit of equality, that is to say, reveals itself by way of its passage through these men and as the means whereby they were rendered equally heroic.

Because neither of these narrators has yet caused the narrative referents of the conditional-intentional clauses that "I" enunciates to exist, the scene does not make reference to an already narrated state of affairs. The narratable actions "I" predicts do not coincide with the instance of their enunciation but designate what may be accomplished out of these asymmetrical statements. Because the "I" who enunciates what "I" shall narrate cannot coincide with the future act of narration, each "I" requires the witness of the spirit of equality to attest to the resolve of the "I" to perform the narration that "I" either intends or promises.

In the here and now of the moment of narrative decision about the fate of the crew, the "I" remains caught up in the process of deciding upon how to narrate the crew's relation to the action. I "gives" the order "bear me out" to the spirit of equality, but the statements to be borne out can be construed either as conditional suppositions or as executable promises. As indices of what might be written, the "If I shall" clauses are at once antecedent to the address to the spirit of equality as the substance of the message that the "I" sends and what "I" receives through and as a consequence of having apostrophized the "just spirit of equality." But when "I" transposes the intentional "If I shall" clauses into conditionals, "I" thereby subordinates the obligation that is linked to the intention to execute this narrative design into the deliberation over the consequences of completing it.

The reader is thus placed into a position to decide between these two performative dispositions of the passage but without determinate criteria. No secure meaning can be ascertained as to which of these idioms should predominate because their irreconcilability exceeds the univocal authority of any metalanguage that would ascertain their significance. Any single set of criteria directing this passage's interpretation would necessarily belong to one idiom at the exclusion of the other.

James's statement that it is clear "that Melville intends to make the crew the real heroes of his book, but he is afraid of criticism" has not merely provided this scene with an interpretive gloss. James's account of the significance of this passage is the result of what Kant has called an indeterminate judgment, which is to say a decision that he arrives at without pre-existing criteria.[15] In describing the signifying practice that James invented to come to terms with this scene, I shall employ an approach that Sylvia Wynter has described as "deciphering aesthetics." An aesthetics of decipherment, Wynter explains, "seeks to identify not what texts and their signifying practices can be interpreted to mean but what they can be deciphered to do, it also seeks to evaluate the 'illocutionary force' and procedures with which they do what they do."[16]

In *Mariners, Renegades and Castaways: The Story of Herman Melville and the World We Live In,* James has refused to adopt a reflexive relation to the passage's conditional clauses. Having removed the attitude of speculation from Melville's scene of writing, James has construed the intentional aspect of the "If I shall" clauses as executive orders so as thereafter to personify an attitude of carrying them out. But James's stipulation that Melville intended to make the men the real heroes of the book involves James in more than a paraphrase of this passage. It entails a decision as to Melville's intention and provides a rationale for Melville's having failed to realize it—"but he was afraid of criticism." In the act of enunciating this statement, James has split himself into at once an interpreter of "the story of Herman Melville" and a narrator-mariner who relays to his fellow mariners the narration Melville was afraid to write.

The question of justice has linked the scene that James interprets with the scene upon which he conducts his interpretation. In its extensive form, Melville's scene of writing includes the site upon which James interprets it as one of the possible referents for the clause, "I shall hereafter ascribe." Whereas Melville deliberates over how to do narrative justice to the crew, James "hereafter" attempts to do interpretive justice to Melville's story. As the novel undergoes a shift in its status from an object of interpretation to the occasion for an indeterminate judgment, James also shifts the locus of his identification from that of an interpreting subject to one of the meanest mariners, renegades, and castaways about whose future narration Melville is deliberating.

Melville's scene of writing thereafter becomes the locus for a change in James's position from the "you" who was subject to the law's power to the "I" capable of doing justice to Melville's crew. As the proleptic actualization of the intention to heroicize the mariners that Ishmael did not, James reenters the scene of narration that, in not having been completely narrativized, remains available as a nonsynchronous narrative resource.

James has not "reimagined" Melville's novel, pace William Cain. After discovering that the position in which he finds himself bears a direct analogy to the forms of protest and power in the novel, James has instead renarrated the narrative that Melville might have written—were he not "afraid of criticism." In rewriting the aspect of the story of Herman Melville to which the already written narrative has not yet done justice, James has also written the narrative that he believes Melville should have written.

Deciphering the Jamesian Aesthetic

Overall, *Mariners, Renegades and Castaways: The Story of Herman Melville and the World We Live In* put into place a multilayered strategy. It produced a frame of intelligibility that supplied James with the categories and themes required to challenge the findings of the McCarran legislation, with the pronominal rights of an interpreting "I," and with an interpretive object through which he could express his grievances against the state. As the continuation of the activity James had undertaken at the time of the state's forcible resettlement, the book was construable as the proximate cause for the state's action as well as documentation of the violence the state had exerted against his person. James's interpretation of Melville brought this example of his activities before the court of public opinion and invited its readers to decide as to the justice of the state's actions.

Upon fashioning his brief against the Cold War state as a renarration of the stateless persons who had not survived the wreck of the *Pequod*, James also constructed an uncanny relationship to the time he served on Ellis Island. The suddenness of the state's interference with James's anticipated project established the temporal as well as the spatial coordinates of the book on Melville. In returning to the work that the federal agents had interrupted, James, who had lost continuity with the time of his project and a secure place in which he could undertake it, produced a connection with Melville's interrupted scene of writing.

After linking the chronologically distinct moments of Melville's past scene of writing with his involuntary incarceration, James imagined himself as if recalled into the past by figures whose present memory depended upon the knowledge that James's reading of Moby Dick constructed out of their traces. These Melvillean figures resembled James in their lacking the condition of belonging to any nation. In establishing imaginary relations with them, James produced an extraterritorial site that was extrinsic to any of the themes through which the state assimilated persons to the national geography and that did not participate in the progressive temporality ascribed responsibility for the development of U.S. history and literature.

In his reading of *Moby-Dick*, James produced a fictive retroactivity whereby he represented the experiences he underwent on Ellis Island as having "realized" in historical time one of the possible national futures Melville had imagined a century earlier. *Mariners, Renegades and Castaways: The Story of Herman Melville and the World We Live In* represented the experiences he underwent on Ellis Island as what became of Melville's past imaginings. James then transformed this temporality into a writing practice which conjoined slightly different orientations toward U.S. citizenship: at once not quite a citizen but also not yet not one, James characteristically split the difference between these dis-positions into the desire for forms of citizenship that while incompatible with I.N.S. categories were consistent with the relationships that pertained among the mariners, renegades, and castaways.

The participants in a transnational social movement, "mariners, renegades and castaways" did not belong to a national community. The irreducible differences and inequivalent cultural features characterizing the "mariners, castaways and renegades" refused to conform to a state's taxonomy and they could not be integrated within a nationalizing telos. Not yet *not* a U.S. citizen, James produces through their motion the capacity to disidentify with the categories through which he would also practice U.S. citizenship.

Forever in between arrival and departure, the elements comprising the composite figure "mariners, renegades and castaways" perform a process of endless surrogation. Each term names the movement of a "we" that is responsible for its constitution and that traces the presence within it of an alterity irreducible to an "I." In and out of the terminological places through which "we" pass, the figure "mariners, renegades and castaways" produces multiple spatial and temporal effects. Each figure would appear to fill the absence in the space evacuated by the preceding figure and to empty that space in turn. Their goings and comings sound forth disparate absences and distant places that emerge from a past that in James's bipolar world order had been territorialized as the "third world."

The temporality that James's writing might be understood to enact in the relationship he adduces between their past and his present is neither the past definite that historians deploy to keep track of completed past actions, nor the present perfect, the what has been of who I now am, of the literary memoirist. It is more properly understood as the future anterior tense. The future anterior links a past event with a possible future upon which the past event depends for its significance. The split temporality intrinsic to the future anterior describes an already existing state of affairs at the same time that it stages the temporal practice through which that state of affairs "will have been" produced.

The future anterior tense provided James with a mode of conjectural reading with which to challenge McCarran's usage. As we have seen, the McCarran bill proposed to have represented a public will that it produced retroactively. The action James has employed the future anterior to produce "will have repealed" McCarran legislation, retroactively. In *Mariners, Renegades and Castaways: The Story of Herman Melville and the World We Live In*, James correlates a past event—the collective revolt that did not take place in the past—as dependent on a future event—the repeal of the McCarran bill—by which the crew's revolt will have accomplished it. When he links the revolt that had not taken place on the *Pequod* with the possible future repeal of the McCarran legislation, the future repeal returns to the past to transform this virtual revolt into what will have been its legal precedent.[17]

Notes

1. William Cain, "The Triumph of the Will and the Failure of Resistance: C. L. R. James's Readings of *Moby-Dick* and *Othello*," in *C. L. R. James: His Intellectual Legacies*, ed. Cudjoe,

Selwyn, and William E. Cain (Amherst: University of Massachusetts Press, 1995), pp. 260–273. Hereafter this work is cited parenthetically in the text.

2. C. L. R. [Cyril Lionel Robert] James, *Mariners, Renegades and Castaways: The Story of Herman Melville and the World We Live In* (New York, 1953), p. 14. Hereafter this work is cited parenthetically in the text.

3. The correlation that he adduced between the state's political judgment and American literature's aesthetic judgment was most clearly evident when Cain retrieved the rhetoric of the Cold War to describe the "disconcerting" chapter in James's text wherein he connected his reading of Melville with the ordeal he underwent as a political prisoner on Ellis Island. Cain complained that James engaged in forms of "special pleading . . . to which he does not stoop in his other writing" (Cain, 271).

4. See Terry Eagleton's detailed exposition in *The Ideology of the Aesthetic* (New York: Routledge, 1996).

5. Louis Althusser has described the procedures whereby an individual gets sutured to a preconstituted subject position in "Ideology and the Ideological State Apparatuses (Notes towards an Investigation)," in *Lenin and Philosophy and Other Essays*, trans. B. Brewster (London: New Left, 1971).

6. The phrase "lawfulness without law" is drawn from Terry Eagleton's essay "The Ideology of the Aesthetic," in *The Rhetoric of Interpretation and the Interpretation of Rhetoric*, ed. Paul Hernadi (Durham, N.C.: Duke University Press: 1989), p. 78.

7. Pierre Bourdieu discusses the notion of structural censorship in "Censorship and the Imposition of Form" in *Language and Symbolic Power*, ed. John Thompson (Cambridge, Mass.: Harvard University Press, 1991), p. 138.

8. According to the itinerary James provided in *Mariners, Renegades and Castaways: The Story of Herman Melville and the World We Live In*, his examination was concluded on August 16, 1950, under the Act of 1918. The Internal Security Act was passed on September 23, 1950, and the Attorney General's decision was handed down on October 31, 1950.

9. Cited by Lisa Lowe, *Immigration Acts: On Asian American Cultural Politics* (Durham, N.C.: Duke University Press, 1996), p. 9.

10. Costas Douzinas and Ronnie Warrington, "'A Well-Founded Fear of Justice': Law and Ethics in Postmodernity," *Legal Studies as Cultural Studies: A Reader in (Post) Modern Critical Theory*, ed. Jerry Leonard (Albany: State University of New York Press, 1995). "Normatives can be seen as prescriptives or commands put into inverted commas that give them authority. The prescriptive says that 'X should carry out Y.' Its normative reformulation adds 'it is a norm (or z decrees) that x should carry out y.' In a democratic polity political and legal legitimacy are allegedly linked with the fact that the addressor of the norm (the legislator) and the addressee of the command (the legal subject) are one and the same. The essence of freedom is that the subjects who make the law are the subjects subjected" (210).

11. James described the limitations the state had imposed on his "I" in his representation of the following exchange when he requested that the District Director of the INS of the Port of New York send him to a hospital for the treatment of an ulcer. "Mr. Shaughnessy's reply was that if I did not like it there I was not going to be detained against my will. I could always leave and go to Trinidad where I was born and drink my papaya juice." C. L. R. James, *Mariners, Renegades and Castaways*, p. 166.

12. A differend "would be the case of conflict between at least two parties, that cannot be equitably resolved for lack of a rule of judgement applicable to both parties." Jean-François Lyotard, *The Differend: Phrases in Dispute* (Manchester, U.K.: Manchester University Press, 1983), p. xi.

13. At a time in which the legal apparatus for surveillance had been put into place to purge universities of politically heterodox activities, Richard Chase's *Herman Melville* continued the state's policing measures by other means. He described the book's purpose as an effort "to ransom liberalism from the ruinous sell-outs, failures, and defeats of the thirties. . . . It must present a vision of life capable . . . of avoiding the old mistakes: the facile ideas of progress and 'social realism . . . the idea that literature should participate directly in the economic liberation of the masses, the equivocal relationship to communist totalitarianism and power politics." Richard Chase, *Herman Melville* (New York: 1949), p. vii.

14. Homi Bhabha has elaborated upon the importance of the scene of writing to the organization of what he calls the Third Space. "The reason a cultural text or system of meaning cannot be sufficient unto itself is that the act of cultural enunciation—the place of utterance—is crossed by the difference of writing. This has less to do with what anthropologists describe as varying attitudes to symbolic systems within different cultures than with the structure of symbolic representation itself—not the content of the symbol or its social function, but the structure of symbolization. It is this difference in the process of language that is crucial to the production of meaning and ensures, at the same time, that meaning is never simply mimetic and transparent. The linguistic difference that informs any cultural performance is dramatized in the common semiotic account of the disjunction between the subject of the proposition (enonce) and the subject of enunciation, which is not represented in the statement but which is the acknowledgment of its discursive embeddedness and address, its cultural positionality, its reference to a present time and specific space. The pact of interpretation is never simply an act of communication between the I and You designated in the statement. The production of meaning requires that these two places be mobilized in the passage through the Third Space, which represents both the general conditions of language and specific conditions of the utterance in a performative and institutional strategy of which it cannot "in itself" be conscious. What this unconscious relation introduces is an ambivalence in the act of interpretation. The pronominal I of the proposition cannot be made to address—in its own words—the subject of enunciation for this is not personable, but remains a spatial relation within the schemata and strategies of discourse. The meaning of the utterance is quite literally neither the one nor the other. This ambivalence is emphasized when we realize that there is no way that the content of the proposition will reveal the structure of its positionality; no way that context can be mimetically read off from the content." Homi Bhabha, "The Commitment to Theory," in *The Location of Culture* (London: Routledge, 1994), p. 36.

15. My analysis of the relationship of prescriptive and interpretive phrases draws upon Jean-François Lyotard, "Levinas' Logic," in *The Lyotard Reader*, ed. Andrew Benjamin (Cambridge: Blackwell, 1989), pp. 275–313.

16. See Sylvia Wynter, "Rethinking 'Aesthetics': Notes towards a Deciphering Practice," in *Ex-Iles: Essays on Caribbean Cinema*, ed. Mbye Cham (Trenton, N.J.: African World Press, 1992), pp. 266–267.

17. Jacques Derrida has famously analyzed this retroactive temporality within the context of the *Declaration of Independence*. "We the people," as Jacques Derrida has explained their emplacement within the paradoxical logic of a representative democracy, "do not exist as an entity; it does *not* exist, *before* this declaration, not as *such*. If it gives birth to itself, as free and independent subject as possible signer, this can only hold in the act of the signature. The signature invents the signer. The signer can only authorize him- or herself, to sign once he or she has come to the end . . . if one can say this, of his or her signature, in a sort of fabulous retroactivity." "Declarations of Independence," trans. Tom Keenan and Tom Pepper, *New Political Science* 15 (1976), p. 10.

Mumbo Jumbo, *Theory,* and the *Aesthetics of Wholeness*

JOHNNELLA E. BUTLER

> Perhaps the most insidious and least understood form of segregation
> is that of the word. And by this I mean the word in all its complex
> formulations, from the proverb to the novel and the stage play, the
> word with all its subtle power to suggest and foreshadow overt ac-
> tion while magically disguising the moral consequences of that ac-
> tion and providing it with symbolic and psychological justification.
> For if the word has the potency to revive and make us free, it has also
> the power to blind, imprison and destroy.
>> Ralph Ellison, "Twentieth-Century Fiction and the
>> Black Mask of Humanity"

> And if I am right in urging the overthrow of the Aryan Model and its
> replacement by the Revised Ancient one, it will be necessary not only
> to rethink the fundamental bases of "Western Civilization" but also
> to recognize the penetration of racism and "continental chauvinism"
> into all our historiography, of philosophy of writing history.
>> Martin Bernal, *Black Athena*

Implicit in African-American literature is the search for an articulation of ways
of viewing the world that accommodate the humanity of the black body and of
black subjectivity. From Olaudah Equiano's descriptions of his Ibo homeland
and Phillis Wheatley's admonitions to Christians to remember that "Negroes
black as Cain, may be refined and join the angelic train," through the vehemence
and urgency of nineteenth-century African-American oratory and fiction, to the
devastating optimism of twentieth-century African-American literature, even in
the most strident nationalism, there is not only the implicit African-American
hope that the United States would live up to its democratic creed, but also, at
the least, the implication that there must be another way to view human beings,
humanity, and the world.[1]

I propose that Ishmael Reed's *Mumbo Jumbo* declares an African-American literary aesthetic, and as a revelatory and pivotal text in the African-American literary

tradition, apprehends the physical and symbolic violence as well as the healing and humanely creative possibilities of the collision, which George Kent called "blackness and the adventure of Western culture."[2] Inherent in that declaratory and revelatory text is a theoretical approach to the text's substance, an approach that reflects the struggle for emotional and physical freedom in eighteenth- and nineteenth-century African-American literature, and that anticipates the explicit search for wholeness present in African-American literature that became most fully articulated by African-American women writers of the 1970s and 1980s. Moreover, in this chapter, I begin to delineate a theoretical position to serve as the foundation for a theory of African-American literature. Such a position provides as well a theoretical approach to the study of American literature, an approach that encompasses the paradoxes replete in African-American and American circumstance and the many aesthetic, cultural, political, social, and economic facets that allow for human possibility to emerge amid sustained oppression.

In spite of the richness of African-American literature—or perhaps because of its richness—African American literature is a literature in search of a theory. Like PaPa LaBas, the HooDoo houngan, the embodiment of the New World expression of the ancient tradition with its roots in Osirian Egyptian spirituality, while it seeks the text of "Jes Grew," both the text (how "to be") and Jes Grew (African-American expression) continue to be under attack. The attack is at least twofold—from the "Atonist," Western, Judeo-Christian, U.S. tradition that insists on fixity and an obsequious indeterminacy, and from the African-American tradition that is riddled with contradictions resulting from the imposition of the Atonist on the Hoodoo.

In her landmark essay, "Unspeakable Things Unspoken," Toni Morrison proffers challenges gleaned from reading American and African-American literatures within the context of U.S. historical, social, cultural, and psychological reality. Thus far, theory has bypassed her challenges, stressing or seeking a middle ground. Morrison calls for three foci in examining our conceptualizations of American literature and the canon. They are "neither reactionary nor simple pluralism, nor the even simpler methods by which the study of Afro-American literature remains the helpful doorman into the halls of sociology. Each of them," she warns, "however, requires wakefulness." Morrison devotes her essay to the second and third foci respectively, "the examination and re-interpretation of the American canon, . . . for the ways in which the presence of Afro-Americans has shaped the . . . meaning of so much American literature. . . . for the ghost in the machine," and the question of "What makes a work 'Black'?" (11). The first focal point Morrison does not address directly. It is, however, the major concern of this paper: the identification of a theory that can accommodate African-American literature, specifically its context.

Key to these issues theoretically is the necessity to engage the conflicts that emanate from the competing individualist and communalist conceptualizations of humanity. These conflicts gird a Du Boisian/Freirean African-American double consciousness. Du Bois, in *The Souls of Black Folk*, seeks the merger of the African and the American; Freire goes beyond the Hegelian dialectic that demands synthesis and describes the self/other dialectic as having the possibility of generative tensions engendering liberation, first of the spirit and of possibility, which, in turn, effects the physical and material.[3] As in Reed's *Mumbo Jumbo*, the objective is a comprehensive, holistic approach evolving from the dialogical[4] framework inherent in African-American culture and literature. By taking up both Barbara Christian's and Toni Morrison's calls for such a theory and doing so in a manner consistent with postpositivist objectivity and realism as defined by Satya Mohanty, I offer a reconceptualization of our approach to African-American literature and of literary theory that provides the necessary foundation for revealing the full significance of the complexities of that literature's aesthetics, their affirmations, denials, rejections, and ambivalences. That reconceptualization has a text in *Mumbo Jumbo*.

Mumbo Jumbo, a mythic, fictional narrative, the name of which invokes a ritual cleansing of the world of troubled, and therefore troublesome ancestors,[5] seeks the missing text, the Book of Thoth. The Book of Thoth (attributed to the Egyptian god, Thoth [Greek: Hermes Trismegistos, translated as Hermes the Thrice Greatest], the inventor of writing and the patron of all the arts dependent on writing) held in its treatises "that the cosmos constituted a unity and that all parts of it were interdependent . . . , and that through divine revelation, one learned the laws of sympathy and antipathy."[6] A social and political satire in the form of a detective story, *Mumbo Jumbo* mythologizes what Chinweizu calls "the West and the rest of us," and depicts allegorically the struggle over the cultural and human manifestations of the irreconciliation of sympathy and antipathy. Jes Grew through PaPa LaBas seeks its text in order to reinstate the long dormant Afro-American aesthetic, while the leader of the first Crusade, Hinckle Von Vampton and his Atonists of the Wallflower Order of the Knights Templar, hunt down PaPa LaBas and the text in order to maintain the hegemony of hierarchical binaries. Without its text, Jes grew is just a "flair-up"—a celebration of style in dress, language, dance, and music and of the less profound manifestations of the joyful spirit that reconciles its opposite, matter. To counter the superficiality of style, Berbelang and his gang rescue from Atonist museums African, Mayan, Peruvian, and other Third World art pieces in order to return them to their proper places. Once the works of art/liturgical pieces are returned to their proper places, the liturgy has its text. Then Jes Grew will no longer only manifest in temporary flair-ups, but rather it will conjure a sustained aesthetic, affecting all aspects of life, freeing human power to do its natural work of building and celebrating the interdependence among humans and among humans and the world. "[I]t will mean the end of Civilization As We Know It" (*Mumbo Jumbo*, unnumbered third page).

At a social gathering at Villa Lewaro (A'Lelia Walker's gathering place for the literati, other artists and critics of the Harlem Renaissance) where PaPa LaBas and his detectives go to arrest Hinkle Von Vampton, LaBas explains the origins of the text of Jes Grew and the battles against it over time, beginning with the retelling of the story of Isis, Osiris, and Set as the basis of the development of Western civilization and the Judeo-Christian tradition. As Reginald Martin, in his book-length study of Reed, his HooDoo African-American aesthetic, and its challenge to the Black Aesthetic, succinctly puts it: "So it is a battle for supremacy between powers which see the world in two distinct, and opposed ways. The separate visions are endemic to the two human types involved: one, expansive and syncretic; the other impermeable and myopic" (88).

The Black Muslim, Abdul Hamid, who wavers between Atonism and Jes Grew, translated the book "into the language of the 'brother on the street'" and sent it off to a publisher who returned only a rejection slip. Hamid then burned the copy of the book because "black people could never have been involved in such a lewd, nasty, decadent thing (231).[7]

The new text, *Mumbo Jumbo* itself, is anticipated by LaBas who sees the end of the 1960s as the return of the 1920s—"Better" (249). Although sixties students and professors honor LaBas as a relic, Jes Grew carriers remain alive and well, despite the Atonists' determination that they have Atonist heads (247). There remains, too, an Atonist ambivalence that harasses PaPa LaBas, an ambivalence born of indecision on the part of Atonists and Carriers, regardless of race, that continues to create confusion, dissonance, maintaining the irreconciliation of sympathy and antipathy in human life and culture. The struggle for wholeness amid the traumatic, binary fragmentations of matter and spirit continues with the possibility for wholeness expressed in the African-American aesthetic. It is a particularly instructive aesthetic for the realization of human possibility, because it is a wholeness articulated amid trauma.

Trauma, Wholeness, and the Word

I usually avoid associating African-American literature with trauma because "experts" are so quick to judge as social and psychological deviance the myriad ways African Americans resist dehumanization. The psychiatric term trauma implies neurotic, irrational responses to an emotional wound or shock. When applied to the African-American group and cultural experience of over 500 years, it does not allow for the ways Africans in America and later African Americans, have not only survived but rebelled, succumbed, resisted, accommodated, excelled, prospered, and as Zora Neale Hurston frequently reminded us, led relatively ordinary lives. Also, evaluating exactly what constitutes trauma and responses to it, is very much dependent upon the cultural, social, political, and economic context of events experienced, those experiencing the events, and those defining the events.

The misjudging and distortion of the African American takes place within the context of a national culture and ethnic and class cultures that share in and reflect what Morrison terms "the trauma of racism [that is], the severe fragmentation of the self, and has always seemed to me a cause (not a symptom) of psychosis—strangely of no interest to psychiatry" (Morrison, 16). What Morrison terms a psychosis is a DuBoisian/Freirean unresolved conflict. For the African American, it is a conflict between the self and the oppressive other (that is simultaneously an outside human interactive force and an internalized psychological one), and between enjoying a limited agency or only existing with the illusion of agency. For the oppressing group—dominated by whites, but as *Mumbo Jumbo* demonstrates, not delimited by race, it is a conflict between the oppressing self and the oppressed other (also simultaneously an outside human force and an internalized, psychological one), and between enjoying an undeserved, oppressive agency or existing with the illusion of a deserved, unoppressive agency. In the essay, "Baldwin and the Problem of Being," George Kent sees the resulting severe fragmentation as denying complexity, and the denial of complexity as paralyzing the ability to know both possibility and limitation. Since "freedom is both discovery and recognition of limitations, one's own and that of society, to deny complexity is to paralyze the ability to get at such knowledge—it is to strangle freedom" (149).

Trauma then, for the African American and for other Americans is the suppression of freedom. And the attainment and maintenance of human freedom is dependent upon the acknowledgment and engagement of complexities: the complexities of the interconnectedness of human beings, of morality, of dialogue and discourse. The resulting cultural conflict for African Americans, experienced since the first Africans arrived in the English colonies, is characterized well in Philip Page's discussion of fusion and fragmentation in Toni Morrison's novels. The freedom sought by Morrison's characters—a spiritual and physical freedom from the legacy of the pain of the trauma—he aptly describes as "dangerous"—dangerous to both individuals and the group because it threatens the hegemonic order of the physical, spiritual, psychological, social, and cultural worlds—or, of civilization as we know it.

From Olaudah Equiano and Phillis Wheatley to Ralph Ellison and Toni Morrison, African-American writers have given expression to an African-American "self" that argues and demonstrates his/her humanity for full participation in humanness; that expresses his/her participation in Western civilization as both a colonized "other" and an assertive "self"; that explores the struggle for freedom to wholeness and offers the possibility of alternatives to the terrain of the African American's encounter with the impoverished Western concept of reality. Ishmael Reed's *Mumbo Jumbo*, to paraphrase Gwendolyn Brooks's poem "The Children of the Poor," civilizes a space wherein all could explore wholeness with grace. In this, it takes us beyond Ellison's *Invisible Man*, which historicizes the struggles caused by the racial and cultural binaries of blackness and its adventure with Western culture. Reed, as Calvin Herndon wrote in 1970, *"explodes* this madness before our very eyes" (222).

The quest for wholeness suggests more than a revision of the way we view racism, slavery, and their legacies in everyday lives. It involves a change of world-view, and a struggle ensues in either consciously attempting to realize that change or, for African Americans, in living in accord with and utilizing the sustaining aspects of African-American culture. Paule Marshall's work, especially in *Praise Song for the Widow* (1983) and *Chosen Place, Timeless People* (1969), for example, por-trays a struggle of worldviews in similar fashion to Alice Walker in her collec-tion of short stories, *In Love and in Trouble: Stories of Black Women* (1973), Toni Cade Bambara in *The Salt Eaters* (1980), Gloria Naylor in *Mama Day* (1988), and Julie Dash in both the film (1991) and 1997 novel, *Daughters of the Dust*. That struggle is fueled by the binaries of materialism and spirituality, the masculine and the femi-nine, good and evil, black and white—binaries that perpetuate the inhumanity of racism, sexism, heterosexism, classism, neocolonialism, and the dominance over and destruction of the environment. Similar to Jean Toomer's *Cane* (1923), their writing expresses the loss of something vital to the affirmation of humankind's frustrated need to understand and live through connections to one another and to the world. With Baldwinian clarity, they express the collision of the fragmented reality of the word, which shapes the Western sense of reality—"Logos"—with the holistic vision of the word, which shapes the traditional African sense of reality—"Nommo."

The following chart clarifies the ramifications of the differences between Logos and Nommo and delineates the fundamental dimensions of African-American double-consciousness and self/other conflict and of the struggle for wholeness:

Logos/Dialogics	*Nommo/Dianommics*
Fragmentation toward exaggerated individualism: separate from the spirit world, from God; alienation from the past, from other human beings; disconnected discourses. Multiple centers unconnected; relativity.	Interconnectedness toward wholeness: connection to a usable but not a defining past; connection to other human beings; recognition of the connection and overlapping of discourse if not in content, purpose, or process, then in time or place, or even connected through opposition. Nommo bridges polarities, voicing and conjuring connections among dissonant multiple centers; all things negotiated as relative to the common good of humanity.
I think, therefore, I am. (Descartes)	I am because we are; we are because I am. I am we. (West African proverb)

Dialogic: across a binary defined word; insists on the destruction of difference through synthesis, either natural or forced. Example: Evil is the binary opposite of good.

Dianommic—generatively defined—accepts difference and sameness as interacting. Writing across the word that creates both through synthesis and through working through contradiction. Example: Evil is the other side of good.

Individualism: confined to the present and the solitude of an unconnected self.

Ancestry: the trope of the past encompassing the present and the future; the company and the interaction of the connected selves in community. Individuality exists in the context of communality.

This concept of Nommo constitutes the worldview of *Mumbo Jumbo*. In *Muntu*, Jahnheinz Jahn relates how the Dogon griot, Ogotomelli, defines it: *Nommo* is "the life force, which produces a life, which influences 'things' in the shape of the *word*" (124). The magara principle is the spiritual birth that arises from the union of the body and Nommo. That union brings about "the wisdom that gives happiness, intelligence, the principle which distinguishes man from all other living things, [and] exists in 'pure' form only in the dead: it is a force from their kingdom" (110–111). The ancestor strengthens the living and the living strengthen the ancestors, "letting the magara flow upon them through honour, prayer and sacrifice" (111). Quoting the renowned philosopher, Leopold Senghor, Jahn explains that through ritual sacrifice, Senghor says that "ritual [is] religion in action", the priest, "who is such purely by virtue of being the oldest descendant of the common ancestor," is "the natural mediator between the living and the dead. . . . the force of the Ancestor flows into the sacrifices and into the community which he embodies" (111). The Ancestor is summoned through the word, Nommo, that first was with the supreme being. We then speak, write, express ourselves dianomically—that is, across a word that is sacred in its evocation and unification of the spirit world, the past, the material world, the present, and the imagined future.

PaPa LaBas, the embodiment of the loa Legba, is also the priest, the oldest descendant of the common ancestor, Osiris. The god Osiris is believed to have been a mortal who became "Egypt's greatest civilizer," and in similar fashion, PaPa LaBas's mission is to bring harmony and balance—civilization—to a world much out of balance, dominated by seemingly irreconcilable binaries and consequent inhumanity. Hermes Thoth, the one Osiris most highly honored, had "unusual ingenuity for devising things capable of improving the social life of man" (224). So the Book of Thoth, the text in *Mumbo Jumbo*, holds not only the written word, but also the "substance," as LaBas refers to it, of life. And that substance

is concerned with the communal, the social life of humankind, or with the possibilities of living dianommically.

In *Mumbo Jumbo* is an implied expression of a possibility, a worldview that is
invigorated by the ancestors, that informs human life socially and culturally
through affirming the connections among past, present, and imaginable future,
and that explores and engages the links and mergers between the spiritual (Reed
uses the word psychological) and physical worlds. This merger of the spiritual
and the physical is possible because of the principle of polarity, recognized by
ancient societies, which makes possible the magara principle that distinguishes
humans from other beings. According to the principle of polarity, opposites are
only opposite according to degree, and it holds the possibility for one to be simultaneously an individual and part of a community, with belonging to a community lived simultaneously in the context of being an individual. One's community, consequently, includes the ancestors, the past, as well as the present and
the imagined future.[8]

Reeds retells and recasts the story of Set, who murders his sister Isis' hus-
band, Osiris, and so doing, lays the foundation for a new religion of monothe-
ism, instituted by Akhenaton, who insisted that Aton was the only god. Thus
began the displacement of the ancestors and an institutionalization of the vulnerability of the past. Reed provides a mythical ancestry of Jes Grew, the opposition to Set and Aton, the way to harmony and wholeness. It is a shared ancestry of the colonized and the colonizer, an ancestry through which the former
seeks and incompletely manifests as Jes Grew, and which the latter, the colonizer, the Atonists, seeks to destroy. This retelling is interestingly close to the
scholarship of Martin Bernal in *Black Athena*, which, among other contributions,
traces the deliberate European distortion of the relationship between Egypt and
Greece; of Richard Poe in *Black Spark, White Fire*, who garners evidence that Egyptian
explorers who were, at the least, partly black, civilized ancient Egypt, and that
the Knight Templar and Masonic Orders (from which Hinckle Von Vampton
emerges, analogous to humanity without the magara principle and its manifestation, Nommo) evolved from distortions of their origins (from texts without the
steps, the dance, the rituals); and to the scientific, laboriously documented work
of the late Cheikh Anta Diop, who stated unequivocally that ancient Egypt was
a Negro civilization that looked to the south of it and to inner Africa as the "old
country." It signifies on the ancestry from the Harlem Renaissance that struggled
with cooptation by white aesthetics. It signifies on the ancestry of America, of
Western civilization, connecting both to the distortion of the primary point of
the ways of knowing and being, the ancient principle of polarity. Hierarchical
binaries cannot exist within the philosophical worldview that sees opposites only
according to degree.

LaBas seeks the text of harmony and balance between good and evil, right
and wrong in a world cosmology that embraces and thrives on the opposition of

difference and similarity and that rewards injustice. Reed traces Christianity, Islam, Mormonism, and all ideologies that demand one way of being (and hence, based on dichotomies, the separation of the physical and the psychological, the material and the spiritual) from the Atonists and Set.

The Book of Thoth, as stated earlier, viewed the universe as a unified whole composed of interdependent parts; the key to understanding the "sympathy and antipathy" of those parts was apprehended through divine revelation. The word, then, writing, was sacred, for it connected and illuminated the physical and spiritual worlds, and, like Nommo, conjured the life force that comes from the divine.[9] Reed places the Book of Thoth as part of what he calls the HooDoo cosmology, the manifestation of African worldview and rituals in the "New World," thereby connecting them with Nommo, the life force.[10]

The text that PaPa LaBas seeks would bring about the unity of astrology and the occult sciences (the intuitive) with theology and philosophy (the rational). He is opposed by Von Vampton, the Knights Templar and the Hierophant 1 (a name Reed deliberately chose as it ironically signifies the Greek "displayer of holy things," the one who determined at the beginning of ceremonies who was unclean and should be cast out and who changed the sacred symbols).[11] Von Vampton and his ilk fight to maintain the binaries that support the greed and power reinforced by the monotheistic hegemony. Assisted by Woodrow Wilson Jefferson, the Talking Android, and Hamid, blacks who act out of self-interest or who see the world in the monolithic way of the Atonists, they descend from Set, who defied Thoth, the protector of Isis and the healer of her son Horus' eye, which Set had wounded. By implication, Set defied the word, Nommo.

Morrison says that she "sometimes know[s] when a work works, when *nommo* has effectively been summoned by reading and listening to those who have entered the text" (33). This is akin to what Reginald Martin calls the "reader-response ambiance [in *Mumbo Jumbo*] which mirrors the HooDoo/oral culture feeling in the text" (90). Writing is then a working, and a text is a work in the HooDoo sense of conjuring. Jahn reminds us that it is the domain of humankind, both living and dead, to use Nommo for good or evil (127–132). "Through Nommo, the word, a man establishes his mastery over things" (132):

> No "medicines," "talismans," "magic horns," no, not even poisons are effective without the word. If they are not "conjured," they are of no use in themselves. They have no activity at all. Only the intelligence of the word frees these forces and makes them effective. All substances, minerals, juices are only 'vessels' of the word, of the Nommo. Nommo is the concrete entity through which the abstract principle magara [life force] is realized. (127)

As a "work," *Mumbo Jumbo* summons through Nommo, African-American expression and life, past, present, and possible future, with its differences and similarities, conflicts and intersections within and outside. It summons wholeness.

Mumbo Jumbo, Ancestry, and Theory

What does this mean, however, to literary theory? What does it mean if we take the concept of Nommo and its cosmology seriously, understanding that feeding the loas (that is, working through and with the past) is vital to divine revelation, to apprehending ultimately the many ways of being and doing that Jes Grew manifests? What if we use the word within the context not of an indeterminate, eternal play, but rather within the context of what is best for a humanity that is connected one to another, to the environment, and to the universe.[12] What if we respond seriously to Morrison's recognition of the evocation of Nommo; go beyond Reed's performing Nommo in his text and his description of HooDoo and its manifestations in his writing process? What if Henry Louis Gates, Jr., in his chapter on *Mumbo Jumbo* in *The Signifying Monkey*, had explored his own implications when he observes that *Mumbo Jumbo* is both a book about texts and a book of texts, a composite narrative composed of subtexts, pretexts, post-texts, and narratives-within-narratives" (220)?

Overarchingly, doing so challenges the philosophical context of American literary theory that is based on the Greek, and ultimately Christian, concept of Logos. Nommo is generative, multiple, changing, interactive, unfixed but connected. Jahn compares the biblical "word" in the gospel of St. John with Nommo:

> "In the beginning was the Word, and the Word was with God, and the Word was God" so begins the gospel according to St. John, and it looks as if Nommo and the *logos* of John agreed. Yet the apostle continues: "The same (i.e., the word) was in the beginning with God. All things were made by it and without it was not anything made that was made." (In the German Gospel.)
>
> In the gospels the word remains with God, and man has to testify to it and proclaim it. Nommo, on the other hand, was also admittedly, with Amma, or god, in the beginning, but beyond that everything comes into being only through the word, . . . Nommo does not stand above and beyond the earthly world. *Logos* becomes flesh only in Christ, but Nommo becomes "flesh" everywhere. According to the apostle, *Logos* has made all things, one for all, to become as they are, and since then all generated things remain as they are, and undergo no further transformation. Nommo, on the other hand, goes on unceasingly creating and procreating, creating even gods. . . . The hierarchy of the *Bantu* ("men" both living and dead) is ordered according to the force of each one's word. The word itself is force. . . . Naming is an incantation, a creative act. What we cannot conceive of is unreal; it does not exist. But every human thought, once expressed, becomes reality. For the word holds the course of things in train and changes and transforms them. And since the word has this power, every word is an effective word, every word is binding. there is no "harmless," noncommittal word. Every word has consequences. (132–133)

Nommo informs the mythological trope of ancestry articulated in *Mumbo Jumbo*, forms the basis of Reed's HooDoo art, and has theoretical implications for terms and concepts rooted in the worldview from which it is derived. That worldview emphasizes not origins but a reflective ancestry, in which the interconnections among the past, present, and future are synchronic, expressing a "changing same" or a sense of "what goes around comes around."

Literary theory that is generative, that is, that engages the text, its context, its intertextuality, and its creator's intention and positionality to the extent that it actively informs the text in some manner, recognizes intersecting and overlapping continua. Thus, for example, the ghost in the machine implies also interactions between and overlaps of the machine and the ghost. The past is recognized as operating either visibly, that is immediately apprehending, or as a ghost in most texts. Its significance is determined by the text, not by our discounting a priori its value.[13] Moreover, *aesthetics*, as approaches, as attitudes, flow from generative being. Life, as a generative process, creates new ways of thinking and being, of engaging difficult situations, engaging conflict not in the sense of "progress" but in the sense of engaging complexity, difference, and opposition for understanding and happiness. While there is no one true meaning, as Martin says of Reed's text, taking Nommo seriously reveals that there is, however, a constancy in the sacredness of the life force and thus, of humanity. All things, even truth, are decided in respect to this sacredness that embodies contradiction.[14] Aesthetics are multiple, connected, overlapping and part of the life force. Reconceptualizations of key theoretical concepts then are implied in taking Nommo seriously.

In the context of Nommo, or of dianommics, *theory* is conceived from within the culture, from within the work. Theory, then, becomes a conceptualization that illuminates the text, that examines the work that has been activated by the word. It seeks repeatable and repeating patterns, identifies the emotional, intuitive connections with the physical world, fact, the rational, and is contingent upon the constants and variables of reality and objectivity as Mohanty demonstrates, is context bound, but not relative.[15]

The *naming* of literary methods dianommically is undertaken, therefore, in continuity with cultural meaning of the text(s). For example, Beloved, Old Wife in *The Salt Eaters*, the unborn child in *Daughters of the Dust* are not examples of magical realism. Rather, they more appropriately are examples of ancestral spiritualism.[16] They are not out of the ordinary within the worldview of the culture from which the text comes. Like PaPa LaBas, like tricksters in HooDoo tradition, they are not magical in the Western sense, out of the ordinary. They are very much part of the everyday cosmology in which the spiritual world interacts with the real world. So *Mumbo Jumbo* is not an "all out assault on Western civilization," nor is it simply a "critique of black and Western literary forms and conventions, and the complex relationships between the two," as jacket blurbs assert, but it is a rereading of Western civilization through the recognition of the power of myth to describe and define. Similarly, "comic" is not a term, in the context of Nommo, to be applied to slave narratives because they begin in slavery and end in freedom.[17]

Diannommically, *binaries* exist alongside generative tensions. They are not simply exposed or disrupted. Something happens to them, they are resolved; they work generatively through and off their tensions toward a possibility of resolution, because opposites are not dichotomous but connected. Difference is not then a deficit but something to be engaged. Consequently, *fragmentation* is a characteristic of life to be engaged, and exists often because of the way we have conceptualized and ordered the world, our power relationships to it and to one another. Fraught with the binaries characteristic of Western logic and emanating from the individualism and abstraction inherent in Descartes's "Cogito, ergo sum" that are in conflict with the basic human need and ancient cultural imperatives for connection and individuality, the African American, the "Third World," and indeed, even those in the position of the dominant "other," struggle with fragmentation, working through and off unresolved tensions, conflicts, and contradictions. Multiplicity, which we read as fragmentation, is part of life, exacerbated by power dominance and imbalance. Fragmentation, however, moves constantly toward unity and exists in tension with it. We choose whether to view it as such.

In this context, *fixity* exists only in so far as the word intends it to be. There is no such thing as a literary work or artistic work that is "fixed," since the word interacts with the reader. One's identity is only fixed when forces outside the self prevent or distort the expression of its agency and multiplicity,[18] and then it is only fixed from the perspective of those outside the self who view it as fixed. In similar fashion, it follows that *hybridity*, then, be read not as dead-end ambivalence, but rather as generative agency. The African-American self, the colonized or objectified self, is never identified as "other" in the context of dianommics. Rather dianommics recognizes the agentive "self" as it encounters the colonizing "other" in texts. That self can be "othered" but is not "other." That dominant "other" likewise enjoys a self, but that self, in the context of dominance is "other" even to itself, to recall Freire. *Agency* is always acknowledged. Even if it has internalized much of the "other," its possibility is acknowledged. Otherwise, the trauma of the self/other conflict has no options, no alternatives. The assumption is that there is a resilient, human spirit, for the self and other, the dominating and dominated. *Otherness* is then, determined by perspective, position, and power relationships, and not simply assumed to be the essential condition of the African American. Likewise, otherness is not assumed to be the essential condition of the dominating.

Indeterminacy in the context of Logos is eternal, unending play. In Gates's influential assertion in "Preface to Blackness: Text and Pretext," he argues that "the correspondence of content between a writer and his world is less significant to literary criticism than is correspondence of organization or structure, for a relation of content may be a mere reflection of perspective, scriptural canon." His argument continues that the relationship between social and literary "facts" that he sees Houston Baker, Addison Gayle, and Stephen Henderson seeking in the

1960s and 1970s can only be found in a relation of structure which, "according to Raymond Williams can show us the organizing principles by which a particular view of the world, and from that coherence of the social group which maintains it, really operates in consciousness'" (Mitchell, 254). Consequently, the role of context, the past and its legacies, the text's present and its history and contours are all diminished as major players, leaving the text—and humanity, for that matter—open to distortion.[19] Gates, then, reads *Mumbo Jumbo* as an indeterminate text, a text that celebrates "indeterminacy, the sheer plurality of meaning, the very play of the signifier itself" (*Signifying Monkey*, 235).

Theodore Mason, Jr., refutes Gates's reading, claiming that Gates "exaggerates the values of indeterminacy and play by masking the degree to which a commitment to these values requires giving up any claim on the 'real,' (a realm Gates views as awfully susceptible to political and linguistic corruption);" however, he overstates "Reed's use of indeterminacy" which he sees as becoming more determinate and hegemonic. Mason then reads Reed's concept of history as making claims on authenticity and determinateness, and therefore sees it as oppressive, the opposite of Reed's goals (106).

Both Gates and Mason miss the point. Play in the context of the generative word, Nommo, which is central to Reed's HooDoo literary method, is generative rather than indeterminate. Generative acts require connection to the past, of humans and events one to another, and an individuality expressed in the context of humanity. *Context* in the Nommo sense is complex, multiple, and interconnected. Thus, Reed's advocacy of different ways of doing things is nonetheless connected and purposeful—seeking human happiness.

I am bold enough to assert that we should dispense with the term *dialogics* and substitute the more descriptive term *dianommics*. However, I doubt that such coinage will catch on. I suggest that we at least redefine dialogics by employing the implications of going beyond the binaries of either/or and both/and, utilizing them where appropriate, and by allowing for paradoxes to generate ideas, ways of being in, and responding to, the complexities of human life viewed as replete with possibility.

Mumbo Jumbo recasts, for the second half of the twentieth century, the African-American trope of ancestry—an ancestry Reed places in the novel as one among multicultural ancestries, shared yet fragmented, divided, and denied. The self that is written, that the reader intuits through the search for the lost text, is a self connected to multiple pasts, connected to others, seeking agency and human happiness.

Jean Toomer first cast that African-American trope of ancestry in *Cane*—"The Dixie Pike has grown from a goat path from Africa" (10)—expressing its U.S. ambivalences, its obscured yet still vibrant African heritage, its sensibility resulting from the divine encounter with historical reality, as James Cone puts it in discussing the spirituals and the blues. *Mumbo Jumbo* gives cohesion to the African-American literary tradition by placing the African-American demand for acknowledged humanity and ancestry smack in the middle of Western civilization, and places Western civilization smack in the middle of its African origins. By signifying on, engaging, correcting, disrupting, and exploding the suppressed contradictions and complexities of Western culture, by reading the present through an evocation of a vital, informing past and voicing the fragmentation detailed in numerous previous African-American texts of the eighteenth, nineteenth, and twentieth centuries, the text demonstrates the need for and directs the reader toward seeking harmony and wholeness through confronting and engaging the complexities and fragmentations that result from the repression of agency. Through the retelling of the Isis and Osiris myth, *Mumbo Jumbo* provides a trope of shared ancestry that contextualizes for the West and the rest of us our power struggles, all the variously positioned postcolonial selves and others.

The implications for theory, performed in *Mumbo Jumbo* and delineated in this chapter, are numerous. They extend not only to white American literature but also to all American literatures. Leslie Marmon Silko, Maxine Hong Kingston, and Rudolfo Anaya, for example, have given us texts that perform similarly to *Mumbo Jumbo*. In so doing they alleviate the trauma of binary, Logos-centered fragmentation and demonstrate possibilities for healing and wholeness. And, as Carol Siri Johnson points out in discussing *Mumbo Jumbo*, they are "expressive of worlds that exist beyond the obvious ideology of the hegemony and in areas where critics have feared to go" (114).

Notes

1. In the essay "The Liberal in Us All" in *Shrovetide*, Ishmael Reed comments that, "Amiri Baraka, formerly LeRoi Jones, recently said . . . that it was necessary in the 1960s to call the white man a devil because many of us grew up thinking he was god" (41).

2. Kent's book takes its title from his essay on Richard Wright, in which he focuses on "three sources of Wright's power: his double-consciousness, his personal tension, and his dramatic articulation of black and white culture" (76).

3. See Sandra Adell's *Double Consciousness/Double Bind, Theoretical Issues in Twentieth Century Black Literature* (1994) which, through close readings of selected major twentieth-century creative and critical texts, begins an examination of "the relation between the black literary tradition" and what she terms "the ensemble of Western literature and philosophy" (3), a relationship that has spawned fierce conflicts among black critics as to their "presumed opposition between the social and political and the aesthetic or beyond the great Afrocentric/Eurocentric divide." Her guiding concept is "W. E. B. Du Bois's notion of 'double-consciousness'" (4). My 1981 *Black Studies: Pedagogy and Revolution* proposed the foundation of a liberatory pedagogy guided by Du Bois's concept of double-consciousness and Paolo Freire's identification of the self/other conflict in oppressed people and their oppressors in major works of African-American literature and theoretical texts of the 1960s and 70s.

Also, see my 2000 essay, "African American Studies and the 'Warring Ideals': The Color Line Meets the Borderlands" in *Dispatches from the Ebony Tower*, ed. Manning Marable.

4. At this point I use the term "dialogical"; however, this essay evolves from a different understanding of that term, which, I propose, is best expressed by "dianommical," a word I have coined and explain later in this chapter.

5. Reed reprints the definition of mumbo-jumbo from the then current American Heritage Dictionary of the English Language on unnumbered page six of the novel: [Mandingo ma-ma-gyo-mbo, "magician who makes the troubled spirits of ancestors go away"; ma-ma, grandmother+gyo, trouble+mbo, to leave.] Interestingly, the 1992 American Heritage edition has no such definition. Instead, it has what Reed would term an antiplague, Atonist definition: 1. Unintelligible or incomprehensible language; gibberish. 2. language of ritualistic activity intended to confuse. 3. A complicated or obscure ritual. 4. an object believed to have supernatural powers; a fetish. [Perhaps of Mandingo origin.]

Could the Atonists be deliberately attempting to distort the text? Regardless, readers who consult this dictionary for a definition of mumbo jumbo will only get the Western version that renders the meaning the title of the text as 'obscure gibberish.'

6. Hermetic Writings, *Encyclopedia Britannica Online*, <http//www.eb.com:180/bol/topic?eu+41022&sctn+1>.

7. Much of *Mumbo Jumbo* is rooted in fact, despite Reed's claim in *Shrovetide* that "sections of *Mumbo Jumbo* were written in what some people call 'automatic' writing or the nearest thing to it. I think you get a lot of help from heritage, you know, 'voices.'" Sufi Abdul Hamid came to Harlem from Lowell, Massachusetts in 1930, founded the Universal Holy Temple of Tranquility, and, like Father Divine, abolished usage of the term "Negro" and offered a political program. He was called "blasphemer, faker, and a fleecer" by the editor of the black newspaper, *The New Age*. See *When Harlem Was in Vogue* (300–301).

8. Jes Grew and wholeness demand a worldview that accepts the magara principle—the bringing together of the human body and the life force, and the Fourth Principle, Polarity, of the Seven Principles Governing Ancient and Traditional Societies (see *The Kybalion: The Hermetic Philosophy of Ancient Egypt and Greece* (Chicago: Yogi Publication Society, 1904). The seven principles are Mind, Correspondence, Vibration, Polarity, Rhythm, Cause and Effect, Gender. (The late Charles A. Frye, to whom I am indebted for many hours of discussion of African-American philosophy and culture, gave me a copy of these principles, with no author cited for *The Kybalion*.)

Dixon and Foster, in *Beyond Black or White*, some years ago named thinking that allows for both the synthesis of binaries and for the generative (read productive, creative) interaction of contradictions, diunital thinking. Their concept did not include, however, the context of Nommo, the life force. That context involves the generative tensions between matter and spirit, good and evil, male and female, and so on, and suggests the existence of a state in which the physical and spiritual fuse. This state corresponds to the time when gods walked the earth, when people had divine knowledge, and in African-American folklore, when people could fly. Any slaves who disappeared after a revolt or who ran away were said to have flown back to Africa. It is well known that Toni Morrison's novel *Song of Solomon* employs this myth. It is also part of the lore of the Caribbean and South America. In African tradition, sound unlocks this state, with the drum and dance relating to the earth. It can be arguably speculated that call response in the black church, musical instruments, chants, high notes in gospel choirs relate to ways of unlocking that state. They are examples of Jes Grew flair-ups.

9. Interestingly, the interpretation of the Supreme Being in the surviving Aton hymn, to the sun god, Aton, is in concert with the European conceptualization of God as the prime source of all, and in opposition to traditional conceptualizations of humankind bringing forth through a life force, called Nommo in West African traditions, what the earth provides. For a discussion of Aton, see *Encyclopedia Britannica Online*, <http://www.eb.com:180/c/s.dll/g?DocFmicro/39/88.html>.

10. Basil Davidson's corpus of works, too numerous to recount here, attest to there being similarities throughout the continent in African traditional religion. Likewise, works like Maya Deren's *The Divine Horseman* (1953), Paul Carter Harrison's *The Drama of Nommo*, and Joseph Murphy's *Working the Spirit Ceremonies of the African Diaspora* (1994), among many others, give credence to Reed's concept of HooDoo in the "New World."

11. *Encyclopedia Britannica Online*, Hierophant: http://www.eb.com:180/cgi-bin/g?DocF+micro/270/45.html>.

12. Diop and others offer historical evidence that Isis and Osiris did exist apart from their legends. The Book of Thoth, Reed equates with the Book of the Dead, which according to Diop contained "cosmogony that leave no doubt about the Negroness of the race that conceived the ideas" (77). Isis and Osiris, Diop and Poe demonstrate to be Negro. I am not here intending to enter the arguments about whether ancient Egypt was black, rather I am offering supporting rationale for Reed's retelling of the Isis and Osiris story.

13. Walter Benn Michael's work most represents the result of the logocentric worldview that dismisses the dynamics of the interconnectedness of past, present, and future. For example, he concludes that "whiteness is not—like class—a social construction. It is rooted instead—like phlogiston—in a mistake ("Position," 143). I think it is significant that he chooses an analogy to phlogiston, not only a mistake but a mistaken hypothetical substance thought to be the volatile constituent in combustion—an apt analogy to whiteness from an African-American historical and contemporary perspective, but one missed by Michaels, it seems. Such an assertion stems from dismissals and distortions of the past and its legacies, an arrogant insistence on the resulting conclusions. It is disheartening to reckon with the overwhelmingly confused yet superficially grounded scholarship on African-American sensibility and aesthetic expression these days, for they are freighted with the contradictions, prejudices, and distortions in much of what Adell calls "the ensemble of Western literature and philosophy." *Mumbo Jumbo* targets these prejudices and distortions.

14. Marie-Sophie in Patrick Chamoiseau's *Texaco* writes in her notebook: "In what I tell you, there's the almost-true, the sometimes-true, and the half-true. That's what telling a life is like, braiding all of that like one plaits the white Indies currant's hair to make a hut. And the true-true comes out of that braid. And Sophie, you can't be scared of lying if you want to know everything" (122).

15. Mohanty offers a postpositivist realist view that sees objectivity as context-specific and offers a realist notion "of scientificity [that] includes an account of the social organization of our current practices of inquiry." A priori notions of knowledge are rejected, and "The realist's postpositivist notion of scientific methodology as epistemically reliable is thus open to the claims of history, that is, to change and revision" (192-193).

His work has enormous consequences for the dominant contemporary conceptualizations of theory and agency. I see much of his analysis and many of his proposals consistent with the theory implicit in *Mumbo Jumbo* and with what I term a dianommic view of the world.

16. I am grateful to Professor Inez Talamantez for this term.

17. This is used in a chapter by Couser in *Teaching American Ethnic Literatures: Nineteen Essays*, ed. Peck and Maitino.

18. Philip Page views African-American identity as plural and not fixed, always in process. However, he also sees it as "necessarily formed in reaction to the controlling mainstream culture." Referring to Ellison in *Shadow and Act* (304), he characterizes it as feeling that "one does not exist in the real world at all," and, invoking Barthold, as always a "variation, a mask, with the constant danger that the mask will slip or, worse, that the disguise will become reality and any real identity will be lost" (Barthold, 45) (22). This is a reading in contradiction to dianommic context, one that denies agency, relegating African-American life and culture simply to reaction to oppression and denying the possibility of agency that exists even within the limitations of oppression.

19. The debates about essentialism, Afrocentrism and the Black Aesthetic, I see as descending from theorists' failure to analyze the function of the historical, social, cultural, political, and economic context. And that context, for the African American, for the postcolonial, and the former colonizer, is defined by forms of multiple competing consciousnesses. For a succinct and poignant analysis and refutation of the ways it has been argued that race, for example, is void of context and thus, essentialist, see Brian Locke, "The Same Drop Rule: Essence, Signification, and Race as an Analytical Category," and Hames-García and Maya, eds., *Realist Theory and the Predicament of Postmodernism*.

Works Cited and Consulted

Adell, Sandra. *Double Consciousness/Double Bind, Theoretical Issues in Twentieth-Century Black Literature*. Urbana: University of Illinois Press, 1994.

Bell, Derrick. *Faces at the Bottom of the Well*. New York: Basic Books, 1992.

Benn Michaels, Walter. "Autobiography of an Ex-White Man, Why Race Is Not a Social Construction." *Transition* 73 (July 1998): 122–43.

Bernal, Martin. *Black Athena: The Afroasiatic Roots of Classical Civilization, Volume I: The Fabrication of Ancient Greece, 1785–1985*. New Brunswick, N.J.: Rutgers University Press, 1987.

Brooks, Gwendolyn. "The Children of the Poor." In *Black Writers of America, A Comprehensive Anthology*. Ed. Keneth Kinnamon and Richard Barksdale. New York: Macmillan, 1972. 717–718.

Butler, Johnnella E. *Black Studies: Pedagogy and Revolution: A Study of Afro-American Studies and the Liberal Arts Tradition through the Discipline of Afro-American Literature*. Lanham, Md.: 1981.

———. "African American Studies and the 'Warring Ideals': The Color Line Meets the Borderlands." In *Dispatches from the Ebony Tower: Intellectuals Confront the African American Experience*. Ed. Manning Marable. New York: Columbia University Press, 2000. 141–152.

Chinweizu. *The West and the Rest of Us*. New York: Vintage, 1975.

Christian, Barbara. "The Race for Theory." In *The Nature and Context of Minority Discourse.* Ed. Abdul R. JanMohammed and David Lloyd. New York: Oxford University Press, 1990. 37–49.

Cone, James. *The Spiritual and the Blues.* New York: Seabury, 1972.

Deren, Maya. *The Divine Horsemen, the Living Gods of Haiti.* New York: Documentext, McPherson and Company, 1953.

Diop, Cheikh Anta. *The African Origin of Civilization: Myth or Reality.* 1967. Ed. and Trans. Mercer Cook. New York: Lawrence Hill, 1975.

Dixon, Vernon J., and Badi G. Foster *Beyond Black or White.* Boston: Little, Brown, 1971.

Du Bois, W. E. B. *The Souls of Black Folk.* [1903]. Ed. David W. Blight and Robert Gooding Williams. Boston: Bedford, 1997.

Ellison, Ralph. *Shadow and Act.* New York: Signet, 1966.

Freire, Paulo. *The Pedagogy of the Oppressed.* New York: Seabury, 1970.

Frye, Charles A. *Towards a Philosophy of Black Studies.* San Francisco: R and E Research Associates, 1978.

Gates, Henry Louis, Jr. *The Signifying Monkey.* New York: Oxford, 1988.

Hames-García, Michael, and Paula Maya, eds. *Reclaiming Identity: Realist Theory and the Predicament of Postmodernism.* Berkeley: University of California Press, 2000.

Harrison, Paul Carter. *The Drama of Nommo.* New York: Grove, 1972.

Herndon, Calvin C. "Blood of the Lamb: The Ordeal of James Baldwin." In *Amistad I, Writings on Black History and Culture.* Ed. John A. Williams and Charles F. Harris. New York: Vintage, 1970. 183–225.

Hord, Fred Lee, and Jonathan Scott Lee. *I Am Because We Are, Readings in Black Philosophy.* Amherst: University of Massachusetts Press, 1995.

Jahn, Janheinz. *Muntu, the New African Culture.* New York: Grove, 1961.

Kent, George. *Blackness and the Adventure of Western Culture.* Chicago: Third World Press, 1972.

Lewis, David Levering. *When Harlem Was in Vogue.* [1979]. New York: Penguin, 1997.

Locke, Brian. "The Same Drop Rule: Essence, Signification, and Race as an Analytical Category." Unpublished paper.

Martin, Reginald. *Ishmael Reed and the New Black Aesthetic Critics.* New York: St. Martin's, 1988.

Mason, Theodore O., Jr. "Performance, History, and Myth: The Problem of Ishmael Reed's *Mumbo Jumbo.*" *Modern Fiction Studies* 34:1 (Spring 1988): 97–109.

Mitchell, Angelyn, ed. *Within the Circle: An Anthology of African American Literary Criticism from the Harlem Renaissance to the Present.* Durham, N.C.: Duke University Press, 1994.

Mohanty, Satya. *Literary Theory and the Claims of History, Postmodernism, Objectivity, Multicultural Politics.* Ithaca, N.Y.: Cornell University Press, 1997.

Morrison, Toni. "Unspeakable Things Unspoken: The Afro-American Presence in American Literature," *Michigan Quarterly Review* 28 (Winter 1989): 1–34.

Murphy, Joseph M. *Working the Spirit: Ceremonies of the African Diaspora.* Boston, Mass.: Beacon, 1994.

Page, Philip. *Dangerous Freedom, Fusion and Fragmentation in Toni Morrison's Novels.* Jackson: University of Mississippi Press, 1995.

Peck, David R., and John R. Maitino, eds. *Teaching American Ethnic Literatures: Nineteen Essays.* Albuquerque: University of New Mexico Press, 1996.

Poe, Richard. *Black Spark, White Fire.* Rocklin, Calif.: Prima Publishing, 1997.

Reed, Ishmael. "D Hexorism of Noxon D Awful." In *Amistad I. Writings on Black History and Culture.* Ed. John A. Williams and Charles F. Harris. New York: Vintage, 1970. 183–225.

——. *Mumbo Jumbo.* New York: Bantam, 1972.

——. *Shrovetide in Old New Orleans.* New York: Doubleday, 1978.

——. "Neo HooDoo Manifesto." In *The Norton Anthology, African American Literature.* Ed. Henry Louis Gates, Jr., and Nellie Y. McKay. New York: Norton, 1997. 2297–2301.

Siri Johnson, Carol. "The Limbs of Osiris: Reed's 'Mumbo Jumbo' and Hollywood's 'The Mummy.'" *MELUS* 17 (Winter 1991): 105–115.

Toomer, Jean. *Cane.* [1923]. New York: Norton, 1975.

PART III

AESTHETIC JUDGMENT AND THE PUBLIC SPHERE

Aesthetics Again?

The Pleasures and the Dangers

PAUL LAUTER

I begin with a portrait of beauty by Tsimshian artist Robert Jackson (figure 1), and with two recent shows of Native American (and Canadian) art. One, *Native Visions: Northwest Coast Art, Eighteenth Century to the Present*, was organized by the Seattle Art Museum; it traveled to the New York State Historical Association museum in Cooperstown, New York, the Anchorage (Alaska) Museum of History and Art, and the Eiteljorg Museum in Indianapolis. The other, titled, *Native Paths: American Indian Art from the Collection of Charles and Valerie Diker*, is a permanent but rotating exhibition at the Metropolitan Museum of Art. The first is impressively represented in a 216-page volume, *Native Visions*, written by Steven C. Brown;[1] the latter is yet to be displayed in print outside a Met newsletter.

The use of "native" in the titles of these shows suggests the widespread rehabilitation of that term from an anthropological marker of status to a distinction of domains of creative expression. Further along the same line is the insertion into the subtitle of Brown's book of the word "Evolution": "Evolution in Northwest Coast Art from the Eighteenth through the Twentieth Century." What the word calls attention to, I think, is the art historical focus of the *Native Visions* show, a focus largely absent from the Met's *Native Paths*. Indeed, the works displayed at the Met, while mostly wonderful in themselves, have primarily been offered in ethnographic terms having to do with their uses rather than their forms, whereas the elaborate exhibit labels of the *Native Visions* show, as well as the text of Brown's book, constitute one of the most complete introductions to the formal properties and, precisely, *evolution* of Northwest Coast Indian art I have ever seen.

I introduce these comparisons not so much to criticize the Met show. Rather, I want to point to what I think is the intellectual engine driving the character of *Native Visions*. Its organizers perceived that for those who stand outside the various native cultures of the Northwest Coast, that is, most of the people who look at its art in shops and museums, certainly in Cooperstown, the aesthetic principles which enable its reading are not at all transparent. On the contrary, the formal structures, the compositional principles, the vision, if you will, through which Northwest Coast native artists work is largely alien to those brought up

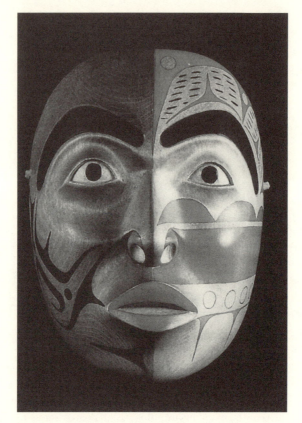

Figure 1 Portrait mask by Robert Jackson, Nagwa.
Courtesy of the artist.

on Western European painting and sculpture. It is therefore necessary for those of us so raised to *learn* the equivalent of a foreign tongue in order for us adequately to read works constituted within its discourse, like this Kwakiutl sea monster mask of 1900 (figure 2). What the Met show reveals, on the other hand, is the curator's notion that certain universal principles of the visual arts are well known to the museum's visitors—or, it may be, that most visitors would have little patience to learn a set of unfamiliar Native American discourses and would simply float down the corridor in which the exhibition is located to something, Warhol or Rauschenberg, say, more familiar and presumably accessible.

I must say at once that I am not proposing that Northwest Coast First Peoples' art exists or has for two hundred years and more existed in some discontinuous vernacular niche, exempt from the influences of Western sailors, buyers, anthropologists, and artists. Such notions of local purity have long been exploded. At the same time, it is impossible not to recognize the ovals, trigons, curvilinear

Figure 2   Sea monster mask, Kwakwaka'wakw.
Courtesy of the Burke Museum of Natural History and
Culture; photo by Eduardo Calderon (Catalog #1-1451).

incisings, and other formal elements (figure 3) that constitute a distinctive group
of two-dimensional formline styles quite peculiar to Northwest Coast sculptures
(figure 4), bentwood boxes (figure 5), masks (figure 6), bowls (figure 7), and other
articles of clothing and feasting (figures 8, 9, 10) and that have marked such work
for many hundreds of years. Reading, responding to such work with feeling,
precision, and depth requires one not only to learn a particular expressive vocabulary, but to see how that vocabulary is deployed in a great variety of works
over time and space and, I believe, to understand something of the changing
cultural roles such works have played.

For example, here is Steven Brown's comment on the art exemplified by late
eighteenth- and mid-nineteenth-century chests (figure 11):

The timeless consistency of the powerfully understated structures and the visual
austerity of the older work can lend us symbolic glimpses of what these original

Figure 3 Chilkat tunic, Tlingit. Courtesy of the Burke Museum of Natural History and Culture; photo by Eduardo Calderon (Catalog #1-631).

societies may have been like for the average members of the communities. The angularity of the movements, the visible weight of individual design forms (as well as the overall structures), and the aristocratic nobility of the images all convey something both beautiful and terrifying about the qualities of life in the millennia of pre-history. . . . By contrast [figure 12], the perceivable feeling of mid- to late-nineteenth-century or classic period formline art is considerably lighter and less austere in character. (*Native Visions*, 67–68)

I am not presenting Brown's comments as a one-size-fits-all model of aesthetic judgment, for it seems to me peculiarly difficult to translate visual (or auditory) responses into the quite different realm of language. Still, I think his words help open the visual discourse of Northwest Coast art for those relatively unfamiliar with its vocabulary and conventions.

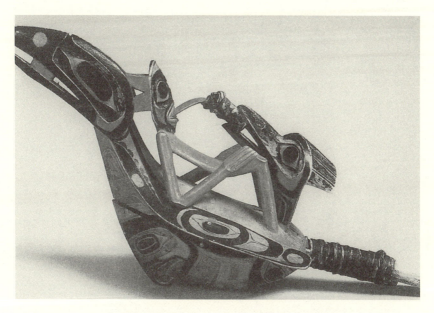

Figure 4 Raven rattle, Tlingit. Courtesy of the Burke Museum of Natural History and Culture; photo by Eduardo Calderon (Catalog #951).

This book is not, of course, one dedicated mainly to the visual arts or to the work of art historians. Still, it seems to me that the case of Northwest Coast art is instructive for those of us who study "aesthetics and difference" principally in literary texts. Though Franz Boas wrote essays about certain formal features of Northwest Coast artifacts,[2] the artistic creations of the people of that area remained part of the province of ethnology among Anglos, certainly until 1965, when Bill Holm (Professor Emeritus of the University of Washington Art School) published his pathbreaking study, *Northwest Coast Indian Art: An Analysis of Form*.[3] Up until then (and obviously still today), one encountered Northwest Coast "objects" in the antique halls of the American Museum of Natural History rather than across Central Park in the rarefied chambers of the Metropolitan Museum of Art. One result of the social movements of the sixties—and, no doubt, of the legacy of Michael Rockefeller's disappearance—has been a certain dissolution of such invidious distinctions, though as I said at the beginning they do persist.[4]

One could argue that the analogies between visual and verbal artistic practices toward which I am obviously heading need to be considered within a framework defined by a discipline like *Comparative* Literature. That what I am looking at are visual *languages*, as different from one another as English is from Tsimshian or either from Creole French. There is a certain truth in this view: nevertheless, I want to maintain that even within one linguistic tradition—that of English

Figure 5 Box drum, Tlingit. Courtesy of the Burke
Museum of Natural History and Culture; photo by
Eduardo Calderon (Catalog # 1-1586).

here—distinctive cultural characteristics and aesthetic understandings exist that
cannot be presumed upon, that are learned as one's original culture or, later, as
objects of collegiate or professional study. But before looking at a specific case,
we need to consider the sources of pleasure in language.

Language use is, with food, drink, sex, sleep, shelter, a necessity of human life.
Above anything else, elaborated language use is what mainly distinguishes humans
as a species from other forms of animal life. Language use, Chomsky has powerfully argued, is based on the hard-wired deep structures of human minds that
enable us to construct ever-new sentences to express or communicate our desires,
objections, anxieties, orders, ideas. Even if one quarrels with the proposition that
language use is peculiarly human, it is certainly true that, as with other human

Figure 6 Kolus mask, Kwakwaka'wakw (Nakwakdakw).
Courtesy of the Burke Museum of Natural History and
Culture; photo by Eduardo Calderon (Catalog #2.5E1605).

needs, we derive pleasure from its exercise. Food is everywhere necessary to people and—at least whenever possible—pleasurable to consume. That's the "universal" element. But the particular form of crab or pepper oil or eel or tofu that tickles one's palate is, in my experience, learned, contingent, particularistic—and changeable. As with food, so with language use: what is learned, contingent, particularistic, and changeable are the exact forms of language use from which pleasure can be derived, the pleasures of play—echo, recognition, association, distinction—of sound—cadence, euphony, repetition and variation—of structure—anticipation, invocation, climax, resolution; these are, among others, the sources of our pleasures.

But such pleasures are embedded in the conventions of a given artistic discourse; discrepancies of convention condition how—or indeed whether—we

Figure 7 Makah, grease disk. Collection of the author.

Figure 8 Bella Coola,
thunderbird frontlet, property
of a chief of Tlatlasikoala
Kwakiutl. Museum of
Anthropology, University of
British Columbia, Vancouver;
photograph by Maximilien
Bruggmann, in Peter R.
Gerber, *Indians of the Northwest
Coast*, trans. Barbara Fritzemeier
(New York: Facts on File,
1989), p. 117. Used by permis-
sion of Maximilien Bruggmann.

Figure 9 Chilikat Tlingit or Tsimshian blanket. National Museum of Man, Ottawa; photograph by Maximilien Bruggmann, in Gerber, *Indians of the Northwest Coast*, pp. 58–59. Used by permission of Maximilien Bruggmann.

Figure 10 Niska-Tsimshian, frontlet. Museum of Anthropology, University of British Columbia, Vancouver; photograph by Maximilien Bruggmann, in Gerber, *Indians of the Northwest Coast*, p. 73. Used by permission of Maximilien Bruggmann.

Figure 11 Tlingit or Tsimshian chest panels, c. 1780. Collection of Eugene and Martha Nester; photograph by Paul Macapia, in Steven C. Brown, *Native Visions: Evolution in Northwest Coast Art from the Eighteenth through the Twentieth Century* (Seattle: Seattle Art Museum in Association with the University of Washington Press, 1998), p. 26. Courtesy of the Seattle Art Museum.

Figure 12 Haida, Tsimshian or Haisla, chest front. Collection of Paul Putnam; photograph by Paul Macapia, in Brown, *Native Visions*, p. 66. Courtesy of the Seattle Art Museum.

value ant stew or even, as I will suggest in a moment, "Aunt Chloe." Conventions can be but are not necessarily transferable. Nor are such conventions permanent fixtures even in one discourse tradition. In the late twentieth century, it takes a deal of specialized work to derive pleasure—ask our students—from *Paradise Lost* or from much of what is now called "sentimental" writing of the last century. Most of us have lost access to certain of the signals that once brought laughter or tears, awe or resignation—or even more commonplace pleasures of writing and reading. For ours is a moment of notable creolization.[5] Is that a bad thing or a good? Some might say that an excess of hybridity threatens to swamp all settled and familiar structures. To be sure, in this carnival, it is easy to undervalue, even to miss, what writers of another century, even within a particular discourse tradition, are about. And it can be easy to read a deceptively hybrid text, like *The Woman Warrior*, through the limiting glasses of Western fictional traditions. It may be that to read in a hybrid manner one has to go back precisely to a less hybrid and anomalous time if there ever was one.

I want to illustrate by looking once again at Frances Ellen Watkins Harper. When we were first putting together the *Heath Anthology of American Literature* in 1989, I was insistent that we include Harper, even though the consultants to whom the publisher had sent the manuscript unanimously proposed her as one writer we might cut. To some extent my insistence was motivated by my understanding of the historical role Harper played both in white and black communities throughout the second half of the nineteenth century: she was an important *figure* in the cultural world of the United States. But I also believed that she was a skilled practitioner of words. Many of us are now familiar with how she captures "Aunt Chloe's Politics" in the poem by that name, how she constructs a voice, in fact, as well as a significant Reconstruction political outlook:

> Of course, I don't know very much
>   About these politics,
> But I think that some who run 'em
>   Do mighty ugly tricks.
>
> I've seen 'em honey-fugle round,
>   And talk so awful sweet,
> That you'd think them full of kindness,
>   As an egg is full of meat.
>
> Now I don't believe in looking
>   Honest people in the face
> And saying when you're doing wrong,
>   That "I haven't sold my race."
>
> When we want to school our children,
>   If the money isn't there,

Whether black or white have took it,
   The loss we all must share.

And this buying up each other
   Is something worse than mean,
Though I thinks a heap of voting,
   I go for voting clean.

I've often asked my students to imagine the actress they see playing Aunt Chloe and to justify their choices from the language of the text. The discussion can plunge us quite deeply into Reconstruction politics—history—the construction of race—sociology—canon theory—the politics of literature—as well as the venues in which such a poem might circulate—cultural studies or anthropology. But is it a "good," a valuable poem?—the central question, I take it, of aesthetics.

When the *Heath* was reviewed in *TLS* in 1990, the writer, Mark Edmundson, complained that most of the poetry we included could be characterized by "thematic intensity" rather than by "intensity of verbal invention."[6] The latter, which he believed characterized significant poetry, was marked by "surprise," growing from the "sophisticated formal concerns" of poets, like James Merrill, we largely omitted. His example of a poet given to "readily accessible narrative" was Garrett Hongo. He might easily have drawn the contrast between Gerard Manley Hopkins and Frances Harper. Hopkins is working in a tradition illustrated also by Christian metaphysical poets like Herbert, Crashawe, and Edward Taylor, for whom the very ability to discipline a prodigal imagination into dense and demanding forms becomes an expression of hope for salvation in a profligate world. The poem emerges as illustration and earnest of that hope, form and function fusing into an ecstasy of language:

Not, I'll not carrion comfort, Despair, not feast on thee;
Not untwist—slack they may be—these last strands of man
In me ór, most weary, cry I can no more. I can. . . .

Harper's discourse is, of course, quite different: it is oral, instructive, and above all performative. She is addressing a cultural community rather distinct from that which functionally overhears the words, often so privately held, of the Christian poets I have named. She is speaking to her community from a platform whereon she stands as a model and a guide. It is a community many of whose members cannot read from the page but whose ears have, from long necessity, been tuned to the nuances of voice, expression, and command, who "read" Aunt Chloe and the folks to whom she refers with great accuracy. Harper's problem is precisely opposite to that of creating a discourse of what Edmondson called "intensity of verbal invention." The effect of that would be alienation, a dynamic of teacherly isolation on her part and withdrawal into respectful silence on the part of her listeners. The illusion she must sustain, somewhat analogous to that of the rapster, is that of speaking her hearers. Her language choices reflect that tension between the knowing and the common "I": thus, "I don't know very much / About *these* politics." "Politics" as a plural object, like horses or dogs, badly "run" by some folks. The kind of folks who look you "in the face" and say—one hears her puffing up to say—"I haven't sold my race." Yes, ma'am, we know that feller. And we know Aunt Chloe, who controls the conditional—"If the money isn't there"— but doesn't fret about the vernacular—"Whether black or white have took it." Is *she* black or white? My students always wonder. But the signal, sparingly registered, clear to Harper's hearers, is there in "Though I thinks a heap of voting." What I am suggesting, in short, is that the verbal invention in "Aunt Chloe's Politics" is quite skillful, but seeing that depends upon *our* learning a discourse quite different from that within which contemporaries like Browning and Swinburne, Sarah Piatt or Emily Dickinson operate.

In fact, the most freighted words in "Aunt Chloe's Politics," those having to do with selling votes, seldom resonate with today's readers. Read among the other poems in the Aunt Chloe series,[7] however, the language of this work takes on greater intensity. The poem immediately preceding "Aunt Chloe's Politics," "The Deliverance," concludes with a series of anecdotes in which black women criticize their men for selling their votes, or force them to return their ill-gotten gains, and in which some black men stand up against the practice:

> You'd laughed to seen Lucinda Grange
>   Upon her husband's track;
> When he sold his vote for rations
>   She made him take 'em back.
>
> Day after day did Milly Green
>   Just follow after Joe,
> And told him if he voted wrong
>   To take his rags and go. . . .
>
> I've heard before election came
>   They tried to buy John Slade;
> But he gave them all to understand
>   That he wasn't in that trade.

Aunt Chloe and likewise Harper are thus responding to the charge of vote-selling, used widely in the Reconstruction South to justify efforts to disenfranchise black men. Moreover, they are encouraging those men, men in the audience, to "rally round the cause, / And go for holding up the hands / That gave us equal laws." In the context of bitter, and often deadly Reconstruction politics, "voting clean" has a different valence with the audience for these poems than the phrase could have with twenty-first-century Americans, more likely to doubt altogether the efficacy of voting than to register its symbolic force.

The question of discourse becomes more complicated, of course, as things get to be more explicitly hybrid, when Claude McKay, for example, appropriates the sonnet form—"since there's no help, come let us kiss and part"—to demand of his kinsmen, "If we must die, let it not be like hogs." Or, working the other way as recent writers like Michael North[8] have noted, when Ezra Pound, e.e. cummings, or William Carlos Williams appropriate dialect and nonstandard personae as spearpoints against gentility. No discourse community is absolutely distinct from any other, and the borrowing and interactions are multiple in as heterogeneous and conglomerate a culture as we now experience. Still, to say that distinctions do not exist is equivalent to arguing that there is nothing to mark off Chinese from French cuisine. That they borrow and interpenetrate is illustrated by Vietnamese cooking, but I am yet to find a person who cannot tell Lutece from Hee Sung Fung.

My food metaphor has not been casual. As the pleasures of their cuisine lead me to value the diverse delights of Hee Sung Fung and Lutece, the pleasures of their language lead me to value the diverse delights of Gerard Manley Hopkins and Frances Harper. But are they equally good? Well, how do you feel about these objects (figures 13, 14, 15, and 16)? They are, all of them, articles of clothing, thus commodities, and thus, at best, crafts, no? But such judgments reflect a fundamental conception of the Western art market: the idea that paint on a canvas surface, carved stone, and etched brass are inherently more to be valued than paint on a bentwood box, or the design woven into a jacket or incised on a mask. What I have been suggesting here is not only that we have been taught to value complex, multilayered texts, especially because they pay off for us in classrooms (as Simon Frith points out, we have more to say about them[9]), but also, in part depending on who defines that "we," certain venues and functions within which art practices are enacted have, in Western culture, likewise been esteemed over others. The visual work hung on an art museum wall has registered more aesthetic coinage for European Americans than the costume worn for ceremonial purposes. Similarly, the poem published in the book carries more weight with that same audience than the poem printed in the magazine or delivered from the platform.

The aesthetic question, then, the question of value, cannot be answered simply by mixing and matching particular texts as if they existed in mutually translatable discourses, in some idealized empyrean venue, and for interchangeable audiences. All these matters—audience, function, conventions—must—and in fact always already do—inform our judgments. To labor under the illusion that they do not victimizes, above all, anyone who maintains such a narrow vision, restricting his or her pleasure to the functional equivalents of what going out to eat meant in Bloomington, Indiana, in 1953: Bob's for hot dogs, and A&W for everything else. Like Whitman, we must embrace contradiction, holding with one hand the reality of hybridity, amalgamation, interpenetration; while, with

Figure 13 Chief Shakes's crest hat of the Nanya.aayi clan in Wrangell, Alaska, Tlingit. Courtesy of the Burke Museum of Natural History and Culture; photo by Eduardo Calderon (Catalog #1-1436).

Figure 14 Haida, Killer Whale hat, 1992, by Don Yeomans. Collection of the *Seattle Times*, photograph by Paul Macapia, in Brown, *Native Visions*, p. 174. Courtesy of the Seattle Art Museum.

Figure 15 Tlingit, beaded neck ornament.

Figure 16 Harold Jacobs,
Tlingit, in ceremonial clothing;
wolf rattle by Reggie B.
Petersen, Tlingit. Photograph
by Maximilien Bruggmann, in
Gerber, *Indians of the Northwest
Coast*, p. 57. Used by permission
of Maximilien Bruggmann.

the other, acknowledging and celebrating the equally real presence of particularity, locality, difference. The task in aesthetics, as in politics, is to hold these seeming contradictions in creative, if often tense and painful, embrace.

Notes

1. Steven C. Brown, *Native Visions: Evolution in Northwest Coast Art from the Eighteenth through the Twentieth Century* (Seattle: Seattle Art Museum in Association with the University of Washington Press, 1998).

2. See Aldona Jonaitis, *A Wealth of Thought: Franz Boas on Native American Art* (Seattle: University of Washington Press, 1995). Boas's essays "The Decorative Art of the Indians of the North Pacific Coast" (1897) and "Notes on the Blanket Designs" (1907) are included in this book.

3. Bill Holm, *Northwest Coast Indian Art: An Analysis of Form* (Seattle: University of Washington Press, 1965).

4. They were further undermined in an important *New York Times* review of an exhibition on Voodou, organized by the Fowler Museum and later mounted at the American Museum of Natural History. As is the case with Northwest Coast art, the flags, altars, and veves of Haitian ceremonial art—and the paintings, too—require a viewer from outside its religious domain to learn a rather different cultural vocabulary. In this case, the problem may be less a matter of stylization than of the use of iconography and of materials—like spangles and filled bottles—not generally associated in Western visual vocabularies with powerful art. See Holland Cotter, "Dazzling and Devout Voodoo Energy," *New York Times*, October 9, 1998, Sect. E, pt. 2, p. 31.

5. I use the term in the sense of "cultural creolization" explored by Rob Kroes in *If You've Seen One, You've Seen the Mall* (Urbana: University of Illinois Press, 1996), pp. 162–164 and thereafter.

6. "Dangers of Democracy," *TLS* (Oct. 19–25, 1990): 1133.

7. These were published in *Sketches of Southern Life* (Philadelphia: Merrihew, 1872). They are most easily found in Frances Foster, ed., *A Brighter Coming Day* (New York: Feminist Press, 1990), pp. 196–208, and in *Complete Poems of Frances E. W. Harper*, ed. Maryemma Graham (New York: Oxford University Press, 1988).

8. Michael North, *The Dialect of Modernism: Race, Language, and Twentieth-Century Literature* (New York: Oxford University Press, 1994).

9. Simon Frith, "John Keats vs. Bob Dylan: Why Value Judgments Matter," *Chronicle of Higher Education* (March 14, 1997): 68.

"Every man knows where and how beauty gives him pleasure"

Beauty Discourse and the Logic of Aesthetics

AMELIA JONES

There can be no rule by which someone could be compelled to acknowledge that something is beautiful . . .
Immanuel Kant, *Critique of Judgment*

Beauty is one of those great mysteries of nature, whose influence we all see and feel; but a general, distinct idea of its essential must be classed among the truths yet undiscovered. If this idea were geometrically clear, men would not differ in their opinions upon the beautiful, and it would be easy to prove what true beauty is.
Johann Winckelmann, *History of Ancient Art*

Every man knows where and how beauty gives him pleasure . . .
John Ruskin, "The Lamp of Beauty"

Each of these great figures in the history of aesthetics—Immanuel Kant, Johann Winckelmann, and John Ruskin—acknowledges the profound instability of *beauty* as a mode of appreciating objects and images that seduce us (in texts from 1790, 1764, and 1849, respectively).[1] There is tension in their acknowledgments, however; while proclaiming the contingency of beauty, each goes on to attempt to recuperate some kind of authority for himself as its arbiter. By stating that "every man knows where and how beauty gives him pleasure," for example, Ruskin blithely and self-confidently naturalizes the determination of "beauty"; at the same time, he explicitly acknowledges the extent to which beauty's obviousness is always subjective ("every man knows . . ."). This dual gesture, which affirms universality even as it admits particularity, structures the aesthetic in its dominant forms of articulation within Western art discourse.

We can at least historicize Ruskin's comment, which was issued in the midst of the heatedly romantic, simultaneously self-assured, and culturally anxious moment of mid-nineteenth-century Europe, with its cultural imperialism and burgeoning capitalist markets. Such hubris in the matter of claiming absolute personal authority for aesthetic judgments is, however, troubling in its renewed formulations in the current era of late-capitalist neonationalist, multicultural, and contentious public vs. private funding debates. Nonetheless, a group of art critics supported by the Los Angeles–based venues the *Los Angeles Times* and the *Art issues* magazine and press has won awards and gained international acclaim for repeating just such authoritative—and, one would have thought, outmoded—claims.

This essay focuses on the writings of this group, most notably Dave Hickey's influential and award-winning book, *The Invisible Dragon: Four Essays on Beauty*, published with Art issues Press,[2] bringing to bear on Hickey's arguments a critique of his perpetuation of certain aspects of aesthetic judgment—a critique that is articulated very much from a contemporary perspective. My text, then, does not pretend to offer a history or theory of aesthetics but, rather, is posed in a polemical way to intervene in a particular position, exemplified by Hickey's work, which holds a great deal of international status within art discourse at this moment. By extension (and it is worth stressing that the tendency to perpetuate a certain authoritarianism within aesthetics and Hickey's own influence are both pronounced in contemporary art criticism), I hope to suggest a way of evaluating works of art that is more in sync with contemporary politics and culture—one that understands rather than veils or occludes the contingency of meaning and value and the role of the interpreter in determining both. It will be clear from my arguments that I do not believe the aesthetic approach to visual culture, which inevitably cleaves to the connoisseurial tradition and perpetuates its authoritarian effects, to be a productive one at this point in our cultural history.

Notably, in the introduction of *The Invisible Dragon* Hickey openly claims allegiance with Ruskin (unctuously citing the latter in the acknowledgments as his "Victorian mentor"), and he stages the book, rather self-contradictorily, as a radical corrective to so-called "political correctness" (or PC)—the supposed hegemony of narrow-minded "art professionals" who currently administer "a monolithic system of interlocking patronage."[3] Hickey, then, strategically poses himself as correcting what he parodically characterizes as a bureaucratization of art through academic discourses of identity and cultural politics. Describing himself as "admittedly outrageous," he offers himself as art's savior from ideology. As many theorists of aesthetics have pointed out, the claim that one is the only critic "free" of ideology is the oldest trick in the long book of aesthetics—it is trick that authorizes the disciplines of art criticism and art history in their more traditional modes.[4] Thus, with the revival of an abstract notion of "beauty," we return not only to Ruskin but, by implication (I will argue thoroughly below), to the imperialist and exclusionary logic of cultural value that gave Ruskin and his contemporaries their social authority as arbiters of taste.

Hickey's book is clearly staged as a polemic (rather close, to my mind, to the melodramatic pronouncements of Howard Stern) and cries out for an equally heated response, which I hope to provide here. It is important to note right away that I am on the defensive here, given that I am just the type of "art professional" Hickey would excoriate for my supposed collusion with what he calls the PC "liberal institution" with its seduction of the nonspecialist beholder by a rigid politics of antipleasure rhetoric—by which I understand him to mean the Marxian and specifically Brechtian emphases in dominant 1980s critical art discourse.[5]

Hickey's conservatism, however, is complicated in that it is intertwined with an overtly staged populism, which takes the primary form of an embrace of popular culture (perhaps it is not a coincidence, to this end, that this discourse has its power base in Los Angeles, the home of the entertainment industry, which conflates social liberalism with a myopic class, gender, and racial politics and an embrace of corporate consumerism). Hickey's admonition implies that the call to political responsibility is nothing but a burden for the "common man." Left alone, Hickey argues, this beholder would otherwise inevitably be impressed by the "beauty" of objects—an aesthetic effect that is, in his words, "*directly*" purveyed to the viewer but at the same time (and contradictorily), all too easily suppressed by misguided purveyors of "PC." Aside from the fact that Hickey himself is an academic, ensconced in the "liberal institution" of the University of Nevada, and the fact that he has been supported by national awards (such as the most prestigious national award for art criticism, given out annually by the College Art Association[6]) the most important points to be made definitively against Hickey's argument are historical and political, rather than personal or institutional.

I want here, then, to dismantle the particular mode of authoritative aesthetic judgment mobilized by Hickey and his supporters such that, by the end of this essay, the reader will no longer be seduced by the rhetoric of beauty that has, unfortunately, once again taken on the legitimacy of a closed and self-evident discourse of "truth." First, through Jacques Derrida's deconstruction of Kant's *Critique of Judgment* in his important book *Truth in Painting,* I retrace the foundations of this authoritative brand of aesthetic judgment;[7] the remainder of the essay then works through a number of images that art history has more or less consensually deemed "beautiful" in order to interrogate the particular exclusions that are at work in any discourse that naturalizes "beauty" as a singular criterion of art judgment and appreciation.

The tension in the "more or less" serves to signal a series of conceptual gaps I spelunk in order to make their edges and chasms more visible, exposing the contradictions at work in this particular kind of aesthetic judgment so as to refuse its attempted lack of closure. I hope to convince the reader that, stripped of its suture effect, the new permutation of beauty discourse (where, in Hickey's words, beauty is made obvious and true as "the single direct route from the image to the individual"[8]) can be laid bare for what it is: yet another version of a very old game that operates to privilege a particular group as having access to the truth. The naturalized discourse of aesthetic judgment ("every man knows where and how beauty gives him pleasure") is itself an "institution" that specifically functions to exclude not only those readers/viewers labeled insensitive (those "art professionals" who happen to disagree with Hickey and his colleagues—such as myself) but the very history of the politics of exclusion within this particular kind of aesthetic judgment.[9]

Exclusion—excluding the nonbeautiful from the realm of objects worth contemplating—is the primary function of aesthetics and the rhetoric of beauty as these have conventionally been wielded, Hickey's stated empathy with what he calls the "secular" or "disenfranchised" beholder aside. My project here is summed up by Roland Barthes's statement of goals in *Mythologies*, his epic study of myth: "I want . . . to track down, in the decorative display of *what-goes-without-saying*, the ideological abuse which, in my view, is hidden there."[10]

Stains on the Passe-Partout

In the history of Western art and the most dominant kinds of aesthetic judgment, the naked white female body has long been staged as the most consistent (if contentious and highly charged) trope of aesthetic beauty, as exemplified by Edmund Burke's description in his 1756 treatise *A Philosophical Inquiry into the Origin of Our Ideas of the Sublime and the Beautiful*: "Observe that part of a beautiful woman where she is perhaps the most beautiful, about the neck and breasts; the smoothness; the softness; the easy and insensible swell; the variety of the surface . . . ; the deceitful maze, through which the unsteady eye slides giddily, without knowing where to fix, or whither it is carried."[11] As Burke's seductive, vertiginous description and bestsellers such as Kenneth Clark's book *The Nude: A Study of Ideal Art* suggest, it is the female nude that, in the words of Lynda Nead, is understood to articulate fully "the alchemic powers of art" to transform through beauty.[12] At the same time, as Nead asserts, the female nude operates *through the aesthetic* as, precisely, a container to enframe and control the threat of unbridled female sexuality.[13] The aesthetic, in this light, can be viewed precisely as a strategic mode of discourse that operates to *cohere* the male subject, always anxious about the perceived power of female sexuality and social access.[14] As object safely contained within the rhetoric of representation, "content" of the commodified painterly or sculpted object, the female nude is presumably made docile, an object of exchange between men (artist and patron or viewer). As I will discuss further later, the female nude is not only disempowered as the object of heterosexual male desire but also retains her status as "art" rather than "pornography" by maintaining an attachment to signifiers of purity (whiteness) that are racially determined.

Viewed through the lens of deconstructive philosophy, the aesthetic model derived from Kant's *Critique of Judgment*, as Jacques Derrida has notably remarked, is a framing device that aims to link the inside (the subject, the interior of the picture) with the outside (the object, the viewer in the world). We might say that the aesthetic is precisely the conceptual structure that enables the traffic in images/in women called the art market, which itself has traditionally supported the vast and intricate system of privilege that might be reduced to the dualistic circuit that opposes the artist (bound by identification to the viewer and, by extension, to "God") to the objects of exchange (women, paintings, slaves). As philosophers from Hegel onward have explored, such oppositional relationships structure not only aesthetics but the philosophical inquiry: lived experience in the Western world is characterized by a partition of subjects into endlessly negotiated dialectics of Master and Slave. Yet, as Derrida points out, the frame is itself both interior and exterior: these relationships are chiasmic, intertwining inside and out even as they work as momentary oppositions.

Through such momentary polarizations, the aesthetic sets itself up as proof of the viewer's mastery and coherence (as in Hickey's discourse, it becomes a "self-authenticating dialogue"[15] that tautologically confirms the viewer's supposed correctness of opinion regarding the beautiful). The aesthetic works both to contain otherness by reducing the other to beautiful object and to erect the subject of judgment as Master; it does this paradoxically by claiming that the judgment of what is beautiful is both spontaneous and individual, sparked by the "harmony of form in the object" (experienced within the subject), and *universal*. Kant, famously, insists that

> the judging person feels completely *free* as regards the liking he accords the object [and is thus fully disinterested]. . . . Hence he will talk about the beautiful as if beauty were a characteristic of the object and the judgment were logical . . . *even though* in fact the judgment is only aesthetic and refers the object's presentation merely to the subject. He will talk in this way because the logical judgment does resemble a logical judgment inasmuch as *we may presuppose it to be valid for everyone.* . . . In other words, *a judgment of taste must involve a claim to subjective universality.*[16]

Kant's model of aesthetic judgment relies explicitly on the capacity of the beautiful object to inspire pure taste and elevated pleasure in the viewer (and it is the "even though" that has been elided by dominant models of art critical analysis that borrow from Kant—*even though* the judgment is resolutely subjective), but, simultaneously, it requires that this viewer maintain his integrity by claiming to be *disinterested*. That is, *even though* the judgment of beauty refers "merely to the subject," it must be disinterested (free of sensory or emotional interest).[17] Aesthetic judgment is both a *bridge* between interior and exterior and, through disinterestedness (which sets the judge definitively *outside*), an inviolable boundary of difference. In proposing to control or master the world of visible objects, the aesthetic points to its own failure: Derrida notes that for Kant, "[while] the purely subjective affect [informing aesthetic judgment] is provoked by what is called the beautiful, that which is said to be beautiful [is] *outside*, in the object and independently of its existence."[18]

The aesthetic is an ideology of control that is obviously highly successful in sustaining the law of patriarchy but also fails by its own internal contradictions; while it attempts to solve the age-old philosophical problem of the relationship between self and world, self and other, it can only function as such by setting apart the philosopher/judge, placing him or her outside the frame of the aesthetic. The frame is a *passe-partout* (which, in French, means both a "pass key" and the matte that sets off the picture inside the frame—a "frame within the frame") and, as Derrida points out, the "internal edges of a *passe-partout* are often beveled."[19] There is always leakage polluting the supposedly disinterested authority of the discourse of beauty (an authority exemplified by Hickey's repeated insistence that the beautiful work has a simple and "direct" relationship to the viewer—a relationship which, naturally, only *he* is authorized to describe). That pollution is, as suggested earlier, the stench of ideology: the arbiter's own psychic and socially conditioned and inflected investments, which encourage him or her to prefer one object over another.

Hickey, like Kant and Ruskin before him, makes recourse to the seductive claims of common sense in his naturalized and never clearly specified notion of beauty, which he only once attempts to define and then tautologically. Hickey's definition—"beauty [is] the agency that cause[s] visual pleasure in the beholder"[20]—thus explicitly parallels (but is far less profound and productively ambiguous than) Kant's fabulous contortion in the *Critique of Judgment*: the "feeling of pleasure or displeasure" that the beautiful inspires "denotes nothing in the object, but is a feeling which the Subject has."[21] Thus, for Kant, as for Hickey, beauty is an agency supposedly emanating from the work of art which causes the viewing subject to judge it beautiful (beauty thus causes its own value), while reciprocally confirming the arbiter of beauty as "correct" in his judgment (the viewer who claims an object to be beautiful is thus, inevitably, right).

Given the role of naked white women in the visual structuration of an ideology of "beauty," it is notable that Hickey chooses Robert Mapplethorpe—the author of images of naked (often black) men engaged in homoerotic postures and acts—as the Genius of beauty (figure 1). The question of the cultural value and interest of Mapplethorpe's work aside, it is worth noting by way of a complaint how convenient it seems to be for white male critics to continue to invoke Geniuses who are white men to secure the authenticity of their aesthetic judgments. The sexualized male bodies of Mapplethorpe's works notoriously mimic the codes of the fetishization of the female body that is at the base of Western aesthetics while, especially in the case of those that are black, aggressively dislocating the expected content. This fabulous contradiction could be productively mobilized to interrogate the bases

Figure 1 Robert Mapplethorpe, *Charles Bowman*, 1980. Copyright © The Estate of Robert Mapplethorpe. Used by permission.

of aesthetic judgment, as it has been in the work of Kobena Mercer, for example.[22] Hickey, however, deploys Mapplethorpe's work to reiterate the ideologically loaded claims of the aesthetic in its most authoritarian guises. There is something insidious at work in Hickey's claim that Mapplethorpe (whom he rather grotesquely insists on calling "Robert") produces images that are dangerous because of their "direct enfranchisement of the secular beholder" and their "Baroque vernacular of beauty that predated and, clearly, outperformed the puritanical canon of visual appeal espoused by the therapeutic institution" (the latter, another Hickey code-term for "PC" academia).[23]

It is the "clearly" of Hickey's text that, in fact, alerts us to the fact that nothing is clear here. The edges of the *passe-partout* are beveled—and stained with ink or some other viscous fluid. Were the "Baroque vernacular of beauty" Hickey invokes so obviously triumphant and transparent in its mechanics of transference, why would Hickey need to mount such an impassioned defense? It is no accident that Hickey claims Mapplethorpe's works have a "direct appeal to the beholder" at the very moment he is so actively manufacturing a particular set of meanings for Mapplethorpe's work.[24] This is the gesture of "self-authentication," based entirely on circular reasoning, that Derrida excavates at the base of Kant's aesthetic. This is the self-authorization that has for so long conspired to support the exclusionary logic and institutions of aesthetic judgment, the most obvious of which is *not* academic art history per se but art criticism, with its basis in connoisseurship (it is the role of art critic that Hickey simultaneously holds and disavows in his self-staging in opposition to the supposed "liberal" or "therapeutic" institution).

At this point, I want to put Hickey in the background as I work to *denaturalize* the notion of beauty in relation, specifically, to the very politics of gendered and racialized identities that Hickey deems beneath his ("disinterested"?) consideration (even while he gets mileage out of the frisson of their transgression by examining works such as Mapplethorpe's homoerotic images of black men). This analysis, which is meant to highlight exactly what is at stake in the revival of "beauty" by Hickey and his followers will pivot around images of naked women that have served as focal points for discussions about the meaning of beauty or, otherwise stated, as magnets for what feminists have perhaps oversimplistically called the "male gaze" of interpretive desire. It is, in my view, by excavating the psychic and social structures of desire at work in such images that we can best interrogate what (or whose) interests are served by the rhetoric of beauty.

God or Goddess? Boucher's Pompadour/Pompadour's Boucher

In François Boucher's elaborate portraits of the extremely powerful Madame de Pompadour (Jeanne-Antoinette Poisson), mistress of Louis XV, the last great Bourbon king of the French monarchy, this extraordinary female intellectual is enframed by an aestheticizing atmosphere of fleshy display.[25] In the 1751 *Toilet of Venus* (figure 2) this "Venus" is depicted as a celestial (yet domesticated) goddess, surrounded by plump pink cupids, typically Rococo swathes of rich silk taffeta, jewels, and exotic gewgaws.[26] Here is a "goddess" (the goddess of love, no less) laid low as paramour, a patroness of the arts sympathetically rendered as willfully open flesh offered for the delectation of Royal viewing pleasure: commissioned by Pompadour herself, the painting hung in the *salle-de-bain* at the Château de Bellevue, favorite trysting place for the King and his mistress.[27]

Figure 2 François Boucher, *Toilet of Venus*, 1751.

However, and paradoxically, within the discourse of beauty, this image stands as both paradigm and antithesis: it both sums up the way in which white women's bodies have historically been produced within the rhetoric of Western painting as "beautiful" objects of male desire and exemplifies that which Kantian aesthetics specifically labors to expel. Madame de Pompadour as Venus instantiates the contradictory logic at the base of the aesthetic. First of all, for Kant, disinterestedness requires precisely the removal of all sensual affect: the arbiter must eradicate corporeal enjoyment in his appreciation of true beauty.[28] This anxiety about corporeal desire is, of course, at odds with the insistent depiction of naked women (in the most obvious sense, sites of arousal for the conventional heterosexual male viewer) in the history of Western art. Pompadour/Venus—as paradigm of the female nude—works to contain just the uncontrollable erotic frisson that she invokes.[29] As Jacques Derrida has noted of this aspect of aesthetics, "The concept of art is . . . constructed with . . . a guarantee in view. It is there to raise man up, that is, always, to *erect* a man-god, to avoid contamination from 'below'. . . . [A] divine teleology secures the political economy of the Fine-Arts."[30]

Pompadour's Bouchers (which are, reciprocally, Boucher's Pompadours) are doubly charged. Not only do they invoke what they are meant to contain and radically confuse female and male authority, such images also signified for revolutionary France and beyond the reprehensible corruption (otherwise viewed as feminization) of the *ancien régime*.[31] The fluffy, Rococo goddess is, above all, excessively sexual and embraced by an environment of hyperornamentality. She threatens to destroy Kant's argument that art, by definition, excludes decoration and artifice: art, Kant writes, "must seem as free from all constraint of chosen rules as if it were a product of mere nature."[32] While being raised to the level of "goddess of love," Pompadour is also arguably disempowered as beautiful object; at the same time, as feminist Eunice Lipton has pointed out, she is also deified and given devastating potency through the very sexual power that Kant's aesthetics labors to contain.[33] It was, in fact, precisely such excesses of the Rococo exemplified by Boucher's flamboyant deployment of color, atmosphere, and symbolism to heighten the erotic appeal (the *im*pure aesthetic pleasure?) of his object which inspired Kant, writing just a few decades later, in his attempt to *expel* artifice (feminizing display) from the realm of the aesthetic.

Pompadour's Boucher and Boucher's Pompadour are thus both at the *center of* the discourse of beauty (by 1765 Boucher was named *premier peintre du roi*) and definitively shut out of its rigorous Kantian borders. Boucher and powerful women such as Pompadour were major targets of the Enlightenment *philosophes* in their articulation of new aesthetic and social standards. By the 1760s, the reaction against Boucher had been fully articulated by Kant's Enlightenment colleague, Denis Diderot, who wrote scathingly of Boucher's compositions as making "an unbearable racket for the eyes." Boucher, continued Diderot, "is showing us the prettiest marionettes in the world."[34] In one swipe, Diderot thus attempts to extinguish both the *feminized* aesthetic of Boucher (which is "pretty" rather than "beautiful") and the female power that lay behind it (with Pompadour having been Boucher's most supportive and prominent patron). Once again, we see a deep anxiety regarding that which can't be controlled at the base of the critic's naturalized claim of judgment.

Such naturalizing claims of value function to position the critic in identification with the artist who is, in turn, conflated with God. Thus, through informed and "disinterested" aesthetic judgment, the critic intuits the meaning and value of the work by discerning the beauty that emanates forth from its contours (as presumably placed there by the divinely inspired artist).[35] This structure of circular identifications, which legitimates artist and interpreter in one gesture by aligning both with a transcendent origin, is what Derrida aptly terms, in the opening quotation of this section, the "divine teleology" of the aesthetic, with its role in "erecting" a "man-god" impervious to the corruption of the feminine and primitive below. In our case, the contamination is signaled by a dangerous feminine sexual *cum* political power (linked, class-wise, to the increasingly questioned privileges of the aristocracy); while the rococo is deemed reactionary by Diderot, it can be viewed at the same time as a radical *freeing* of otherwise enframed and forbidden sexual power.

Given this divine teleology, it is worth returning to Ruskin, who, in the 1849 essay, states that "God has stamped those characters of beauty which He has made it man's nature to love."[36] It is "clear," as Hickey would claim for his judgment of Mapplethorpe, that it is God—the ultimate patriarch—who secures such claims of beauty. Only God can act as origin and end of beauty, incontrovertible enough to stop the seepage that pollutes the ostensibly closed, otherwise "pure" system of aesthetic judgment (staining the *passe-partout*). In fact, as noted, the history of aesthetics as it developed in the work of Kant and others in the eighteenth and nineteenth centuries, is a story about one of the last covertly theological attempts to bridge the seemingly unsurpassable chasm between "man" and "nature," inside and outside, subject and object. Kant's notion of aesthetic judgment proposed precisely to bridge this gap by defining a mode of experiencing beauty that would leap the abyss between the natural, the source of all that is beautiful, and the human-made.[37]

By proposing a "divine teleology," where the figure of the Genius secures a "divine agency in art" the meaning of which can only be determined by the disinterested critic (who, by extension, claims his own "divine agency" as judge), this model of the aesthetic reconfirms a system of privilege that can only be called patriarchal (with all of the colonialist, sexist, and heterosexist assumptions it sustains).[38] The artist/critic circuit—that divine teleology—is given authority by reference to an originary genius, God. It is *as goddess* that Pompadour threatens to disrupt this naturalized circuit of authority—both because of the uncontainability of the erotic pleasure she promises and because of the anxiety invoked by the social and economic power that enabled her to sponsor a painter such as Boucher.[39] Thus, per Diderot's analysis, Pompadour/Boucher must be shut down. Diderot derides Boucher's paintings (Pompadour's body?) as a grotesque "invitation to pleasure." The heatedness of Diderot's denunciation alerts us to the fact that this pleasure the pictures supposedly invite is dangerous because it is flamboyantly not "disinterested" or wholesome.

It is of great interest, then, that the very naked white women's bodies that the aesthetic deploys to defuse the threat of femininity are the vehicles through which this threat is publicly extended and proclaimed. At the same time, the aesthetic is successful enough in its framing exercise such that white women are, to be sure, not ruling the world—nor are academic feminists, Hickey's anxieties aside. As Peggy Phelan has pointed out in her brilliant critique of the common faith in theories of identity on the power of visibility, "[i]f representational visibility equals power, then almost-naked young white women should be running Western culture."[40] The very ambivalence that destructures the aesthetic at its core also points to the slipperiness of meaning and value in relation to all images, not the least those assumed to be "beautiful" by one critic or another.

At this point, it is certainly worth thinking about other works that might be seen as performing an equally dangerous invitation to forbidden pleasures. In this way, I would like to suggest that there are other "almost-naked" or even fully clothed women whose bodies disrupt the aesthetic from within—even more dramatically than that ambiguous figure of the white female nude.

"Olympia's Maid"

Two contemporaneous texts relating to Édouard Manet's *Olympia* (figure 3), the scandal of Paris's 1865 salon, indicate the dangers posed by the *black* female body to the aesthetic:

> *Quand, lasse de songer, Olympia s'éveille*
> *Le printemps entre au bras du doux messager noir;*
> *C'est l'esclave, á la nuit amoureuse pareille,*
> *Qui vient fleurir le jour délicieux à voir:*
> *L'auguste jenue fille en qui la flamme veille*
>
> [*When, weary of dreaming, Olympia wakes,*
> *Spring enters in the arms of a gentle black messenger;*
> *It is the slave, like the amorous night,*
> *Who comes to make the day bloom, delicious to see:*
> *the august young girl in whom the fire burns*][41]

What's to be said for the Negress who brings a bunch of flowers wrapped in a paper, or for the black cat which leaves its dirty footprints on the bed? We would still forgive the ugliness, were it only truthful, carefully studied, heightened by some splendid effect of colour.[42]

Manet's *Olympia* holds a crucial—because highly conflicted—place in the trajectory defining the codification of the aesthetic in Western thought. The painting, conflated with its nude, was widely condemned by critics at the time. Olympia, wrote one critic, is "a sort of female gorilla, a grotesque in India rubber outlined in black [who] . . . apes on a bed, in a state of complete nudity, the horizontal attitude of Titian's *Venus* [of Urbino, 1538]."[43] *Olympia*, as art histo-

Figure 3 Édouard Manet, *Olympia*, 1863. Musée d'Orsay, Paris.

rian T. J. Clark has argued, travestied conceptions of the beautiful (specifically through its explicit parody of Titian's Renaissance "masterpiece") such that critics became almost hysterical, scarcely veiling their anxiety in a sarcastic rhetoric of exaggerated disgust (not only is Olympia a "rubber gorilla," she is dirty, corpse-like, decrepit, stupid, and "of a perfect ugliness").[44]

Olympia's radical unhinging of accepted conventions of "beauty"—as summed up by contrasting it to Alexandre Cabanal's *Venus*, which had been effusively praised as the masterpiece of the 1863 salon—resulted in feverish attempts to *close her down*. Olympia must be kept out—or *en-framed*—at all costs, lest the resistance signaled by her rubbery flesh and defiant gaze destroy the pretension of (erotic) disinterestedness held forth by the aesthetic.

And yet, there is something even more disturbing here. Leaving Boucher's boudoir-encased fluffy pink nudes behind, by the early to mid-nineteenth century, French painters highlighted the delectable whiteness of their naked or almost naked women by posing them against dark bodies.[45] As Lorraine O'Grady has so importantly asked in this regard, what about "Olympia's Maid"? Once brought back into the frame, as it were, the maid points to the fact that it is not, strictly speaking, Olympia who is the greatest threat to the conventional gaze of aesthetic judgment, but the maid herself; surely the tendency to label Olympia a "gorilla" is a displacement of racial anxieties generated by the maid. As O'Grady notes, the maid (painted after a professional model named Laura) is the "chaos that must be excised [from the picture], and it is her excision that stabilizes the West's construct of the female body, for the 'femininity' of the white female body is ensured by assigning the not-white to a chaos safely removed from sight. Thus, only the white body remains as the object of a voyeuristic, fetishizing male gaze."[46] While Olympia is clearly a challenge to the unbridled privilege of sexual ownership claimed by the upper-class European white male viewer, the chaos signified by the maid *exceeds* that proposed by Olympia to such a degree that the maid cannot even be mentioned in contemporaneous critical reviews without an immediate reference to her object status as Olympia's possession (reinforced by Manet's choice of the Astruc poem, which makes reference to a black slave, to accompany the picture in the catalogue).[47] The maid, whose "hypersexuality possesses the white woman," threatens to "stain" Olympia black, as Jennifer Brody has noted of the painting.[48]

Olympia's maid thus throws into relief not only the anxious misogyny at the base of aesthetic judgment but its classist and racist dimensions. J. A. D. Ingres's 1839–1840 painting *Odalisque with a Slave* (figure 4) allows a further elaboration of these dimensions, which were linked to Europe's colonial exploits abroad. Thus, in the Ingres painting a range of racial desirability serves to sustain the conflicted logic of the aesthetic and thereby labors to secure the viewer in his sexual, racial, class, and national superiority. The apparently "white" woman in the foreground is clearly thrown forth as the primary object of sexual desire, her blank genital

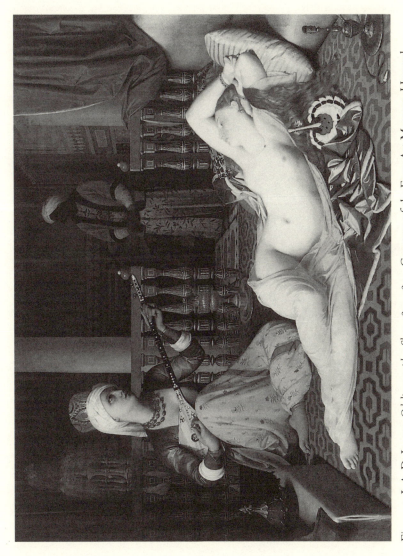

Figure 4 J. A. D. Ingres, *Odalisque with a Slave*, 1839–1840. Courtesy of the Fogg Art Museum, Harvard University Art Museums, bequest of Grenville L. Winthrop. © President and Fellows of Harvard College.

region coyly offered up through a diaphanous veil of chiffon, her arms thrown back in seeming ecstasy. At the same time, she must not, cannot "really" be white in the European sense since Ingres clearly shows us a Middle Eastern or North African harem (the two vastly different cultures being virtually interchangeable in French painting from this period).[49] Yet she is assigned symbolic whiteness *by contrast* to her harem mates—a somewhat darker skinned female musician, taut reddish nipple peeking out from green silk robe, and a eunuch servant whose black and emasculated body recedes into the depths of the painting's rich, exaggeratedly "Oriental" interior. (And one might ask, which figure, musician or eunuch, is the "Slave" of the title?) The Orient, produced in relation to all three bodies in the painting, is rendered exotic and strange, "feminized as a passive cipher to be governed by an active (and superior) Western civilization."[50]

Notably, too, as the skin gets darker, it is more fully covered—to the point where the servant's body (except for hands and face) is entirely draped in fabric: molded into a phallic sheath as if to palliate the (castration) anxiety that the idea of the eunuch—as well as the image of the female nude—produces in the European masculine imagination. The white European male viewer is offered a cornucopia of exotic/erotic delights, with the threat of racial and sexual otherness defused either by its transformation into whiteness or its veiling and class subordination (the covered eunuch, the objectified musician gazing upwards as if in an opium-induced stupor).[51] Like Olympia's maid, the olive-skinned musician and reserved black servant function to highlight the available *difference* and, by comparison, supposed "purity," of the seemingly white odalisque: fleshy, open, penetrable, erotic.

The harem, as contrived through the nineteenth-century French male imaginary, functions as the perfect site for the circulation of uninhibited desires (after all, European men viewed harems as equivalents to bordellos). As Malek Alloula has written, "[t]he phantasmatic value of the harem is a function of this presumed absence of limitation to a sexual pleasure lived in the mode of frenzy." He adds that it is in the nature of pleasure "to scrutinize its object detail by detail, to take possession of it in both a total and a fragmented fashion. It is an intoxication, a loss of oneself in the other through sight."[52] While the white European male produces an "intoxication" in such images, proposing a "loss" of the white male subject in the "other through sight," he also, as discussed, attempts to defuse the threat posed by such an intoxication through the colored ranking of bodies and through their hierarchical regimentation in space.

This regimentation is, within art discourse, codified as aesthetic composition, its political dimension effectively veiled. Thus, in the major survey book on nineteenth-century art, Robert Rosenblum sums up the evasive exclusions of dominant modes of aesthetic judgment in his rhapsodizing description of the painting, in which he argues that, "[a]s rigorous as his master David in his ability to interlock a multitude of rectilinear volumes and surfaces, Ingres evokes here a feminine ambiance of voluptuous relaxation and engulfing sensuousness."[53] Even as Ingres exposes and unveils his erotic object(s) he labors to contain her/them through rigid codes of aesthetic display—codes that specifically reiterate differences of class, nation, and race as they function both to incite desire and to allay psychosexual, cultural anxieties about these very differences. This, as Rosenblum's description confirms, is the goal of the mode of aesthetic judgment that has come to define how and what is talked about in art discourse.

Yo Mama! Renée Cox's Phallus

Through this rather extended analysis of paintings by Boucher, Manet, and Ingres I hope to have persuaded my readers that anxieties regarding gender are not by any means the only terrors motivating the aesthetic's logic of enframing (either in terms of the production or reception of works of art). In concluding, I want to take a look at a stunning life-sized photographic self-portrait by the young artist Renée Cox. Entitled *Yo Mama*, this 1993 image (figure 5), which I read as exemplifying the efforts on the part of many young women artists working today to dislocate and discredit claims for the neutrality of "beauty" as a label of aesthetic judgment, can be seen as a definitive talking-back, an aggressive challenge to the still potent institutional force of beauty discourse.

Hickey might well criticize such work—and certainly my reading of it—as motivated by the desire to be "politically correct"; by such a gesture, he would legitimate his own preferences as inherent rather than ideologically motivated. I would like to stress here again that such rhetoric merely veils privilege (and this is where the crux of my argument against continuing this authoritative aspect of aesthetic judgment lies). Hickey privileges Mapplethorpe's works for their "enfranchise[ment] of the non-canonical beholder," with no consideration of who this beholder might be and under what circumstances she or he would become "enfranchised" through an encounter with an image of, for example, a picture of a young girl with her naked legs spread or two men fist-fucking. Too, Hickey's argument shows a complete and surely strategic lack of any element of self-consciousness that might take into account why *he in particular* finds "Robert's" works so obviously and directly to convey such *jouissance*.

Like Kant's transcendental subject, Hickey must, in the words of Susan Buck-Morss, "purge . . . himself of the senses which endanger autonomy not only because they unavoidably entangle him in the world, but, specifically, because they make him passive . . . instead of active . . . , susceptible, like 'Oriental voluptuaries,' to sympathy and tears."[54] Self-consciousness would eliminate Hickey's naturalized claim to critical authority—placing him, as it were, in the harem or conspiring with Mapplethorpe in the latter's eroticization of black male bodies; an

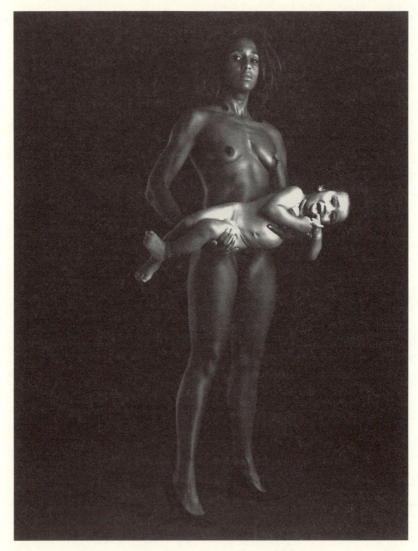

Figure 5   Renée Cox, *Yo Mama!*, 1993. Courtesy of the artist.

admittance of his own erotic interpretive investments—his desire to *penetrate* the mysteries of "Robert's" works—would expose what is at stake in his attempt to establish his view as inexorably correct.[55]

Returning to Cox, let me propose an alternative way to interpret visual art works that we find compelling, politically astute, entertaining, or, for that matter, "beautiful" (whatever that may mean). Let me project my own partiality for Cox—her body (I want it for my own, to *be* it as well as, perhaps, but this is deeply repressed, to *possess* it) and her mind (I want to mimic what I perceive as her conceptual brilliance and ironic sense of humor). I want to align myself definitively with Cox's strength of mind and body, as I perceive these being expressed in this taut body-image of a strong naked woman who is at once sexualized object, threatening (masculinized) muscular black female subject, and maternal subject. In my sometimes pain at being white, with the negative responsibilities this entails in Western patriarchy, and experiencing the inevitable privilege that my "visible" bodily appearance assigns me in this culture, I want to *be this someone else*.

This is an impassioned response to Hickey's dismissal of PC, and here I will strategically continue my lapse into self-consciousness. I've always attempted to incorporate a sense of my own responsibility within my judging subjectivity rather than projecting it outward into claims for authenticity; if this is "PC," then so be it (though this catch-all term certainly, to say the least, profoundly oversimplifies the complexity and heterogeneity of the vast range of politicized and informed positions on art and culture which Hickey and others attempt to join together under its rubric). As Jennifer Faist recently argued, beauty is Hickey's "camouflage to lobby for his own ethical and political agendas."[56] Refusing to camouflage myself, I have to emphasize here that my readings are fully contingent and willfully tendentious; this does not, I hope preclude their being experienced as informed and compelling, at least for some.

I am here, I judge and give meaning—on the basis of what my particular investments are, on the basis of a specific, highly politicized, argument I am trying to make. I am cognizant that I thereby participate in the circuit of meaning ascribed to the author-subject Renée Cox. If I am persuasive, I may entice some of my readers to identify with the positions I outline here (and to agree with my admiration for the "beauty," power, and political efficacy of Cox's fantastic image). If I am not, you may dislike the picture and even continue to believe in the immutable authenticity of Dave Hickey's judgments. Either way, it behooves all of us to recognize that beauty—there's no doubt about it—is in the eye of the beholder.[57]

Notes

This essay was originally written as a talk and given at the Society for Photographic Education's regional conference entitled *Skin Deep: Beauty, Displeasure, Agency*, in Los Angeles, in 1997; a shorter version was given at the Center for Ideas and Society, University of California, Riverside conference *Aesthetics and Difference: Cultural Diversity, Literature, and the Arts* in 1998. An earlier version of this published text was published in *X-Tra* 2, no. 3 (Spring 1999), 7–13. I am very grateful to Ken Gonzales-Day of the SPE, Emory Elliott of the Center for Ideas, and to the editors of *X-Tra* for the opportunity to develop this material.

1. Immanuel Kant, *Critique of Judgment* (1790), trans. Werner S. Pluhar (Indianapolis: Hackett Publishing Co., 1986), 59; Johann Winckelmann, *History of Ancient Art* (1764), reprinted in Eric Fernie, ed., *Art History and Its Methods: A Critical Anthology* (London: Phaidon,

1995), 75; and John Ruskin, "The Lamp of Beauty," *The Seven Lamps of Architecture* (1849), reprinted in *The Lamp of Beauty: Writings on Art by John Ruskin*, ed. Joan Evens (Ithaca, N.Y.: Cornell University Press; and Oxford: Phaidon Press, 1980), 197.

2. Dave Hickey, *The Invisible Dragon: Four Essays on Beauty* (Los Angeles: Art issues Press, 1993). Hickey's book precipitated his being awarded the 1994 Frank Jewett Mather Award, the most prestigious national recognition for art criticism, given out by the College Art Association (the major professional institution for artists, art historians, and other arts professionals). For those readers outside the discipline, it is important to note the pervasive power held by Hickey and his colleagues and followers. For example, the interwoven power effects of the *Los Angeles Times/Art issues* crowd have been played out in the Mather committee itself: in 1997, the committee (consisting of Suzanne Muchnic, Dave Hickey, and Lowery Stokes Sims) granted Christopher Knight, chief critic of the *Los Angeles Times*, the award; Muchnic is Knight's colleague at the *Times* and Hickey, like Knight, publishes with Art issues Press and in the journal.

3. Hickey, *The Invisible Dragon*, on John Ruskin, in the unpaginated "Acknowledgments"; on "art professionals," 13.

4. Among many inspirational critiques of the authoritarianism embedded in this kind of aesthetic judgment, three have been particularly important for my understanding: Donald Preziosi's *Rethinking Art History: Meditations on a Coy Science* (New Haven, Conn.: Yale University Press, 1989); Pierre Bourdieu's *Distinction: A Social Critique of the Judgement of Taste*, trans. Richard Nice (Cambridge, Mass.: Harvard University Press, 1984); and Jo Anna Isaak's feminist analysis, "Seduction without Desire," *Vanguard* 16, no. 3 (Summer 1987), 11–14.

5. It has been suggested to me by Natasha Boas that Hickey is reacting specifically against the dominance of the writers associated with the journal *October* in New York City, scholars and art critics who developed a highly theoretical avant-gardist model of analyzing postmodern art in the 1980s. Indeed, during this period, British and U.S. art discourse (particularly that generated from New York and associated with *October* and local art magazines and institutions such as the New Museum of Contemporary Art) promoted ideas drawn—often secondhand—from Brecht (such as distanciation as a mode of politicizing the spectator of the work of art) and French poststructuralism (the split subject of Lacan, Derridean deconstruction, etc.). Art work that seemed to follow through these values was generally privileged as "radical" in that it followed avant-gardist strategies, overtly politicizing the visual. Needless to say, while there is a point to be made about this rather reified discourse, Hickey caricatures it unfairly, collapsing what has been a contested arena of discussions into a singular "PC" line. At the same time, I am willing to admit that I am conflating Hickey's arguments (from his early 1990s *Invisible Dragon*) with those of other *Los Angeles Times* and *Art issues* writers such as Christopher Knight and Libby Lumpkin.

6. See note 2.

7. Jacques Derrida, *Truth in Painting*, trans. Ian McLeod and Geoff Bennington (Chicago: University of Chicago Press, 1987).

8. Hickey, *The Invisible Dragon*, 20.

9. In commenting on an earlier draft of this chapter, Colin Gardner made the excellent point that, not only does Hickey naturalize beauty, but he also conflates it with both the Burkeian and the Kantian sublime. The latter, Gardner points out, is actually clearly

differentiated from Kant's notion of beauty; far from "reinforcing human subjectivity's complicit harmony with bounteous nature (the innate role of beauty-as-idea [in Kant]), . . . [the sublime] makes us aware of our disjuncture from it. The sublime underlines the fact that we are split subjects, divorced from an Other that partially constructs us." Gardner stresses the link between this disjunction and the "wondering self-estrangement [that] lies at the core of what Russian Formalism will later dub 'defamiliarization,' and what Brecht will eventually systematize as the [alienation effect]" or distanciation. Hickey cannot acknowledge this aspect of the sublime because it would align him with the *Octoberists* (see note 5), and it interferes with his desire to reinforce the power of the viewer and thereby "reinforce the validity of his own subjective role as connoisseur," à la Ruskin, I might add. Hickey's vaunted populism is thus inherently corrupted by the desire to promote himself as the arbiter of beauty and its, in his terms, sublime effects. I am very appreciative of Gardner's close reading and these excellent comments, transmitted by e-mail February 27, 1999.

10. Roland Barthes, preface to *Mythologies* (1957), trans. Annette Lavers (New York: Hill and Wang, 1972), 11.

11. Edmund Burke, *A Philosophical Inquiry into the Origin of Our Ideas of the Sublime and the Beautiful* (1756), cited by Peggy Zeglin Brand, "Disinterestedness and Political Art," *n. paradoxa*, issue 8 (Nov. 1998), published on-line at <http://web.ukonline.co.uk/n.paradoxa/brand.htm>, this quote p. 1 of the web text.

12. Kenneth Clark's book was originally published in 1956 (*The Nude: A Study of Ideal Art* [London: John Murray, 1956]) and has since been reprinted in numerous subsequent editions. See Lynda Nead, *The Female Nude: Art, Obscenity, and Sexuality* (New York: Routledge, 1992), 12–14.

13. Nead states, categorically, "one of the principal goals of the female nude has been the containment and regulation of the female sexual body," *The Female Nude*, 6.

14. I am leaving the castration complex (the unconscious level of this dynamic) aside for this analysis, but one could easily analyze this problematic from the point of view of castration anxiety. I am grateful to Thomas McCullough for sharing his excellent paper on the hidden role of castration anxiety in masculine judgments of women's naked bodies as signs of beauty or the sublime; "The Soulless 'Sublime,'" unpublished paper, 1998.

15. D. N. Rodowick, expanding on Derrida's ideas in "Impure Mimesis, or the Ends of the Aesthetic," *Deconstruction and the Visual Arts: Art, Media, Architecture*, ed. Peter Brunette and David Wills (Cambridge: Cambridge University Press, 1994), 111.

16. Kant, *Critique of Judgment*, 54; my emphases.

17. For an interesting feminist read on disinterestedness, see Peggy Zeglin Brand, "Disinterestedness and Political Art."

18. Derrida, *Truth in Painting*, 47.

19. Ibid., 13.

20. Hickey, *The Invisible Dragon*, 11.

21. Kant, *Critique of Judgment*, 42. This translation is modified according to the 1978 edition, translation by James Creed Meredith (Oxford University Press).

22. See Mercer's "Skin Head Sex Thing: Racial Difference and the Homoerotic Imaginary," *How Do I Look? Queer Film and Video*, ed. Bad Object Choices (Seattle: Bay Press, 1991), wherein he effectively discusses the way in which Mapplethorpe's aestheticizing

strategy operates to make the "glossy allure of the photographic print . . . consubstantial with the shiny texture of black skin," fetishizing black men and thus "lubricat[ing] the ideological reproduction of racial otherness as the fascination of the image [which thus] articulates a fantasy of power and mastery over the other" (174). He goes on to note the "important question of the role of the reader and how he or she attributes intentionality to the author" (179), a key issue in relation to Hickey's authoritative pronouncements of the meaning and value supposedly inherent in this work (the implication being, as placed there or intended by Mapplethorpe).

23. Hickey, *The Invisible Dragon*, 21, 22.

24. Ibid., 24.

25. It is up for debate whether the numerous nudes Pompadour commissioned from Boucher are actually portraits of her. The faces of the nudes are typically abstracted and idealized (as are, in fact, the faces in the official portraits of Pompadour); furthermore, Boucher had a favorite model, "Mlle. O'Murphy," for some of his erotic nude portraits (such as *Odalisque*, also titled *Mlle. O'Murphy*, 1743, at the Musée du Louvre). However, it is justifiable to analyze them as portraits to the extent that they were clearly used as points of self-reference for their patroness, who had them hung throughout the palace where she held her romantic trysts with the king. This is especially justifiable in the case of the *Toilet of Venus*, since Pompadour had just played the role of Venus in a play by the same name, making the element of self-identification strong. See the exhibition catalog *François Boucher 1703–1770* (New York: Metropolitan Museum of Art, 1986). Albert Boime identifies this painting as a portrait of Pompadour in *Art in an Age of Revolution 1750–1800* (Chicago: University of Chicago, 1987), 18.

26. With the incongruous addition of a Grecian urn, marking the beginning of the rage for all things Greek among European cultures at this time. I am very grateful to Stephen Ostrow for this and other insights into these portraits.

27. The painting hung as a pendant with the *Bath of Venus*. See *François Boucher 1703-1770*, 256.

28. "*Taste*," Kant writes, "is the ability to judge an object, or a way of presenting it, by means of a liking or disliking *devoid of all interest*. The object of such liking is called *beautiful*." Kant, *Critique of Judgment*, 53. Edmund Burke also noted this necessity. As Peggy Zeglin Brand points out, he cites (but also rhapsodizes over, as in the quotation at the beginning of the last section of this essay) the "female body as a beautiful object which can be perceived as beautiful only if the sole interest of the perceiver is in perceiving for its own sake and not in the desire for possession"; Brand, "Disinterestedness and Political Art," 1.

29. Nead explores a similar dynamic in *The Female Nude* but analyzes the framing apparatus of the aesthetic in terms of the opposition of "art" and "obscenity." My analysis sees a more subtle and mutually sustaining series of terms at work as exemplified in the conflicted reception of Boucher's work—as both high art, paradigmatic of beauty, and as debased, frivolous, kitsch—that against which Enlightenment philosophers such as Diderot and Kant reacted.

30. Derrida, "Economimesis," trans. R. Klein, *Diacritics* 2, no. 2 (Summer 1981), 9, 5; my emphasis on "erect."

31. Thomas Crow notes that Pompadour's name "is one of the most familiar in the cultural history of the period, standing itself for Rococo elaboration and excess." Crow, *Painters and Public Life in Eighteenth-Century Paris* (New Haven, Conn.: Yale University Press,

1985), 110. This links up to the way in which images of Marie Antoinette were, thirty years later, also highly coded to align her with the corruption of Rococo culture and the depravity of the aristocracy, as viewed by revolutionary culture. See Boime, *Art in an Age of Revolution*, 45, 467.

32. Kant, cited by Rodowick, "Impure Mimesis," 105.

33. See Eunice Lipton's essay "Women, Pleasure and Painting (e.g., Boucher)," *Genders* 7 (Spring 1990), 69-86.

34. Cited by Michael Fried in *Absorption and Theatricality: Painting and Beholder in the Age of Diderot* (Chicago: University of Chicago Press, 1980), 41. Fried discusses Boucher's reputation at some length and this discussion is indebted to his research. That Fried uses Boucher's reception to confirm the antithesis between absorptive painting (which he, along with Diderot, privileges) and a debased theatricality cannot be a matter of critique here, though I have elsewhere critically examined these terms as Fried plays them out in relation to contemporary art. See my essay "Art History/Art Criticism: Performing Meaning," *Performing the Body/Performing the Text*, ed. Amelia Jones and Andrew Stephenson (London: Routledge, 1999), 39–55.

35. See Donald Preziosi's deep analysis of this dynamic in *Rethinking Art History*.

36. John Ruskin, "The Lamp of Beauty," 196.

37. It was Hegel, following the ideas of Winckelmann, who changed the emphasis of the aesthetic by arguing that the Ideal could be found not in nature, with its vastness and imperfections, but in the creations of humankind. The Ideal is precisely that which bridges nature and "man" by taking that which is the most superior in nature but combining these elements to create a greater beauty. See Hegel's *Philosophy of Fine Art* (1835), trans. F. P. B. Osmaston (London: G. Bell and Sons, 1920), especially "The Ideal as Such."

38. See Rodowick's thorough discussion of this aspect of Derrida's argument in "Impure Mimesis," 105.

39. Pompadour came from a thoroughly bourgeois family with aristocratic pretensions. As Crow has suggested, her support of the arts was useful in raising her family's social position: "lavish support for the arts" was a means of "legitimizing *arriviste* pretensions to aristocratic status"; see Crow, *Painters and Public Life in Eighteenth-Century Paris*, 110–113. The power of Pompadour was thus itself secured by the aesthetic in a perversion of the masculinist divine teleology of which Derrida writes.

40. Peggy Phelan, *Unmarked: The Politics of Performance* (New York: Routledge, 1993), 10.

41. Poem by Zacharie Astruc. Manet placed Astruc's poem under *Olympia* in the salon catalogue. See T. J. Clark, *The Painting of Modern Life: Paris in the Art of Manet and His Followers* (Princeton: Princeton University Press, 1984), 83. Clark's research into the criticism published in relation to *Olympia* is an invaluable resource.

42. From Gautier's review of the salon of 1865 in *Le Moniteur universel*, cited in *Art in Theory 1815–1900: An Anthology of Changing Ideas*, ed. Charles Harrison and Paul Wood with Jason Gaiger (Oxford: Basil Blackwell, 1998), 516–17.

43. Amédée Cantaloube, writing in *Le Grand Journal* in 1865; cited by T. J. Clark, *The Painting of Modern Life*, 94.

44. All cited by Clark, *The Painting of Modern Life*, 96–98.

45. Sander Gilman has noted that "[b]y the eighteenth century, the sexuality of the black, both male and female, becomes an icon for deviant sexuality in general. . . . By the

nineteenth century, as in [Manet's] *Olympia* . . . , the central female figure is associated with a black female in such a way as to imply their sexual similarity." Gilman, "Black Bodies, White Bodies: Toward an Iconography of Female Sexuality in Late Nineteenth-Century Art, Medicine, and Literature," in *"Race," Writing, and Difference*, ed. Henry Louis Gates, Jr. (Chicago: University of Chicago Press, 1986), 228. Ultimately, he argues, the black body during this period, through insidious medical ("scientific") discourse as well as in visual imagery, acts as an antithesis to highlight not only the "purity" of white female sexuality but the "superiority" of white subjectivity in general.

46. Lorraine O'Grady, "Olympia's Maid: Reclaiming Black Female Subjectivity," in *New Feminist Criticism: Art, Identity, Action*, ed. Joanna Frueh, Cassandra L. Langer, and Arlene Raven (New York: HarperCollins, 1994), 153.

47. Thus, Théophile Thoré, in a contemporaneous review of the 1865 salon in *L'Indépendance Belge*, noted that "Manet's *Olympia* has caused all Paris to run to see this curious woman with her magnificent bouquet, *her Negress*, and her black cat," typically placing the maid on the level of the pet cat; my emphasis. Cited in *Art in Theory 1815-1900: An Anthology of Changing Ideas*, 517.

48. Jennifer Brody, "Shading Meaning," in *Performing the Body/Performing the Text*, 103. Another interesting discussion of race and gender in *Olympia* can be found in Rebecca Schneider's *The Explicit Body in Performance* (New York: Routledge, 1997), 27–28. Ultimately, she is rather harder on Manet than I would be, since I read his painting as (whether consciously or not) enacting sexist, classist, and racist relations that had until that point been aestheticized (as in the Ingres painting discussed below) or otherwise veiled; by unveiling them, the painting contributes to the beginning of their critique and dissolution. Schneider also stresses the implication of white women in mobilizing black femininity as a way of "seeking to control their [our?] displacements—to render invisible or to manipulate the signs of their symbolic fallen doubles: persons of color," 28.

49. Robert Rosenblum and H. W. Janson evasively call the scene "Islamic" in *19th-Century Art* (New York: Abrams, 1984), 149.

50. Mark Antliff and Patricia Leighton, "Primitive," in *Critical Terms for Art History*, ed. Robert S. Nelson and Richard Shiff (Chicago: University of Chicago Press, 1996), 176.

51. And yet, per Brody's argument vis-à-vis *Olympia*, this structure is never complete or fully successful—the "slave(s)" stain(s) the female odalisque.

52. Malek Alloulla, *The Colonial Harem*, trans. Myrna Godzich and Wlad Godzich (Minneapolis: University of Minnesota, 1986), 49.

53. In Rosenblum and Janson, *19th-Century Art*, 150.

54. Susan Buck-Morss, "Aesthetics and Anaesthetics: Walter Benjamin's Artwork Essay Reconsidered," *October* 62 (Fall 1992), 9; she is citing Kant with "Oriental voluptuaries."

55. Even the most seemingly sophisticated scholars and theorists are often tempted to revert to a kind of base-line subjectivism, posed as fact, when discussing the issue of whether or not something is "beautiful" (in this sense Hickey's claims can be viewed as at least consistent with his overt project of rehabilitating premodern aesthetics). Hence, in a recent interview, Buck-Morss herself contradicts her own earlier insights by arguing that "beauty is the experience of material reality as something that resists instrumentalization," and, by definition, is not "culturally mediated"; in "Aesthetics after the End of Art," an

interview with Susan Buck-Morss by Grant H. Kester, in *Art Journal* 56, no. 1, "Aesthetics and the Body Politic" special issue (Spring 1997), 39. Such claims fly in the face of her own recognition of the interpreter's fear of being rendered passive and the role of this fear in conditioning his or her relationship to images and objects. Since when are the bodily sensations she ascribes to her experience of aesthetic objects unmediated by our thoroughly socialized experience of the world? Even most doctors and cognitive psychologists today would stress the role of social conditioning in our physiological responses to the world and even our neurological make-up (the way in which we are "wired" to respond to things). The two special issues of *X-Tra* on beauty discourse and art criticism (2, no. 3 [Spring 1999], and 2, no. 4 [Summer 1999]) cover the "beauty" debates from multiple points of view (including my own, in an earlier version of this essay; see the unnumbered note that begins these "Notes"), and Margaret Morgan's review of the Spring 1999 Los Angeles conference "Practical Criticism, Art and Theory in the Nineties" addresses the tendency of participants to fall back on clichéd notions of beauty and personal taste (Summer issue, 20–21). She calls eminent art historian Thierry de Duve to task for making "bland pronouncements about merely loving or hating certain works of art" and notes how disappointing it was to see "the distinguished scholar . . . taking his own tastes so seriously," 21.

56. Jennifer Faist, "Wrapping for the Rhetoric: Dave Hickey and Beauty in Art," *Coagula* 26 (March 1997), 36.

57. Joseph Leo Koerner and Lisbet Koerner note that "to speak of value today is rarely to reach a judgment on the beauty of an art object. Such evaluations, held to be mere relative judgments of values that are themselves relative, have been largely purged from academic practice and annexed to the journalistic practices of 'art criticism.' . . . Art, it is discovered [in contemporary art history], is not a quality of the object, but a valuation by the subject; like beauty, art is in the eyes of the beholder." Koerner and Koerner, "Value," in *Critical Terms for Art History*, 293. Hickey and his followers have thus bypassed the insights of the new art history in their return to eighteenth- and nineteenth-century views on the aesthetic.

The Aesthetics of Wounding

Trauma, Self-Representation, and the Critical Voice

KATHLEEN MCHUGH

Trauma involves a violent event and a body which registers its effects. Historically a medical term deriving from the Greek "wound" and "to pierce," trauma referred to a bodily wound, especially one produced by sudden physical injury that usually pierced or ruptured the skin (Laplanche and Pontalis, 465). Today, trauma has come to shape or haunt many and diverse discourses. Two features are crucial to its contemporary applications: the sudden, unexpected occurrence of the traumatic event and the disturbance it wreaks on organs or systems that otherwise would receive, "understand" and incorporate the significance of the event on the organism. These organs or systems typically provide a boundary and/or facilitate interaction between outside and inside, object and subject. Psychoanalysis, philosophy, and aesthetics provide three examples of such applications, each apprehending very differently violent breaches and disturbances in systems that articulate the distinctions between subjective and objective phenomena. I want briefly to review these encounters to give a context or frame to the topic that ultimately concerns me: that of trauma and self-representation and the possibility of an aesthetics predicated on their explicit interaction.[1]

In his later work, Sigmund Freud expanded the clinical meaning of trauma to encompass the effects of different kinds of violence on the psyche. His most famous formulation, in *Beyond the Pleasure Principle*, articulates an "economic" correlative to physical assault which affects the psyche. Freud argued that the mind possessed "a protective shield" against external stimuli. The "external world," he argued, was "charged with the most powerful energies," energies that would kill human consciousness with an overwhelming excess of stimulation were it not for this protective shield (30). After noting consciousness's liminal function in regulating the flow of external and internal stimuli, he asserts:

> We describe as 'traumatic' any excitations from outside which are powerful enough
> to break through the protective shield. It seems to me that the concept of trauma
> necessarily implies a connection of this kind with a breach in an otherwise effica
> cious barrier against stimuli. Such an event as an external trauma is bound to pro-

voke a disturbance on a large scale in the functioning of the organism's energy and to set in motion every possible defensive measure. (33)

In addition to theorizing how the mind is implicated in the traumatic event, Freud also notes that the excessive excitations permanently disturb "the manner in which the energy operates" (quoted in Laplanche and Pontalis, 465). The mind cannot take a measure of, cannot gauge the significance of the overwhelming influx of stimuli. And so the mind and its very capacities to mediate and negotiate internal and external stimuli are altered and disturbed.

In contemporary trauma studies, Freud's insights regarding the permanent psychic disturbances provoked by traumatic events, whether world-historical or individual, inform theories of witnessing, testimony, memory and self-representation. Such events are "unspeakable," "unrepresentable," their traumatic character defined precisely as the inadequacy of any expression to apprehend, represent or recollect them. Language, narrative, history, and self-representation must grapple with material stimuli which exceed the capacity of their symbolic systems. And thus, these systems suffer a breach, a permanent disturbance.

Because the stimuli generated by the traumatic event ruptures and disturbs the very coherence and orientation of subjectivity in its capacity to receive and assimilate experience, Cathy Caruth argues that the event is not experienced as it occurs but only belatedly and only with "the surprising literality and nonsymbolic nature of traumatic dreams and flashbacks, which resist cure to the extent that they remain, precisely, literal" (5). But the malaise extends beyond that of the traumatized subject him or herself:

> It is this literality and its insistent return which thus constitutes trauma and points toward its enigmatic core: the delay or incompletion in knowing or even seeing, an overwhelming occurrence that then remains, in its insistent return, absolutely true to the event. It is indeed this truth of traumatic experience that forms the center of its pathology or symptoms; it is not a pathology, that is, of falsehood or displacement of meaning, but of history itself. (5)

Not only is the relation between subject and object vis à vis experience disrupted, but insofar as the traumatic event outdistances the subject's ability to experience, possess, and represent it, the very possibility of historical truth and representation is put into question. As Caruth eloquently puts it, "Such a crisis of truth extends beyond the question of individual cure and asks how we in this era can have access to our own historical experience, to a history that is in its immediacy a crisis to whose truth there is no simple access" (6). The radical temporal and perceptual disjuncture between the subject and his or her experience constituted by trauma in turn radically disturbs the question of historical reference.

In this context, representation—historical, fictional, autobiographical, memorial—constitutes the most highly charged stake in trauma studies, confronting historians, survivors, theorists, and artists with an ethical contradiction that in-

exorably raises aesthetic questions. The traumatic event, whether world historical or individual, simultaneously challenges the conventions and structures of
objectivity and truth while it also exerts an ethical imperative to remember, record,
and testify to its occurrence. In addressing the consequent dilemma—how to
testify to and represent that which irrevocably exceeds representation—history
must collude with aesthetics. That is, no one, from survivors to historians, can
sustain the illusion of language's capacity to apprehend the (traumatic) referent.
The question of how to proceed with representation is an aesthetic one, a question of style. Representation's inevitable referential failure weds aesthetics to
trauma.

For my purposes, it is a telling coincidence that the very question of aesthetics itself has been considered traumatic in contemporary philosophical discourse, a necessary frame to any consideration of trauma and self-representation.
The fundamental problem of aesthetics since Kant—the incommensurability of
the particular and the universal, the object and the ideal, the affective and objective—constitutes a philosophical trauma, if you will. For Kant, the determining
ground of the aesthetic "can be no other than subjective." But this subjective
ground gives rise to "disinterested" and "universal" judgment. That is, in the
particular, subjective yet disinterested moment of aesthetic reception, the subject "implies in his judgment a ground of satisfaction for all men." This determination, furthermore, is predicated on the formal, objective, and therefore pure
qualities of the work itself (Kant, 379–385).

Insofar as Kant's theorization of the aesthetic insinuates the reception of beauty
or the sublime (subjective) with the formal qualities of the object (objective) which
instigate that reception, it articulates an impossible, if necessary relation, one which
contemporary philosophers and theorists have understood as a trauma. This
trauma haunts and troubles the thought of Hegel and Heidegger and shapes,
though in different ways, Jacques Derrida and Paul de Man's re-readings of Kant's
Critique of Judgment.

For Derrida, Kant attempted in the third Critique to bridge "the irresolvable
differences determined in the first two Critiques." What was required was "an
analogy between two absolutely heterogeneous worlds, a 'third' for crossing the
abyss, cauterizing the gaping wound, and binding the separation" (Derrida, 5).
While Derrida's reference to the "gaping wound" invokes the etymology of the
word 'trauma,' de Man characterizes the threat in Kant's third Critique and in
the sublime as having to do precisely with surprise, excess, and failures of representation and perception:

> But the notion of danger occurs in Kant not as the direct threat of a natural force
> to our physical well-being, but, first of all, as you remember, in the shock of sur-
> prise, of *Verwunderung*, which we experience when confronted with something of
> extreme magnitude. We feel that our faculties, including the imagination, are un-
> able to grasp the totality of what they encounter. It occurs, the danger occurs in

Kant as a failure of representation, and it has to do, and will be explained . . . with the structure of the imagination. (139)

De Man goes on to argue that, for Kant, the imagination was the symptom of the impossibility "of a pure intellect entirely separated from the material world, entirely separated from sensory experience." For him, "it is this failure of the imagination that leads to aesthetic contemplation" (146). The imagination marks that place where the material world pierces any illusion of pure intellect.

De Man and Derrida both invoke traumatic figures ("gaping wound") and significations ("shock," "extreme magnitude") to structure their readings of the *Critique of Judgment*. Derrida reads with and through the paradoxical figure, the parergon, that Kant mobilizes to attain the effect of resolution or coherence (in relation to what is, essentially, irresolvable), while de Man insists that Kant's work registers the material trace that cannot be eradicated from any universal or ideal. The third Critique is of special interest to both of them because it stages the incommensurability of philosophical discourse to apprehend "the enigma of the aesthetic," an encounter which breaches the integrity of philosophy itself.[2]

In the culture wars, this incommensurability has shaped the usually repressed relation of aesthetics to the social, a relationship whose trauma is difference. Properly "aesthetic" criticism tends to ignore the social and subjective fact of aesthetic reception, while cultural criticism foregoes considerations of aesthetic merit. I would like now to map out the structure and challenge of this trauma as it relates to critical aesthetic practice by looking at two critics who contend, in very different ways, with self-representation and trauma: Arlene Croce and Roland Barthes. Though these two critics are worlds apart in their intellectual presumptions, concerns, and milieux, I would argue that Barthes very self-consciously confronts and works through the critical crisis that Croce rather dramatically and provocatively stages.

In the December 1995 issue of the *New Yorker*, Arlene Croce published what quickly became an infamous piece of art-criticism, "Discussing the Undiscussable," her nonreview of Bill T. Jones's dance piece "Still/Here." Baldly stating in the first line that she had not seen Jones's work and had no intention of reviewing it, she proceeded to critique his AIDS-themed choreography as "victim art" and to declare any such work "a menace to all art forms" (16–17). Though somewhat rambling and contradictory, her argument does make manifest the one-sided neo-Kantian principles at the heart of a mainstream aesthetics which finds the explicit self-representation of trauma anathema to the idea of art. To begin with, as she argues, "victim" art is utilitarian. It speaks for and to social groups (18–19). Its social utility disqualifies it as "disinterested" and therefore as truly aesthetic material, which is to say, universal.

Even more problematic for Croce is that such work disarms critics and criticism in a very particular way. She asserts that "Still/Here" is "undiscussable." Because Jones employs the words and images of "dying people," his "act" is "beyond the reach of criticism" (16). Later in her article, Croce concedes that many nineteenth-century artists lived with, battled or succumbed to various kinds of trauma, but that their "personal disease and impending death were unmentionable"; in their art, "the individual spirit could override them both." Art for Croce should be about "the grandeur of the individual spirit" rather than "the political clout of the group" (24). Contemporary artists have used this clout to declare war on critics; their work deals with issues that, by Croce's own admission, are beyond the reach of [her] criticism—AIDS, death, age, deformity, racism, violent abuse of all kinds, and disenfranchisement due to identity based on difference. In short, this art features people whom she is "forced to feel sorry for because of the way they represent themselves" (17).

Croce's reaction to Jones's piece manifests all the classic qualities of a resistance response. A resistance response at once constitutes the repression of psychic forces and their revelation, though in the form of "acting out." The coincidence of Croce denouncing "victim statements" with considerable affect and vehemence, while at the same time acting out her own victimization is a perfect example of this defensive structure. Thus, as with any resistance response, Croce's piece is an example of exactly that against which she inveighs; it is an instance of victim art criticism in which the victim/critic lashes out at art work which has exceeded the frame of the Kantian aesthetics that shape her perspective.[3] The encounter is traumatic; her critical system cannot accommodate the magnitude of its stimuli.

In Croce's view, trauma may inspire art, but it should be transcended (a contradiction in terms, because trauma is precisely that which cannot be transcended). But to do so, it must remain unmentionable as a specific social or autobiographical referent. Her reason? Because actual trauma is particular, "interested," and therefore cannot attain the universality of true art. It also silences critics. Needless to say, Croce's position does not allow for an art that bears witness, as Joyce Carol Oates points out, nor does it begin to account for scores of autobiographical masterpieces that render the traumas their authors or makers suffered (Oates, 34). What it does do is protect the institutional turf of the critic precisely by identifying that which exceeds her balliwick. Croce's defense of her institutional turf reveals a kindred ideological investment in a humanist subject capable of transcending trauma by sheer force of will. In contradistinction to Freud, who asserted that trauma, by definition, trumps all aspects of human experience, especially representation and perception, Croce proclaims that art trumps trauma, albeit by denying its presence.

Before going on, I want to specifically address aesthetics as an issue of reception with respect to Croce herself, an aspect she would like to repress or foreclose altogether. Croce's tacit assumptions are that, as an art critic, she is an individual responding to the aesthetic production of other individuals. Her identificatory logic with the artists she judges runs like this: "I am an individual; you are an individual; we share an abstracted sameness. Thus I can speak to the universalized value or lack thereof of your work." In this way Croce speaks from, even as she suppresses, the basic social contract the critic makes with the artist and the art world—an identification with their universal sameness.

Confronted with hearsay about Bill T. Jones's "Still/Here," however, Croce's presumption of sameness is violated. We can imagine her amended, imaginary reaction to go something like this: "I am an individual. I used to think that you were an individual, but I have heard otherwise. That fills me with a terrifying sense of my own difference, a difference which also compromises my ability to speak, to judge art for everyone. Therefore, I will not even look at your work." I have focused on and simplified Croce's resistance response because it so clearly manifests the tacit social contract based on an imaginary sameness brought to crisis by Bill T. Jones's invocation of trauma. It is noteworthy that self-expressions of trauma at once signal this crisis and offer a way of conceptualizing the aesthetic through difference. In other words, rather than repressing reception and affect in the interests of disinterest, autobiography and self-representation provide another mode of reception for aesthetic expressions and critical apprehensions of trauma.

For the first steps in that direction, I would like to consider the work of Roland Barthes.[4] Barthes offers a useful contrast with Croce because his sustained investigation of photographs and film stills turned ultimately to Kantian questions bearing on aesthetic judgment. His theorization of the ontology and aesthetics of photographic representation depends on exactly those elements condemned as nonaesthetic by Croce—the "undiscussable," the traumatic, and the autobiographical.

Although Barthes's work on the semiotics of photographic meaning goes back to the early 1960s, in his 1970 essay "The Third Meaning," he raised aesthetic problems and concerns when he began to try to pinpoint an "obtuse" meaning that captivated him in certain film stills. Barthes identified this meaning as a feature of (his) reception, a component of a poetical grasp or reading of the image. Significantly, this meaning resisted analysis, description; its sense was (conceptually) unspeakable. As he says, "In short, what the obtuse meaning disturbs, sterilizes, is metalanguage (criticism)" (61).

Though Barthes has no professed interest in the question of beauty, his desire to describe an image's power to "captivate" him and the difficulty of doing so in the registers afforded by the metalanguages of criticism and ideology invoke what are very clearly Kantian concerns. These concerns become more pointed and engaged in *Barthes by Barthes* and especially *Camera Lucida*, autobiographical works in which Barthes continues to pursue these questions. In the latter, both the issue of poetic reception and the indescribable third meaning resurface in Barthes's notion of the *punctum*, a term which he uses to reformulate a central feature of Kantian aesthetics.

Barthes writes that the punctum is "this element [in the photograph] which rises from the scene, shoots out of it like an arrow, and pierces me. A Latin word exists to designate this wound, this prick, this mark made by a pointed instrument . . . A photograph's punctum is that accident which pricks me, but also bruises me, is poignant to me" (*Camera*, 26–27). His language ("pierces me") pointedly references significations of trauma. The punctum refers to that in the photograph which solicits a subjective, affective, and passive response to it. Anthony Cascardi observes:

> Kant's insistence on the purposelessness of aesthetic production and on the disinterestedness of aesthetic pleasure is . . . meant to isolate what pertains irreducibly to the subject in the peculiar mode of production that is characteristic of art. For Kant this is the element of feeling or affect, and it reveals subjectivity in its passive mode. Coming to grips with the agency that is associated with this peculiar form of productivity represents an abiding interest of aesthetic theory following Kant, ranging from Hegel and Heidegger to Barthes, whose notion of the photographic punctum depends largely on a characterization of subjectivity in terms of affect. (48–49)

Barthes's inquiry into the spectatorship of the photograph jettisons beauty as the occasion for the punctum and replaces it with trauma and loss. In so doing, he invokes but transforms the leitmotif of death and mortality that runs through all the major critical statements on the photographic image, including his own.[5] Yet Barthes is no longer seeking, as they do, to define photography's essence:

> But at the moment of reaching the essence of Photography in general, I branched off; instead of following the path of a formal ontology (of a Logic), I stopped, keeping with me, like a treasure, my desire or my grief . . . As Spectator, I was interested in Photography only for "sentimental" reasons; I wanted to explore it not as a question (a theme) but as a wound: I see, I feel, hence I notice, I observe and I think. (*Camera*, 21)

Though he identifies photography "as a wound," the field in which he considers its meaning and effects is his affect, not that of the objective meaning of photography.

Barthes thereby enacts in *Camera Lucida* a contemporary rewriting of the problems and paradoxes that motivated Kant's *Critique of Judgment*. Though the feelings of pleasure and pain provoked by the aesthetic object are particular and subjective, they are nevertheless, as Cascardi argues, "endowed with a universality independent of the laws of cognition and morality." For Kant, "the validity attributable to judgments that are grounded in our particular responses to moments of beauty and sublimity supports his conviction that the concept-driven fields of cognition and morality cannot account for all there is of knowledge" (Cascardi, 42). Barthes's meditations on the photographic punctum make use of an aesthetic genre (autobiography) and a personal trauma (the death of his mother) to revisit questions of the aesthetic. Working with those aspects of his subject which he found undiscussable, indescribable, he shifted his critical approach from semiotic, ideological analyses to a very personal aesthetic inquiry in order to apprehend subjective forms of knowledge "for which the concept-driven fields of cognition and morality cannot account."[6] That these have precisely to do with trauma, both his own and those relating to crises in representation and criticism, suggest that far from being antithetical to the aesthetic, trauma is central to its concerns and its expression.[7]

Barthes uses the photograph and his experience of it as an exemplar of a fundamental enigma addressed by Kant—the incommensurable yet necessary relation between the particular, subjective moment and the formal generality or judgment that together make up aesthetic reception. Croce exemplifies the tendencies of that contemporary criticism which positions "beauty" and formal achievement as the standard for aesthetic experience where subjects and their responses have all but dropped out. These types of readings and their perpetuation of such limited ideas set a trap for all critics who respond by jettisoning aesthetics for the social. That is, by accepting Croce's terms (art versus victim art), they never question the limits such a binary imposes on the scope and relevance of aesthetic experience. Accepting such a binary, they can only choose to reiterate or invert her hierarchy.

Yet in Kant's formulation of the aesthetic, though the work itself and its "internal purpose" are foregrounded, the social is always involved. Kant argues that the aesthetic satisfaction prompted by the beautiful object in one person can be "presuppose[d] in every other person" (381). While this inference is somewhat abstract, in the contemporary examples to which I refer, the social connection is much more concrete and pronounced. To begin with, there are Croce and Barthes's function and effects as critics and theorists. I would like to consider these in a bit more detail.

Against what Croce criticizes in Bill T. Jones's work as the "undiscussable," she institutes a paradox of the unseeable. That is, the social is reintegrated into aesthetic expression via Croce's not seeing Jones's piece. What she does not see motivates her impulse to public speech, to criticism which is, by definition, affective and unknowing and thereby not concerned with the aesthetic. It raises the question of what one is seeing when one is not seeing something, adding a twist to our notion of the blind review. This same phenomenon is at work in Congressional debates over NEA grants for "ob/scene" art in which no one has seen the work (Cheryl Dunye's *Watermelon Woman* would be one important example). But this phenomenon also suggests that Croce et al. never see certain aspects of the work they do review.

Croce's version of Kantianism, which represses aesthetic reception to secure critical pretensions to objectivity, induces blindness of the particular, whereas the autobiographical response of someone like Barthes seems to avoid the big questions of the universal and the social. To put this dichotomy and Barthes's thought within it in a larger, political perspective, one which addresses cultural receptions of trauma on a larger scale, here is Benedict Anderson,[8] speaking on trauma at the beginning of *Imagined Communities*:

> The extraordinary survival over thousands of years of Buddhism, Christianity or Islam in dozens of different social formations attests to their imaginative response to the overwhelming burden of human suffering—disease, mutilation, grief, age, and death. Why was I born blind? . . . The religions attempt to explain. The great weakness of all evolutionary/progressive styles of thought, not excluding Marxism, is that such questions (of disease, mutilation, grief, age and death) are answered with impatient silence. (10)

Anderson's critique of "progressive styles of thought" and their inability to deal with trauma measures that failure against the success of religion and all other modes of thought which offer transcendental and mythological panaceas for trauma. Interestingly, his dichotomy provocatively echoes Barthes's own earlier (1957) formulation of myth on the right and on the left. In "Myth Today," Barthes also diagnosed what has turned out to be a significant problem for the left in the latter half of this century. Barthes argues that myth on the right is, first and foremost, "depoliticized speech" that ceaselessly converts history into nature; it is "essential; well-fed, sleek, expansive, garrulous," taking hold of "all aspects of the law, of morality, of aesthetics." Myth on the left, however, is "inessential," impoverished; "it never reaches the immense field of human relationships." As it "always defines itself in relation to the oppressed, [it] can only be poor, monotonous, immediate." Myth on the left is particular, specific; it springs from objective, ideological analysis (142–151). Vested in history, it cannot, does not address (and mystify) trauma as does religious discourse or myth on the right, wherein individual tragedy is linked to transcendental continuities and ahistorical forces.

So where does Barthes's later work fit in this scenario? It does not seem far-fetched to suggest that the trajectory of Barthes's thought produces a mode which evades the perniciousness and denials of myth while also critically and creatively confronting the representational enigmas of trauma. His later texts engage (his own) personal trauma through the theoretical trauma posed by photographic representation and its affiliation with death. Barthes accomplishes this complex insinuation through self-representation, clearly a mode of expression which answered critical questions he had pursued for years.

In the "The Third Meaning," Barthes attempts to locate something in film stills which holds him, which evades the reach of critical analysis, yet which nevertheless compels "an interrogative reading." In *Barthes by Barthes* and *Camera Lucida*, he takes his own reception, his own poetic and personal grasp of certain photographs to aestheticize the critical impulse itself. The inadequacies of critical theory and discourse as such led him to experiment and continually innovate and revise his approach to literary (*S/Z*, *Fragments of a Lover's Discourse*, *The Pleasure of the Text*) and visual (*Barthes by Barthes*, *Camera Lucida*) texts. Key to these innovations was an impulse to fuse genres of criticism and creativity, a project that marked his work from the publication of *S/Z* on (Ray, 94–96).

He speaks to these aspirations in a passage from *Camera Lucida* where he testifies to an autobiographical desire which would exceed his individuality: "I have always wanted to remonstrate with my moods, not to justify them; still less to fill the scene of the text with my individuality; but on the contrary to offer, to extend this individuality to a science of the subject, a science whose name is of little importance to me, provided it attains (as has not yet occurred) to a generality which neither reduces nor crushes me" (18). In his late work, Barthes introduces autobiography as the only legitimate form of aesthetic criticism. In this mode, he is always speaking for himself, which is not to say that he is only speaking as himself: he is using autobiography to allegorize the aesthetic, which is to say, to allegorize his own affect. What is seemingly left out of his account is also, precisely, the social, which he cannily leaves to speak powerfully through the photographs that pierce him (a young man awaiting execution; a self-portrait of Mapplethorpe; nuns in Nicaragua). Barthes offers one possible methodology that suggests how aesthetic criticism might enunciate the difference, the trauma, the social and the self that are anyway already there.

Barthes is by no means the only critic/artist who works within what I am calling an aesthetics of wounding. Rising to the demands, the impossibilities of representing trauma and of confronting the trauma that representation itself constitutes, numerous filmmakers (Sadie Bening, Cheryl Dunye, Mindy Faber, Su Friedrich, Bill Jones, Lourdes Portillo, Renee Tajima, Rea Tajiri), writers (Dorothy Allison, Jamaica Kincaid, Sara Suleri, Jeannette Winterston), therapists (Kay Jamison, Annie Rogers), theorists and critics (Henry Louis Gates, bell hooks, Cherrie Moraga, Jo Spence, Carolyn Kay Steedman, Gregory Ulmer), film critics (Michelle Citron, B. Ruby Rich), philosophers (Jacques Derrida) and performance artists (Karen Finley, Harry Gamboa Jr., Holly Hughes, Carmelita Tropicana, Guillermo Verdecchia) have seized upon autobiography as a mode in which the aesthetic negotiates between the traumatic and the social *cogito* of the critical voice.

These otherwise very diverse writers and artists share an approach which transcends conventional distinctions between creativity and criticism, event and critic, aesthetics and politics, cognition and affect. What gives rise to this kind of approach is their recognition that something is always beyond the reach of cognition, morality, and affect, an ineffable and mysterious remainder.[9] Self-representation provides a way to apprehend more fully this remainder. As with

Barthes's late work, autobiography also offers a mode in which the critic or artist may speak with authority, but never with an authority that presumes to know for all or to know objectively. It also allows for the insinuation of critical and aesthetic practices that resist ideology while not denying the political. In so doing, this type of work explores the possibilities that arise from bringing together the impossible, the irreconcilable, the unrepresentable. Thus, if aesthetics is the affect that thought cannot represent and trauma is the experience that affect cannot contain, then the aesthetics of wounding testify to the experiences which we can neither represent nor contain within ourselves but which happen nonetheless.

Notes

1. I would like to thank the research group on autobiography at the Center for Ideas and Society, especially Traise Yamamoto and Tiffany Lopez, as well as Robert Miklitsch, Chon Noriega, Randy Rutsky, and Vivian Sobchack, whose astute suggestions enhanced both the scope and focus of this piece.

2. Deconstruction and trauma studies's engagement with representation, reference, aesthetics and history overlap most provocatively in the case of Paul de Man. While an extensive critical literature exists, Shoshona Felman explicitly addresses self-representation, autobiography and de Man's aesthetic theory in "After the Apocalypse: Paul de Man and the Fall to Silence" (1992). She carefully reads de Man's biography, his wartime journalism, and his silence according to his reading of Rousseau's theft of the ribbon and false accusation of Marion in the Confessions. Her essay reads his theoretical work and his silence as a conscious and ethical accounting for his wartime writings.

3. See Laplance and Pontalis (1973) on "Resistance" in *The Language of Psychoanalysis*, 394–397.

4. Anthony J. Cascardi's cogent and illuminating essay "The Difficulty of Art" (1998) led me to consider Barthes's work on aesthetics in relation to trauma. For other compelling accounts of Barthes's methods as models for new critical practices, see Robert B. Ray (1995), whose arguments about Barthes's synthesis of creative and critical practices has shaped my account here; and Craig Saper (1997), who looks at the use of humor in Barthes's work which he also uses to theorize a mode of cultural invention.

5. See, for example, Andre Bazin (1967), where he identifies the "ontology of the photographic image" as aligned with the embalming of the dead; Susan Sontag (1977), who asserts that "all photographs are memento mori," comparing them with death masks (15); and Noel Burch, who observes that Edison's audio-visual aspirations represented "the pursuit of a class phantasy . . . to conclude the conquest of nature by triumphing over death through a substitute for life itself" (6).

6. In English and French, the word "point" refers both to a focused summation of meaning and to a sharp edge capable of pricking or piercing someone. Barthes marks the transformation in his critical practice by means of this pun; he uses the punctum to move his critical practice from concerns with abstract meaning to those having to do with his

own affect and wounding. The latter strategy refuses to banish the material trace, the subject, from considerations of textual effects.

7. One question which poses itself is whether trauma lies at the origins of the aesthetic or is a more contemporary manifestation.

8. Benedict Anderson (1991) cites Regis Debray, "Marxism and the National Question," *New Left Review*, 105 (Sept.–Oct. 1977), 29, in relation to this passage.

9. Gregory Ulmer's concept of mystory, elaborated in *Teletheory: Grammatology in the Age of Video* incorporates mystery and autobiography in a critical practice committed to invention.

Works Cited

Anderson, Benedict. *Imagined Communities*. New York: Verso, 1991. (Original work published 1983.)

Barthes, Roland. *S/Z*. Trans. Richard Miller. New York: Hill and Wang, 1970.

———. "Myth Today." *Mythologies*. Trans. Annette Lavers. New York: Hill and Wang, 1972. 109–159.

———. *Barthes by Barthes*. Trans. Richard Howard. New York: Hill and Wang, 1977.

———. "The Third Meaning: Research Notes on Some Eisenstein Stills." *Image—Music—Text*. Trans. Stephen Heath. New York: Hill and Wang, 1977. 52–68.

———. *Fragments of a Lover's Discourse*. Trans. Richard Howard. New York: Hill and Wang, 1978.

———. *Camera Lucida*. Trans. Richard Howard. New York: Hill and Wang, 1981.

Bazin, Andre. "The Ontology of the Photographic Image." In *What is Cinema?*, vol. 1. Trans. Hugh Gray. Berkeley: University of California Press, 1967. 9–16.

Burch, Noel. "Charles Baudelaire versus Doctor Frankenstein." Trans. Tom Milne. *Afterimage*, nos. 8–9, Spring 1981: 4–21.

Caruth, Cathy. "Introduction" and "Preface." *Trauma: Explorations in Memory*. Ed. Cathy Caruth. Baltimore, Md.: Johns Hopkins University Press, 1995. 3–12, vii–ix.

Cascardi, Anthony J. "The Difficulty of Art." *Boundary 2*, vol. 25, no. 1, Spring 1998: 35–65.

Croce, Arlene. "Discussing the Undiscussable." *The Crisis of Criticism*. [1995]. Ed. Maurice Berger. New York: New Press, 1998. 15–29.

De Man, Paul. "Kant and Schiller." *Aesthetic Ideology*. Ed. Andrzej Warminski. Minneapolis: University of Minnesota Press, 1996. 129–162.

Derrida, Jacques. "The Parergon." Trans. Craig Owens. *October* 9, Summer 1979: 3–41.

Felman, Shoshona. "After the Apocalypse: Paul de Man and the Fall to Silence." *Testimony: Crises of Witnessing in Literature, Psychoanalysis, and History*. Ed. Shoshona Felman and Dori Laub. New York: Routledge, 1992. 120–164.

Freud, Sigmund. *Beyond the Pleasure Principle*. [1920]. Trans. James Strachey. New York: Norton, 1989.

Kant, Immanuel. "Critique of Judgment." *Critical Theory since Plato*. Ed. Hazard Adams. New York: Harcourt Brace Jovanovich, 1971. 377–399.

Laplanche, J., and J. P. Pontalis. *The Language of Psychoanalysis*. Trans. Donald Nicholson-Smith. New York: Norton, 1973.

Oates, Joyce Carol. "Confronting Head-on the Face of the Afflicted." *The Crisis of Criticism*. [1995]. Ed. Maurice Berger. New York: New Press, 1998. 15–29.

Ray, Robert B. "Roland Barthes: Fetishism as Research Strategy." *The Avant-Garde Finds Andy Hardy*. Cambridge, Mass.: Harvard University Press, 1995. 94–119.

Saper, Craig. *Artificial Mythologies: A Guide to Cultural Invention*. Minneapolis: University of Minnesota Press, 1997.

Sontag, Susan. *On Photography*. New York: Delta, 1977.

Ulmer, Gregory. *Teletheory: Grammatology in the Age of Video*. New York: Routledge, 1989.

Beautiful Identities

When History Turns State's Evidence

CHON A. NORIEGA

Buried in the Federal Trade Commission Library are several intragovernmental documents from the 1960s and 1970s that can be found in no other archive, but that signal an attempt within the state itself to create an autonomous space outside its own corporate liberalism and the emerging global media. That space was an aesthetic space, instrumental neither for political representation nor for mass communication; instead it served the needs of a social movement for beautiful identities. That space is now called "Chicano cinema" and its mode—initially at least—is that of the documentary, and its location, television.

Ironically, the history of Chicano cinema has been told in ways that link aesthetic analysis to the contingency of social movement activities that are considered discrete from and contestatory of the state. Thus, that history has been bounded by the essential terms of cultural nationalism: first, as a narrative of resistance to dominant cinema, and, second, as an internal matter that distinguishes between two paths—one good, the other bad—toward such resistance. Such a history seeks to define difference—something one can call "Chicano"—against the backdrop of an industrial and national sameness from which it remains excluded, and with which it also seeks incorporation by way of difference. The choice between "good" and "bad," then, is not about whether to assimilate, but rather *how* to do so and remain beautiful.

To a large extent, the contradictions of this historiography can be attributed to its articulation within the institutional and disciplinary boundaries of the university. But this situation is more complicated than it first appears, since Chicano histories claim to speak from (or, at the least, for) another space—the community. And, this "speaking for" reflects not so much a naive idealism within the Ivory Tower as it does the ambiguous location of the minority scholar in the first place. In other words, if such "speaking for" is similar to that of cultural nationalism expressed outside of (or even *before*) university-based Chicano studies, that is because the inclusion of Chicanos within the university has been structured along the lines of their prior exclusion. This inclusion/exclusion places clear limits on the type of history that can be told, especially insofar as the uni-

versity and minority scholar want the same thing—a "minority discourse"—
though each places emphasis on a different word. Of course, all histories can be
read as allegories of employment. While histories may speak to an outside community or another time, they are also—as Michel de Certeau notes in *The Writing
of History*—"the product of a place" (64). That is, histories speak from a social
institution and its constellation of peers, methods, sources, practices. Thus, to
paraphrase David James in *Allegories of Cinema*, a historical text never fails to tell
the story of how and why it was produced (5). Within "body" programs of race,
gender, and sexuality, however, that story is qualitatively different than for "traditional" appointments insofar as job recruitment and critical analysis are explicitly tied to the same object: a body marked by difference. This situation raises
fundamental questions, not about affirmative action per se, but about an institution that cannot imagine, let alone enact, an alternative to racial and gender exclusion. For this reason, then, the minority historian often engages in a strategic
conflation of critical discourses rooted in an academic professional culture with
social practices outside the university.

The literature on minority cinemas tends to deal with the expressive qualities
and sociohistorical context for cultural production—that is, defining a vernacular aesthetic, cinema movement, and corresponding community, usually against
a backdrop of mainstream exclusion. Despite the theoretical range of these efforts,
more than anything else they have contributed to the construction of minority-
produced media as distinct *genres* within critical discourse, funding practices, and
public exhibition. In fact, quite often minority cinemas are named and become
functional within discourse and institutional practices *before* they exist as a text-
producing phenomenon. Historiography precedes History. There is a catch-22
at work here that speaks to the dynamic of racially marked expression and its
circulation within popular and academic discourses. It is necessary to posit
subnational histories in order to locate texts and, thereby, incite discourse; but,
at the same time, any specific text will necessarily exceed the history within which
it then circulates, and within which it is, more or less, contained.

What we end up with, then, are a series of body genres for, by, and about
women, blacks, Chicanos, queers, and so on that are problematic as "genres" for
the same reason that they are so effective: these social-cum-aesthetic categories
create a space for filmmakers to move into in a very practical and consequential
way. Films and videos *do* get funded, produced, and distributed. But that space
often ends up being another, more public, version of the home, ghetto, barrio,
and closet from which the filmmakers were trying to escape. For my current
purposes, I am concerned with the historiographic impulse behind the construction of body genres—that is, with a recent *critical* activity that attempts to write
a particular community, subject, or identity into history by way of "film" genre.
What must be repressed in such a move is the fact that one is doing a form of
genre analysis that effectively reduces institutional analysis and social history to

a textual effect; that is, these social phenomena exist only as signs circulating within a closed set of texts. But there is another consequence embedded within the inherent formal and textual limitations of genre analysis: insofar as one tends to look within and not across genres, the analysis also looks within and not across racial and sexual identities.

Drawing upon extensive archival research, I want to offer a theoretical model for understanding "Chicano cinema" as a practice created and regulated by the state. For the purposes of this essay, as well as the confluence of aesthetics and historiography, I propose that the aesthetic is always instrumental, or, rather, put to instrumental purposes; but, depending on one's vantage point, either beauty or purpose will be the only thing perceived; and that the state holds the evidence wherein the two come together. I do not, however, subscribe to a simple binarism within aesthetics between the autonomous and the instrumental, positions usually mapped onto Kant and Bourdieu, respectively. As a reluctant theorist of what could be called autohistoriography, I am partisan to neither position in and of itself. Thus, I am not arguing that the aesthetic transcends the particular into the universal or, conversely, that it represents the false consciousness of a particular class. Instead, I will attempt to show the structure of the particular through which "beauty and truth" took shape within the state in the 1960s and 1970s, giving rise to a "Chicano cinema" of beautiful identities. Herein lies the paradoxical origins of Chicano cinema.

Before starting, let me explain that while I will be talking about minority "cinemas," I will focus my attention on broadcast policy—which is to say, television—since it is here that most activity has taken place, whether media reform, state regulation, or even textual production. In fact, despite our claims to examine a "cinematic" practice, most of the relevant texts we study are products of television, including half of the dozen or so Chicano-directed feature films. The reason minority cinemas emerged vis-à-vis television is political: broadcasting, and not film studios, represented the one potential site of state intervention in response to minority demands for access to the public sphere. Beginning with the Civil Rights Act of 1964, the courts and new regulatory agencies challenged and, in some cases, changed or superseded broadcast policy, thereby introducing a conflicted state apparatus as mediator between the mass media and disenfranchised groups. Thus, in addition to addressing the industry, the state appeared to be regulating its own regulators, too. In general, this intervention came from two sets of institutions: those that directly oversaw the "core institutions" for broadcast policy, such as the U.S. Court of Appeals, and those that "regulated the social consequences of business behavior" (Horwitz 76), including the Equal Employment Opportunity Commission and Civil Rights Commission. Rather than functioning as a "neutral" domain, the state actually *created* both the market and that which contests the status quo, largely by defining and subordinating political struggles within an overall corporate liberal framework. In policy- and legal-oriented scholarship, this process is seen as one that generates "irony" (Horwitz), "illusion" (Rowland, Jr.), or a "contradictory situation" (Haight and Weinstein) as protest groups are brought within the administrative control of the state (see also Streeter). The internal "conflicts" between federal agencies, then, represent an adaptive feature of the state, rather than its Achilles' heel. This double bind is no more evident than in the way in which unregulated social protest is converted into the ritual of "expert" testimony before the state.

For the most part, Chicano testimony fell outside the interpretive framework of the various agencies that solicited it in the first place. Chicano media activists understood neither the style nor the substance of the "appropriately neutral and expert policy language" for mass media. After all, they were *not* policy experts, nor were they professionals within the industry; they were outsiders demanding to be let inside. At the same time, however, they were part of a growing social movement defining its own boundaries, language, and demands. By the late 1960s, the Chicano movement had begun to theorize its location within power relations, largely by providing a deeply historical and, hence, transnational dimension to the current socioeconomic and political situation of Chicanos in the United States. In starting with the conquest of the Americas, this historical orientation led to an investment in defining and reproducing a culture of resistance that stood outside the historical forces of the state, whether of Spain (1492–1821), Mexico (1821–1848), or the United States (since 1848). To be inside the Chicano movement, then, was to be outside the state, albeit on *cultural* grounds more than anything else. Needless to say, this position colored the demands for access to the mass media, that is, the demands to be let inside, and it helps to explain why the state had to come to Chicano media groups rather than vice versa.

Which brings me back to my opening remark: the state itself attempted to resolve this impasse between a viable, yet unassimilated social movement and an exclusionary mass media, and it did so by creating the concept of Chicano cinema via broadcast television. Between 1968 and 1973, state functionaries working within both the new civil rights bureaucracy and key executive departments produced a series of reports and letters outlining the features of a Chicano cinema vis-à-vis the state and corporate media. The most influential document, *Chicanos and Mass Media*, entered the Congressional Record twice during 1970 (U.S. Congress, Senate; U.S. Congress, House). The next year, the authors published an abridged version as a pamphlet in support of their ongoing media reform; although that pamphlet now appears to reside only in the Federal Trade Commission Library (Rendón and Reyes).

Chicanos and Mass Media proposed "amalgamating the two extreme concepts" of Chicano media and Establishment media through the "intermediary agencies" of the state: "A balance must be struck between total insulation from outside media contact and influence and the co-opting of Chicano thought and news-reporting by the non-raza communications system" (U.S. Congress, Senate,

928AP; U.S. Congress, House, 75). Pushing this argument even further, the report demanded support for developing a Chicano media through industry "reparations" rather than state-regulated "equal opportunity," while it also announced the need to utilize the regulatory arena to bring about reforms in mass media content and hiring practices (see also Reyes).

In many ways, *Chicanos and the Mass Media* is an astonishing document that presents a fullblown theory that builds upon historical and statistical analyses in a more complex way than anything put forth by either the FCC or Chicano grassroots activists in the Southwest. What the report proposed was nothing less than "amalgamating the two extreme concepts" of inside and outside by allowing both to coexist on equal terms; in short, it offered a real solution to the problem of exclusion rather than the FCC's "dance of delay, limits, cooptation, and quiescence" (Haight and Weinstein, 141). But this approach also questioned the very legal framework for mass media, suggesting that a noncorporate alternative, "Chicano media," could exist alongside the industry. In this way, the report exceeded the interpretive community within which it was presented. It didn't make sense. What it *did* do, however, was to rearticulate the political rhetoric of the Chicano movement through the state itself. In fact, when read as a part of the published Congressional hearings within which it appeared, *Chicanos and the Mass Media* comes across more as an act of "thinking aloud" within the context of the Chicano movement than of speaking to an addressee within a legally defined set of power relations. Actually, it did the latter through the former.

If concurrent broadcast law and policy placed television outside representational politics, in both senses of the phrase (democracy and mediated public identities), then difference necessarily became the *bête noire* within the public sphere that television produced. After all, difference signalled a body politic, whereas television addressed a mass audience; and, for this reason, media reform based on civil rights often found itself subordinated to the logic of consumer rights. In the 1950s and 1960s, racial difference brought this dynamic into high relief insofar as racial minorities did not have the requisite rights of citizenship that television could then rearticulate as consumer rights. Thus positioned "outside" the corporate liberal imaginary for the citizen-consumer, racial minorities encountered the complexities and paradoxes of seeking social change. While the state responded to social unrest by constructing avenues through which racial minorities could seek adjudication, it also did so in a way that did not foster structural assimilation. Instead, the state compelled these groups to participate in a "discourse of violence" as well as base their claims on supplemental racial categories for citizenship. Thus, in their negotiations with the state, racial minorities oscillated between injured party and unlawful threat, while their status as citizens was itself marked as exceptional in both senses of the word: an exception (rights) and superior (identity). These paradoxes pitted a nonwhite racial identity against an unmarked national imaginary from which it remained excluded.

In the late 1960s and early 1970s, the struggle over access to and control of the mass media brought together conflicting notions of ethnic community and national identity, communication and capital, stereotypes and employment, while violence provided a rationale for linking these social spheres, basic infrastructures, and symbolic and material representations into an agenda for social equity. And here's how it happened: When Chicanos protested the broadcast media, the state intervened and redirected their protest to the policy arena, offering them a *quid pro quo*: the state would participate in constituting minorities as distinct groups, each with an identity and place within the body politic; and, in exchange, that place would be an informal one that did not challenge the structure of rule. Thus, for example, this period of state activism resulted in the heyday of minority public affairs programming, which offered highly charged public symbols of an identity and community marked by otherness, but did little to integrate the executive ranks. By the mid-1970s, amid the recession, the state would defer issues of social equity to the marketplace, and broadcasters would quickly cast themselves as the victims of the symbolic violence of minority cultural citizenship. Minority and local public affairs series were quickly cancelled, replaced by syndicated game shows, conservative talk shows, and corporate-funded investment series. We call this deregulation, but it was also deracination, in which minority groups' already problematic toehold in the public sphere was lost.

In arguing that the state created Chicano cinema, I am being at once deeply ironic and deadly earnest. Having just finished a book-length study on the topic— *Shot in America: Television, the State, and the Rise of Chicano Cinema*—I set myself the challenge of writing a parody of my own book that would be as true as the book itself. If historiography precedes history, then it seemed only appropriate that the parody precede the original. But I am less concerned with generating a simple reversal than with exploring the implications of a subtle shift in emphasis. Whereas my book stresses social movements, here I foreground the state; but in both cases I draw upon the same evidence. So if I am being deeply ironic and deadly earnest, I do so to reveal something that neither the state nor social movements care to manifest: their complicity. By complicity, however, I am talking about structural relations, not ethical choices. It is aesthetics, the search for the good and the beautiful, that serves to obscure these relations; not because it is in the nature of the aesthetic to do so, but because both the state and social movements turn to the aesthetic at precisely that moment when their complicity threatens to manifest itself. What we lose in the process is a history that concerns itself with the good, the bad, and the ugly, acquiring beautiful identities, instead.

As a methodological issue, then, I want to end by stressing the need to examine the relationships and tactical maneuvers that locate social protest both inside *and* outside the state. The archival holdings suggest the complex self-othering required for minorities to approach the state in order to gain access to television. The irony is that television itself was often understood as an intermediate step toward Hollywood. It is in this circuitous relationship among social movements, the state, broad-cast television, and Hollywood that beautiful identities emerged. Such an approach does not deny the fact that certain groups have been clearly excluded from equal participation in political representation, economic opportunity, and mass commu-nication, but neither does it fetishize exclusion into an identity out of step with the complexities and paradoxes of seeking social change. The evidence *does* exist, but it becomes invisible when we hold other truths to be self-evident.

Note

This essay appears in a slightly different form in *Television and New Media* 1, no. 1 (Feb. 2000): 117–124.

Works Cited

de Certeau, Michel. *The Writing of History.* [1975]. Trans. Tom Conley. New York: Colum-bia University Press, 1988.

Haight, Timothy R., and Laurie R. Weinstein. "Changing Ideology on Television by Changing Telecommunications Policy: Notes on a Contradictory Situation." *Com-munication and Social Structure: Critical Studies in Mass Media Research.* Ed. Emile G. McAnany, Jorge Schnitman, and Noreene Janus. New York: Praeger, 1981. 110–144.

Horwitz, Robert Britt. *The Irony of Regulatory Reform: The Deregulation of American Telecommu-nications.* New York: Oxford University Press, 1989.

James, David E. *Allegories of Cinema: American Film in the Sixties.* Princeton: Princeton Uni-versity Press, 1989.

Noriega, Chon A. *Shot in America: Television, the State, and the Rise of Chicano Cinema.* Minne-apolis: University of Minnesota Press, 2000.

Rendón, Armando, and Domingo Nick Reyes. *Chicanos and the Mass Media.* Washington, D.C.: National Mexican-American Anti-Defamation Committee, 1971. Pamphlet archived in the Federal Trade Commission Library; an abridged version of U.S. Con-gress, House, and U.S. Congress, Senate.

Reyes, Domingo Nick. "Anti-Defamation Committee Says Media Do Not Depict Mexi-can Americans Fairly." *TV Code News* 3, no. 12 (Feb. 1971): 2.

Rowland, Jr., William D. "The Illusion of Fulfillment: The Broadcast Reform Move-ment." *Journalism Monographs* 79 (Dec. 1982): 1–41.

Streeter, Thomas. *Selling the Air: A Critique of the Policy of Commercial Broadcasting in the United States.* Chicago: University of Chicago Press, 1996.

U.S. Congress, House Subcommittee on Communications and Power, "Chicanos and the Mass Media," *Films and Broadcasts Demeaning Ethnic, Racial, or Religious Groups,* hearings held September 21, 1970 (Washington, D.C.: U.S. Government Printing Office, 1970), 67–97.

U.S. Congress, Senate Select Committee on Equal Educational Opportunity, "Chicanos and the Mass Media," *Hearings on Equal Educational Opportunity,* Part 2—Equality of Educational Opportunity: An Introduction—Continued, 91st Cong., 1st sess., 1970 (Washington, D.C.: U.S. Government Printing Office, 1970), 928AH–928AR.

Toward a Pluralist Aesthetics

HEINZ ICKSTADT

There is widespread agreement that, in our contemporary late-capitalist culture, the aesthetic has spilled over into all areas of life, connecting art and everyday experience, inciting to "living beauty," as Richard Shusterman phrased it, from fashion to self-fashioning. This "general drift towards the aesthetic" is perhaps most strikingly confirmed in the area of philosophy, where, although "aesthetics" as an independent field of theoretical inquiry has lost the status and prestige it had acquired in the previous two centuries, the erasure of the metaphysical has nevertheless resulted in the "total aestheticization of the *logos*" (Grabes, 1994, 4).[1] If art has ceased to be the object of philosophical reflection, it now provides models for such reflection, since—as another critic argues—it is aesthetic thinking more than any other that appears adequate to help us understand our contemporary, largely fictionalized reality (Welsch, 1998, 110).

It may therefore seem all the more surprising that in the humanities, and particularly in American Studies, the aesthetic—mostly for political and ideological reasons—has fallen into disrepute. Although one could well argue that such aversion is only the flipside of a radical cultural critique which, in its attempt at purging American Studies of the aesthetic by politicizing it, has, in fact, aestheticized its politics (Fluck, 1994). Yet there have also been attempts to reverse that trend. Most recently, Elaine Scarry has put the matter of the Beautiful back on the agenda. Yet in relating it to the notions of the "true" and the "just," she seems to combine an understanding of "Beauty" as perception with aspects of a substantialist aesthetics which may inadvertently confirm, more than refute, prevailing prejudice.

However, it is indeed worthwhile to remember that the present distrust is a comparatively recent phenomenon. In Europe, the aesthetic (its value and its social function) had been a thriving topic even during the Marxist revival of the late-1960s and the decade after, when in the heated debates on Structuralism and Marxism the neo-Marxist theories of Lucien Goldman and Pierre Macherey were published, in the French avant-garde journal *Tel Quel* and in the German *Alternative*, next to the essays of the then recently rediscovered Russian formalists and Prague structuralists.

And yet, on the agenda of the new American Studies (as outlined not too long ago in Janice Radway's Presidential Address at the 1998 conference of the American Studies Association) such issues do not figure (Radway, 1999). The aesthetic has been denounced from various positions as repressive, as immoral, as hopelessly fetishistic and ideological. It has been accused of elitism (always a major sin), even of "fraudulence;" indeed the list of its transgressions as well as that of its detractors is long.[2] Culture and cultural theory have so much been the all-encompassing focus of American Studies during the last twenty years, that to raise questions about the literariness of texts and their aesthetic function may appear suspiciously reactionary, or perhaps as a sure sign of one's approaching old age—in any case, as a questionable return to the New Criticism of the now ancient 1950s. No doubt, neither Poststructuralism, nor Deconstruction, nor the New Historicism, nor Cultural Studies in general have had much use for, or interest in, questions of literariness[3] or fictionality.

Since Text has become a universal category, differences between texts (or between classes of texts) no longer appear to be relevant; or, more precisely, such differences have been defined primarily in cultural and ideological, not aesthetic terms. Although this pantextuality has gone hand in hand with a heightened sense of textual complexity—so that, as Sacvan Bercovitch once remarked about the New Historicism, "history may be understood through the subtleties of literary criticism" (Bercovitch, 1983, 322)—all specifically literary or aesthetic questions have been consigned to the background at best. The effort to understand its "cultural work" (Tompkins, 1985; Lauter, 1999) has pushed aside as irrelevant all questions pertaining to the text's specific literary work: why it can do the cultural work it does; why it can do it better (or differently) than a nonliterary text; or why fiction has the power to even subvert its own ideological complicity.

Many revisionist critics have avoided the ideologically treacherous ground of the aesthetic altogether. In reinterpreting the acknowledged masterpieces of the American Renaissance they have taken the aesthetic quality of these canonical texts for granted and then proceeded to read them culturally, politically, or theoretically.[4] In doing so, they might argue (possibly with Derrida in mind) that *not* to read aesthetically was a deliberate choice and their rightful option, since the category of the aesthetic is indeed not a textual category in the first place but constituted by the act and manner of our reading. As Derrida says, ". . . there is no text which is literary *in itself*. Literarity is not a natural essence, [not] an intrinsic property of the text." On the other hand, he also declared that "there are 'in' the text features which call for the literary reading and recall the convention, institution, or history of literature" (Derrida, 1992, 44). Therefore literary texts are able to do things that nonliterary texts cannot do: they are, he says, "potentially more potent" (43). They form a "counter-institution," "a place at once institutional and wild, an institutional place in which it is in principle permissible to put in question [. . .] the whole institution" (58).

And yet, the reflection on what makes the literary text "potentially more potent" definitely refers to its aesthetic dimension.[5] Refusing to deal with it (i.e.

not to try to understand the literary text's specific 'potency' for doing the cultural work it does) is to ignore a dimension of textual analysis that is a vital and genuine aspect also of cultural studies. In other words, I argue for the reinstatement of the aesthetic as a distinct discourse not *separate* from or *against* American (Culture) Studies but emphatically *within* it, since the aesthetic does not deny the political, ethical, or historical dimensions of literary texts but engages them and mediates between them.[6] If the historical, the social, and the political could have once been said to be the Repressed of the New Criticism (to return with a vengeance in the new theories), might not now the aesthetic be the Repressed of Cultural Theory? Perhaps we have, for too long a time, connected issues of aesthetic theory exclusively with the New Critics who, as we all seem to remember (without even having to go back to read them), made aesthetics a form of politics: a politics of aesthetic discrimination and exclusion. To subsequently exorcise this spirit of elitist formalism, of political aloofness, and of repressive value judgment by emphasizing the cultural and political (as well as the culturally and politically marginalized) has had a great liberating effect. It has brought texts into view that had not been seen before, and it has posed questions that had not been asked before. Without any doubt, it has enlarged and enriched our awareness of what constitutes American literature.

Yet it is quite unlikely that the problem of the aesthetic which has occupied critics for centuries should have become obsolete because it has been falsely identified with a modernist aesthetics of autonomy, or a hegemonial European philosophical tradition, or associated with individualism and the bourgeoisie, or simply because it does not 'fit' contemporary cultural theory which has therefore chosen to ignore it. The aesthetic does not go away with our determination not to see it since, although it can surely be used ideologically, it is always more than ideology. In the words of Terry Eagleton: "The aesthetic is at once [. . .] the very secret prototype of human subjectivity in early capitalist society, and a vision of human energies as radical ends in themselves which is the implacable enemy of all dominative or instrumentalist thought" (Eagleton, 9). We might add, that it is also not at all a purely academic issue but a matter of everyday life. We live and survive by aesthetic experience and we pass aesthetic judgment constantly, whether we care to reflect upon it or not.

In sum, it should be clear that I am not pleading for a return to formalism but for locating the aesthetic within the scope of the new cultural studies. Will it be possible to write a theory of literature that has incorporated and digested poststructuralism, the new cultural anthropology, and the new historicism? Wellek's and Warren's old *Theory of Literature* was based on the certainties of the Enlightenment (although less rigorously than legend has it): on certainties of status and of value, on criteria of objectivity, universality, hierarchy. These certainties gone (or at least fundamentally put in doubt by the prevalent epistemological scepticism), the question of aesthetics can be raised only on highly unstable and constantly shifting ground. Such a theory would have to give account of a fundamental plurality of aesthetic production and reception, of different and rivalling aesthetics, i.e. of aesthetics different in purpose, use, and function at different historical moments or for different social groups. It would have to be highly inclusive as well as highly inconclusive since it could never provide more than preliminary answers, and whatever "certainties" it propagated would have to be constantly questioned and renegotiated.

If anyone should ever want to write such a theory of literature, she or he could make use of the theories of American pragmatism. Pragmatism saw the aesthetic as a realm of creative self-assertion but also as a laboratory of thought and action, refusing to divorce "the aesthetic function of things . . . from the practical and moral," as George Santayana has it in his "Reason in Art" (216), or to separate "art from the objects and scenes of ordinary experience," as John Dewey argues in *Art as Experience* (Dewey, 6). And she or he could also make use of the theories of the Prague structuralist Jan Mukařovský who, in his attempt to reconcile Marxism with Modernism, placed his theory of aesthetic function and aesthetic value firmly within a context of social practice. Both theories, although quite different in origin and manner of argument, overlap in their emphasis on process, in their anti-essentialism, in their blurring of boundaries between the aesthetic and the practical, and in their disregard, their contempt even, for traditional aesthetics and traditional notions of Art. Both see the aesthetic and the social as interconnected, see the aesthetic as formed by the historical and social and, at the same time, as functioning—in the words of Dewey—as "enhancements of the processes of everyday life," as deepening "the sense of immediate living" (6). Both share an open, pragmatic, and flexible pluralism, focusing on multiple functions rather than on singular states or conditions. In addition, both see these practical, moral, and aesthetic functions as mutually dependent. When they are isolated they turn into mere abstractions: "Aesthetic and other interests," I quote Santayana this time, "are not separable units, to be compared externally; they are rather strands interwoven in the texture of everything. Aesthetic sensibility colours every thought, qualifies every allegiance, and modifies every product of human labour" (340).

For Mukařovský, too, the boundaries between the aesthetic and the non-aesthetic, between art and life, are fluid, defined and redefined by social habits and cultural conventions: "There are neither strict borderlines nor unmistakable criteria that would distinguish art from what is external to it" (Mukařovský, 28). He sees all texts (or objects) potentially as semiotic or communicative signs that may have, or may still acquire, many different functions, all competing with each other, of which the aesthetic function is only *one*. Literary texts (as art objects in general) differ from others because, with them, the aesthetic function is dominant—which does not mean, however, that its other functions (let's say: its pragmatic functions in the widest sense) have been suppressed or made to disappear. Rather, the literary text (or the artistic object) is a dynamic ensemble of competing and often antagonistic functions organized by the aesthetic function.

There are literary texts in which the didactic or the political functions are prominent and others in which the aesthetic function itself is explicitly emphasized. In all these different texts all functions are present yet interrelated differently. Yet although they form distinct hierarchies of functions, each is organized and held together by the aesthetic function. We might therefore say that they create various kinds of aesthetics: the aesthetics of the didactic novel, for example, in which appellative strategies of narrative persuasion are foregrounded, or those of the documentary novel, whose strategies pursue entirely different goals and effects. These different aesthetics give evidence as to how many different uses literary texts may be put (and have been put in the past), even to the use of creating an antiaesthetic that openly denounces the dominant aesthetic mode but, in doing so, inevitably advances (often against its stated intentions) another kind of aesthetics (an aesthetics of disruption, distortion, or silence, for instance).

Are functions qualities of texts, or are they socially and culturally created attitudes that we bring to them? Mukařovský, like Dewey, denies one of the main tenets of traditional aesthetics, namely, that the aesthetic should be considered as a "real quality" inherent in the "beautiful object."[7] Instead Mukařovský distinguishes between the material art product and the aesthetic object. It is the latter that constitutes the actual work of art which is actively (re)created in a dialogic exchange between object and recipient. Although there are elements or qualities in the art object that influence this interaction by provoking our response, Mukařovský stresses its contextual aspects since our attitudes and ways of perception are socially and culturally formed and thus subject to historical change. The aesthetic function, however, is connected more with the form, the organization, of an object than with its practical purpose. It is a disposition, an attitude we bring to the object when we see or read it aesthetically—a subjective attitude that is nevertheless shaped, if not determined, by cultural situation and social context.

Thus the African masks and sculptures, that Picasso so famously encountered in the Trocadero in 1907, could help him solve a problem he had long labored with, precisely because he looked at them with aesthetic eyes. Yet in the culture from which they had been taken, they were considered religious or ritual objects, and their function was therefore not primarily aesthetic. Such historical shifts and such differences between cultures leave the definition of what constitutes art (or literature) open, dependent on changing social and cultural conditions, individual situations, and subjective or collective attitudes. When we see an object in the street (a car, let's say, or a piece of junk) we define it predominantly by its practical (or its once-practical) function. Even though we may surely be aware of its aesthetic function, that is most likely not dominant in our perception of it.

But by a mere change of context, if we encounter it in a museum, for instance, we are compelled to look at it aesthetically; that is, we appreciate its 'made-ness', its color and design, and make it the object of our mental and emotional engagement.

Much avant-garde and postmodernist art depends on such unexpected changes of context: the dominance of the pragmatic function is replaced here by the dominance of the aesthetic function.[8] Of course, it is always possible for any reader or observer either to refuse such a shift or to not be aware of it (as in the case of the cleaning woman in a Cologne museum who inadvertently destroyed one of Josef Beuys's junk sculptures while cleaning up). To quote Mukařovský once again: "[p]recisely because the aesthetic function does not own a specific 'content,' it can become transparent, not antagonistic *vis-a-vis* the other functions but supportive of them. . . . It organizes their mutual tensions and relations, in order to bring out the multiplicity of functions concentrated [. . .] in the work of art" (quoted in Guenther, 19). In this process, the various pragmatic functions (as, in fact, all nonaesthetic functions) cease to be unequivocal and gain a polysemic richness they do not have in the context of everyday existence. "Therefore, they cannot be isolated and compared to a 'reality' outside the text; such a relation can only be established when mediated through the whole text and its internal structure" (Guenther, 20).

Obviously, such hierarchies of functions are highly unstable since they depend on subjective or, even more so, on collective dispositions. We may read aesthetically what was once considered a scientific, political, or religious text (be it the Bible, the Declaration of Independence, Marx's Communist Manifesto, or Freud's psychoanalytical work) because we, formed by the culture we live in, consciously ignore, or do not know, or cannot sufficiently appreciate anymore the text's original purpose and function. Inversely, we may choose to read literary texts as a form of theory or politics and thus willingly disregard their aesthetic function. The latter procedure, of course, risks a reductionism that, apart from being called "inappropriate" (as Mukařovský calls it), must eventually provoke the question why it should be necessary to read literature in the first place, if what we discover in it might not be more easily available through other (non-literary) texts. Indeed, the importance of the aesthetic depends largely on our willingness to raise the issue *as* important, thereby insisting, by implication, on the importance of the object of our mutual inquiry: literature. What may once have been intended to increase the social relevance of the literary text and to save it from the 'restrictions' and 'irrelevancies' of the merely aesthetic may thus well have added to what John Guillory has diagnosed as a conceptual and institutional crisis of literary studies.

But what *is* the aesthetic function? According to Mukařovský it is a dynamic, yet transparent principle of organization: It creates a reflective distance between observer and object by de-pragmatizing it, by putting "its referential and pragmatic function into brackets" (Fluck, 1999), thus forcing the reader/observer to contemplate the specific manner of its 'made-ness' and to engage the whole range of the text's various, often contradictory functions. Since Mukařovský subsumes the literary text within the much larger field of aesthetic objects in general, he has comparatively little to say about its specific strategies and procedures. Nor does either he or Dewey analyze to any great extent aesthetic experience as an individual process of reception: what happens in the act of reading or of seeing. Both focus almost exclusively on placing the aesthetic within the larger context of experience and on the interaction between the aesthetic and the other functions. Although this interrelation and interaction is constantly up for cultural redefinition, the dominance of the aesthetic function nevertheless marks the literary text's difference: it is not theoretical, political, documentary, etc. but able, through the specific organization of its functions, to open up and test theoretical or political discourse by pushing it to its limits, by staging it in terms of lived life, i.e. in terms of practice and experience, of the concrete and the particular.[9]

Mukařovský and Dewey sound remarkably similar here: "Esthetic experience is always more than esthetic. In it a body of matters and meanings, not in themselves esthetic, become esthetic as they enter into an ordered rhythmic movement toward consummation" (Dewey, 26); and Mukařovský: "The functional perspective allows for seeing things in terms of activity and process without ignoring their material reality. It shows the world as movement and, at the same time, as a secure basis for human action" (quoted in Guenther, 13); and again: "The autonomy of the art work and the dominance of the aesthetic function and value within it appear not as destroyers of all contact between the work and reality—natural and social—but as constant stimuli of such contact" (Mukařovský, 105).[10]

Once a text is marked, by genre signal or cultural convention, as an aesthetic object, it cannot easily escape the conditions created by the dominance of the aesthetic function. Even if the text would struggle against these conditions (as many fictional texts of the 1930s did), even if it would signal to the reader its interest to be read, let's say, politically, it would still have to stage its politics aesthetically; this is most evident in the extreme tension between aesthetic and nonaesthetic functions in, let's say, Tillie Olson's *Yonnondio* or James Agee's and Walker Evans's *Let Us Now Praise Famous Men*—both texts that advance an aesthetics of the nonaesthetic by denouncing an obsolete and elitist concept of Art ("For God's sake, don't look at it as Art").

In other words, the value of a literary text can never be determined by its politics alone, or by the cultural work it does, since all the values it projects are aesthetically mediated or staged. For illustration, let us briefly look at a statement of Toni Morrison's. In one of her essays she writes:

> The novel should try deliberately to make you stand up and make you feel something profoundly in the same way that a Black preacher requires his congregation

to speak, to join him in his sermon. . . . And, having at my disposal only the letters of the alphabet and some punctuation, I have to provide the places and spaces so that the reader can participate. Because it is the affective and participatory relationship between the artist and the speaker that is of primary importance. (Morrison, 1984, 341)

Note that she is not talking about the novel as sermon, nor about the subject matter of the sermon nor of the artist as a preacher but about a very specific effect to be created by the mere use of the written word; it is *all* aesthetic strategy and although that strategy is not all of Morrison's novel, whatever is being communicated cannot be had without it. In other words, the social value we recognize in her work can affect us only because it "works" culturally as well as aesthetically. Here, social value *is* aesthetic value and *vice versa*. In fact, although she specifically refers to modes and characteristics of African-American culture, Morrison sounds very much like Dewey here when he writes in *Art as Experience*: "For communication is not announcing things. . . . Communication is the process of creating participation, of making common what had been isolated and singular; and part of the miracle it achieves is that, in being communicated, the conveyance of meaning gives body and definiteness to the experience of the one who utters as well as to that of those who listen" (244).

But what constitutes aesthetic value and in what way is it tied to the social values projected in and through the text? It is perhaps especially interesting to raise this question now because in much ethnic and neorealistic writing of the last fifteen years or so, there has been a remarkable emphasis on shared values and shared experience, on identity-building and communication, in short, an emphasis on the pragmatic functions of the text. Whether its authors are aware of it or not, as in the case of Morrison such emphasis seems to echo Dewey's definition of the communal function of art, for instance, when he writes that "[w]orks of art that are not remote from common life, that are widely enjoyed in a community, are signs of a unified collective life. But they are also marvelous aids in the creation of such life. The remaking of the material of experience in the act of expression is not an isolated event confined to the artist and to a person here and there who happens to enjoy the work. In the degree in which art exercises its office, it is also a remaking of the experience of the community in the direction of greater order and unity" (81). Although Dewey conceived of the work of art predominantly as individual expression and included in his discussion the abstract art of the modernist movement, he nevertheless believed that the purpose of art, even of 'experimental' art, was ultimately communal—not communicative in any superficial sense, but demanding participation and fulfilling itself in participation.

The contemporary emphasis on the communal (and communicative) function of art is especially evident in texts that address themselves to the experience of specific groups (be they defined in terms of ethnicity or gender). The communicative or even therapeutic function of such novels is most striking in Lisa Alther's *Other Women* (1984). Inverting the strategies of more experimental (or postmodern) fiction almost programmatically, the novel does not pursue the *de*construction of narrative order but its *re*construction, creating meaning out of confusion, identity out of psychic disturbance. Alther's novel is particularly relevant in this connection because therapeutic conversation becomes a metaphor for the possibility of explaining and thus reconfirming the "real"—an explanation based on the gradual consensus of those engaged in communication about "truth." Although, through the discovery or reconstruction of personal history, reality cannot be made whole again, it can nevertheless be healed for those able to communicate about it (in this case, by and large a community of women).

This may be an extreme example but it is nevertheless indicative of a general tendency in contemporary narrative. It is certainly true of much ethnic fiction, especially Native American and African American. (One might think of *Ceremony* or *Beloved*, for example, but there are many others.) Yet even what is frequently called neorealistic fiction has reintroduced the topic of common values and shared experiences. In his essay "On Writing," Raymond Carver seems to reach back to earlier concepts of realist fiction when he speaks of the "sense of proportion and a sense of the fitness of things," which definitely rings a Howellsian note, although Carver applies the phrase somewhat differently (Carver, 27). Or let us take DeLillo's *White Noise*, in which the family endlessly discusses what constitutes the "real" and the quality and meaning of their shared experience. And yet, even though such scenes may seem to evoke similar conversations in the classic realist novel, DeLillo's "neorealism" is based on a common experience that no longer provides a basis for a clear or firm sense of reality. Perhaps one could say that DeLillo's text fully brings out what Richard Brodhead once called the paradox of realism: "when the Howellsian realist performs his proud office of telling the truth in fiction, he is always actually engaging, by his own covert admission, in an act of fabrication: a use of fiction's power to *make* real what it cannot *find* real, outside itself" (Brodhead, 102). In other words, the staging of communication may be indicative of the desire for successful social interaction and for a consciousness of shared experience, but in fact arises from the experience of an actual lack or absence of such consciousness.

Let us, once more, go back to Toni Morrison. In an interview she gave to Thomas LeClair in the early 1980s she said: "I write what I have recently begun to call village literature, fiction that is really for the village, for the tribe. Peasant literature for my people" (Morrison, 1983, 253). And then she claims to see her role as related to that of the griot, "the traditional African guardian of personal, familial and tribal history." It is hard to take this statement literally, and it is hard to believe that Toni Morrison herself meant every word she said. It is perhaps best understood as a gesture of desire: the desire for a group to exist that she could call "my people" and to be accepted by "her people" as their voice, their memory, their conscience. The very self-consciousness of this claim is an indication of her uncertainty, however, of the very paradox Brodhead had talked about. What she in fact practices in her fiction is not only an attempt to tell the lost, forgotten, or suppressed stories of black people but to create a fiction of the oral, making use of, and adding to, a tradition of orality in writing—so that the term "griot" may be at best a metaphor, at worst a self-deception. Indeed, in all of her novels community is surely a resource, but even more so a problem beyond the easiness suggested by the term "my people."

In other words, we may accept a grounding in the collectively shared as a condition of recent ethnic writing, perhaps as the very basis of its particular aesthetics. (Although we should keep in mind that, at least according to Dewey, such grounding is the condition of all aesthetic experience and expression.) At the same time, we have reason to expect an awareness of the problematics implied in the concept of a collectively grounded art. Toni Morrison, in her theoretical statements, may come close to a questionable claim of origin, or to a nostalgic (at times even sentimental) evocation of an unbroken connection between her art and the much wished-for community of "her people." In her best fiction she gives evidence of the tensions and contradictions hidden in such a concept—of the fact that it attempts to construct a presence against the conscious knowledge of its absence. Brodhead had talked about this, but also Dewey. For his *Art As Experience* can be understood as a passionate attempt to establish a philosophical basis for a universalist claim of art against what he considered the growing evidence of contemporary "diffuseness and incoherence," "the manifestations of the disruption of a consensus of beliefs" (340).

Although Dewey emphasizes tensions and conflicts, a breaking with convention and taboo, as the liberating potential of art and its experience, and although he rejects the pressure of totalizing visions, it seems clear that his concept of art still implies a unifying faith as much as a unifying project: i.e. that art, although an individual object of expression, is nevertheless grounded in participation; and that its "office" is "a remaking of the experience of the community in the direction of greater order and unity" (81).[11]

However, what constitutes community is of course the question and the burning issue here. Although Dewey's universalism seems to reveal itself as almost painfully outmoded and unacceptable from a position of argued "difference," it is interesting to note how easily his universalist claim applies to the level of the local and particular (be it defined in terms of class, race, or gender). Whether it is possible to use this argument in the name of anti-universalism without privileging (and thus universalizing) *one* particular is surely a matter of some relevance. More important, however, is the question whether, in "remaking the experience" of a particular community, art (or literature) may yet (re)open the particular toward something shared beyond the boundaries of difference. "Expression," I quote Dewey again, "strikes below the barriers that separate human beings from one another" (270). Such openness, such "potency" of the literary text for crossing boundaries, going off limits, imaginatively taking the place of the Other, or exploring oneself in the Other is, it seems to me, the very essence of literature as much as the very condition of its social and economic existence and survival; and even though such exploration is inevitably also self-projection and self-invention, it nevertheless opens possibilities of understanding and of sharing. It could thus be considered the basis for a pluralist as "a comparative aesthetics" (Grabes, 3) which accepts difference without discarding the notion of a universal, however tentative and hypothetical, however 'questionable' (in a very literal sense), it may have become.

In referring to Morrison's "best fiction," I have implicitly connected the question of "aesthetic value" with that of aesthetic judgment, the most touchy of issues in the present debate. One could argue that in choosing Morrison, I, like some of the "new Americanists," have played it safe after all, since she represents what has been already affirmed as aesthetically valuable, as masterful and complex, thus claiming, at least by implication, that complexity not only constitutes aesthetic value but ensures cultural relevance. Yet complexity is not the point. There is an aesthetics of complexity as well as an aesthetics of simplicity. Neither of them constitutes or guarantees aesthetic value. To raise the question of aesthetic value (and with it, unavoidably, that of aesthetic judgment) would seem to be a self-defeating enterprise. For it raises a universalist question for which there are, and can only be, relativist answers, that is, answers that, although necessary, are also necessarily inconclusive since they are open to controversy and to change. And yet this inevitable discrepancy between the universal question and the plurality of possible (and relative) answers it generates should not make evaluation a matter of frustration but a welcome challenge. It gives energy to a process through which the importance of literature as aesthetic *and* social fact is reinstated through argued contestation. To be sure, in a culture that rejects what it considers 'repressive' universalism in favor of cultural difference, the primary goal of such a contestation cannot be the creation of consensus. Yet it should also not content itself with a happy assertion of mere pluralist disagreement.

Aesthetic evaluation could probably not do without the category of the text's "well-madeness"—whether it "works" within the framework of its particular aesthetic or not. Dewey evokes the tradition of "craft" and "craftsmanship" which, for him, is more than technical perfection but an act of "loving," of caring "deeply for the subject matter upon which skill is exercised" (48).[12] It could also not do without the time-honored criterion of the "sincere": the text's honestly exploring the limits as well as the possibilities of its medium and of the various conditions (social, historical, literary, linguistic) under which it "works" to engage the imagination of the reader. I do not deny that criteria such as the "well made" (with its Jamesian connotations of "craft" and "craftsmanship") and "honest" may sound unforgivably modernist (and thus hopelessly obsolete in our postmodernist context); yet they are categories relevant for all aesthetics—even if they apply to each of them in different ways.[13] To be sure, what defines the "well-made" and the "honest" is again a question that can only generate tentative answers—answers that will differ in different historical and cultural contexts. After all, how many texts of American literature were once considered "untruthful" and "badly made" before their value was recognized within the context of a new aesthetics that they embodied as well as helped to bring about? It is precisely for this reason that such questions should not be avoided but posed again and again, in a dialogue that, even though it can, at best, achieve only partial or temporary agreement, should have as its premise the possibility of reaching agreement.

Indeed, the house of fiction has room for many different functional models and thus for many different aesthetics of the novel, so that one could indeed speak of a coexistence of the heterogeneous (Welsch, 149–156). These aesthetics may compete with one another, may be of use to certain groups at certain times. They answer, in any case, to the communicative, the pragmatic, or aesthetic needs of author and/or audience in specific social contexts or at a specific historical moment. To view fiction functionally would do away with a number of false oppositions that have marred the debate on canon and curriculum. The functional view would thus acknowledge the culture-work of the women writers Jane Tompkins wrote about in *Sensational Designs,* as much as it could recognize the identity-creating function of much recent ethnic fiction, without having to either ignore the question of aesthetics altogether or claim aesthetic value (in the old New Critical sense) for texts that respond to different needs and "work" under a different aesthetics. But it would also take into consideration that for some writers, regardless of their ethnic origin or gender, writing implies not only a commitment to communication, or to the assertion of racial and cultural identity, or to social and political change, but also to the craft of writing itself. Although their sense of difference may surely be defined through opposition against the power of dominant social, cultural, and aesthetic assumptions, they may yet see such opposition most radically enacted in their own dedication to the power of the word.

Notes

1. Grabes sees this process at work in all areas of contemporary theory, from philosophy to cultural anthropology: "Whilst on the surface the aesthetic, in the turn towards cultural studies, seems to be dissolving in a broader concept of culture, this broader concept is itself conceived of as a complex text claiming much of the autonomy and irrationality of the traditional work of art" (11; my trans.). For a related argument, see Wolfgang Welsch, "Zur Aktualität ästhetischen Denkens," *Ästhetisches Denken,* 1998, 41–78.

2. "The recent widespread dismissal of the aesthetic [...] is based not only on those who attack it as a mystification, a sort of fetishism, but even more severely, by those who attack it as a dangerous [...] tool of a reactionary politics. That assault upon the aesthetic, now several decades in building, has come from many quarters, as structuralist, poststructuralists, and—more recently—historicists and socio-political and cultural theorists, have joined in it for reasons as different as their different agendas" (Krieger, 1994, 21–22; see Grabes, 1994, for a similar account). Efforts to reclaim the aesthetic have also got underway—if with much soul-searching and ideological trepidation: "breathlessly and nervously" as George Levine writes in the introduction to his *Aesthetics and Ideology* (1994). The fact that many of those who attempt to bring the aesthetic into the theoretical debate feel compelled to invoke their working-class background is another indicator of how marginalized the topic has become during the last twenty-five to thirty years.

3. As Bredella points out, for deconstructionists, "literariness" is not an aesthetic category but "a linguistic category which helps to deconstruct the relationship between language and the world" (REAL, 1994, 172–173).

4. Cf. among many others Bercovitch/Jehlen, 1986, Bercovitch, 1983, as well as the various reinterpretations of 'classic' American writers by Donald Pease, Jonathan, Arac and a number of other "new Americanists." In all these cases "it is striking to see how revisionism remains dependent on a traditional view of the aesthetic" (Fluck, 1994, 41).

5. If, in his earlier essay on "Structure, Sign and Play . . .," Derrida had modeled his notion of "free play" after the "specific joy of aesthetic experience" as described by Kant (Grabes, 5), he seems to reconnect it here with the specific "potency" of the literary text.

6. In a similar argument George Levine speaks of the aesthetic "as a mode engaged richly and complexly with moral and political issues, but a mode that operates differently from others and contributes in distinctive ways to the possibilities of human fulfilment and connection" (Levine, 1994, 3).

7. Elaine Scarry seems to evoke this essentialist (and premodernist) tradition when she links the perception of the Beautiful to an awareness of the Just. This ethical or enlightening notion of the inherent power of "Beauty" to guide or incite us to truth and justice seems difficult to maintain when we think how often the Beautiful not only failed in this educative purpose but was put into the service of the Unjust throughout the twentieth century. Thus, the failure of Victorian and, in particular, of German culture could be called a failure of the concept of the Beautiful, of social and ethical improvement through aesthetic education, a failure that had already become Henry James's great despair during the first years of World War I. In contrast, the 'potency' of the literary text—which is the work of the aesthetic function—is not dependent on either the existence or the creation of the Beautiful. Although it has power to question, undermine, or reveal, to enhance our understanding or assault our consciousness, its direct application to the practice of living is limited, as is evident in the case of, say, the political novel whose aesthetics of persuasion, in its effort to deny the distance between symbolic and social action, can only create a fiction (or illusion) of direct applicability.

8. In retrospect it is striking to what extent Mukařovský's theories anticipate, within the frame of Marxism, the aesthetic recognition and valuation of contemporary art, especially of works that Harold Rosenberg called, thirty years later, "anxious objects," since they could never be quite sure whether they were art or junk.

9. Derrida, in comparing literature and jurisdiction, makes a related argument:

[Literature] is an institution which consists in transgressing and transforming, thus in producing its constitutional law; or to put it better, in producing discursive forms, 'works' and 'events' in which the very possibility of a fundamental constitution is at least 'fictionally' contested, threatened, deconstructed, presented in its precariousness. Hence, while literature shares a certain power and a certain destiny with 'jurisdiction,' with the juridico-political production of institutional foundations, the constitution of States, fundamental legislation, and even the theological-juridical performances which occur at the origin of the law, at a certain point it can also exceed them, interrogate them, 'fictionalize' them: with nothing, or almost nothing, in view, of course, and by producing events whose 'reality' or duration is never assured, but which by that very fact are more thought-provoking. (Derrida, 1992, 72)

10. Mukařovský occasionally seems to approach Kant's "pleasurable disinterestedness" in his various definitions of the aesthetic function. Nevertheless he pushes his argument into a different direction. When he speaks of the "self-referential" and "de-pragmatizing" effect of the aesthetic function, he is not far from Dewey's anti-Kantian statement that "'[d]isinterestedness' cannot signify uninterestedness. But it may be used as a roundabout way to denote that no specialized interest holds sway. 'Detachment' is a negative name for something extremely positive. There is no severance of self, no holding of it aloof, but fullness of participation" (257–258). It is true that Mukařovský's notion of an aesthetic function appears to underline the contemplative aspects of aesthetic experience (whereas Dewey insists on its active, almost orgasmic, quality). Yet he also stresses its dynamic potency since it brings out (yet also holds together) the conflicting or contradictory nonaesthetic functions of the work of art in a precarious, yet highly energetic balance. On the "esthetics of pragmatism" in general, see Jonathan Levin, 1994; on Dewey and Mukařovský in particular, see Lothar Bredella, 1994 and 1996. Perhaps it is worthwhile to remember that both theories were developed at practically the same time—Dewey's book appearing in 1934, Mukařovský's in 1936. This may be one of the reasons why they both insist that the aesthetic is not removed from, but grounded in, social and historical processes; that it is, in the last instance, a social category.

11. If this sounds rather old-fashioned, if not conceptually crude, to contemporary ears, we should remember, as Bredella and Fluck have justly pointed out, that for Dewey "unity," "whole," "order" are not metaphysical but pragmatic terms. That is, they do not suggest essence or transcendence but refer to "a process in which tensions and divergences are not eliminated but experienced" (Fluck, 1999, 240). The power of aesthetic fusion is a precious but impermanent moment in this process of experience; and such moments enrich and stabilize our lives "in a world which is indifferent and even hostile to our needs and desires" (Bredella, "John Dewey's Art of Experience," 1994, 187).

12. However, I am well aware that the category of the "well-made" does not seem to apply to an aesthetics of the antiaesthetic—to Duchamp's early "ready-mades," for instance, although one could argue that all aesthetics generate their own standard of achievement, as is the case even in Duchamp's later work.

13. This became apparent to me when I interviewed a number of Turkish-German rappers in Berlin who insisted that what mattered to them most was to gain "respect" for their skills and for the quality of their work.

Works Cited

Bercovitch, Sacvan. *The Rites of Assent: Transformations in the Symbolic Construction of America.* New York: Routledge, 1983.

Bercovitch, Sacvon, and Myra Jehlen, eds. *Ideology and Classic American Literature.* New York: Cambridge University Press, 1986.

Bredella, Lothar. "John Dewey's Art of Experience." *REAL* 10 (1994): 169–201.

———. "Two Concepts of Art: Art as Truth or as Dialogue." *Affirmation and Negation in Contemporary American Culture.* Ed. G. Hoffmann and A. Hornung. Heidelberg: Winter, 1994. 89–134.

———. "Aesthetics and Ethics: Incommensurable, Identical, or Conflicting?" *Ethics and Aesthetics: The Moral Turn of Postmodernism.* Ed. Gerhard Hoffmann and Alfred Hornung. Heidelberg: Winter, 1996. 29–52.

Brodhead, Richard. *The School of Hawthorne.* New York: Oxford University Press, 1986.

Carver, Raymond. *Fires: Essays, Poems, Stories.* London: Picador, 1985.

Derrida, Jacques. "Structure, Sign and Play in the Discourse of the Human Sciences." *The Structuralist Controversy.* Ed. R. Macksey and E. Donato. Baltimore, Md.: Johns Hopkins University Press, 1972. 247–265.

———. *Acts of Literature.* Ed. Derek Attridge. New York: Routledge, 1992.

Dewey, John. *Art as Experience.* New York: Perigee, 1980.

Eagleton, Terry. *The Ideology of the Aesthetic.* London: Blackwell, 1990.

Fluck, Winfried. "The Americanization of Literary Studies," *American Studies International* 28 (Oct. 1990): 9–21.

———. "Radical Aesthetics." *REAL* 10 (1994): 31–48.

———. "Literature, Liberalism, and the Current Cultural Radicalism." *Why Literature Matters: Theories and Functions of Literature.* Ed. R. Ahrens and L. Volkmann. Heidelberg: Winter, 1996. 211–231.

———. "Pragmatism and Aesthetic Experience." *REAL* 15 (1999): 227–242.

Grabes, Herbert. "Contemporary Theory and the Aesthetic: Rejections and Affinities." *REAL* 10 (1994): 1–18.

Guenther, Hans. *Struktur als Prozess: Studien zur Ästhetik und Literaturtheorie des tschechischen Strukturalismus.* München: Fink, 1973 [my translation].

Guillory, John. *Cultural Capital: The Problem of Literary Canon Formation.* Chicago: University of Chicago Press, 1993.

Krieger, Murray. "The Current Rejection of the Aesthetic—and Its Survival." *REAL* 10 (1994): 19–30.

Lauter, Paul. "Reconfiguring Academic Disciplines: The Emergence of American Studies." *Through the Cultural Looking Glass: American Studies in Transcultural Perspective.* Ed. H. Krabbendam and J. Verheul. Amsterdam: VU University Press, 1999. 229–243.

Levin, Jonathan. "The Esthetics of Pragmatism." *American Literary History* 6 (Winter 1994): 658–683.

Levine, George. "Introduction: Reclaiming the Aesthetic." *Aesthetics and Ideology.* Ed. G. Levine. New Brunswick: Rutgers University Press, 1994.

Morrison, Toni. "An Interview with Toni Morrison." *Anything Can Happen: Interviews with Contemporary American Novelists.* Ed. T. LeClair and L. McCaffery. Urbana: University of Illinois Press, 1983.

———. "Rootedness: The Ancestor as Foundation." *Black Women Writers (1950–1980): A Critical Evaluation.* Ed. Mari Evans. New York: Doubleday, 1984.

Mukařovský, Jan. *Kapitel aus der Ästhetik.* Frankfurt: Suhrkamp, 1970 [my translation].

Radway, Janice. "What's in a Name? Presidential Address to the American Studies Association, 20 November, 1998." *American Quarterly* 51, no. 1 (1999): 1–32.

Rosenberg, Harold. *The Anxious Object.* Chicago: University of Chicago Press, 1966.

Santayana, George. *The Works of George Santayana,* vol. 4, *The Life of Reason.* New York: Scribner's, 1936.

Scarry, Elaine. *On Beauty and Being Just.* Princeton, N.J.: Princeton University Press, 1999.

Shusterman, Richard. *Pragmatist Aesthetics: Living Beauty, Rethinking Art.* Oxford: Blackwell, 1992.

Tompkins, Jane. *Sensational Designs: The Cultural Work of American Fiction, 1790–1860.* New York: Oxford University Press, 1985.

Welsch, Wolfgang. *Ästhetisches Denken.* Stuttgart: Reclam, 1998.

Afterword

LOUIS FREITAS CATON

Among literary critics, the notion that one might situate the word "multicultural" alongside "aesthetics" in the title of a single volume of articles probably generates more dissensus than consensus. After all, many of the terms associated with each word appear antithetical. Consider the following group of words often identified with the "multicultural" part of the title: particular, relativism, constructed conditions, mediation, otherness, self-interest, and ideology. Compare those to a list related to the term "aesthetics": universal, excellence, human condition, immediacy, commonality, disinterest, and metaphysics. Paired off on a one-to-one basis, the words in their respective vocabulary pools could not be much more contested; the clash presents an oppositional dynamic, a turbulent rather than tranquil mixture. Moreover, the intellectual field of aesthetics and American multiculturalism often arises from the already divisive debates over canonicity and national identity. So discord must play a role. Because such conflict can be anticipated, however, does not mean that this controversial topic has had sufficient exposure or academic analysis. In fact, despite its anecdotal reputation as one of the sources for the heated polemics in the "cultural wars," this particular battle has only recently started to come under needed scrutiny.[1] One of the reasons is the pervasive notion of aesthetics itself.

According to Terry Eagleton, the aesthetic is "nothing less than the whole of our sensate life together—the business of affections and aversions, of how the world strikes the body on its sensory surfaces, of what takes root in the gaze and the guts and all that arises from our most banal, biological insertion into the world" (13). And yet, at this moment in literary criticism, the aesthetic is also radically suspect, often "denigrated or reduced to [a] mystified ideology" (Levine, 3). Its classical vocabulary of disinterest, immediacy, wholeness, universal value, genius, and the like, strikes one as dated, naive, and perhaps as even a covert collaboration with a self-interested hegemonic politics. In that formulation, aesthetic rhetoric needs to be deconstructed, dismantled, and defeated.

The time-honored and hopeful definition of an ideal aesthetics—one that wants to confirm what Eagleton calls a "compassionate community, of altruism and natural affection, which along with a faith in the self-delighting individual represents an affront to ruling-class rationalism" (60)—describes a community yet to be. For many, the aesthetic no longer represents individual liberation. Seemingly without much resistance, it has been "effectively captured by the political right," especially in figures like Coleridge, Arnold, and Eliot. Unpopular, conservative, and dangerous, the failure of aesthetic platitudes, well-intentioned as they may have been, has led to "a devastating loss to the political left" (Eagleton, 60). "Because of that association, an interest in literary form is sometimes thought to grant "second class citizenship to cultural diversity in the narrative" (Paley, 3). As Jerome McGann advises, a savvy critic should never accept traditional aesthetic presentations on their own merits; instead, the critic needs to "expose" aesthetic "dramas of displacement and idealization" (1) in order to find "their raison d'etre in the socio-historical ground" (3).

Certainly the commentary above on the pitfalls of a universal aesthetics is supported by many of the multiculturalist's efforts to ignore cultural similarities as she celebrates diversity. Moreover, if certain "aesthetic" works are labeled transhistorical, transcendent, and universally valid, will that not lead to "the repression of the oppositional voice, and the illusion that there is only one genuine 'culture'" (Jameson, 87)? In other words, too many references to transcultural principles of knowledge may cause the polycultural ethnic narrative either to lose its distinction or to be left out of the discussion completely. With worries such as these, then, invoking universals would seem to block the proper reception of the literary work. With the above weighty concerns in mind, why has the combination of "multiculturalism" and "aesthetics" not received an adequate hearing? Perhaps this academic neglect derives from the vexed reputation of the two terms themselves.

The term "aesthetic" would, indeed, seem to reference something "universal." It amounts to a ubiquitous sensory relation to the world, a response seemingly all cultures embrace and never completely circumvent. But recognizing this feature, what Kant termed the aesthetic's "universally valid subjectivity," also draws attention to the other side of the aesthetic: the contrasted force of reason's "objectivity." The two famously play off each other: feelings demand their universal assent while they necessarily elude conceptual thought. Hence, aesthetic writings indirectly reveal the well-known abyss between the classic poles of Descartes's consciousness. When Kant and Baumgarten tried to bridge that Cartesian gap, the traumatic duality of the human condition seemed suddenly less pressing. Of course, according to the German Romantic interpretation of Kant's *The Critique of Judgement*, the sensible was able to reconnect to the intelligent, art mended to science, and the imagination healed the mind.

Even today, in the middle of late capitalism, globalization, and a deep postmodern skepticism, the holistic dream of a healthy aesthetic remains. In fact, ironically, due to the current academic climate of pervasive relativism, hermeneutic solipsism, and the loss of a vocabulary for authenticity, the aesthetic's utopian hope of unity and idealism seems, at the same time, both oddly retrograde and strikingly imperative: retrograde because in an age of cultural studies many critics assume an affective incommensurability between separate discourses, and yet creative due to the aesthetic's ability to see beyond a culture's oppression and into a discourse of solidarity and emancipation.

The term "difference" may be just as vexed, yet it has slowly become the dominant star of conventional academic enterprises. Recent literary critical deployments all too often emphasize difference, discrimination, and the uniqueness of a disclosed excellence. That is, as the literary critic increases her magnification of the work, each element under investigation has the potential to become more brilliant, singular, and, in a word, "different." Since enhanced specificity defines the orthodox commentator, why would a critic want to investigate works in order to theorize about their commonalities or their universals? When one *does* retraverse this traditional route and, accordingly, *de*creases the sharpness of the gaze for a more communal perspective—to see the human forests among the individual trees—various literatures *do* appear similar and related. Critics like Joseph Campbell, Karl Jung, and Northrop Frye have sometimes taken this more general comparative approach with uneven success. Certainly their work carries influence, but their conclusions regarding human commonality have not been endorsed by the academy in the way that human difference, seen through anthropological or sociological methods, has. And this latter interest in these ideologically and scientifically oriented strategies obviously fits less well into the older aesthetic paradigm than the newer one of "difference" or cultural studies.

If a critical preference for discussing and evaluating the difference of multiculturalism is taken as a given in current literary studies, then how might "universalism," the primary aesthetic term opposed to difference, be better understood? Although too complex a question for this afterword, I will risk some observations since many of our essayists struggle with it. To begin with, if difference depends upon a cognitive awareness of social conditions and historical specificity, according to Kant, it will (and should) clash with the universal and transcendental axis of aesthetic judgment. Kant searches for universal principles to underwrite the non-cognitive concepts needed for a fully disinterested aesthetics. As such, his investigation is not directed to "taste," which might depend on cultural experiences of difference, but to the aesthetic's transcultural and "transcendental aspects" (Kant, 6). Critics interested in difference quite reasonably view such a search for a pure aesthetics as a suppression of the social realities that *do* make an aesthetic judgment interested rather than disinterested. Dividing history from aesthetics, as Kant's use of the universal seems to do, is nothing if not a particular (and thus ironic) historically determined act. In other words, "difference" critics often hope to correct Kant's supposed naivete by exposing the ideology left out of his supposedly "disinterested" equation.

Using this sketch of one of many clashes embodied in the convergence of aesthetics and multiculturalism leads me next to briefly review three key arguments that surface from the oppositional energy of these conflicting vocabularies. Each argument radically reconfigures chief features of a traditional aesthetic and literary study. All three investigate the political and ideological consequences that occur when material particularity ("emotions," "feelings," and/or "subjectivity") is analyzed apart from conceptual abstraction ("rationality," "reason," and/or "objectivity"). After all, this was the gap that aesthetic discourse had attempted to traverse. How successful was that bridge-work? To answer that question I will consider Terry Eagleton, Anthony Easthope, and Susanne Kappeler. All three mount strong arguments for a radical re-evaluation that might demote aesthetic harmony from an enlightened project to a strong form of mystification: Eagleton claims the aesthetic covertly suppresses the potentially revolutionary power of the feelings, Easthope exposes the false notions of aesthetic organicity, and Kappeler sees aesthetics as always hurtful, exclusionary, and merely an alibi for the pornographic.

In his *The Ideology of the Aesthetic*, Eagleton sees aesthetic understandings as traditionally mediating the clash "between the generalities of reason and the particulars of sense" (15).[2] A certain conceptual-less reasoning constructively negotiates the metaphysics of universals by placing them always within the context of a specific sensuality. But this is only the received cultural opinion, what we are supposed to believe. At the deeper end of the pool, the issue becomes how aesthetic discourse, through the imagination, validates reason's control of the feelings. Kant and Baumgarten immediately come to mind; they keep the sensual experience within the domains of the known, bridging the mind/body duality with a new understanding of reason's imagination. In so doing, intellectual power can remain in the hands of the enlightened (that is, within the Enlightenment legacy, the ruling class). Eagleton believes that if this is the case, then those in power might want to encourage aesthetic, philosophical literature: "[Absolutist] power needs for its own purposes to take account of 'sensible' life, for without an understanding of [feelings] no dominion can be secure" (15).

Understanding how aesthetics, a rational discourse aligned with the power of a dominant leisure class, could theoretically threaten authority with its attention to sensuality and the body, Kant and Baumgarten locate "feelings," the central subjective concern of aesthetics, into the "majestic scope of reason itself" (15). In effect, the theory of literary judgment eventually uses reason to colonize and subsume the feelings until the aesthetic becomes "the moment of letting go of the world and clinging instead to the formal act of knowing it" (66). With such a formulation, no authority risks rebellion from its subordinates; the aesthetic becomes quietly internalized and habituated into "a source of one's social cohesion" (23), the inhibiting but universal covenant of humanity. After all, "what bonds could in any case be stronger, more unimpeachable, than those of the senses, of 'natural' compassion and instinctive allegiance?" (23). Richard Schusterman usefully summarizes this major point of Eagleton's:

[T]he aesthetic and its discourse served a crucial project of politico-cultural hegemony, through which the order and consensus of a ruling ideology were not to be
coerced on our senses and desires from without by external law or concept but rather
introjected into the heart of our subjectivity and 'natural' affections through the
unforced force of aesthetic pleasure. (260)

Eagleton recognizes how the aesthetic comes to internalize repression, colonizing and subjugating the masses so that they give away "interested" particularism
for a "disinterested commitment to a common well-being" (25).

In an equally strong challenge to the heritage of a self-contained, "disinterested"
aesthetics, Easthope, in his *Literary into Cultural Studies*, cites self-defeating contradictions inherent to the crucial notion of organic unity in literary studies.[3] Formalism and aesthetics rely upon a disclosure of organicity in order to claim a text to be
an independent object, a work upon which one could practice theoretical operations. The belief in the unity of the text assures the reader that the literary object is
secure, as Easthope phrases it, "sufficient to itself" (12). The creation of this paradigm became institutionalized in literary studies so that the subject/object poles
could be transparent for an empiricism, the reader autonomous to what she reads.
This modernist approach preserved the reader's independence from the text and
secured a literary object for the subject to pseudoscientifically disassemble. From
Aristotle to Northrop Frye, critics have proclaimed unity to be inside the text, allowing for metaphorical coherence and thematic stability. A text declared itself
intransitive: not a transformation of information but an undivided event, complete
in and of itself (16).

Most late twentieth-century theorists now disavow that belief in organicity.
Whether drawing upon psychoanalytic distinctions, deconstructive aporias, or
Marxist historicisms, they now view the literary object as a multivocal, self-divided
collection of signifiers that remain distinct and absent from their signifieds. Aesthetic theory gets unmoored; it must define itself without the benefit of a free-
standing, independently known literary work. It must now accept the profusion
of meaning as a crucially redefining characteristic. Hence, accepting not unity
but polysemy, aesthetics risks "losing its identity" (36). Before the recognition of
radically plural signification surfaced, the concept of a self-sufficient unity kept
polysemy under control. Organicity was the lid suppressing various competing
notions of meaning. Even if we had disagreed over the extent of the ambiguity
and disparate meanings, an ordered sense of aesthetics still managed to contain
signification with some sense of consistency, albeit arbitrary in nature.

But as early as the iconoclastic *Seven Types of Ambiguity* (1961), Easthope reminds
us, William Empson was already warning his readers that an "ever greater plurality of meanings in a text" had the potential of disrupting "signification all
together" (20). Late twentieth-century criticism highlights these examples of

conflicting meanings and claims that unity is nothing more than one of many unsteady reading strategies. Readers independently declare valuations, hierarchies, and unities to control their various meanings. Hence, "the wholly incoherent text may exist but we will never know about it" (35) since the concept of unity resides in and is deployed by the reader. As the work discloses an ever greater plurality of signification, the reader must rescue the text and declare, more or less unpredictably and inconsistently, which features create "unity" and which do not.

If the text resists unification by language—if language, in fact, disarticulates rather than articulates meaning—then there is no stable ground upon which aesthetics can build its house. Accepting this insufficiency within the work leads one to devalue not only the aesthetic but the category of the literary itself. Without a distinctive object for literary study, it is difficult to have literary studies. Without agreed upon, inherent, or essential material particulars (upon which we can agree) that might cohere thorough transhistorical notions of form, the aesthetic project becomes crippled, if not completely destroyed.

For Kappeler, these problems only point to a much more pervasive and corrosive concern: the oppressive canonical position of the literary project itself.[4] The historical project of the aesthetic, its concern over distinction, exclusivity, and elitism, is similar to a self-defined membership in a restricted club. The aesthetic critic does not honor universal values when considering whether or not a work should be deemed canonical. In practical terms, critics depend on similarities, associations, and the opinions of the "already adjudged member[s] of the literary elite" (116). Instead of an aesthetic that focuses on the merits of a work, we have one based on club members' recommendations: "The quality itself, the inherent literary values [that supposedly the previously inducted literary works initially had pronounced], need neither be stated, nor analyzed or demonstrated" (117).

Kappeler recognizes that the "principal concern of the literary is exclusion" (123), but exclusion without clear criteria. The aesthetic escapes responsibility in this matter because, as a discourse, it stands in opposition to practical or instrumental reason. Using Kant, Kappeler reminds her readers that the aesthetic is disinterested in any cognitive understanding of the literary object. After all, the aesthetic contributes nothing to knowledge and has "no direct correspondence with or relevance to any real objects in the world" (56). The aesthetic sense of delight comes under the name of feelings and, as Kant states, is "completely *free* in respect of the liking he accords to the object" (emphasis in original, quoted in Kappeler, 54). Aesthetic disinterest, then, could inadvertently but easily double as an incentive for irresponsibility. Quoting Pater, Kappeler reinforces this point: "Art . . . is thus always striving to be independent of the mere intelligence, to become a matter of pure perception, to get rid of its responsibilities to its subject or material" (quoted in Kappeler, 55). Here the aesthetic allows for pornography, since the critic should not be concerned with "the mere intelligence," that is, with the potentially hurtful content of the aesthetic.

Kappeler suggests that support for aesthetic theory encourages the notion that art should be disconnected from political realities. The, at once, scriptural and playful attitude towards art helps place the critic and writer outside any healthy politics of the human community (133). Due to the writer's residency in this protected domain of aesthetic artistry, the ills of society will only increase. For Kappeler, the whole category of the aesthetic must be dismantled: "The concept of 'aesthetics' is fundamentally incompatible with feminist politics" (221). That is, the concept of "the arts themselves will necessarily also have to change, [*sic*] Art will have to go" (221).

My aim in presenting these challenges is to comment on the depth of the theoretical and pragmatic issues circulating within this volume. Our collection of original essays attests to the variety of ways critics interpret the issues outlined above. No longer can one have a resigned acceptance of Cartesian and Kantian positions that provides a more or less stable subjectivity from which a discussion of aesthetics might proceed. The loss of that vantage point echoes throughout these articles.

In our first article, "Can Our Values Be Objective? On Ethics, Aesthetics, and Progressive Politics," Satya Mohanty wonders if a renewed understanding of "objectivity" under the current conditions of radical difference and relative value might actually invigorate multiculturalism. Rather than suggest a criteria of set standards or, on the other hand, endorse a far-reaching indeterminacy, Mohanty envisions a nonabsolutist empirical approach that acts as a cultural laboratory. That is, while shying away from both an a priori rejection of empiricism and firm hierarchical norms, Mohanty salvages a transcultural minimal model of rationality. Objectivity can still aid our seeing beyond familiar cultures since "questions that might be asked in local cultural conditions . . . are not thereby limited to the local." His paradigm of productive objectivity leads him to a "healthy multicultural society."

In "The Pragmatics of the Aesthetic," Giles Gunn takes a different route. He enlists a beleaguered term like "unity" and reinvigorates it specifically for our age of cultural studies. Noting that life's infinite experiences outpace our abilities to describe them, Gunn charges the aesthetic with organizing and representing this surplus. Citing observations by B. Herrnstein Smith, Gunn points to those occasions when perceptions are only marginally articulated, minimally recognized, "a sense, barely grasped, of the import of some incident." He argues that at these moments aesthetic discourses "seem eminently suited to help remedy" the disproportionate relation between life and expression. The "literary" enters this gap with gusto since it offers an opportunity whereby "the unspeakable may be spoken and the potentially lost retrieved." In this way, the aesthetic is "less interested in confirming or interpreting the known than in extending the realm of the knowable." Hence, the aesthetic moves "into the precincts of the ordinary" as it enlarges our "public world of meaning" with "a debate about what things are most worth valuing." The problem, of course, is that this universalism might reduce/devalue diversity or replace it with sharable traits that would then be used to essentialize notions of culture. But that risk, Gunn implies, might be worth the effort if, at some level, this universalism leads to larger and larger recognitions of human value, rights, and justice.

Similarly, Winfried Fluck sees the split between the aesthetic and its politics not as a problem but as an opportunity for deeper knowledge. Like John Carlos Rowe and Gunn, Fluck in his essay "Aesthetics and Cultural Studies" would take us beyond New Critical theories. For Fluck, form is not the depoliticized structure while content becomes the devalued political significance. Rather than move down that worn path, Fluck reveals aesthetics to be more of an attitude. Replaying some of Ickstadt's notions, Fluck wants the aesthetic to tell us *how* we see rather than *what* we see. Fluck might tell Robyn Wiegman (a writer from our next section), for example, that the epistemological challenge that she wants "difference" to provide could be deployed without sacrificing the discourse of aesthetics or the literary. All political observations, for Fluck, are aesthetic in that they must imagine or envision an answer. But, at the same time, Fluck would seem to agree with those who want the category of the literary to include a deep questioning about its own legitimacy. Under Fluck's understanding, the aesthetic relies on such extreme interrogation, an activity he calls the "discourse of the real." Thus political insights of difference would "in fact, [be] mutually constitutive" with aesthetic ones. In other words, the aesthetic can never be an evasion of history or ideology since those concepts make up part of its very being.

Writing from a more overarching, descriptive vantage point, John Carlos Rowe ends this section by reporting on the partnership between aesthetics and social activity. In "The Resistance to Cultural Studies" he sees little danger of the aesthetic being replaced by an exclusive cultural interpretation because "culture" itself becomes "the horizon of interpretation." Aesthetics turns out to be one of many "scholarly projects" that compose "the larger 'horizon' of the specific 'cultural'" realities that the critic explores. In other words, aesthetics is not embraced as a grand narrative but neither is it dismissed wholesale as an aggressor or oppressor. Defending the aesthetic value of canonical authors promotes "just the sort of intellectual debate that makes for valuable teaching, useful scholarship, and historically vital intellectual exchange." Conversely, cultural studies also reminds us that aesthetic knowledge is no less exciting or enlivening when analyzed as a political/social force.

As if in some ways to respond to these prompts by our previous critics, part II of our volume, "Redefining Categories of Value and Difference," addresses in more depth the question of aesthetics and assessment. Shelly Fisher Fishkin, the first writer of this section, begins her article "Desegregating American Literary Studies" by posing two contested forces. In Fishkin's terms, the two sides are "elite white men" and everyone else. Not a dialectic, these two camps instead have traditionally kept their distance from each other. Fishkin's essay begins by asking if and when a "rich and complex cultural dialogue" will connect them or if and when "essentialist paradigms" will divide them. A way at these two questions is to explore the dynamics of "transgressive" texts—the ones where black writers showcase white heros and white writers black ones. Such stories could be used as crossover texts, ambiguous narratives that do not wholly belong in any black/white category. By advocating their use in the classroom, Fishkin suggests that the cultural moment has arrived to go beyond identity politics and segregated survey courses. This is a position slowly gaining acceptance. For example, Werner Sollors, in "A Critique of Pure Pluralism," seems to agree with Fishkin when he asks if the same racial categories that generated exclusion before should be used as organizing concepts in future texts. By not advancing transgressive texts, we "bury an intriguing chapter in American literary history, and [a portion of] the history of American race relations." For Fishkin, the white authors who imaginatively portray black characters as protagonists and heros in fiction need to be publicized: "an identity politics that assumes that only black writers may be relied upon to write truthfully about African Americans" hurts everyone.

In "Difference and Disciplinarity," our next essay, Robyn Wiegman disputes the notion that "difference" needs to be "transdisciplinary." In fact, she also feels that "theory" will not essentially help in the effort to transgress identity models. Difference should not be viewed as a marker of culture and diversity but, instead, as an "object" that "transforms the knowledge practices of the university itself." In another of her examples, difference cannot disrupt feminism's disciplinary reproduction since it does not act as a "qualifier for the diversity of 'culture.'" Other critics, Wiegman acknowledges, still hold out that the aesthetic might "function to found for feminism a literature-based disciplinary tradition." Specifically, Wiegman cites Susan Gubar as one of these critics who claims that the solidarity undergirding feminism has been injured by the specialized concerns for racial, gendered, cultural concerns. For Wiegman, however, a strong form of difference might only emerge by separating it from this history of aesthetics and the literary. With such an autonomy, difference would then encourage, if not propel, feminism "out of the discipline" and into a deep question of the term "woman" itself. By sacrificing the aesthetic, women move more easily beyond the institution, beyond "the nationalist ontology of cultural diversity." In such a fashion, they will better see themselves in other underrepresented groups and together renew a commitment to determine why they have been overlooked. Discussed in this manner, difference becomes a legitimate "epistemological" challenge to institutions and not a literary marker to recapture "roots."

But Wiegman's bid to define difference outside the aesthetic in order to politically challenge institutional epistemology would probably conflict with Donald Pease's notions of politics and aesthetics. In "Doing Justice to C. L. R. James's *Mariner, Renegades and Castaways*," Pease reviews and challenges William E. Cain's

1995 literary condemnation of James's text, in which he claims that James assaulted the "aesthetic integrity" of *Moby-Dick* by "reimagining" the core of the plot to correct Melville's refusal to allow the crew members of the *Pequod* to "rebel against their diabolical captain," based on James's identifying his own incarceration as a "subversive" in 1954 with the plight of the mariners, renegades, and castaways of the crew who were oppressed by authoritarian control (Ahab in *Moby-Dick*); in James's view, the oppressor was the political state that sought to deport him.

Pease sees this conflict as one between aesthetic criteria—perhaps privileged and self-interested—and political complexity, which claims the comparable privilege of "critical witness against an injustice." Pease challenges Cain and aesthetic privilege, claiming that James refused "to ratify art's autonomy in order to disclose the social inequalities . . . that the political ideal of autonomous expression covered over." James, by linking the events of the *Pequod* with his in-time incarceration, creates a grammatical and political condition, what Pease calls the "future anterior," in which injustice in the present "will have been" transformed by "renarrating" a literary past event which, by its precedent, will have already effected the potential for change in the future. Contrary to the irrevocable loss of Walter Benjamin's "angel of history," Pease sees James's project as one in which "the future . . . returns to the past to transform" both the literary past and the political present.

Rather than move towards the Kantian embrace of a dynamic relation between universalism and the particular, as many of our above writers have reconsidered, Johnnella E. Butler ends this section by using Ishmael Reed's *Mumbo Jumbo* as "an archetypal myth" that "anticipates the explicit search for wholeness" evinced by African-American women writers. In her "*Mumbo Jumbo*, Theory, and the Aesthetics of Wholeness," Butler calls for a rich theoretical vocabulary for African-American literature. Just as characters in *Mumbo Jumbo* seek "the missing text," so does Butler desire a "text" or theory to interpret African-American literature. Like Kathleen McHugh (a writer in our third section), who is aware that the aesthetic projects various gaps, wounds, and traumas, Butler notices the pain within African-American literature that "'experts' are so quick to judge as social and psychological deviance." Such trauma seeks a theory of wholeness, a theme that arises as "a leit motif throughout African-American literature." An aesthetic of wholeness helps us realize the tragic force of hierarchical binaries that produced "slavery, the colonization of and genocide against the American Indian, and all the 'isms' that flow from racism." An African-American aesthetic should underwrite a concept of holistic polarity because it "holds the possibility . . . for one to be both an individual and part of a community simultaneously." Butler's advocacy for polarity—or what she calls the "dianonmical"—is an attempt to offer a "literary theory that provides the necessary foundation for revealing the full significance of the complexities" of African-American literature.

Paul Lauter's article "Aesthetics Again? The Pleasures and the Dangers" introduces our third and last section: "Aesthetic Judgment and the Public Sphere." Lauter compares two American Indian art shows to reveal the role history plays. In one show, the artifacts were presented without any commentary on their form or aesthetic composition. In the other, a detailed account of formal, cultural properties was given. The organizers of the first show apparently felt that most visitors would discern "universal principles," or that visitors would not care about an exotic discussion of Native American aesthetic principles. The curators of the other exhibition, however, seemed to realize that Indian art, like all art, has a complex relation to history and culture. They provided the particular compositional principles necessary for an uninformed viewer. For Lauter, this contrast between their approaches displays one of the many important dynamics in the study of "aesthetics and difference" for literary texts. He submits that just because art is universally pleasurable does not mean that the particulars of art are any less "learned, contingent, particularistic—and changeable." Using Francis Ellen Watkins Harper, Lauter shows that readers need to learn the individual and community discourse before passing judgment on a text. Since no discourse community is absolutely distinct from another, hybrid acculturation and communication inevitably occurs. Questions of aesthetics, then, "cannot be answered simply by mixing and matching particular texts as if they existed in mutually translatable discourses, in some idealized empyrean venue, and for interchangeable audiences." Instead, "the reality of hybridity" must hold hands with "the equally real presence of particularity," even if the embrace is often "tense and painful."

Lauter's conclusion that pictures human commonality holding hands with difference, although conscious of history, may not invoke it deeply enough for our next writer, Amelia Jones. Jones disrupts the more or less conciliatory approaches of the preceding chapters with some hard-hitting claims that echo and then expand on a more separatist vision of aesthetics and difference. Jones's article, "'Every man knows where and how beauty gives him pleasure': Beauty Discourse and the Logic of Aesthetics," declares that "the logic of cultural value" becomes "imperialist" if it returns to the doctrines of earlier ages that promoted and practiced a politics of exclusion. The history of the aesthetic cannot escape its legacy of a powerful, aristocratic elite wielding dominance over the less influential. By invoking Dave Hickey's book *The Invisible Dragon: Four Essays on Beauty* as a bad example, Jones asserts that art, contrary to Hickey, is neither natural nor what Hickey calls "a closed system of aesthetic and political judgement." Jones reminds us of what Hickey forgets: that "the fetishization of the female body . . . is at the base of Western aesthetics." Rather than theorize about the historical, cultural implications of that gendered appreciation, Hickey claims that art can bypass politics and register a "direct appeal to the beholder." For Jones, this misguided belief in a natural, transhistorical moment risks creating "hubris" in the critic. When understandings of a "natural" art emphasize a separation from the social and the political, the critic hazards an "absolute personal authority for aesthetic judgements." That move, in turn, generates "an ideology of control" that sustains "the law of patriarchy." Thus invoking the history of aesthetics risks continuing a history of oppression.

As if to modify those claims a bit, Kathleen McHugh suggests that the aesthetic might be more of an injury or wound than an ideology of control. In "The Aesthetics of Wounding: Trauma, Self-Representation, and the Critical Voice," McHugh reflects and expands on Fredric Jameson's claim that "history is what hurts." McHugh points to the gaps and openings that lead to pain in the legacy of aesthetic theory. Using Kant as a paradigmatic figure for this concern with linkage and breakage, McHugh makes sense of the aesthetic through Kant's need to bridge the universal with the individual, the subject with the object, and the real with the ideal. Enlisting help from Freud, Barthes, and the infamous "non-review" of Arlene Croce, McHugh shows how classical notions of a disinterested aesthetics may not be capable of understanding the "interested" trauma of art, a force that cannot be transcended "by sheer force of will." For example, Croce's rigid separation of art from propaganda justifies her refusal to attend Bill T. Jones's dance piece "Still/Here" since she claims it is overtly interested in making a political statement about the AIDS epidemic. Contrary to Croce, McHugh feels that rigid aesthetic understandings will always fail art because art and politics can never be separated cleanly. In this case, Croce's declaration of why she refuses to see the play simply brings politics through the back door. That is, when she gives a public hearing to explain why she vetoed the production, Croce is ironically and actually reintegrating the political into the aesthetic. From the method Croce uses to delimit the aesthetic, then, one can see how underrepresented literary genres, like journals, letters, autobiographies, etcetera, acquire their marginalized status. Even though only recently coming into the realm of the literary, those forms, according to McHugh, have always evinced a trauma indicative and worthy of aesthetic representation.

The next article, "Beautiful Identities: When History Turns State's Evidence," Chon A. Noriega gives her account of the minority artist trying to find a place in the world of government bureaucracy. She shows how the state, even as it apparently opens the door to "artistic freedom," tends to create and regulate Chicano cinema. Using Noriega's analysis that "the aesthetic is always . . . put to institutional purposes," Noriega claims that the "beautiful identities" of Chicano cinema are linked and indebted not only to a social activism that contested the rights of the state but also to that very state itself. In other words, the history of Chicano cinema should not be construed as only "a narrative of resistance." To do so will perpetuate an understanding of difference—of the Chicano—that arises from "an industrial and national sameness," one that tends to exclude not include.

Hence, the question "is not about whether to assimilate, but rather *how* to do so and remain beautiful" (emphasis in original). After all, Noriega suggests, the state and movements against the state have structural relations that are complicitous. And it is chiefly through aesthetics, "the search for the good and the beautiful," that such relations are obscured; "not because it is in the nature of the aesthetic to do so, but because both the state and social movements turn to the aesthetic at precisely that moment when their complicity threatens to manifest itself."

Heinz Ickstadt ends our collection with his article, "Toward a Pluralist Aesthetics." Ickstadt wants to locate aesthetics, if not entirely within the scope of cultural studies, then at least in deep relation to it. One way of doing this is to suggest how aesthetics emerges not as an absolutist set of standards but, instead, as a reading strategy. In this fashion, aesthetics "would be different in purpose, use, and function at different historic moments or for different groups." Ickstadt envisions literary appreciation as partly attitudinal, but "an attitude that is nevertheless determined by situation and context." Aesthetic organization depragmatizes the object and "turns it into an autonomous sign which forces the reader/observer to contemplate the specific manner of its 'made-ness.'" Hence, the politics of a text can also be defined aesthetically. By constructing a nonpolitical role for the formal concerns of aesthetics, Ickstadt makes room for those writers who, "regardless of their ethnic origin or gender," write not only with "a commitment to communication, to cultural assertion, or to social change but also to the craft of writing itself." After all, Ickstadt concludes, even though difference often gets defined "through opposition against the power of dominant cultural assumptions," some artists "see such opposition most radically enacted in their dedication to the power of the word."

All of these essays represent the climate of change spreading through the academy, wherein "difference" has emerged as a marker for the present era. Oppression, power, dominance, and associated terms vie for attention in the midst of earlier preferences for terms like irony, ambiguity, and complexity. Our writers testify, though, that these new understandings have emerged from the rethinking of past claims. This eclectic assemblage of methodologies and theoretical positions confirms that the category of the literary ought to remain open-ended. If nothing else, these writers show how the topic of "aesthetics and multiculturalism" helps define the academy in multiple ways at the current moment.

Notes

1. Emory Elliott organized a conference on this topic in late 1998. A selected collection of articles from that meeting forms the basis of this text. There are very few other specific book-length treatments of multiculturalism and aesthetics. Some collections come close, like Levine's *Aesthetics and Ideology*, Siemerling and Schwenk's *Cultural Difference and the Literary Text*, Soderholm's *Beauty and the Critic*, and Wonham's *Criticism and the Color Line*. For example, two excellent collections that investigate aspects of multiculturalism with

some specificity, Goldberg's *Multiculturalism: A Critical Reader*, and Melzer, Weinberger, and Zinman's *Multiculturalism and American Democracy*, contain no essays directly on aesthetics at all.

    2. For critical responses similar to Eagleton's, see Benhabib, Althusser, and de Man.

    3. For critics who generally support Easthope's views, see Tompkins, Macherey, and Williams.

    4. For additional support for Kappeler's argument, see Russ, Bennet, and Smith.

Works Cited

Althusser, Louis. *Lenin and Philosophy*. Trans. Ben Brewster. London: New Left Books, 1977.

Benhabib, Seyla. *Critique, Norm, and Utopia*. New York: Columbia University Press, 1986.

Bennet, Tony. "Really Useless "Knowledge': A Political Critique of Aesthetics." *Literature and History* 13.1 (1987): 38–57.

de Man, Paul. "Form and Intent in the American New Criticism." *Blindness and Insight*. Minneapolis: University of Minnesota Press, 1996. 20–36

————. "Phenomenality and Materiality in Kant." *Aesthetic Ideology*. Minneapolis: University of Minnesota Press, 1996. 70–91

Eagleton, Terry. *The Ideology of Aesthetics*. Cambridge: Blackwell, 1990.

Easthope, Antony. *Literary into Cultural Studies*. London: Routledge, 1991.

Goldberg, David Theo, ed. *Multiculturalism: A Critical Reader*. Cambridge: Blackwell, 1994.

Jameson, Fredric. *The Political Unconscious: Narrative as a Socially Symbolic Act*. Ithaca, N.Y.: Cornell University Press, 1981.

Kant, Immanuel. *The Critique of Judgement*. Trans. James Creed Meredith. Oxford: Oxford University Press, 1991.

Kappeler, Susanne. *The Pornography of Representation*. Cambridge: Polity Press, 1986.

Levine, George, ed. *Aesthetics and Ideology*. New Brunswick, N.J.: Rutgers University Press, 1994.

Macherey, Pierre. *A Theory of Literary Production*. Trans. Geoffrey Wall. London: Routledge and Kegan Paul, 1978.

McGann, Jerome. *The Romantic Ideology: A Critical Investigation*. Chicago: University of Chicago Press, 1983.

Melzer, Arthur M., Jerry Weinberger, and M. Richard Zinman, eds. *Multiculturalism and American Democracy*. Lawrence: University of Kansas Press, 1998.

Paley, Karen Surman. "Religious Skirmishes: When the Ethnic Outsider Cannot Hear 'The Loudest Voice.'" *Literature and Ethnic Discrimination*. Ed. Michael J. Meyer. Atlanta: Rodopi, 1997. 3–16.

Russ, Joanna. *How to Suppress Women's Writing*. Austin: University of Texas Press, 1983.

Schusterman, Richard. Review. of *The Ideology of the Aesthetic*, by Terry Eagleton. *Journal of Aesthetics and Art Criticism* 49.3 (1991): 259–61.

Siemerling, Winfried, and Katrin Schwenk, eds. *Cultural Difference and the Literary Text*. University of Iowa Press, 1996.

Smith, Barbara H. *Contingencies of Value: Alternative Perspectives for Critical Theory*. Cambridge, Mass.: Harvard University Press, 1988.

Soderholm, James, ed. *Beauty and the Critic: Aesthetics in an Age of Cultural Studies*. Tuscaloosa: University of Alabama Press, 1997.

Sollors, Werner. "A Critique of Pure Pluralism." *Reconstructing American Literary History.* Ed. Sacvan Bercovitch. Cambridge, Mass.: Harvard University Press, 1986. 250–79.

Tompkins, Jane. *Sensational Designs: The Cultural Work of American Fiction 1790–1860.* New York: Oxford University Press, 1985.

Williams, Raymond. "Base and Superstructure in Marxist Cultural Theory." *Problems in Materialism and Culture.* London: Verso, 1980.

Wonham, Henry B., ed. *Criticism and the Color Line: Desegregating American Literary Studies.* New Brunswick, N.J.: Rutgers University Press, 1996.

Index